MAURITIUS, RÉUNION & SEYCHELLES

Seychelles
p207

Madagascar

Mauritius
p55

Réunion
p131

Paula Hardy, Fabienne Fong Yan, Rooksana Hossenally

CONTENTS

Plan Your Trip

The Journey Begins 4
Mauritius, Réunion & Seychelles Map 6
Our Picks 8
Regions & Cities 26
Itineraries 28
When to Go 34
Get Prepared 36
Diving in Mauritius, Réunion & Seychelles 38
Hiking in Réunion 40
The Food Scene 42
The Outdoors 48

The Guide

Mauritius 55
Port Louis 60
Beyond Port Louis 70
Mauritius' Best Hikes 76
Flic en Flac 79
Beyond Flic en Flac 82
Chamarel 87
Hiking the Black River Gorges 90
Beyond Chamarel 92
South Coast Road Trip 94
Grand Baie 97
Beyond Grand Baie 104
Trou d'Eau Douce 108
Beyond Trou d'Eau Douce 110
Blue Bay 114
Beyond Blue Bay 117
Hike & Drive the Deep South 120
Rodrigues 124
Arriving 128
Getting Around 129

Réunion 131
St-Denis 136
Beyond St-Denis 143
St-Paul 147
Beyond St-Paul 150
St-Pierre 159
Beyond St-Pierre 165
The Road to the Wild South 174
St-André 176
Beyond St-André 179
Salazie 186
Cilaos 190
Mafate 194
Hiking the Haute Mafate 196
Piton de la Fournaise & the Plains 198
Arriving 204
Getting Around 205

Seychelles 207
Mahé 212
Hiking Morne Seychellois National Park 224
Beyond Mahé 229
Praslin 233
Beyond Praslin 239
La Digue 242
La Digue Beaches 246
The Outer Islands 249
Arriving 252
Getting Around 253

Hindu statue, Grand Bassin (p95), Mauritius

Toolkit

Money 256
Accommodation 257
Family Travel 258
Health & Safe Travel 259
Food, Drink & Nightlife 260
Responsible Travel 262
LGBTIQ+ Travellers 264
Accessible Travel 265
Nuts & Bolts 267
Language 268

Storybook

A History of Mauritius, Réunion & Seychelles in 15 Places 272
Meet the Mauritians 276
Meet the Réunionnais 278
Meet the Seychellois 280
Séga: Mauritian Soul Music 282
Réunion's Spiritual Heritage 285
Seychelles: Green Pioneer 288

Cirque de Cilaos (p190), Réunion

PLAN YOUR TRIP

Beach, Seychelles

La Digue (p242), Seychelles

MAURITIUS, RÉUNION & SEYCHELLES
THE JOURNEY BEGINS HERE

Born and raised in East Africa, like millions of people around the Indian Ocean I'm a product of the massive migration of people who moved both voluntarily and under duress across continents, and over centuries. Those journeys were no easy task, and neither were the nation-building projects they necessitated. An embrace of diversity was essential for this – as local historian Tony Mathiot told me, most Seychellois have five or six ancestral heritages.

That's what I find so inspiring about Seychelles. It has taken a history of slavery and natural exploitation and transformed it into a fantastic Creole culture and pioneering conservation projects.

Paula Hardy

@paulahardy

Paula has been an Africa-based travel journalist for over 20 years.

My favourite experience A bike ride to La Digue's Grand Anse (p247), then a walk in the forest to Anse Coco (p247), where there's a shack serving the best barbecued Creole fish. Paradise!

WHO GOES WHERE

Our writers and experts choose the places which, for them, define Mauritius, Réunion & Seychelles

Whenever I come back home, I travel to the Wild South and drive along the coastline to experience the spectacular deep-blue waves battling the sculpted volcanic rocks – in Cap Méchant and Le Baril, for instance. But one of my favourite places is Le Tremblet beach. It is a place where you can sense a sort of mystical energy born from fire meeting water. It's the essence of the island.

Fabienne Fong Yan
@a.fab.journey

French-Chinese born and raised in Réunion, Fabienne is a travel writer now based in Paris.

Cap Méchant (p175), Réunion

Port Louis is where the rich blend of French, British, Indian, Chinese and Creole cultures comes together in a clash of colours and flavours. In many ways, the Mauritian capital is where it all began, where traces of colonial rule can still be seen, and where thousands of Indian labourers arrived at Aapravasi Ghat World Heritage Site, to be dispatched across the island's sugarcane plantations to do much of the hard graft done by enslaved people before them.

Rooksana Hossenally
@rooksana_hossenally

Rooksana writes about travel for various magazines and newspapers.

Central Market, Port Louis (p60), Mauritius

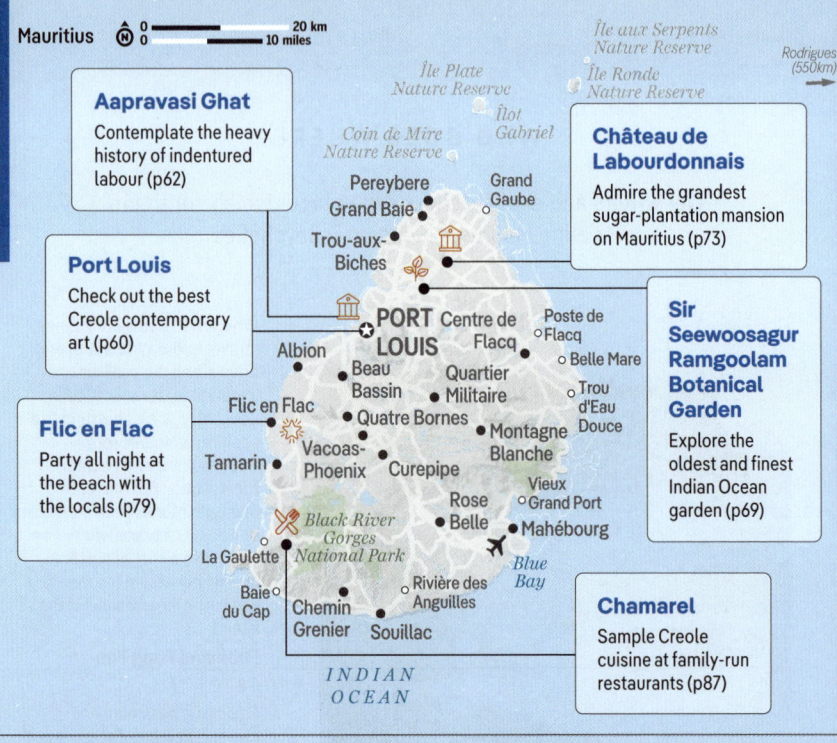

Mauritius

0 — 20 km
0 — 10 miles

Aapravasi Ghat
Contemplate the heavy history of indentured labour (p62)

Port Louis
Check out the best Creole contemporary art (p60)

Flic en Flac
Party all night at the beach with the locals (p79)

Château de Labourdonnais
Admire the grandest sugar-plantation mansion on Mauritius (p73)

Sir Seewoosagur Ramgoolam Botanical Garden
Explore the oldest and finest Indian Ocean garden (p69)

Chamarel
Sample Creole cuisine at family-run restaurants (p87)

Île aux Serpents Nature Reserve
Île Plate Nature Reserve
Île Ronde Nature Reserve
Rodrigues (550km)
Coin de Mire Nature Reserve
Îlot Gabriel
Pereybere
Grand Baie
Grand Gaube
Trou-aux-Biches
PORT LOUIS
Albion
Beau Bassin
Centre de Flacq
Poste de Flacq
Belle Mare
Quartier Militaire
Trou d'Eau Douce
Flic en Flac
Quatre Bornes
Montagne Blanche
Tamarin
Vacoas-Phoenix
Curepipe
Vieux Grand Port
Rose Belle
Mahébourg
Black River Gorges National Park
La Gaulette
Blue Bay
Baie du Cap
Chemin Grenier
Rivière des Anguilles
Souillac

INDIAN OCEAN

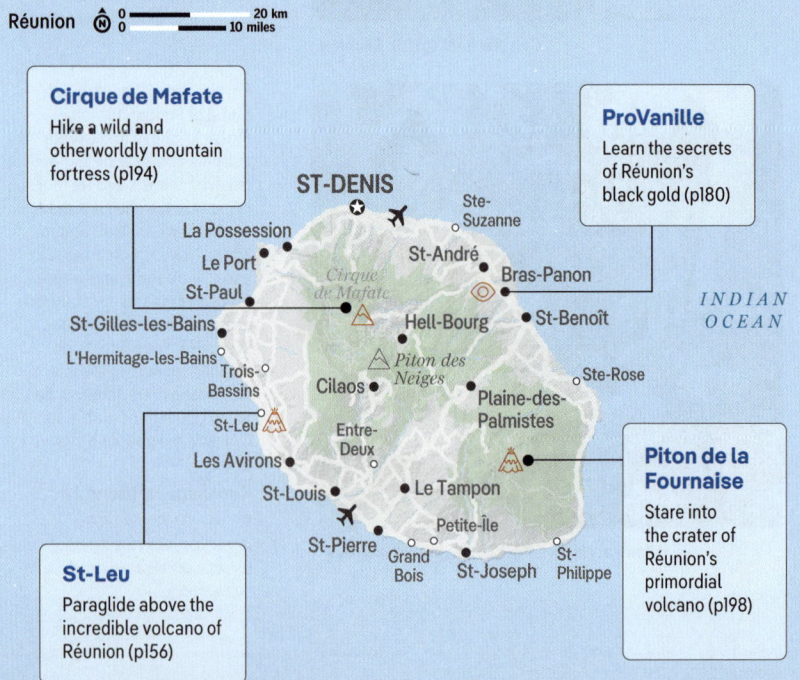

Réunion

0 — 20 km
0 — 10 miles

Cirque de Mafate
Hike a wild and otherworldly mountain fortress (p194)

ProVanille
Learn the secrets of Réunion's black gold (p180)

Piton de la Fournaise
Stare into the crater of Réunion's primordial volcano (p198)

St-Leu
Paraglide above the incredible volcano of Réunion (p156)

ST-DENIS
La Possession
Le Port
St-Paul
Ste-Suzanne
St-André
Bras-Panon
Cirque de Mafate
Hell-Bourg
St-Benoît
St-Gilles-les-Bains
L'Hermitage-les-Bains
Trois-Bassins
Cilaos
Piton des Neiges
Ste-Rose
St-Leu
Plaine-des-Palmistes
Les Avirons
Entre-Deux
St-Louis
Le Tampon
St-Pierre
Petite-Île
Grand Bois
St-Joseph
St-Philippe

INDIAN OCEAN

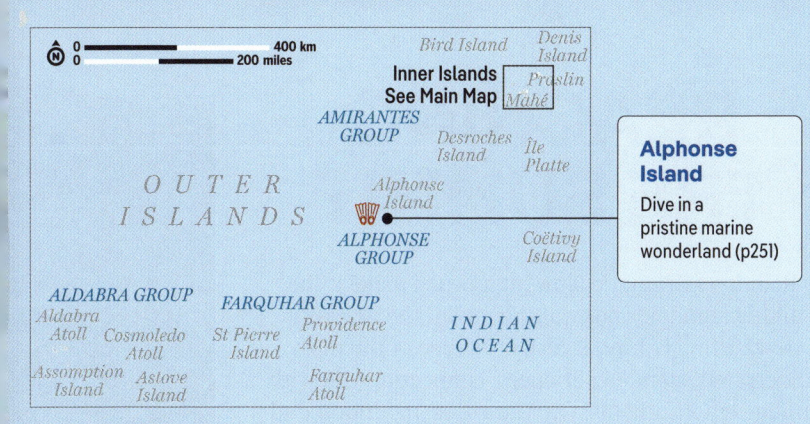

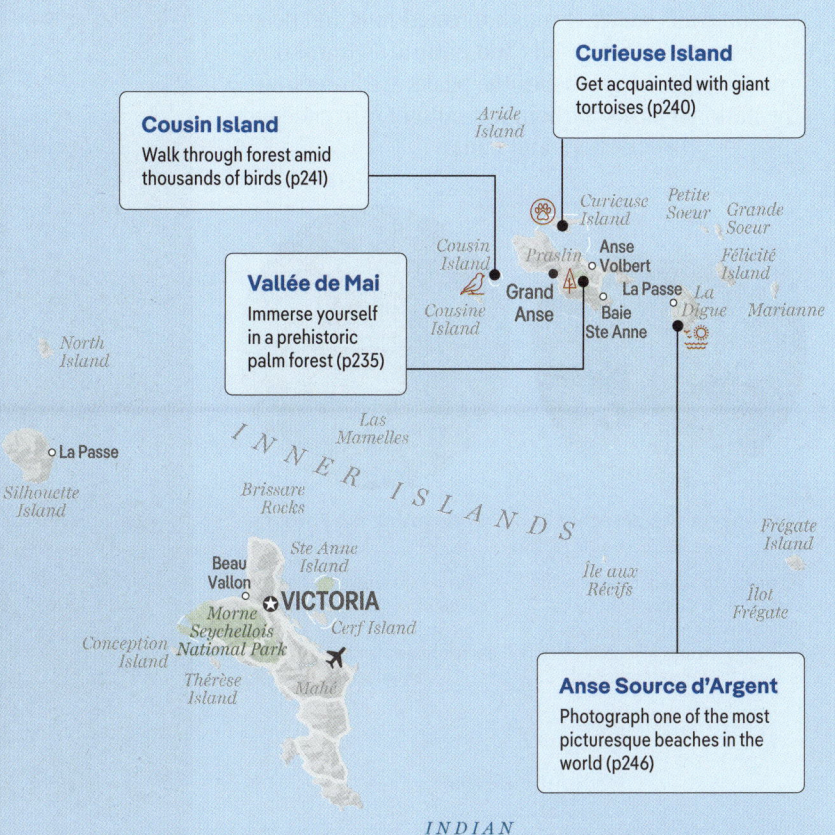

Seychelles

PLAN YOUR TRIP

Inner Islands See Main Map

- Bird Island
- Denis Island
- Praslin
- Mahé
- AMIRANTES GROUP
- Desroches Island
- Île Platte
- OUTER ISLANDS
- Alphonse Island
- ALPHONSE GROUP
- Coëtivy Island
- ALDABRA GROUP
  - Aldabra Atoll
  - Cosmoledo Atoll
  - Assumption Island
  - Astove Island
- FARQUHAR GROUP
  - St Pierre Island
  - Providence Atoll
  - Farquhar Atoll
- INDIAN OCEAN

Alphonse Island
Dive in a pristine marine wonderland (p251)

Curieuse Island
Get acquainted with giant tortoises (p240)

Cousin Island
Walk through forest amid thousands of birds (p241)

Vallée de Mai
Immerse yourself in a prehistoric palm forest (p235)

- Aride Island
- Curieuse Island
- Petite Soeur
- Grande Soeur
- Praslin
- Anse Volbert
- Félicité Island
- Cousin Island
- Grand Anse
- La Passe
- Baie Ste Anne
- La Digue
- Marianne

INNER ISLANDS

- North Island
- La Passe
- Silhouette Island
- Las Mamelles
- Brissare Rocks
- Ste Anne Island
- Beau Vallon
- VICTORIA
- Morne Seychellois National Park
- Conception Island
- Cerf Island
- Thérèse Island
- Mahé
- Île aux Récifs
- Frégate Island
- Îlot Frégate

Anse Source d'Argent
Photograph one of the most picturesque beaches in the world (p246)

INDIAN OCEAN

REACHING THE SUMMIT

Réunion's dramatic 3km-high peaks make it the hiking standout, but walking on all the islands is rewarding. Hiking is also often one of the most underrated island experiences, connecting you with unique environments. On Mauritius, mountain and coastal trails weave through forested hills and deep gorges full of waterfalls and natural swimming pools, while in Seychelles the peaks are lower and the national parks harbour a wealth of rare endemic flora and fauna.

Dress for the Weather

These tropical islands have humidity around 80%. Choose light, loose-fitting clothes and long trousers to guard against mosquitoes, or cover yourself in insect repellent.

Navigating the Forest

Hiking trails are well defined, clearly signposted and easy to follow. That said, a guide is a huge asset in understanding the forest environment.

High-Altitude Hiking

High-altitude hiking in Réunion requires extra care and warm, waterproof clothing. April to October is the best season. Note that the weather is extremely changeable.

Black River Gorges National Park (p90), Mauritius

PLAN YOUR TRIP OUR PICKS

BEST HIKING EXPERIENCES

Climb to the rim of one of the world's most active volcanos, the ❶ **Piton de la Fournaise** on Réunion. (p198)

Wander through a bird-rich wilderness in ❷ **Black River Gorges National Park**, Mauritius' last great forest. (p90)

Go off-grid for a multiday hike in the wild ❸ **Cirque de Mafate** and visit the most remote mountain communities in Réunion. (p194)

Trek through spice trees and endemic palms in ❹ **Morne Seychellois National Park** for summit views of idyllic offshore islands. (p224)

Scale the Indian Ocean's highest peak and watch the sunrise above the cloud-line on Réunion's epic ❺ **Piton des Neiges**. (p192)

OUR PICKS | PLAN YOUR TRIP

Sea coconut, Vallée de Mai Nature Reserve (p235), Seychelles

EXCEPTIONAL ECOSYSTEMS

Adrift in the Indian Ocean, over 1500km from anywhere else, these islands harbour unique environments, prehistoric geology, unusual microclimates and marine wonderlands. This adds up to some very special ecosystems that are worth exploring. Réunion with its unique volcanic character and Seychelles with its mosaic of islands are particularly wild and wonderful.

Gondwanaland

Seychelles' inner islands are granite rather than coral. That's because they're a fragment of the Gondwana supercontinent, left behind when it split Madagascar from India.

Volcanic Hot Spot

Réunion sits on a volcanic hot spot that created it two million years ago and may also have caused the extinction of the dinosaurs.

BEST ENVIRONMENTAL EXPERIENCES

Be amazed by the gigantic coco de mer palm trees that make up the prehistoric forest of the ❶ **Vallée de Mai**. (p235)

Climb through Réunion's primary ❷ **cloud forest of Bébour-Bélouve** and marvel at its giant ferns and Japanese cryptomeria. (p189)

Walk among thousands of nesting birds on the nature reserves of ❸ **Cousin** (p241), **Aride** (p240) and **Bird Islands** (p231).

Experience a unique indigenous ❹ **Ebony Forest**) and learn how it provides sanctuary for Mauritius' rare pink pigeons. (p88)

Dive into a marine wonderland in ❺ **Seychelles Outer Islands**, where you'll be joined by turtles, manta rays and a million other fish. (p249)

Meet Aldabra giant tortoises at their exclusive island home, ❻ **Curieuse**. (p240)

ISLAND DINING & DRINKING

One of the great pleasures of island life is the fabulous Creole cuisine. With African, Indian, European and Asian influences, it sings with rich, tropical flavours. This is the home of some of the world's great spices and tropical fruit, as well as the finest oceanic fish – the islands' cuisine deserves recognition alongside the glorious beaches.

Street-food Scene

Street food and takeaway are a big part of the local food scene and offer a great chance to graze island specialities, so join the queue.

Seasonality

Most tropical fruit trees produce multiple harvests each year, although some (such as mangoes) are best between November and January.

Dinner Dress

Although island culture is very casual, most locals still dress up a little when dining out, which is a treat. Anything smart-casual is fine.

BEST TASTE EXPERIENCES

Seek out the food-focused mountain village of ❶ **Chamarel** in Mauritius for its family-run restaurants such as Le Palais de Barbizon. (p87)

Do a taste tour of Mahé's ❷ **beachside restaurants**, where you'll find some of the best Creole food right by the water. (p235)

Spend a delightful day in historic ❸ **Mahébourg**, browsing the daily market, grazing the food stalls and exploring the town's restaurants. (p119)

Cruise the ❹ **St-Pierre food trucks** on the seafront in the early evening and sample such Réunionnais favourites as *Americain bouchons* and pork dumplings. (p159)

Rum is the drink of choice everywhere; sample it at ❺ **Rhumerie de Charamel** (p89), ❺ **Savanna Rum Distillery** (p178) and ❺ **Takamaka Rum Distillery**.(p220)

Anse Source d'Argent beach (p245), LaDigue, Seychelles

BEST BEACH EXPERIENCES

Join the influencers photographing one of the world's most famously beautiful beaches, ❶ **Anse Source d'Argent** in Seychelles. (p246)

Take in the sunset as you enjoy the warm, silvery waters of Mahé's west-facing ❷ **Beau Vallon beach** in Seychelles. (p213)

Seek out Mauritius' tranquil ❸ **Trou d'Eau Douce** for great fresh fish, unspoilt breezy beaches, and island excursions to even better beaches. (p108)

Hang out with local families, snorkel in the marine reserve and snooze under filao trees at Réunion's 7km-long ❹ **Plage de l'Hermitage.** (p153)

Kayak, paddleboard and snorkel around Chauve Souris off Praslin's ❺ **Anse Volbert** in Seychelles. (p235)

WORLD-CLASS BEACHES

There's no doubt about it: Indian Ocean beaches are among the best in the world. They're picture perfect, with soft white sand, leaning palm trees, protective barrier reefs and warm, translucent waters in extraordinary shades of blue. With 115 islands and islets, Seychelles has the most variety, with many beaches framed by millennia-old granite boulders. The scene in Mauritius is more lively and sociable, and in Réunion the volcano has created some of the world's newest black-sand shores.

Southeastern Trade Winds

Between May and October the southeastern trade winds blow, bringing breezes and choppy seas to southeastern beaches, making some of them unsafe.

Shark Safety on Réunion

Réunion sits on the shark highway between Australia and South Africa. Since 1913 there have been 56 attacks. For safety, swim off designated beaches only.

Beachwear

In Mauritius, Réunion and Seychelles, avoid wearing beachwear into town or in restaurants. Nude and topless sunbathing are prohibited.

OUR PICKS | PLAN YOUR TRIP

Eureka (p71), Mauritius

ISLAND ARCHITECTURE

What do Saint-Louis (Senegal), New Orleans (USA) and Port Louis (Mauritius) have in common? Surprisingly for such disparate places, the answer is their Creole architecture. The result of the long reach of the French colonial empire, the 18th- and 19th-century architecture of these former colonies displays an interesting and particular blend of European, Indian and African styles.

The Features

The classic Creole building has a gable roof, wraparound porch, symmetrical floor plan and absent interior hallways. Valued goods were stored below, with living quarters above.

The Verandah

The most recognisable feature of Creole architecture is a deep porch or 1st-floor gallery with a decorative trim. This is certainly an African and/or Indian influence.

BEST ARCHITECTURAL EXPERIENCES

Walk around the multicultural Mauritian capital of ❶ **Port Louis** to see its wealth of preserved Creole architecture and 18th-century street names. (p60)

As the political HQ of the French Indian Ocean plantation system, Mauritius has some grand plantation mansions. Seek out ❷ **Eureka** (p71) and **Château Labourdonnais**. (p73)

Wander Mauritius' World Heritage-listed ❸ **Aapravasi Ghat** immigration depot and contemplate the thousands of enslaved people and indentured workers who passed through here. (p62)

Drive up into Réunion's mountains to find the quaint, colourful town of ❹ **Hell-Bourg** with its well-preserved provincial Creole houses. (p187)

Visit Seychelles' Takamaka Rum Distillery, and after the tour check out the beautifully restored adjacent plantation villa of ❺ **La Plain St André**. (p220)

ADRENALINE RUSHES

Although diving and hiking hog the headlines on these tropical islands, their varied geography provides a natural adventure playground for a huge range of thrilling experiences. Choose from canyoning, whitewater rafting, caving, rappelling, paragliding, climbing, horse riding, deep-sea fishing, seasonal whale-watching and even the odd scenic helicopter ride if you want to splash out.

Paragliding Tips

It might seem challenging, but paragliding is very accessible and requires no special skill. First flights are done in tandem with an instructor. Simply bring sunglasses.

Cirque de Cilaos

Réunion's almost alpine Cirque de Cilaos is the epicentre of adventure activities on the island. Canyoning is particularly big, and climbing is increasing in popularity.

Réunion's Weather

Given the high altitudes on Réunion, you'll need to consider the weather when planning an adventure holiday. Wet season runs December to March, sometimes April.

BEST ADVENTURE EXPERIENCES

Check into Mauritius' chilled ❶ **Tamarin Bay** for a few days' surfing off a picturesque beach backed by tropical forest. (p83)

Hook up with local-activity fanatics Yanature, who can take you on guided kayaking trips or mountain-trail running in ❷ **Mauritius**. (p83)

If you fancy some thrilling canyoning or river rafting in Réunion, let Rando Aqua Reunion show you the ❸ **Rivière des Marsouins** and **Rivière des Roches**. (p182)

Want even more Réunion thrills? Throw yourself off a volcano and go paragliding in ❹ **St-Leu**. (p156) You can thank us later.

It's not all James Bond–level action on Réunion, though; the ❺ **Cilaosa Parc Aventure** has family-friendly adventure circuits in a cryptomeria forest. (p192)

TECHNICOLOUR DIVING

Although largely overshadowed by what's on offer in the Maldives, scuba diving in Mauritius, Réunion and Seychelles is more varied, with stunning underwater landscapes forged by volcanic eruptions and continental fractures. There's also a wealth of rainbow-coloured fish and large pelagics, including rays, swordfish and myriad shark species. Good sites are found off the west coast of Mauritius and Réunion, and the diving around Seychelles guarantees sensory overload with its amazing reefs and marine wildlife.

When to Dive

It's possible to dive year-round, but the best months are October to December, March and April. Visibility reduces when the south-eastern trade winds blow.

Snorkelling

If you don't want to dive, all the islands have great snorkelling opportunities near the barrier reefs that protect most beaches.

High Standards

Virtually all dive centres are affiliated with internationally recognised organisations such as PADI, SSI or CMAS and cater to all levels, including beginners.

Coral structure, Seychelles

BEST DIVING EXPERIENCES

Immerse yourself in the Outer Islands' colourful ❶ **Astove 'Wall'**. (p251)

Choose from the canyons of Colorado and Roches Zozo, the Trou Moutou anemone gardens and the wreck of the *Sirius* around ❷ **Blue Bay** in Mauritius. (p114)

Swim with barracudas, wahoos and sprats at lively Sprat City, then seek out the rays and trevallies of Morane, both in Seychelles' ❸ **Silhouette marine park**. (p232)

Explore spectacular seascapes just off Mauritius' busy ❹ **Flic en Flac beach**, including the Cathedral, Snake Reef and Colline Bambous. (p81)

Enjoy relaxed reef dives off Réunion's ❺ **St-Gilles-des-Bains**, with prolific fish life and cool wrecks. (p153)

PLAN YOUR TRIP — OUR PICKS

Heritage Le Telfair (p93), Mauritius

IDYLLIC OFFSHORE ISLANDS

Once you've landed on Mauritius, Réunion and Seychelles, you'll realise they are little worlds with even more exotic and secluded islands scattered around their shores. Many in Seychelles are stunning private-island resorts, while others are dedicated nature and marine reserves you can visit on day trips, replete with beach barbecues. They offer a vicarious castaway experience.

Private-Island Central

Seychelles is home to some of the world's most exclusive private-island resorts, such as North Island, Desroches, Félicité, Frégate, Alphonse and Platte.

Natural Reserves

Islands offer perfect self-contained conservation laboratories where endemic plants and animal populations can be revived and monitored by environmental scientists.

BEST ISLAND EXPERIENCES

Commit to a once-in-a-lifetime adventure on the incredible coral island of ❶ **Alphonse** in Seychelles' Outer Islands. (p251)

Turn back time on the ❷ **Île aux Aigrettes**, where the Mauritian Wildlife Foundation is nurturing rare endemic species back to health. (p115)

Go way off-piste in the ❸ **Cirque de Mafate** (p194), Réunion's most inaccessible mountain crater. It's not strictly an island, but it may as well be.

Walk with giant tortoises on Seychelles' ❹ **Curieuse Island** (p240), where 150 roam freely in the forest. They're also found on the island of Aldabra, but it's largely closed to all except scientists.

Book yourself a romantic getaway on charming ❺ **La Digue** (p242) or the coral cay of **Denis Island** (p232).

FROM LEFT: JESSE KENJI/500PX ©, WESTEND61/GETTY IMAGES ©, DIMITRI COUTANDY/SHUTTERSTOCK ©

VOLCANIC ADVENTURES

Réunion's iconic Piton de la Fournaise is one of the most active volcanoes on the planet, regularly putting forth explosive founts of magma that tourists flock to see. You can drive to its rim, hike the crater, traverse its sand desert and burrow beneath in its lava tunnels. Whatever you do, visiting it is an incredible experience.

The Schedule

La Piton de la Fournaise (pictured) erupts nearly every eight months. Eruptions are generally confined to the caldera, but activity sometimes flows down the eastern flank.

Mother Mountain

Near the Piton de la Fournaise, the Piton des Neiges erupted to create Réunion two million years ago but is now considered extinct.

Shield-Volcano Science

Shield-volcano eruptions are easy to predict and feature runny, low-viscosity magma that bubbles out in a gentle stream, thus making them relatively 'safe'.

BEST VOLCANO EXPERIENCES

Stand at the edge of the awesome 8km-wide crater at the ❶ **Pas de Bellecombe** (p199), in view of the central cone where all the eruptions take place.

Check out Bourg-Murat's immersive ❷ **City of Volcanology museum** (p200), full of lava facts, samples and interactive exhibits. Great for families.

Drive the Lava Rd across the blackened landscape of the ❸ **Grand Brûlé** (p184), a solidified lava flow.

Hike from the Pas de Bellecombe or walk from the Pas de Sables around the ❹ **Plaine des Sables** (p199), a rust-coloured lunar desert made of volcanic mineral dust.

Spelunk into the dark, hot lava tunnel of ❺ **Bassin Bleu** (p155), one of the oldest on the island, where endemic birds nest.

Sir Selwyn Clarke Market (p216), Victoria, Seychelles

BEST CULTURAL EXPERIENCES

Catch live local music performances in Mauritius at the nightclubs of ❶ **Grand Baie** and **Flic en Flac**, as well as dozens of local music festivals. (p81)

Participate in cool cultural workshops or take an off-the-radar tour with Mauritian insiders ❷ **My Moris**. (p62)

Dig into the secrets of Creole cooking with home-based cookery workshops in the lovely countryside around ❸ **St-André** on Réunion. (p179)

Stock up on the best island souvenirs – local spices and condiments – at Victoria's lively ❹ **Sir Selwyn Selwyn-Clarke Market** in Seychelles. (p216)

Party at Seychelles' week-long ❺ **Festival Kreol** in October, celebrating traditional food, music and dance. (p35)

COLOURFUL CREOLE CULTURE

With the focus firmly on those amazing beaches and impossibly blue sea, visitors are often surprised to discover the unique Creole cultures that thrive on these islands. They are the upshot of the interesting integration of once-segregated European, African, Indian and Asian communities after the abolition of slavery. The result is rich, island-specific blended cultures with their own unique music, food, art and traditions.

Hindu Festivals

The large Mauritian Hindu community celebrates lots of colourful festivals, including Holi, Diwali and Teemeedee (p92).

Tropical Fusion Food

Creole food is one of the big highlights here, blending African, Indian, Asian and European flavours with the freshest fish and incredible tropical fruit.

The Local Lingo

Each of the islands has its own Creole language, derived from French with African and Indian influences. English and French are also widely spoken.

FROM LEFT: JUERGEN RITTERBACH / ALAMY STOCK PHOTO ©; THE VISUAL EXPLORER/SHUTTERSTOCK ©; GOWTUM/SHUTTERSTOCK ©

21

PLAN YOUR TRIP | OUR PICKS

Cilaos (p190), Réunion

CONTEMPORARY ART SCENE

Music has traditionally been the islands' main art form, but contemporary art is a growing area of creative expression. Mauritius has the biggest scene, with several large galleries, an annual salon and prizes, and artists' studios to visit. The scene in Réunion and Seychelles is smaller but developing, and young artists are putting out some thought-provoking work.

Salon de Mai

May is a good art month in Mauritius, with such cultural events as the Salon de Mai and the Laguna Art Prize. (p78)

Collectible Embroidery

The village of Cilaos is famous for its delicate embroidery, which is now much sought after by collectors. (p190) You can purchase pieces at the Maison de la Broderie.

BEST ART EXPERIENCES

Plan an art day in the Mauritian capital of Port Louis and visit the ❶ **Caudan Art Centre**, **ICAIO** and **EDITH**, all showcasing local and regional talent. (p65)

Follow Port Louis' ❷ **street-art trail**, a great way of exploring the city while getting an art fix. (p66)

Discover the ❸ **Lieu d'Art Contemporain** in St-Pierre, Réunion, where street artists, painters, photographers and sculptors showcase their work. (p171)

Visit the studio of ❹ **Michael Adams**, in Mahé, Seychelles. His work is on display alongside that of his talented son and daughter. (p226)

Look out for George Camille's galleries in ❺ **La Digue** (p243) and **Victoria** (p217). He's one of Seychelles' most celebrated artists, participating in two Venice Biennales.

FROM LEFT: KLETR/SHUTTERSTOCK ©, ARAKO SPACE/SHUTTERSTOCK ©, JAN BURES/SHUTTERSTOCK

LAVISH TROPICAL GARDENS

Horticulturalist and one-time administrator of Mauritius and Réunion, Pierre Poivre (1719–86), introduced spices to all these islands. He stole them from the Dutch in Indonesia and planted them in the garden of Pamplemousses in Mauritius in 1769. Thus began the Mascarene spice trade, which resulted in the creation of modern-day Mauritius, Réunion and Seychelles.

The Value of Spice

Vanilla (pictured) remains one of the world's most expensive spices. After a devastating cyclone in Madagascar in 2017, the price of vanilla exceeded that of silver.

Spices Versus Endemics

Although these Indian Ocean islands are known as 'spice islands', spice trees are invasive species. Some, like cinnamon (pictured), crowd out rare endemics if not controlled.

Turmeric Tales

Demand for spices is increasing due to their reported health benefits. This is particularly true of turmeric, which is taken as an anti-inflammatory.

PLAN YOUR TRIP — OUR PICKS

BEST BOTANICAL EXPERIENCES

Delight in Mauritius' vast, gorgeous garden of ❶ **Pamplemousses**, the oldest botanical garden in the Indian Ocean. (p69)

Walk through Réunion's lovely ❷ **Botanical Garden of Mascarin**, which is landscaped into themed areas, then buy some spices in the shop. (p157)

Head for the lovely ❸ **Ferney Valley conservation area** (p122) in Mauritius, where you can visit a traditional spice garden, then dine at the farm-to-table **Falaise Rouge**. (p122)

Cycle down La Digue's sandy roads to ❹ **L'Union Estate**, a heritage Seychellois spice plantation that still produces and sells vanilla and coconut products. (p243)

Learn the wildest and wackiest facts about Seychelles' endemic plants and spices on a brilliant guided tour at the ❺ **National Biodiversity Centre**. (p222)

23

PLANTATION HISTORY & LEGACY

Given the natural beauty of these islands, it's easy to overlook their difficult history of slavery and exploitation. But there's an increasing desire to recognise the complexities of that history in new museums, heritage experiences, and cultural tours and workshops. Their aim is to recognise the huge financial and cultural contribution of enslaved peoples, acknowledge the hardships borne by them, and celebrate the rich legacies they left in the language, music, food and art.

Vanilla Tea

Bois Chéri's vanilla tea is one of Mauritius' most popular beverages, dating from the late 19th century, when the island had numerous vanilla and tea plantations.

Island Souvenirs

The best souvenirs to take home from these islands are spices (particularly vanilla, cinnamon and nutmeg), tea, rum and coconut products.

Musical Heritage

Tracing their origins to the era of slavery are Creole musical styles such as séga, moutya and maloya. They are the soul music of enslaved peoples. (p282)

Stella Matutina Museum (p158), St. Leu, Réunion

BEST HERITAGE EXPERIENCES

Dig deep into plantation-system history at the Mauritian World Heritage Site of ❶ **Aapravasi Ghat**. (p62)

Learn about enslaved 12-year-old Edmund Albius' remarkable technique of vanilla pollination at Réunion's ❷ **ProVanille plantation**. Albius linked the island and the spice forever when he devised an efficient pollination method. (p180)

Walk through spice and fruit trees at Seychelles' ❸ **Le Jardin du Roi**, then taste old Creole recipes in the open-air dining room. (p221)

Explore sugar-cane's industrial history at Réunion's ❹ **Stella Matutina Museum** (p158) and **L'Aventure du Sucre** (p73) in Mauritius.

Join savvy Seychellois grandmas to learn local crafts and cookery at plantation house ❺ **Domaine de Val des Près**. (p218)

REGIONS & CITIES

Find the places that tick all your boxes.

Seychelles

ISLAND HOPPING AND WORLD-CLASS BEACHES

Seychelles is a storybook paradise with dozens of islands to explore, fringed by some of the world's best beaches and surrounded by some of the Indian Ocean's most pristine marine parks. On land, you may be surprised to find tropical forests, nesting sites with thousands of seabirds, islands devoted to giant tortoises, and even a prehistoric palm forest with a legendary sea coconut. Seychelles' Creole culture is another great discovery, particularly its fantastic seafood.

Seychelles
p207

Seychelles Outer Islands

MARINE MARVEL & OFF-GRID LUXURY

Scattered across the deep ocean at distances of 210km to 1150km from Mahé, Seychelles Outer Islands consist of 72 coral cays and four immense atolls surrounding vivid blue lagoons. Most are uninhabited (except for three private island resorts) – they're miniature worlds containing largely untouched marine habitats teeming with wildlife. Few visitors remain unmoved by what they see: pristine reefs, millions of nesting seabirds and a marine wonderland that scientists use as a baseline for what the world once looked like.

Seychelles Outer Islands
p247

Rodrigues

BLISSFUL ESCAPISM AND UNSPOILT NATURE

An hour from Mauritius by plane is tiny Rodrigues, a vintage volcanic throwback a million miles away from its multicultural sister island. It's characterised by laidback fishing villages, gorgeous island scenery, pristine offshore islands and one of the most beautiful coastal walks in the world, running between Graviers and St François.

Rodrigues
p124

Mauritius
p55

Mauritius

CREOLE CULTURE AND ALL-ROUND ADVENTURE

Multicultural Mauritius has it all: mountains, beaches, surfing, diving, river gorges, waterfalls, tea plantations, conservation projects, joyful Hindu festivals, and a dynamic urban scene full of food markets, art galleries and music venues. Food and culture aficionados shouldn't miss Port Louis and Chamarel; Flic en Flac has some of the Indian Ocean's best dives; and hikers should head for the dramatic hills and waterfalls of the Black River Gorges.

Réunion
p131

Réunion

VOLCANIC DRAMA AND WHALE WATCHING

Soaring peaks 3km high, plunging green valleys, the scorched desert landscapes of Le Grand Brûlé and the bubbling volcano of Piton de la Fournaise – Réunion will take your breath away. Adrenaline seekers will be in heaven here as they hike the great Cirque de Mafate, canyon in the Cirque de Cilaos, and white-water raft, paraglide and whale watch on the west coast. But don't forget to check out the Creole restaurants, heritage sites and street art of St-Denis, and the food market and music festival of SAKIFO in St-Pierre.

MADAGASCAR

PLAN YOUR TRIP REGIONS & CITIES

Caudan Waterfront, Port Louis (p60)

ITINERARIES

A Tour of Mauritius

Allow: 14 days **Distance:** 202km

This itinerary will give you a snapshot of the very best of Mauritius, from its vibrant cities to its stunning mountain landscapes, beautiful gardens, gorgeous beaches and idyllic islets. Throw in some great cultural tours, Creole cuisine, hiking and diving, and you'll have a perfect fortnight.

❶ PORT LOUIS ⏱ 2 DAYS

Start in the lively city of **Port Louis** (p60) getting to grips with the island's multicultural character. Visit temples, churches, forts and Unesco-listed sites on immersive My Moris tours. Then spend the day exploring island flavours in city markets and at popular food stalls. The Natural History Museum (pictured) is a good intro to island fauna, including the now-extinct dodo. Then pick up a hire car and head south.

❷ TAMARIN ⏱ 3 DAYS

Drive south past Flic en Flac's beach. It's the longest strand on the island, with fabulous snorkelling and diving. Stop for lunch and a swim, then push on to nearby **Tamarin** (p83), a laid-back surf town (pictured). Stay a couple of days to catch some breaks, go kayaking upriver and head out on boat trips.

Detour: The **Tamarind Falls** is a 40-minute drive east of Tamarin. It's an easy hike through the forest. ⏱ 6 hours.

❸ MAHÉBOURG ⏱ 2 DAYS

Make a stop in historic **Mahébourg** (p119), a quiet market town with a history of naval battles and a museum covering colonial history. It's also a great food town with an open-air market and brilliant restaurants, while the Rault factory still turns out handmade manioc biscuits.

Detour: Drive 15 minutes north to **Vieux Grand Port** (p117) to see where the first settlers landed. ⏱ 2 hours.

PLAN YOUR TRIP ITINERARIES

❹ BLUE BAY ⏱ 3 DAYS

When you arrive in **Blue Bay** (p114) you'll never want to leave. It's gorgeously tranquil. No speedboats are allowed, to protect the coral, and the snorkelling here is excellent. Two kilometres north, Pointe d'Esny also has great dive sites. There's some lovely accommodation, so give yourself a few days to enjoy.

🐾 *Detour: Boats depart Pointe d'Esny for **Île aux Aigrettes** (p115), 1km offshore.* ⏱ 5 hours.

❺ TROU D'EAU DOUCE ⏱ 1 DAY

Driving up the eastern side of the island, you'll want to stop in at **Trou d'Eau Douce** (p108). It offers a great slice of local life, with villagers still making a living from fishing. That means there are some excellent seafood restaurants. You can pick up snacks at Les Alizées or dine on perfect fish at Lacaz Poisson.

🐾 *Detour: Spend another day and head to **Île aux Cerfs** (p107; during the week is best).* ⏱ 6 hours.

❻ CAP MALHEUREUX ⏱ 2 DAYS

Cap Malheureux (p105) gets its name from all the ships wrecked off its shores. The coastline here is full of character, the village has a charming church and there's boutique accommodation. If you fancy a night out, the bars of Trou-aux-Biches are just 20 minutes away, but devote yourself to beach walks and boat trips.

🐾 *Detour: On the drive back to Port Louis, take the route to **Pamplemousses Botanical Garden** (p69).* ⏱ 2–3 hours.

FROM LEFT: LOVEMELOVEMYPIC/SHUTTERSTOCK ©, DMITRY VERYOVKIN/SHUTTERSTOCK ©, SERENITY-H/SHUTTERSTOCK ©

Formica Leo, Piton de la Fournaise (p198)

ITINERARIES

Highlights of Réunion

Allow: 10 days **Distance:** 325km

Réunion's southern shores and central high plains offer dramatic scenery, with volcanic landscapes, massive ravines, wave-lashed cliffs and some of the world's best hiking. You can discover the highlights in a 10-day tour with a few days of beach time and some small-city exploration.

❶ BOUCAN CANOT ⏱ 2 DAYS

On arrival, drive 30 minutes down the west coast to Senteur Vanille near **Boucan Canot** (p153). Take the Nouvelle Rte du Littoral coast road for amazing views. Boucan Canot is a seaside enclave with a safe beach. Nearby is the marine park of L'Ermitage-les-Bains and the small town of St-Paul, site of Réunion's first settlement.

*Detour: The 2190m-high **Maïdo Belvedere** (p151) is one of the island's best viewpoints. ⏱ 5 hours.*

❷ ST-PIERRE ⏱ 2 DAYS

Drive down to **St-Pierre** (p159), the main city of the south, with a buzzing seafront and pleasant beaches. You can stop en route at Le Blue Margouillat in St-Leu for a super meal. Explore St-Pierre's temples, churches and contemporary-art museum, LAC; visit the local market (pictured); and eat greedily at the seaside food trucks and restaurants..

*Detour: Take a day trip to isolated **St-Joseph** (p172). ⏱ 7 hours.*

❸ PITON DE LA FOURNAISE ⏱ 1 DAY

Get up *early* for a day of adventure on the **Piton de la Fournaise volcano** (p198). From Plaine des Cafres you'll drive up through an Alpine-like landscape and a canyon-like valley until you reach the Pas de Bellecombe (2311m). Walks and hikes start from here. Take one of the easy walks before making your way down to Ste-Rose on the eastern side of the island.

④ STE-ROSE ⏱ 2 DAYS

Stay a night in **Ste-Rose** (p179), where you'll find the Notre Dame des Laves (pictured), a Catholic church revered for its supernatural force in arresting a lava flow almost at its doorstep in 1977. The lava wall is still there in front of the church.

Detour: Twenty minutes south of Ste-Rose, **Le Grand Brulé** (Great Burnt Land; p184) is the eerie lava field left after the last eruption of the Piton de la Fournaise. Get lunch at La Case Volcan. ⏱ 5 hours

⑤ ST-ANDRÉ ⏱ 1 DAY

On your way back north, overnight in agricultural **St-André** (p176), which was shaped by the sugar-cane industry and where you can visit the Bois Rouge factory and Savanna rum distillery. There's a huge Hindu community here and Tamil celebrations are big. Take a guided tour of the Maryen Péroumal temple and consider a cooking class with La Sirandane.

⑥ ST-DENIS ⏱ 2 DAYS

Finally, land in **St-Denis** (p136), Réunion's capital and hub of history. Check out the street art, visit the art centres and museums, and hunt down some Creole meals. Le Reflet des Îles is an institution, serving traditional dishes. If you're lucky enough to be visiting in December, try to catch the celebrations on the 20th commemorating the 1848 Abolition of Slavery.

La Passe, La Digue (p242)

ITINERARIES

Essential Seychelles

Allow: 14 days   **Distance:** 200km

You really need two weeks to do justice to Seychelles and explore its mosaic of islands. The different characters of each island often come as a surprise to visitors, and there's a wide range of nature-based activities – as well some of the world's finest, most unspoilt beaches to lounge on.

❶ BEAU VALLON ⏱ 3 DAYS

Start off in **Beau Vallon** (p213), with a safe beach that offers stunning sunsets. It's near some great restaurants and bars. From here you can organise snorkelling and diving adventures to the marine parks of Baie Ternay and Port Launay. You won't need a car, as most things are within walking or taxu distance.

Detour: Take a half-day away from the beach to hike in **Morne Seychellois National Park** (p224). ⏱ 4 hours.

❷ VICTORIA ⏱ 1 DAY

The world's smallest capital city, **Victoria** (p213) deserves a full day to explore its fantastic market, vibrant art galleries and super Marie Antoinette Creole restaurant. Also here are the National History Museum and the archipelago's oldest cemetery, which are worth visiting to understand Seychelles' origin story of slavers, pirates, exiles and revolutionaries – as well as the birth of Creole culture.

❸ ANSE À LA MOUCHE ⏱ 2 DAYS

Head southwest on Chemin Sans Souci. Stop at the Mission Ruins and then drive down the western coast admiring the beaches until you get to the prettiest, **Anse à la Mouche** (p222). Base yourself here and visit the artists' studios that cluster on Baie Lazare and dine in the fine restaurants.

Detour: A 10-minute drive north is the **Biodiversity Centre** (p222) and Turquoise Trails, if you fancy horse riding.

FROM LEFT: NICK FOX/SHUTTERSTOCK ©, VIDEO MEDIA STUDIO EUROPE/SHUTTERSTOCK ©, GABRIELE MALTINTI/SHUTTERSTOCK ©

④ ANSE ROYALE ⏱ 2 DAYS

Take the long way round the south of the island to Mahé's second city, **Anse Royale** (p228). On the way, go to Petit Police to see the wild southern tip of the island, before heading back northeast. Sleepy Anse Royale offers great snorkelling, kayaking and some surfing as well as a laid-back village vibe.

↪ *Detour: The Takamaka Rum Distillery (p220) and Domaine de Val de Prés are an easy excursion.* ⏱ *4 hours.*

⑤ PRASLIN ⏱ 2 DAYS

Take the 8am ferry across to **Praslin** (p233), Seychelles' second-largest island. Base yourself on Anse Volbert beach. Also, visit the extraordinary Unesco heritage site of the Vallée de Mai to see the famous coco de mer love nut. A tour is well worth it to understand this unique prehistoric palm forest.

↪ *Detour: If you can squeeze it in, book a trip to Curieuse Island (p240) or Cousin Island (p241).* ⏱ *6 hours.*

⑥ LA DIGUE ⏱ 3 DAYS

Make sail for **La Digue** (p242), 15 minutes away. You'll need three days here to do justice to the island's beaches. Don't miss Anse Source d'Argent, Anse Sévère and Anse Coco. Also worth a visit is L'Union Estate, a heritage plantation where you can still buy vanilla, cinnamon and coconut products.

↪ *Detour: Snorkelling and diving trips are possible to surrounding islets such as Île Cocos (p247).* ⏱ *4–6 hours.*

WHEN TO GO

These balmy subtropical islands are year-round destinations. The best time to go really depends on what you want to do.

Mauritius, Réunion and Seychelles all have subtropical climates, with sea temperatures averaging 24°C and humidity hovering around 80%. Across all the islands the UV index is a high 10 to 11.

Situated in the southern hemisphere, Mauritius and Réunion have summer in November–December. This is also the wettest season, particularly in mountainous Réunion. In fact, Réunion's south-eastern side is one of the wettest places on the planet! The island's temperature variation from coast to peak is some 10°C to 15°C. Mauritius experiences its coldest weather in August, when average temperatures are 17°C.

Sitting almost on the equator outside the cyclone belt, Seychelles always stays in a balmy window of 24°C to 32°C. Its slight weather variations are dictated by the north-western (December to March) and south-eastern (May to October) trade winds. The former bring tropical rains and the latter a cooler wind, which is lovely but makes some beaches unsafe for swimming.

I LIVE HERE

TALL FISHING TALES

Keith Rose Innes (roseinnes.com) is a world-class fly-fisherman and co-founder of marine-safari outfit Blue Safari. @bluesafariseychelles

I've been exploring Seychelles Outer Islands for over 20 years. In my opinion, it's the most thrilling place to fish in the world. In 2011 I was one of the first to see giant trevally leap from the water and catch a baby bird – a scene we helped capture for Blue Planet II. Now Blue Safari works with the government to protect these pristine islands from illegal fishing and monitor climate change.

Deep Sea Fishing, La Digue (p242), Seychelles

CYCLONES

Cyclones occur in the southern Indian Ocean in summer (December to March). They're most likely in Mauritius in January and February and in Réunion in February and March. There are around four cyclones a year, but most dissipate offshore. Seychelles sits outside the cyclone belt.

Weather through the year

MAURITIUS DRY SEASON
June to Sept
Avg daytime max: **25°C**

MAURITIUS DRY SEASON
Days of rainfall per month:
10-13

MAURITIUS WET SEASON
Nov to April
Avg daytime max: **28°C**

MAURITIUS WET SEASON
Days of rainfall per month:
14-17

RÉUNION DRY SEASON
June to Nov
Avg daytime max: **28°C**

RÉUNION DRY SEASON
Days of rainfall per month:
7-10

TRADE WINDS

When the sun is in the north (May to September), the south-eastern trade winds blow 10 to 20 knots, whipping up waves on south-eastern beaches. When the sun's in the south (November to March), light, north-westerly winds mean clear seas that are great for diving.

Big-Ticket Festivals

On Mauritius and Réunion, **Chinese New Year** sees homes decked out in red (the colour of happiness) and fireworks rain down, particularly in Port Louis (Mauritius). Around the same time, the Tamil Hindu festival Cavadee involves fire walking.
Late January, early February

Maha Shivarati, the biggest Hindu festival on Mauritius, involves a pilgrimage of 500,000 people to the holy lake of Grand Bassin. Colourful **Holi** follows hot on its heels.
February or March

The Indian Ocean's biggest music festival is **SAKIFO**, celebrated in St-Pierre (Réunion). Some 40,000 people attend for the diverse program, including Creole maloya, salsa, funk and blues.
June

The **Feast of the Assumption** on La Digue (Seychelles) is the archipelago's biggest religious celebration, drawing visitors from all the islands for a blessing, procession and street party. **August**

I LIVE HERE

WEDDING SEASON

Natasha St Ange is a descendant of a spice-farming family on La Digue and runs Le Nautique guesthouse.
@lenautiqueseychelles

My ancestors came to Seychelles from Réunion in 1811 and farmed coconuts, patchouli and vanilla. When farming collapsed, the family turned to tourism. My grandfather opened one of the first hotels on La Digue and repurposed the farm's ox carts as tourist transport. During wedding season you still see them around the island decorated with palm leaves and bougainvillea.

Ox Cart, La Passe, Seychelles

HOT & HUMID

In summer Mauritius has relative humidity of 92% – uncomfortable if you're not on a beach. Réunion is less humid, but even moderate humidity can make an easy hike feel difficult. April to mid-December has the best hiking weather.

Under-the-Radar Local Events

LA ISLA 2068 showcases the best of the local music scene on small stages while the audience picnics on street-food favourites. Fun kids' workshops in the day; dancing after dark.
May

September is great for small local festivals in Mauritius, including the **Trou d'Eau Douce** book festival and the **All Waves** music festival. On 9 September Christians undertake the **Père Laval** pilgrimage to the priest's shrine at Ste-Croix to pray for miracles. **September**

Seychelles' island-wide **Festival Kreol** offers an opportunity to see heritage dances such as the moutya and séga, taste local recipes at food stalls and check out the latest in Creole art and music.
October

The **Grand Raid** is Réunion's cross-country trail run, covering 165km across the lofty cirques from St-Pierre to St-Denis. Not for the fainthearted. **October**

RÉUNION WET SEASON
Dec to March
Avg daytime max: 30°C

RÉUNION WET SEASON
Days of rainfall per month: 11-14

SEYCHELLES DRY SEASON
May to October
Avg daytime max: 29°C

SEYCHELLES DRY SEASON
Days of rainfall per month: 3-6

SEYCHELLES WET SEASON
Nov to April
Avg daytime max: 30°C

SEYCHELLES WET SEASON
Days of rainfall per month: 6-9

Beach, Balaclava area, Mauritius

GET PREPARED FOR MAURITIUS, RÉUNION & SEYCHELLES

Useful things to load in your bag, your ears and your brain

Clothes

Beachwear For children and those prone to sunburn, consider UV-protection swimsuits or tops and a hat with a decent brim. If snorkelling, your own snorkel, mask and flippers are best. Reserve beachwear for the beach only. Nude and topless bathing are prohibited.

Hiking gear Avoid lycra and heavy safari clothes; instead, pack light, long trousers and some loose, long-sleeve shirts. On Réunion, you'll need a fleece and lightweight waterproof jacket for altitude and comfortable hiking boots (river runners are also good). Also pack binoculars, a torch and mosquito spray.

Fishing kit Pack flat boots for reef wading, and a waterproof rucksack and polarised sunglasses.

Manners

Cultural diversity is integral to the social fabric. Universal immigrant ancestry, shared Creole cultures and an emphasis on family life are strong unifiers.

Religious tolerance is the norm, and churches, temples, mosques and pagodas are found in close proximity. Dress modestly if you visit.

Gossip is a national pastime everywhere. In Réunion it's called *la di la fé* and is best enjoyed via Radio Free Dom (freedom.fr).

📖 READ

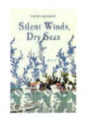

Silent Winds, Dry Seas
(Vinod Busjeet; 2021)
A debut novel about identity, place and the legacy of colonialism in Mauritius.

Voices: Seychelles Short Stories (Glynn Burridge; 2014) Descriptions of life on the remote Outer Islands.

Blue Bay Palace
Nathacha Appanah; 2009) Life in a developing country: this is a novel of love, poverty and tourism.

Tête Haute (Memona Hintermann; 2009) This is a personal rags-to-riches tale tackling issues of colonialism and immigration.

Words

'Allo', 'Bonjour', 'Bonzour' is how you say hello in Mauritian Creole, French and Seychellois Creole.

'Bonzour, ki manier?' is Mauritian Creole for 'Good morning, how are you?' You reply, **'Mo bien, mersi'** ('I'm fine, thanks'). In Seychelles, 'How are you?' is **'Comman sava?'**

'Ki dir?' is a casual 'What's up?' in Seychellois.

'Je ne comprends pas' means 'I don't understand' in French; **'Mo pas kompran'** is the equivalent in Creole.

'Excusez moi' ('Excuse me') and **'Pardon'** ('Sorry') are useful French niceties.

'Pa met pima' is what you say in Mauritius if you don't want chilli on your food.

'Ey, kass ene poz' – literally, 'break for a pause' – translates as 'Hey, chill out' in Mauritius.

'Parlez-vous Anglais?' is French for 'Do you speak English?' Most people do, but less commonly in rural Réunion.

Zorey (literally, 'the ears') is what Réunionnais call French mainlanders. It implies that mainlanders are constantly straining to hear what's being said about them in the local patois.

La pasians i geri la gal is one of Réunion's bon mots. It means patience cures everything, but it translates literally as 'patience heals scabies'!

'S'il vous plaît' is please in French; the equivalents are **silvouple** in Seychellois Creole and **siouplé** in Mauritian.

Je suis allergique is how you tell people you have an allergy in French; **'appelez un médecin'** is 'call a doctor'.

'Où sont les toilettes?' is how you ask where the nearest toilets are in French; in Seychellois, say **'Oli toilet?'**

Anse Soleil (p226), Seychelles

Snorkelling, Seychelles

🎧 LISTEN

Remember Me
(AnneGa; 2021) The debut album from pop artist Anne Gaëlle Bourquin, a Mauritian singer and songwriter influenced by the likes of Coldplay.

Maligasé
(Trans Kabar; 2019) A maloya rock band inspired by the music and songs of enslaved Réunionnaise ancestors, with an electronic twist.

Seychelles – Nouvelle Tendances (various artists; 2018) A mixed album featuring Seychellois greats such as Jeny Letourdie, Jean-Marc Volcy and Patrick Victor.

Sanpek (Patyatann; 2016) A contemporary group putting out a dreamy, spiritual-sounding fusion music performed on traditional instruments.

Diving, Seychelles

TRIP PLANNER

DIVING IN MAURITIUS, RÉUNION & SEYCHELLES

Diving off these Indian Ocean islands is a world-class experience. All are surrounded by barrier reefs, which are home to a huge variety of rainbow-coloured fish and large pelagic species, including sharks, barracudas, rays, trevallies and turtles. The underwater scenery, particularly around Seychelles and Réunion, is stunning, with giant granite boulders, steep drop-offs, caves and tunnels.

Diving in Mauritius

Abundant marine life, dramatic seascapes, atmospheric wrecks – Mauritius has it all, not to mention well-established, high-quality dive operators run by Mauritius Scuba Diving Association (msda.mu). The island is surrounded by a barrier reef, creating turquoise lagoons that provide great possibilities, although some sites are affected by currents, plus cyclones in January and February. Mauritius is diveable year-round, but the best months are March, April and October to December.

WHERE TO DIVE

North Coast A magnet for divers of all levels given its combination of wrecks, drop-offs and easy dives. The offshore islands (Île Plate, Coin de Mire) are a highlight. Trou aux Biches is the main departure point.
West Flic en Flac is one of the best places for diving, with good conditions year-round as it's protected from the prevailing winds.
South-east More impressive underwater terrain with a profusion of caves, tunnels and giant arches as well as large pelagics. However, between June and August visibility is poor and the sea choppy.
East Not great for diving, with the excep-

tion of two sites: Belmar Pass and Passe de Trou d'Eau Douce.

Rodrigues An absolute highlight, with virgin sites and outstanding fish life.

Diving in Réunion

Réunion is less well known for its diving than for its hiking, but there's a good variety of dive spots inside the lagoon for novices, and deeper dives (25m to 40m) just outside for experienced divers. Most sites are found off the west coast between Boucan Canot and St-Pierre. Dive centres concentrate around St-Gilles-les-Bains, St-Leu, Étang-Salé-les-Bains and St-Pierre. Most instructors speak English. You'll need a medical certificate stating you're fit to dive, which is compulsory in France. The best time for diving is October to April.

WHERE TO DIVE

St-Gilles-les-Bains The main dive area, with relaxed diving around reefs, which slope gently away in a series of valleys to a sandy bottom in about 25m. Prolific fish life.
St-Leu Splendid wall diving and good coral fields, but with less fish. The Tombant de la Pointe au Sel is considered Réunion's best all-round site for experienced divers.
St-Pierre Less well known is the area between St-Pierre and Grand Bois. The main draw is the interesting topography characterised by ridges, canyons and drop-offs.

Diving in Seychelles

One of the Indian Ocean's great diving destinations, Seychelles has spectacular underwater landscapes and is a hot spot for large pelagics. There's a huge variety of sites here, with something to suit all abilities. Dive centres maintain high standards. You can dive around all three main islands – Mahé, Praslin and La Digue (at a depth of 10m to 30m) – as well as in the marine park around Silhouette and Curieuse. Diving in the Outer Islands is simply out of this world.

Although you can dive year-round, some sites are very weather dependent. The seas are calmest and clearest from April to May and October to November.

WHERE TO DIVE

Mahé Sites off Mahé include abundant fish life (including large pelagics), coral-clad granite islets, offshore wrecks and plenty of shark species around Shark Point.
Praslin & La Digue There's a mix of easy sites around La Digue, Curieuse and Cousin, as well as more pristine, deeper dives near Aride Island and Booby Islet.
Silhouette & North Island Pristine marine-park diving between the two islands. Sprat City is an aptly named site on a large reef north of Silhouette; Turtle Rock and Barracuda Rock have great underwater formations.
Outer Islands Diving in the Amirantes and Alphonse Group is the stuff of legend. The biomass here is six times that of the inner islands, and the coral is some of the most abundant and healthy in the Indian Ocean.

Diving responsibly

- Practise and maintain proper buoyancy control.
- Avoid touching living marine organisms with your body or equipment.
- Never stand on corals, even if they look solid and robust.
- Take care in underwater caves, as your air bubbles can damage fragile organisms.
- Minimise your disturbance of marine animals.
- Take home all your rubbish, and any litter you find as well.
- Do not collect seashells (or buy seashells, turtle shells or products made from them).

CORAL BLEACHING

The western Indian Ocean has significant coral biodiversity, with literally hundreds of species that in turn support a wealth of fish. It's all the more distressing, then, that the ocean's reefs were badly hit by coral bleaching in 1997 and 1998, and again in 2016. Bleaching is caused by sea-temperature rises exacerbated by climate change. The International Union for Conservation of Nature now considers these reefs to be endangered. Although there are some signs of new growth, in Seychelles there are several conservation projects (particularly on Cousin Island) whereby scientists are transplanting new corals to affected areas.

Cirque de Mafate (p194)

TRIP PLANNER

HIKING IN RÉUNION

From the seashore to the top of Piton des Neiges (3069m), Réunion is a dream for hikers. About 900km of marked tracks go through and around the island, from bottom to top. From easy to very hard, there's something for everyone who wants to explore Réunion's glorious environment at close quarters.

Réunion's Sensational Terrain

Covering 42% of the island, Réunion National Park is a Unesco World Heritage Site. Hiking is almost mandatory here if you want to follow the island's rugged volcanic coastline, explore the greener inland areas, discover the most concealed waterfalls and reach remote 'islets' – hamlets nestled in the mountains. All types of landscapes are accessible on a hike: heathland in Le Maïdo, rainforest in Bélouve, a car-free Mafate cirque, volcanic coast in Ste-Rose, and even the slopes of active Piton de la Fournaise volcano, to mention only a few.

Paths for All

Many paths are accessible and easy, and don't require specific training or experience. These include a short hike to a waterfall pond or the entrance to a lava tunnel, or an educative forest loop. But the challenge goes gradually up to 'medium' (a five-hour loop in a cirque with some steep sections) and then 'very difficult' (as in, 'not recommended without a guide and being in excellent physical condition') – these go up to the top of peaks or down to the bottom of riverbeds. Réunion is also home to one of the most spectacular and demanding trails on the planet: the Grand Raid, which takes you across the island from south to north.

Hiking with Kids

Hiking paths are for everyone in Réunion! If you're hiking with children, look for the words Sentier Marmailles (Children's Path).

This designation indicates that the path is suitable for children, with no technical difficulty or dangerous zones. Keep in mind, though, that some of these might still be a bit steep!

Preserving a National Park

Much of the island is part of the protected national park, with many endemic and indigenous species, some in danger of extinction. To help preserve this heritage, there are two basic rules: never pluck any flower or plant along your way, and clean your shoes between hikes to avoid transporting seeds from one site to another.

Prepare for Your Hike

WEATHER

Always check conditions on your route before you leave, on dedicated websites (randopitons.re is the best if you can read French) or with the tourist office. These resources can provide updates on whether hiking paths are closed due to natural disasters or bad weather (landslides, forest fires, heavy rainfall…). Don't go hiking after long periods of rain, since paths can be slippery and rivers may have flooded. Be aware that the weather can change rapidly during your trip, especially in the heights.

CAMPING

Some hikes might require an overnight stay for a better or more complete experience, or simply because of their length. This is often the case for hiking in the cirques (Mafate, Salazie, Cilaos) as the drive there can take a big part of your day before you even reach the starting point. Climbing Piton des Neiges, the highest peak in Réunion – and indeed in the Indian Ocean – is also an overnight trip. If you're doing one of these hikes, book your accommodation first, especially in high season. Most refuges or mountain guesthouses can offer meals, which you'll need to book in advance as well.

GUIDES

A guide can be helpful for particularly adventurous hikes, but they're a good idea in general. With mountaineering guides

---

HIKING CHECKLIST

Make sure you inform somebody of your intended route before you leave, and tell them when you expect to return. The following are recommended items to take with you.

- A paper map, or instructions about your intended itinerary, even if the paths are well marked overall. Don't rely on online resources, as phone signals can be poor in some areas.
- A rain jacket, as the weather can change very quickly, especially inland.
- A jacket or pullover, as temperatures can drop when you reach the heights and elevations above 1000m.
- High hiking boots for mountain paths. Light closed shoes are adequate for the easiest paths.
- Mosquito repellent can be useful, especially in rainforest areas, along riverbeds and near water spots.
- Sun protection (a hat and some sunscreen), as some parts of your hike might be directly exposed to the sun at certain times of day (for example, a steep cliffside at midday or an open path on a ridge at 10am).
- Adequate water for the length of your intended hike.
- Snacks to keep you going (dried fruit, energy bars, chocolate…).
- A headlamp if you plan to stay overnight, or if your hike might last after the sun goes down.
- Your fully charged mobile phone.

---

who know Réunion's paths like the back of their hand, you will be safer and will avoid losing your bearings, and you'll have help with preparing your itinerary. Along the way, guides might also tell you more about local vegetation and the history of some paths (such as old routes used by fugitive enslaved people, and ways carved in the mountains to reach former thermal sources). Ask at tourist offices for guide recommendations.

Traditional Mauritian dishes

THE FOOD SCENE

The Creole cuisines of Mauritius, Réunion and Seychelles are born of the islands' spice-plantation history and rich larders of fish and fruit.

The food of the islands reflects a rich variety of Malagasy, African, Indian, Anglo-Indian, Asian and French influences. Much of this heritage derives from the cooking of enslaved and indentured peoples brought in to cultivate the fruit and spices that funded empires. In Seychelles, where enslaved Malagasy and East African people dominated the population, African tastes are most evident; in Mauritius, where there were large communities of indentured Indian and Asian workers, their food staples are to the fore; and the French department of Réunion has developed a Franco-African fusion, with traditions such as apéritif (a habit of French plantation owners) and elaborate picnics (a tradition of enslaved people) still popular today.

Fish, fruit and spices reign supreme, and although cooking techniques tend to be simple (things spoil quickly in the tropical heat), dishes pack a mighty flavour punch. Sensations that might be new to you include a huge variety of tropical fruit chutneys, soursops (custard apples), bilimbi (sour, succulent fruit used for flavouring) and bat curry.

Mauritian Fusion

Today, nearly two thirds of Mauritians are of Indian descent, just under a third are African Creoles and the rest are Franco-Mauritian and Chinese. This makes for an intoxicating Creole cuisine reflecting the strong food cultures of these communities, which have been adapted

---

Best Mauritian Dishes

BOULETTE
Local dumplings filled with meat, fish or tofu.

DHAL PURI
An Indian flatbread filled with ground split peas.

ROUGAILLE
Tomato-based ragout base for several dishes, most typically salted fish.

to local ingredients. While some dishes and traditions remain as they were in their parent culture, there has been a lot of crossover, such as the signature dish of *rougaille* (tomato-based ragout). That dish has its origins in southern France, but when it's mixed with saltfish and chilli it takes on an African Creole flavour. If you add more ginger and serve it with prawns, *dhal puri* and chutney, then it feels Indian instead. Also of French origin, the table d'hôte (a meal in a local home; p103) is a wonderful way to try Mauritian food.

Do yourself a favour and enrich your visit still further by taking a food tour with Taste Buddies (p62). You'll soon discover gastronomy incorporating hot curries from southern India, milder curries typical of the north of India, Chinese dim sum, French beef (or wild boar) bourguignon and Creole *rougaille*.

Staples

Rice and noodles are two staples of everyday life in Mauritius. A Sino-Mauritian may choose to start the day with tea and noodles, a Franco-Mauritian might enjoy a café au lait and a croissant, and an Indo-Mauritian may breakfast on a chapatti. While

Dholl Puri, Mauritius

VEGETARIANS & VEGANS

Creole cuisines feature lots of tropical salads and Indian dishes based on lentils or vegetables. In particular, look out for *carri de légumes* (vegetable curry). Chinese restaurants also offer some good options, such as chop suey and noodles (pictured), although these are more prevalent in Mauritius.

In Réunion you'll find lots of salads and vegetable-based *gratins* (a baked dish). You'll certainly come across *chouchou* (choko; a speciality in the Cirque de Salazie), lentils (a speciality in the Cirque de Cilaos), *bois de songe* (similar to a leek) and *vacoa* (pine fronds), not to mention *bringelles* (aubergines) and *baba figue* (banana flower).

Vegans will find things harder but not impossible – most resorts offer vegan options with notice.

meat is widely eaten, the mainstay of Mauritian cuisine is fish and seafood. Marlin, often smoked, is a big favourite, as are mussels, prawns, lobster and calamari. Octopus (*ourite*) is a highlight and appears in various guises – salads, cooked in saffron, or in a curry (sometimes with green papaya). When it comes to street food, boulettes (tiny steamed Chinese dumplings) are delicious and unmissable.

Best Mauritian Dishes

BOL RENVERSÉT
'Upside-down bowl' of rice topped with stir-fry.

ACHARDT
Pickled mix of carrots, cabbage, French beans and chillies.

BRIANI
One-pot rice dish with herbs, spices and meat or seafood.

OCTOPUS CURRY
One of the most popular of the many local seafood dishes.

Pwason griye, Seychelles

There are many candidates for the title of national dish, but few have the mass appeal of *dhal puri* (which you'll also see spelt as *dholl puri*). Inspired by the Indian bread known as paratha, it diverged from the original recipe due to a lack of key ingredients locally. The Mauritian version, using a thin flat bread known as *farata*, is filled with ground yellow split peas and prepared with curries, *rougaille* and pickles or chutney. The best ones wear a fiery crown of chillies.

Réunionnais Curries

Like Mauritius, Réunion has a blended cuisine, but here French and African influences are strongest. That said, the staple dish is *carri* (curry) with a base sauce made of tomatoes, onions, garlic, ginger, thyme and saffron or turmeric. Endless variations incorporate fish, seafood, chicken, pork, duck and even fruit bat. Another popular main course is *rougail boucané*, a tomato ragout prepared with meat smoked over a wood fire. Seafood *carris*, such as tuna (*carri thon*), swordfish (*carri espadon*), toothfish (*carri légine*), lobster (*carri langouste*), freshwater prawn (*carri camarons*) and saltfish are the most exalted. Octopus curry, an all-round favourite (and also beloved in Mauritius and Seychelles), is called *civet zourite* in Réunion.

Local vegetables can also be prepared *carri*-style – try *carri baba figue* (banana-flower *carri*) and *carri ti jaque* (jackfruit *carri*) – but some incorporate fish or meat, so ask ahead. *Carris* are invariably served with rice, grains (lentils or haricot beans), *brèdes* (local spinach) and *rougail*. A common Tamil stew is *cabri massalé* (goat carri), while *roumazaf* (a meat-and-greens hotpot) is a typical Malagasy dish.

French Customs

French habits have shaped many food and drink customs in Réunion. Coffee drinking, pastry eating and *le goûter* (afternoon

---

Best Réunionnais Dishes

SAMOUSSAS
Deep-fried pastries filled with meat and/or vegetables.

CABRI MASSALÉ
Typical Tamil stew of spicy goat.

BONBON PIMENT
'Chilli candy': mix of cape beans and chilli, deep fried.

BICHIQUES
Sprat-like small fish cooked in *carri*.

tea), where cakes such as *gâteau patate* (made with sweet potato) are served, are popular rituals. The popular Beignets de Bananes are banana fritters, and as good as they sound. Appetisers – in this case Indian *samoussas* and *bonbon piments* (spiced doughnuts) – are enjoyed as part of a meal. And the tradition of the pre-dinner *apéritif* is well established on the island.

Seychellois African Flavours

In Seychelles, African and French influences dominate, although as the majority of the nation's ancestors came from Madagascar, Mozambique and East and West African countries, African traditions are strongest here. You'll find plenty of sweet potato, cassava, taro, breadfruit, jackfruit and plantains – Seychelles has 23 banana species alone. Even the popular dessert *ladob* is made with tubers (sweet potatoes, yam and cassava) and plantains, which are peeled and cooked in coconut milk, brown sugar, vanilla and some nutmeg.

Before they came to the archipelago, Mozambiquans were familiar with salt, onions, bay leaves, coriander, chillis, red peppers and garlic because these flavours had been introduced to the East African coast by Arab and Portuguese traders. The Portuguese also introduced cassava, maize, cashew nuts and *pwason sale* (saltfish), an easily preserved food used to feed enslaved people. The latter is still popular, appearing in chutneys and curries (introduced by Indian migrants), and Seychellois *rougay*, a tomato-and-onion based Creole ragout with plenty of garlic, ginger and chilli.

French Techniques

Finally, from the French era (1756–94) Seychelles inherited cooking techniques such as pot roast (*roti dan marmit*), baking, *daube* (a sweet-and-sour sauce, as in *daube de banana*), smoking and smoke-grilling (*boukannen*), which is used to preserve fish – most popularly to make smoked sailfish or marlin. French *bouillon* (seasoned broth), locally called *bouyon*, also appears here as *bouyon blan* (fish soup), spiced with tangy, sour bilimbi fruit, and *bouyon bred*, a cabbage soup typically eaten with fried fish.

Islanders love local pork products, another French import, including blood pudding, fresh and dried *sosis* (sausages), tripe, and salted and smoked pork.

DARE TO TRY

Mazavaroo Fiery Mauritian condiment of red chillies and garlic.

Sea-cucumber salad Prepared with dried, salted and chopped sea cucumber.

Fish vindaye Strongly flavoured curry of pickled fish cooked with turmeric.

Alouda Mauritius' favourite milkshake (pictured), made with milk and agar agar (similar to gelatin, but vegetarian friendly) and topped with *tookmaria* (basil seeds).

Fruit-bat curry Made with the large local flying foxes (fruit bats), which are marinated in wine and vinegar and cooked with herbs and spices. Common on all the islands.

Shark chutney Popular Seychellois chutney of boiled and mashed shark mixed with fried onions and chilli.

Blood pudding and apples

Spices & Fruit

Cinnamon, cloves, allspice, vanilla and nutmeg are the signature spices of these islands. Cinnamon leaves are used in everything and give a more delicate flavour than the bark, and coconut milk is the base of most curries, along with masala spices, curry leaves, turmeric and saffron, introduced by South Asian communities. Indian and Anglo-Indian chutneys (*chatini or satini*) are also hugely popular, the former are vegetable-, herb- or nut-based and are sweetened with tamarind, while the latter are usually based on a tart fruit like the golden apple, and look like a thick-cut jam similar to marmalade. These can be made with almost anything, but the most popular is made with green papaya.

In Réunion, lychees and *ananas Victoria* (Victoria pineapples) are iconic. In Seychelles, go for papaya, mango and passionfruit, and also try Satini, a side salad made of finely grated unripe fruit. In Mauritius, lychees, longans and mangoes are favourites, particularly José mangoes and Maison Rouge mangoes. Also look out for soursops (custard apples), carambolas, guavas, *pamplemousses* (grapefruit), *jamalac* (rose apple) and *jamblon* (damson plum).

Fish, Fish, Fish!

Pwason ek diri ('fish and rice' in Seychellois) is at the heart of most meals in the Indian Ocean. These fishing grounds are some of the richest in the world and fish and seafood are the main source of protein for islanders. In fact, the Seychellois are one of the world's greatest fish eaters, consuming about 59kg per person per year. Hundreds of different fish feature in traditional recipes, although this is narrowing as the fishing industry focuses on fewer species. Expect to see familiar names like tuna (this is one of the tuna capitals of the world), grouper, sailfish, jobfish, snapper, parrotfish, capitaine, bonito, jackfish, barracuda, conch, mackerel, leatherjacket, rays, eels, crabs, rabbitfish, caranx, sturgeon and shark...you get the picture.

To bring variety, fish are grilled, steamed, minced, smoked, smoke-grilled, stewed, salted, baked and wrapped in banana leaves. Best of all is a whole fish marinated in lemon, ginger, garlic, tomatoes and chilli, and simply barbecued.

Fish curry with coconut rice, Seychelles

Best Seychellois Dishes

PWASON GRIYE
Marinated fish grilled on a barbecue over coconut husks.

SOSIS ROUGAY
Sausages stewed in a tomato, onion, garlic and ginger ragout.

KOKO KARI
Coconut curry made with meat or seafood, frequently octopus.

BREADFRUIT
Staple eaten as crisps, or baked, grilled or mashed.

Spices used in Mauritian dishes

View from Le Morne (p77), Mauritius

THE OUTDOORS

It may be hard to see past the dazzling peacock-blue sea, but these Indian Ocean islands are also natural playgrounds, full of exciting adventure activities.

Each of the islands has a unique character and offers something different. Mauritius is the best all-rounder, with varied topography where you can hike, horse ride, play golf, mountain bike, kitesurf and surf. Réunion is one of the world's most stunning hiking destinations, with some canyoning, caving, whitewater rafting and whale watching on the side. And Seychelles' myriad islands offer lower-level tropical forest hikes, cycling, reef walking, kayaking and incredible deep-sea and fly fishing.

Hiking

Réunion's volcanic landscape offers the most varied trails (see p40), but Mauritius and Seychelles also have good hiking. Mauritius' mountainous profile means more dramatic options, including Black River Gorges National Park (p90), the Central Plateau, the Ebony Forest at Chamarel and Unesco-listed Le Morne. Rodrigues' Northeastern Coastal Walk is one of the finest hikes in the Indian Ocean.

Seychelles' peaks only reach 905m, so hikes are less strenuous and focus on the tropical flora and summit views of offshore islands. Highlights include Morne Seychellois National Park (p224), Silhouette's cloud forest, the Fond Ferdinand Reserve on Praslin and La Digue's coastline. The best time to hike is dry season (late April to the end of October).

Best of the Rest

GOLF
In Mauritius, golfers head to the Heritage Golf Club at **Château de Bel Ombre** (p96) for fabulous greens and out-of-this-world tropical views.

HORSERIDING
Forest-and-beach hacks are possible on the west coast of **Mahé** (p228; Seychelles) and in Réunion's primary **Bébour rainforest** (p189).

CANYONING
Réunion's **Cirque de Cilaos** and **Cirque de Salazie** offer canyoning – **Fleur Jaune** (p192) is a favourite spot with the locals.

FAMILY ADVENTURES

Go **snorkelling** in **Baie Ternay** (p213), Seychelles, where you'll see rays, and probably turtles. In Réunion, learn turtle lore at **Kelonia marine observatory** (p157).

Search for **waterfalls** with local guides in **Tamarin** (p83), Mauritius.

Seychelles' **La Digue** (p242) is a virtually **car-free cyclists' haven**. Combine a bike ride with **sea kayaking** at **L'Union Estate** (p243).

Réunion's **Grand Étang lake** (p183) offers an easy **hike** and an enjoyable **horse ride** (p183). Another good walk is along the **Rivière des Marsouins** (p182).

Cilaosa Parc Aventure (p192) and **Parc de la Luge** (p152) are two **adventure parks** in Réunion. One offers canopy trails; the other a luge slide through the lush forest.

Fishing

The seas around Mauritius and Seychelles support large predators such as marlin, sailfish, wahoo, tuna, sharks and trevallies. Serious big-game anglers from around the world come to fish here and there are annual fishing competitions in Black River, Mauritius, in November and February. In Seychelles, Denis and Bird Islands are top spots for their proximity to the deep water at the edge of the Seychelles Bank. Closer to Mahé, the catch is more likely to be jobfish, groupers and red snappers.

Most big hotels run deep-sea fishing boats, which usually take three anglers and three guests. Tag-and-release allows you to enjoy the thrill of the sport without further impacting the marine environment. Make this clear when booking.

Seychelles' Outer Islands are also world-renowned for catch-and-release fly-fishing (p251). Species include bonefish, triggerfish, milk fish and – the holy grail – giant trevally.

Boating & Water Sports

Diving (p38) and snorkelling are popular ways to enjoy the islands' waters. You can snorkel almost anywhere. Shark safety is an issue in Réunion, and note that when the southeastern trade winds blow, southern and southeastern beaches can be dangerous.

In Mauritius, boat trips run from Flic en Flac, Mahébourg, Grand Baie or Trou d'Eau Douce. In Seychelles, trips run from Mahé (Beau Vallon is the hub), Praslin (to Curieuse and Cousin Islands) and La Digue. Réunionnais boat trips focus on dolphin and whale watching.

Otherwise, there's windsurfing and kitesurfing in Mauritius off Le Morne, as well as off Cap Malheureux. There's a small surfing scene in Tamarin (Mauritius) and Grand Anse (La Digue, Seychelles). Sea kayaking is also possible in Seychelles and Mauritius. On Réunion, it's possible at Trou d'Eau and L'Ermitage.

BEST SPOTS

For the best outdoor spots and routes, see map on page 50

Helicopter ride, Seychelles

PARAGLIDING
Take flight near **St-Leu** (p156) for jaw-dropping views of Réunion's volcanic cone.

WHALE-WATCHING
From June to October, whales migrate past Réunion's west coast; watch them aboard boats heading out from **St-Gilles** and **St-Leu** (p153).

HELICOPTER RIDES
Corail Helicopteres (p156; Réunion) and **ZilAir** (p248; Seychelles) (pictured) will take you up for a thrilling ride and cinematic views.

WHITEWATER RAFTING
Réunion's **Rivière des Marsouins** and **Rivière des Roches** rivers (p182) are the most thrilling.

ACTION AREAS

Where to find Mauritius, Réunion & Seychelles' best outdoor activities.

Snorkelling
1. Blue Bay Marine Park, Mauritius (p115)
2. Flic en Flac, Mauritius (p79)
3. L'Ermitage-les-Bains, Réunion (p153)
4. Anse Sévère, Seychelles (p245)
5. Île Cocos, Seychelles (p247)

Seychelles

0 – 20 km
0 – 10 miles

Hiking
1. Black River Gorges National Park, Mauritius (p90)
2. Le Morne, Mauritius (p77)
3. Le Pouce, Mauritius (p76)
4. Cirque de Mafate, Réunion (p194)
5. Piton des Neiges, Réunion (p192)
6. Morne Seychellois National Park, Seychelles (p224)
7. Nid d'Aigle, Seychelles (p244)

Diving
1. Flic en Flac, Mauritius (p79)
2. Rodrigues, Mauritius (p124)
3. St-Gilles-les-Bains, Réunion (p39)
4. Curieuse Island, Seychelles (p240)
5. Seychelles' Outer Islands (p249)
6. Silhouette Island, Seychelles (p231)

Boat Tours
1. Grand Baie, Mauritius (p97)
2. Rodrigues, Mauritius (p124)
3. Trou d'Eau Douce, Mauritius (p108)
4. Rivière des Marsouins, Réunion (p182)
5. Mahé, Seychelles (p212)

National Parks
1. Black River Gorges National Park, Mauritius (p90)
2. Bras d'Eau National Park, Mauritius (p113)
3. Réunion National Park (p40)
4. Morne Seychellois National Park, Seychelles (p224)
5. Ste-Anne Marine National Park, Seychelles (p229)

PLAN YOUR TRIP THE OUTDOORS

THE GUIDE

MAURITIUS, RÉUNION & SEYCHELLES
THE GUIDE

Seychelles p207

Chapters in this section are organised by hubs and their surrounding areas. We see the hub as your base in the destination, where you'll find unique experiences, local insights, insider tips and expert recommendations. It's also your gateway to the surrounding area, where you'll see what and how much you can do from there.

Mauritius p55

Réunion p131

Brissare Rocks (p213), Seychelles

Above: Sockalingum Meenatchee Ammen Kovil Temple (p68); Right: Coconut seller, Blue Bay (p114)

THE MAIN AREAS

PORT LOUIS
Capital steeped in history.
p60

FLIC EN FLAC
Dive sites and local beach life.
p79

CHAMAREL
Canyon hiking and boutique rum.
p87

GRAND BAIE
Beaches, bars and boutiques.
p97

MAURITIUS
CREOLE CULTURE AND ALL-ROUND ADVENTURE

Climb a canyon in the morning, be in Chinatown for lunch, see dolphins in the afternoon and enjoy a local beer on the beach at sunset.

Mauritius packs a lot into its compact 2000 sq km. Glorious beaches are just the beginning: inland is a scenic landscape of forest-draped mountains, and everywhere historic sites recall Mauritius' time in the sugar trade. The country's growing art and music scene is led by homegrown talent, and its dynamic food culture mixes Indian, Chinese, French and Creole influences. These diverse ethnicities have woven a colourful – though not always happy – 425-year history. From the 10th century, Arab seafarers used the island as a layover, and later Portuguese explorers on the old East India trade route between India and Africa helped put the unoccupied paradise on the map. But it wasn't until 1598 that the Dutch became the first people to inhabit the island. Their brief stay was followed by the arrival of the French and the British, who brought enslaved people from Africa. Hundreds of thousands of workers later arrived from India, and as the country prospered, Gujarati (Muslim) and Chinese tradespeople arrived. Today, South African and Bangladeshi communities are growing, and 60% of the population is Hindu. There are 14 spoken languages in Mauritius. The official language is English, which is taught in most schools, but most people speak French and almost everyone speaks the local Creole dialect. Despite its history of slavery, Mauritius has become a rare example of diverse cultures living peacefully together.

TROU D'EAU DOUCE
Local life, food scene and castaway beaches.
p108

BLUE BAY
Diving and sailing, market and museum.
p114

RODRIGUES
Laid-back island of fishing villages.
p124

Find Your Way

Journeys rarely take more than 1½ hours and it's easy to get around. Explore beyond the country's famed beaches to see the places that showcase Mauritius' thought-provoking history, impressive array of cultures and sublime landscapes.

Grand Baie, p97
The area is known for its pretty, beachy coves, while the town has a handful of shops and comes alive at night.

Port Louis, p60
Home to the Unesco-recognised Aapravasi Ghat immigration depot, plus prime examples of colonial architecture and various religious sites.

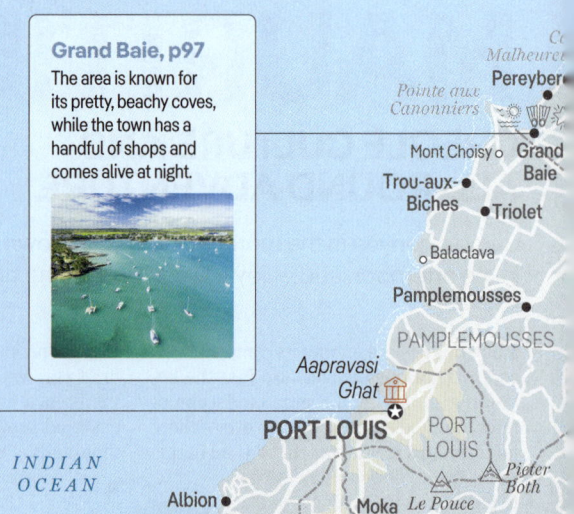

Flic en Flac, p79
Serves up nightlife and white-sand beaches; outside town, surfing and a seven-tier waterfall beckon.

Chamarel, p87
Fantastic food and boutique rum distilleries, hiking trails, religious sites and tea plantations. Le Morne mountain, Mauritius' second World Heritage Site, and the island's best beaches are close by.

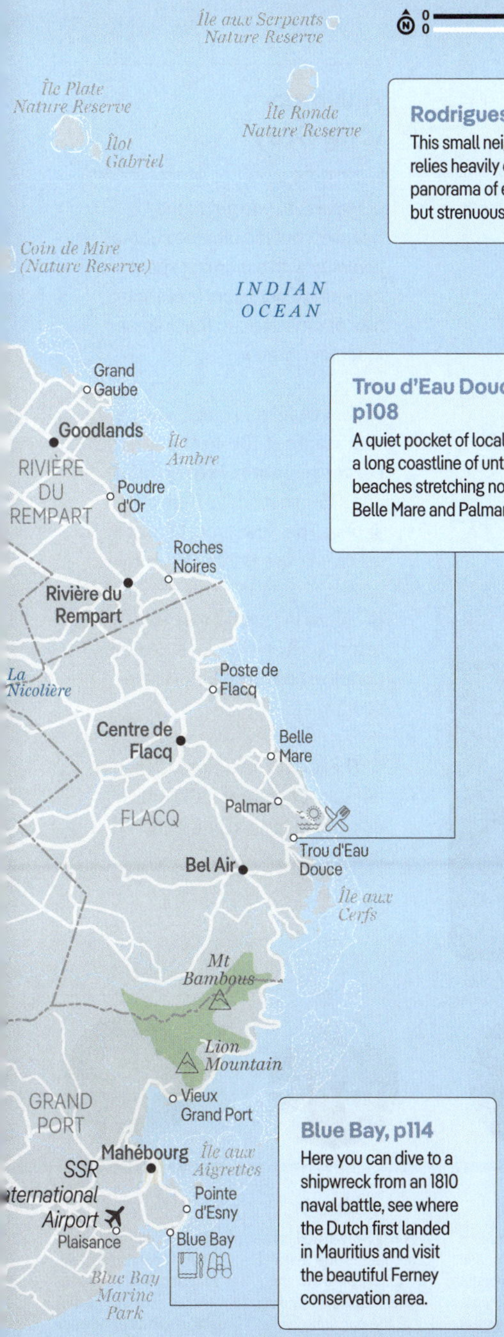

THE GUIDE

MAURITIUS

Île aux Serpents Nature Reserve

Île Plate Nature Reserve

Île Ronde Nature Reserve

Îlot Gabriel

Coin de Mire (Nature Reserve)

INDIAN OCEAN

Grand Gaube
Goodlands
Île Ambre
RIVIÈRE DU REMPART
Poudre d'Or
Roches Noires
Rivière du Rempart
La Nicolière
Poste de Flacq
Centre de Flacq
Belle Mare
FLACQ
Palmar
Bel Air
Trou d'Eau Douce
Île aux Cerfs
Mt Bambous
Lion Mountain
Vieux Grand Port
GRAND PORT
Mahébourg
Île aux Aigrettes
SSR International Airport
Pointe d'Esny
Plaisance
Blue Bay
Blue Bay Marine Park

Rodrigues (550km)

Rodrigues, p124
This small neighbouring island relies heavily on fishing and offers a panorama of empty beaches, plus short but strenuous hikes.

Trou d'Eau Douce, p108
A quiet pocket of local life, with a long coastline of untamed beaches stretching north to Belle Mare and Palmar.

Blue Bay, p114
Here you can dive to a shipwreck from an 1810 naval battle, see where the Dutch first landed in Mauritius and visit the beautiful Ferney conservation area.

METRO EXPRESS LIGHT RAIL
Still in phase one, the tram runs between Port Louis and central plateau cities such as Rose-Hill and Quatre Bornes. The website (mauritiusmetroexpress.mu) has a useful map and schedule information.

BUS
Mauritius has an extensive bus network, but the many stops mean travel time is often quadrupled. A bus trip is a good way to experience local life, as you'll see villages off the beaten track.

CAR
The quickest and most reliable way to get from place to place. There are several car-rental companies in a concrete block in the airport car park. Taxis are very costly.

Plan Your Time

In Mauritius you can do as much (hiking, surfing, diving, art galleries, music festivals) or as little (sunbathing, beach barbecues, spa days) as you want and still soak up the local culture.

Rivière Noire (p84)

A Week-long Stay

- Make sure you get to the beaches, but dip into the cultural diversity with a morning spent exploring **Port Louis** (p60) and a hike or drive around the dramatic mountain interior.

- For instant relaxation, start with a night at 200-hectare conservation area **Ferney** (p122), just a 15-minute drive from the airport. The views from here of lush green hills are extremely soothing.

- Follow that with a stay at a resort, B&B or villa close to beach paradise **Le Morne** (p86) in the southwest.

- The town is also close to foodie hot spot **Chamarel** (p87), which also offers canyon and waterfall hikes.

Seasonal Highlights

Sunny, hot and humid summers run from November to April; the rest of the year is drier but greyer. There's plenty to keep visitors busy all year round.

JANUARY
Chinese New Year is one of many Chinese festivals celebrated on Mauritius. January also sees the spectacular Tamil Hindu festival **Cavadee**.

FEBRUARY
Maha Shivaratri is the biggest Hindu festival, celebrated all over the country, including at the pilgrimage site **Grand Bassin**.

MARCH
The Hindu festival of **Holi** is celebrated by Mauritians of all faiths. March also marks the island's **independence** from British rule in 1968.

Two Week-long Stay

- Split your 14 days between the east and west coasts. In the west, stay in surfy **Tamarin** (p83) or **Le Morne** (p86) for the fantastic beaches.

- To change coasts, take the scenic route through the **Black River Gorges** (p90); down to the island's biggest Hindu temple, **Grand Bassin** (p92); and through the tea plantations of **Bois Chéri** (p95) and the island's **Moka** mountain range.

- Stay in **Belle Mare** (p112), where the beaches are long ribbons of white sand alongside bright turquoise waters.

- Glimpse local life in nearby **Trou d'Eau Douce** (p108), where boats leave for **Île aux Cerfs** (p107), a popular Robinson Crusoe–style island day trip.

If You Have More Time

- Stay on both coasts, but spend a couple of nights in the **deep south** (p93) for the ultimate peaceful getaway.

- Stop in charming **Mahébourg** (p114) to look around its market and get a feel for the town.

- Mauritius is surrounded by smaller desert islands, and an **island-hopping tour** is a truly relaxing experience.

- Energy to burn? Hikers can explore some of the best trails with **Yanature** (p117), including the south's waterfalls, the **Black River Gorges** and the **Moka range**.

- Catch an hour-long flight to neighbouring **Rodrigues** (p124), an island of fishing villages, to see Mauritius as it once was.

MAY
Mingle with locals at music events like **Mama Jaz**, **LA ISLA 2068** and **Underground Rock**. Salon de Mai showcases Mauritian artists.

SEPTEMBER
All Waves and **Momix** music events, the **Trou d'Eau Douce** book festival, the Hindu **Ganesh Chaturthi** ritual and the Christian **Père Laval** pilgrimage.

NOVEMBER
The Hindu festival **Diwali**, the family-friendly **Anba Pie** festival, and the commemoration of the arrival of indentured labourers at Aapravasi Ghat.

DECEMBER
Festival Kiltir celebrates the local culture, and Tamil temples across the island host the **Teemeedee** fire-walking festival.

PORT LOUIS

Nestled between the undulating Moka mountain range – peeping through a cluster of small malls and office blocks – and the deep blue sea where ships sail in from all over the world, Port Louis is more a large town than an intimidating metropolis.

Once you get past the stifling heat and the roar of traffic on the main road, the port town is quiet and pleasant, its tangle of streets hiding fascinating pockets of culture and history. Visit the handful of small museums and smattering of centuries-old architectural gems to dip into the island's riveting past as it was handed from Dutch to French and British settlers before obtaining independence.

Experience the country's rich cultural heritage by delving into the dynamic food scene, visiting religious landmarks of Mauritius' Hindu, Catholic, Chinese and Muslim communities, and hunting down local and international artists' colourful murals that bring the island's history alive.

TOP TIP

Port Louis might be the busiest city in the country, but absolutely everything closes down by 4pm. Roads tend to be choked with traffic, so avoid rush hour by leaving before 7.30am or after 9am in the mornings and before 3pm or after 5pm in the afternoons.

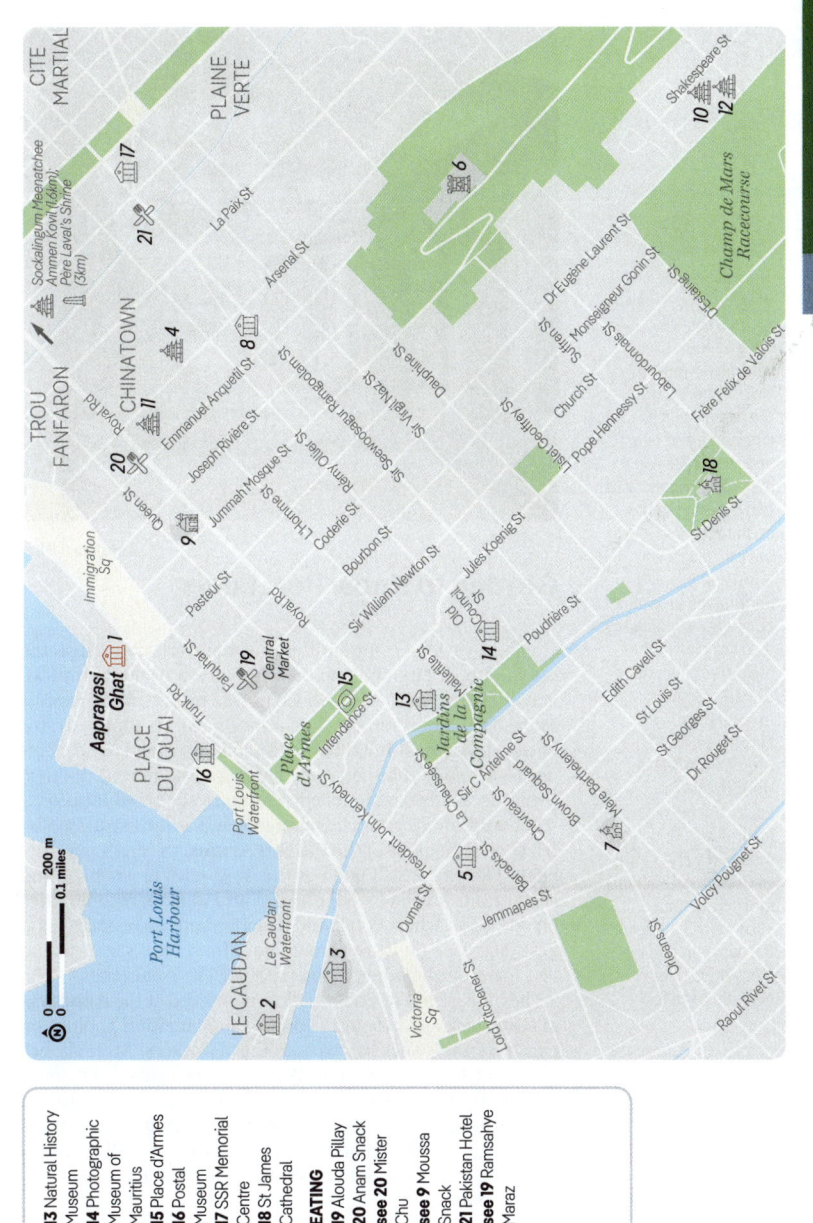

HIGHLIGHTS
1 Aapravasi Ghat

SIGHTS
2 Blue Penny Museum
3 Caudan Arts Centre
4 Chan Chak Pagoda
5 EDITH
6 Fort Adelaide
7 Immaculate Church
8 Institute of Contemporary Art Indian Ocean (ICAIO)
9 Jummah Mosque
10 Lam Soon Pagoda
11 Lawkwanthion Pagoda
12 Nam Shun Fooy Koon Pagoda
13 Natural History Museum
14 Photographic Museum of Mauritius
15 Place d'Armes
16 Postal Museum
17 SSR Memorial Centre
18 St James Cathedral

EATING
19 Alouda Pillay
20 Anam Snack
see **20** Mister Chu
see **9** Moussa Snack
21 Pakistan Hotel
see **19** Ramsahye Maraz

Aapravasi Ghat

Getting to Know Port Louis
CRADLE OF HISTORY AND CULTURE

Home to various communities and their religious sites, the bustling port city and capital is the heart of multiculturalism in Mauritius. It was founded in 1736 by Bertrand-François Mahé de La Bourdonnais (Labourdonnais), an administrator of the French East India Company commissioned to bring order to a colony that had gone awry, and he moved the port from the windy east to its current more sheltered location.

Labourdonnais created commerce and administration districts on either side of the **Place d'Armes**, the city's main avenue. The city is still laid out this way, with most shops and restaurants owned by the Chinese and Muslim communities on one side – where you'll find pagodas and the country's biggest mosque – and government buildings, banks, courts and law firms on the other, along with the city's churches.

The bulk of the country's workforce arrived at the **Aapravasi Ghat** here – it's thought 70% of the Mauritian population can trace their ancestry back to these workers. After slavery was abolished on 1 February 1835, workers were drawn mainly from India to staff the numerous sugar-cane plantations. For a time Mauritius was one of the world's biggest exporters of sugar (it's currently 22nd in the world). Still extremely active, Port Louis remains the country's main export and import point.

TRACKING DOWN PORT LOUIS' BEST SITES

The best way to find the sites worth leaving your sunlounger for is to book a tour with Jaya from **My Moris**. She knows the history of the city inside and out, and she'll take you to below-the-radar cafes and secret pagodas in Chinatown's backstreets. Jaya is great at keeping information clear and concise. The company also has many other highly recommended tours and immersive experiences. **Mauritian** foodie Adrien from **Taste Buddies** takes you to the belly of Mauritius through a mouth-watering array of street food, markets and restaurants, allowing you to delve into what unifies the many ethnicities of Mauritius: the food.

WHERE TO STAY IN PORT LOUIS

Labourdonnais Waterfront Hotel
A resort-style hotel with luxury rooms and a pool; close to Caudan mall. €€

Kirin Guesthouse
Steps from Jummah Mosque, this very simple guesthouse has comfortable beds. €

Citadelle Mall Apartments
Inside the Citadelle mall, with great views; apartments are simple but fully equipped. €

A WANDER THROUGH HISTORY

This tour takes you past hallmarks of Port Louis' colourful past and diverse cultural fabric. Start at the **1 Caudan Waterfront mall**, facing Place d'Armes. Head left along the port past the 1850s **2 Central Post Office**, and then a white windmill (once a grain storage warehouse) and an old hospital being converted into the Museum of Slavery. Beyond is the must-see **3 Aapravasi Ghat** (p64).

Cross Trunk Rd into **4 Chinatown** for a bite to eat. Next, head southwest along Royal Rd past the gleaming white **5 Jummah Mosque**. Take Queen St behind the mosque to the bustling Victorian **6 Central Market**. Follow Queen St back to Place d'Armes. On the far side of the broad avenue, **7 HSBC** and **8 AfrAsia** banks are prime examples of 1700s architecture. Walk southeast past **9 Government House** (built 1738), one of the country's best-preserved French colonial houses.

Take Jules Koenig St past the classical **10 Port Louis Theatre** to the **11 Champs de Mars racecourse**, established by the Mauritius Turf Club, said to be the second-oldest racing club in the world.

Retrace your steps north along Jules Koenig St towards the theatre, then turn left down little Rue du Vieux Conseil to reach the **12 Photographic Museum**. Slip through the open gate at the end of the street to find a wooden Creole house, the **13 Port Louis Fire Station** (1906). Inside is a huge Merryweather steam engine mounted on a wall. Walk via Rue du Vieux Conseil and Poudrière St towards the **14 Jardins de la Compagnie**, marked by a huge banyan tree and statues of local sculptor Prosper d'Epinay and godfather of séga music Ti Frère. Round off your tour with a visit to the **15 Natural History Museum**, where in-depth displays showcase Mauritian wildlife.

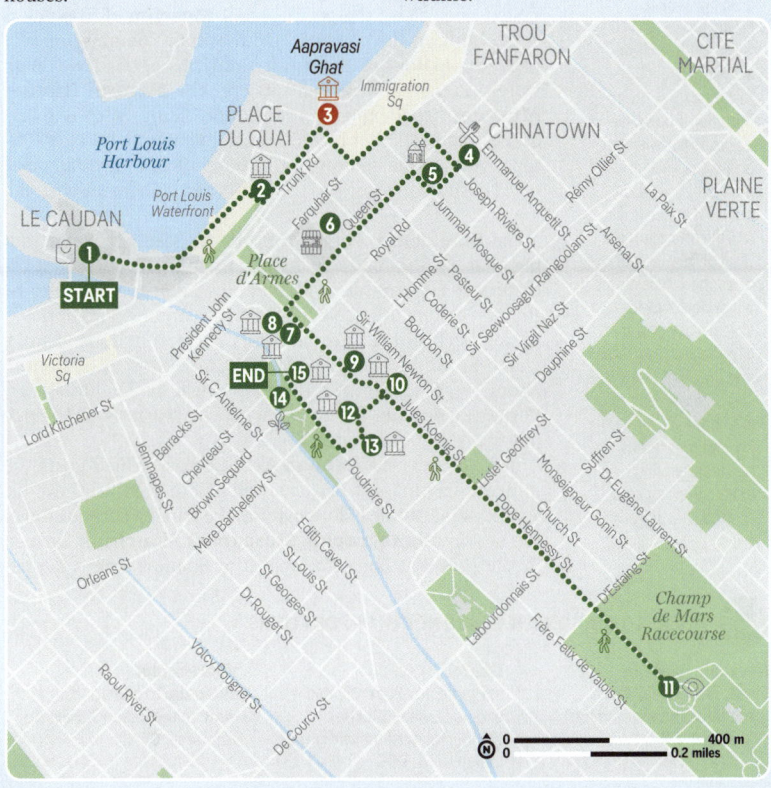

Other clues to the city's past can be seen in the form of **line barracks** (now the police station), **Fort Adelaide** and numerous street names pertaining to battles between the French and British.

Outside Port Louis, Labourdonnais added residential districts for people of colour, designating these areas the '**black city**'. Stretching all the way to the Moka mountains, the districts still exist today, among them Plaine Verte (for Muslims) and Sainte-Croix (for Hindus and Christians of Indian descent).

Deeper Discovery

PORT LOUIS' MUSEUMS

If you visit just one museum in Port Louis, make it the **Aapravasi Ghat World Heritage Site** (free). A well-designed visitor centre tells the story of how half a million indentured labourers were drawn from India under British rule for what was called the 'great experiment' in the use of free labour following the abolition of slavery. The labourers toiled on the island's sugar plantations between 1834 and 1920. Set across a 1.64-sq-km site, the buildings of Aapravasi Ghat are among the earliest manifestations of what was to become a global economic system and one of the greatest migrations in history.

Next door along the port, a small **Museum of Slavery** is being built on the site of an old hospital. The museum will trace the history of slavery in Mauritius under the rule of Dutch, French and British settlers. The **Natural History Museum** (free) explains the island's fauna, with displays of fish and birds that include two fully mounted dodo skeletons – Mauritius' national bird that suffered an infamously rapid extinction after less than 200 years of contact with humans.

The **Blue Penny Museum** inside the Caudan Waterfront mall has well-annotated maps and paintings that recount the history of the capital, including how Mauritius came to be the first colony to issue British Empire stamps. Two of these, dating back to 1847, are on display here and are said to be worth around €5 million. There is also a small exhibition about *Paul et Virginie*, the 1788 novel by Jacques-Henri Bernardin de Saint-Pierre that is set on Mauritius and helped put the island on the map.

Steps away is the **Caudan Arts Centre**, which hosts the midyear Laguna Art Prize as well as other cultural events. Check the schedule before making the trip. Be sure to stop at the nearby **Photographic Museum of Mauritius**, opened in the 1960s. It houses a wealth of fabulous snaps depict-

---

WHY I LOVE PORT LOUIS

Rooksana Hossenally, writer.
@rooksana_hossenally

I've been lucky enough to travel widely and live in many parts of the world, but I keep coming back to Mauritius.

Yes, the beaches are fantastic – but there's a lot more to this island paradise. Its cultural diversity is unique, and for me Port Louis is on par with major Asian street-food capitals.

Full of vestiges of the past, the city is also a wonderful place to learn about the island's rich heritage and colonial history.

My number-one tip is to book a tour with My Moris to really appreciate what makes the city so special. Ask for Jaya.

WHERE TO STAY ON THE BEACH NORTH OF PORT LOUIS

Ravanela Attitude	**Oberoi**	**Villa Maridul**
This four-star stay has a great pool and a waterside restaurant. €€	In Pointe aux Piments, this exquisite villa hotel has wonderful gardens and great Indian food. €€€	Sleeps up to eight and is right on the beach in Baie du Tombeau. €

ing Mauritius through the years, from life on sugar plantations to the creation of cities such as Rose Hill and Port Louis, as well as photography memorabilia from the 19th and 20th centuries. At 6 Edith Cavelle St, inside a grey-brick storage space, contemporary-art gallery and events venue **EDITH** hosts great exhibitions and concerts. Art-lovers should also keep in mind local artist and designer Salim Curimjee's **Institute of Contemporary Art Indian Ocean (ICAIO)**: it's a platform for the Art Education and Public Art Programme and often hosts exhibitions of work by local and regional artists.

The **Postal Museum** inside the old Central Post Office, inaugurated in 1870, is an example of local colonial architecture using volcanic stone. Inside, the exhibition runs through the history of the postal system under British rule. There's also a small but very modern museum inside the central **Bank of Mauritius**, containing some 500 artefacts. Among them are extremely rare gold and silver coins, including Arab dinar and British Indian Mohur, which found their way to Mauritius via a flourishing trade.

The **SSR Memorial Centre** was the home of Sir Seewoosagur Ramgoolam, the well-liked first governor of the independent Mauritius from 1935 to 1968. It's a listed example of Creole architecture. Inside you can see some of his belongings as well as footage of the man himself.

THINGS TO DO AT CAUDAN WATERFRONT MALL

Pause for a juice
Seek respite from the heat with a freshly pressed pineapple or mango juice at a breezy waterside cafe while watching ships sail in and out of the port.

Take in an exhibition
Visit the Caudan Art Centre, which often shows the most prominent local artists' work, or the Blue Penny Museum for a sense of history.

Pick up a souvenir
The Caudan Craft Market is a one-stop shop for all types of souvenirs, from dodo-shaped magnets to spices and vanilla.

Blue Penny Museum

BRUSH UP ON HISTORY

Don't miss the small **Mahébourg Museum (p119)** in the southeast. Descriptions and paintings vividly recount Mauritius' fascinating history under Dutch, French and British rule.

The Westin
A modern luxury resort with all the trimmings, plus a small, palm-fringed beach. €€€

Voile Bleue Boutique Hotel
Good value, clean and well maintained; the beach here isn't great for swimming, but there's a pool. €

Récif Attitude
Well priced and right on the water, this adults-only hotel has attractive interiors and a fun atmosphere. €

ART ON THE STREETS

A few years ago street-art festival Porlwi asked artists to create murals showcasing Port Louis' highlights. Looking out for their work is a delightful way to explore the city.

Start at Aapravasi Ghat (p64), where local artist **1 RYMD**'s spiralling underwater scene can be spotted on rue du Quai. Next, cross Trunk Rd into Chinatown. At the corner of Queen and Emmanuel Anquetil Sts is Chinese artist **2 Wenna**'s vivid depiction of characters from a Chinese tale. A block south, along Royal Rd, glimpse murals by **3 The Ink & Clog** from Singapore (corner Emmanuel Anquetil St) and Austrian artist **4 Frau Isa**'s three women (near Jummah Mosque).

Turn right onto Bourbon St to see the murals around Central Market, including Réunionnais duo **5 Kid Kreol & Boogie**'s floating bubble spaceman (Sir William Newton St, behind the market). Return to Bourbon St and head south. Clustered at the corner of Rémy Ollier St, are local artist **6 Brian Lamoureux**' black-and-white depiction of old and new Port Louis, **7 Armand Gachet**'s Chinese girl playing the flute and Berliner **8 44 Flavours**' cheerful mural of a cartoon courtyard.

Continue along Bourbon St, turn left onto Dauphine St and walk to the corner of Dr Eugène Laurent St for French artist **9 Seth**'s *Under the Pavement*. The face of its kneeling figure melts into the ground.

Double back on to Dauphine St, and turn right at Poudrière St and left at Mère Barthélemy St to walk through the Jardins de la Compagnie towards **10 Dévid**'s black and white eyes lined up on a wall (corner Louis Victor de la Faye St). Further on are **11 Evan Sohun**'s bright-blue fresco (corner Edith Cavell St), then *Curvy Lady* by **12 Floe** from Réunion, at the corner of St Louis and Chevreau Sts.

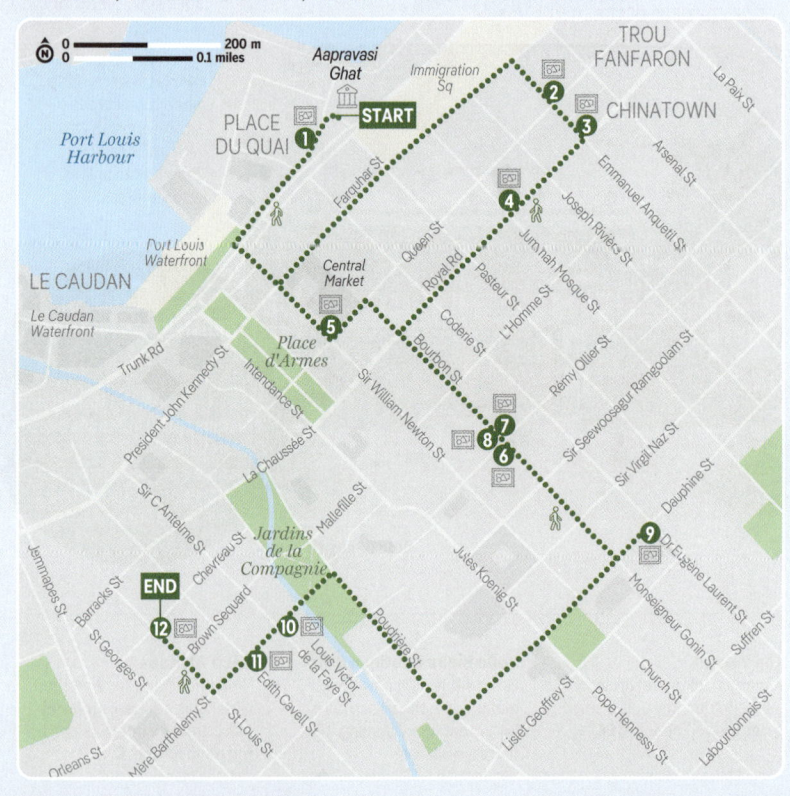

Immaculate Church

Get Your Cultural Bearings

A DOSE OF MAURITIAN DIVERSITY

The eastern side of Port Louis brims with shops selling everything from *puja* (Hindu prayer) garlands and candles to fabric and hardware. These are largely run by the Chinese and Muslim communities. It's here, steps from the Chinese arches, that you'll find the ornate **Jummah Mosque**, which was built in the 1850s by Indian workers and consequently has Hindu-style carvings inside and out, reminiscent of temple decorations. It's possible to visit the mosque every day except Friday. Nearby in Chinatown are several pagodas, such as the **Lawkwanthion** and **Chan Chak**; the **Lam Soon** and **Nam Shun Fooy Koon** pagodas are near the Champ de Mars.

The western part of the city is the business district, with government ministries. Here is also where the city's various churches are located, such as the colonial-style wooden and volcanic-rock **St James Cathedral** and the British-style **Immaculate Church**.

Père Laval's shrine, in Ste Croix outside the main city centre, is the most important site for Catholic Mauritians. The priest was beatified in 1979 during a visit by Pope John Paul II, and buried here. Every 9 September, pilgrims from all over the world travel to commemorate his death.

LOCALLY MADE SOUVENIRS

Goyave sandals
Simple, stylish and well priced, these are summer must-haves. Nab a pair from the showroom (p99) in Grand Baie.

My Ceramic Adventure
Séverine Tyack makes spectacular homewares that resemble seashells in her workshop (p85) in Rivière Noire.

Vacoa baskets
Close to the east-coast Frederik Hendrik Museum, artisans in a women's association (p123) use vacoa leaves to weave baskets. Pre-order a week ahead.

Ravanne drums
Bring back a *ravanne* drum, used for local séga and seggae music, from the craft market at Caudan Arts Centre (p64)

WHERE TO STAY ON THE BEACH SOUTH OF PORT LOUIS

Villa Anakao
A villa of several rooms for rent, this is a pleasant abode right on the sea in quiet Pointe aux Sables. €

La Maison de la Plage
Close to Port Louis in residential Albion, this beachfront house has a handful of clean, basic rooms and a pool. €€

La Case Bois Créole
Charming wooden house with tasteful rooms and beautiful gardens; close to the sea and Albion beach. €

THE FATHER OF SPICE

A name you'll often hear as you explore Mauritius is that of Pierre Poivre, an intendant of the French East India Company for the Mascarene Islands (Mauritius, Réunion and Rodrigues) in the 1760s.

The rather aptly named horticulturist (*poivre* means 'pepper') introduced spices to the islands, having seen the territory's potential to become a hub of spice cultivation for the company.

Poivre also created the wonderful **Sir Seewoosagur Ramgoolam Botanical Garden** (p69) near Port Louis, devoting his life to the breeding of some of the island's most beautiful plants and spices. He was made administrator of the colony in Mauritius in 1765, and it's said he governed rather well.

Street food, Port Louis

Close to the shrine is the Hindu temple **Sockalingum Meenatchee Ammen Kovil**. With its brightly coloured sculptures, it is one of the island's most impressive temples.

When visiting religious sites, take a sarong with you to cover your legs and shoulders.

Street-food Capital

RICH HERITAGE IN EVERY BITE

A mix of Indian, African, French and Chinese influences, Mauritius brims with stands, motorbike vendors and *snacks* (small cafes) selling street-food favourites. Locals have high expectations, so you'll be hard-pressed to find bad street food anywhere on the island. The star dish is *dhal puri* (lentil pancakes with a tasty curry sauce) – try it at **Ramsahye Maraz** in the Central Market. It also has roti or *farata* (a sort of flour flatbread that melts in the mouth). For fried *gajaks* such as *gâteaux piment* (deep-fried ground-lentil balls with coriander and chilli), go to **Pakistan Hotel**, a *lotel dité* (tea house)

WHERE TO STAY ON THE BEACH SOUTH OF PORT LOUIS

Sugar Beach
A beachy resort in Flic en Flac with comfortable rooms, crisp decor and nods to colonial architecture. €€€

La Pirogue
One of the oldest hotels on the island, with thatch-roofed rooms and a beach bar. €€€

Les 2 Canons
A pretty villa with simple, sea-view rooms, a terrace and an infinity-edge pool. €€

in Chinatown. Head to another tea house, **Moussa Snack** (no bigger than a corridor), for beef *samoussas* and minced-chicken *catless* (cutlet) patties with milky vanilla tea made with powdered milk; it's next to the Jummah Mosque. You can try the popular *boulettes* (steamed chouchou vegetable or fish dumplings served in broth or with noodles) or *mine bouilli* (boiled noodles) all over town, but **Anam Snack** is a favourite spot for them. When at the market, try **Alouda Pillay**'s fruity milkshake with basil seeds. In Chinatown, don't miss **Mister Chu**, a local institution from 1942 where all the Chinese pastries are made fresh. Other popular street food includes *haleem* broth, green mango or cucumber with chilli paste sold from huge jars, sticky *bilimbi* (tamarind seeds) in packets to suck on, and sweet treats such as *gâteaux banane* (banana fritters) and *Napolitaines* (delicate sandwich biscuits topped with icing).

Reading Between the Lines
TALENTED WOMEN WRITERS

With cultural diversity inevitably comes complexity. Jean-Marie Gustave Le Clézio, winner of the 2008 Nobel Prize in Literature, Carl de Souza, Marcel Cabon and Malcom de Chazal might be familiar names in Mauritian literature, but a generation of women writers has also been getting underneath the island's glossy surface and telling it like it is.

Journalist **Nathacha Appanah**'s prize-winning novels often give accounts of Mauritius from the shadows. Coming-of-age tale *The Last Brother*, set during WWII, is based on a true story.

Shenaz Patel's work accurately depicts real hardship. *Silence of the Chagos* is a poignant account of the Chagossian people's forced exile from the Chagos Islands, which used to be part of Mauritius, by the US military and the British government.

Ananda Devi shines a new light on the paradise island tourists never see. *Eve Out of Her Ruins* is the heartbreaking tale of a group of teenagers from Port Louis trapped in a cycle of fear and destruction.

South African activist and staunch feminist **Lindsey Collen** has lived in Mauritius since the '70s. Her dark novel *The Rape of Sita*, banned in Mauritius, tells a story of oppression.

Priya Hein's children's books recount traditional Mauritian tales passed down from generation to generation. In *Riambel* she describes a conservative society dictated by a racial hierarchy rooted in colonialism.

LOTUSES & LAVISH LILY PADS

Sir Seewoosagur Ramgoolam Botanical Garden (p69) was created by Mahé de Labourdonnais in 1735 for his Mon Plaisir château. In 1768 the grounds came into their own under French horticulturist Pierre Poivre, who had transformed Mauritius by introducing spices to the island.

Fortunately, he also ensured endemic flora was properly conserved. Stroll alleys of elegant palms, admiring the lotus flowers growing high above the water and the giant *Victoria amazonica* water lilies (native to South America) with their round, tray-shaped pads, some them 2m across.

The garden is also home to trees planted by Nelson Mandela, Indira Gandhi and British royals. It's a 20-minute drive north of Port Louis in the district of Pamplemousses.

GETTING AROUND

Roads in and out of Port Louis are usually heavy with traffic, especially at peak times, when you may lose the will to keep exploring the island. There are also very few parking spots in town. Another way of reaching the capital is to drive to one of the plateau cities and park close to the tram, which will take you straight into Port Louis in 15 to 20 minutes. See mauritiusmetroexpress.mu for times and stops.

Beyond Port Louis

Lively towns and mountain hikes

Port Louis' immediate surroundings are mountainous, offering some of the island's best hiking. Skirt the jungly peaks, and big malls such as Tribeca and Bagatelle, and you'll come to the island's corridor of towns. Scattered across the island's central plateau, they run to the dormant volcano of Trou aux Cerfs (p77) with its 300m crater, which is testament to the country's volcanic formation millions of years ago. Authentic pockets of local life, these cities are where the majority of Mauritians live. They're pleasant places to visit, but not worth sacrificing beach time for, especially if you've thoroughly explored Port Louis. The region's hikes, on the other hand, are a definite highlight.

TOP TIP

All central plateau towns are accessible from pretty much anywhere on the island in 1½ hours or less.

Chateau de Bel Ombre (p73)

Eureka

Central Plateau Towns

EXPLORING MAURITIAN-STYLE CITY LIFE

Drive 15 minutes from Port Louis and the first town you'll come to is **Moka**, in the foothills of its namesake range, with dramatic mountainous scenery. The president's home is here, but the main attraction is **Eureka**, a well-preserved Creole mansion built in the 1830s. It's pleasant to stroll through its cool interiors looking at the period furniture imported by the French East India Company. Wander outside and follow the jungly trail down to a small waterfall. If you can stay awhile in Moka, art shows, artist residencies, concerts and sports events are held around **Moka Smart City** – consult moka.mu/fr/evenements for information about what's on.

Nearby are **Beau Bassin-Rose Hill** and **Quatre Bornes**, which are largely residential with bustling centres. Quatre Bornes has a giant **clothing market** on Thursday and Sunday, which is great if you like to dig for a bargain. Don't miss the **street food** stands on the side, especially the freshly made *gâteaux piment*. In **Rose Belle**, north of Quatre Bornes, check out artists' residence **Bactory**, where you'll find local artists such as Evan Sohun (p74) and Skizofan.

LOCAL BEERS

The Phoenix brewery has had a beer monopoly in Mauritius since its creation in the 1960s, but newcomers are diversifying the scene.

Phoenix
The golden Phoenix lager is the brewery's most popular tipple. You could also try its Blue Marlin and Guinness Foreign Extra beers.

Flying Dodo
Produced by the only microbrewery on the island, which uses traditional but also innovative brewing methods to brew Belgian-style ales and an IPA.

Thirsty Fox
Launched by the Oxenham group, this is the island's first craft beer. Thirsty Fox also makes a lager, an amber ale, a pale ale and a Bavarian-style *Weissbier*.

WHERE TO EAT ON THE PLATEAU

Escale Créole
A leafy wooden patio restaurant in Moka serving excellent home-cooked Creole dishes. €

Maison Eureka
In Moka, visit Eureka mansion house around lunchtime to sit down to traditional Creole food. €€

King Dragon
Upmarket Chinese restaurant in Quatre Bornes; locals come for the seafood dishes. €€

A MODEL HANDICRAFT

While you're in Curepipe, grab a handmade souvenir at model-ship maker **Voiliers de l'Océan**, whose name means 'sailboats'. The large store is packed with wooden dodos, pashmina scarves and other appealing wares, but the main draw is the model ships, each more intricate than the last. Don't miss the upstairs workshop, where a handful of highly skilled artisans pour hours of painstaking labour into their creations. Their passion is contagious and may inspire you to buy a ship of your own just to support the craft.

Model ships are traditional Mauritian handicrafts that highlight the country's naval past. The tradition is hanging on, but support of its artisans is essential for its long-term survival.

Hand crafting a model ship, Curepipe

Head to the heart of the island higher up the plateau and you'll feel temperatures get cooler from **Vacoas-Phoenix**, known for its **hand-blown glass** factory and gallery where you can pick up decorative objects. Try the local **Phoenix beer**, a mainstay across the island.

Curepipe, 25 minutes from Port Louis, is the last and highest town of the plateau, sitting at 550m above sea level. Don't miss **Les Aubineaux** (built 1872), a wonderfully evocative colonial manor house with white walls and turquoise shutters, and surrounded by lush, leafy gardens. In 1889 it was the first residence to be kitted out with electricity. Today it's a cosy restaurant mainly serving local Creole dishes. It's also the first stop on the historic Route du Thé (p74), which leads south to Bois Chéri.

While you're in the area, head up to chic, leafy suburb **Floréal**, where enormous mansions hide behind tall bamboo hedges and imposing camera-guarded gates. At the top, surrounded by jungle slopes, is the crater of the Trou aux Cerfs volcano (p77). (This is said to be the volcano that formed the island of Mauritius.) Be sure to take in the views from here: they span all the way across the Moka mountains.

BEST MAURITIUS ACTIVITIES FOR KIDS

La Vanille Crocodile Park
Crocodiles and giant tortoises, plus an insectarium with 23,000 species. (lavanille-naturepark.com)

Under the Sea
The island is home to 200 species of aquatic creature. Visit some at Port Louis' Odysseo. (odysseomauritius.com)

Casela
Zoo offering wildlife safaris, activities with big cats, and zip-lining in a beautiful park (p81).

Plantation-House Museums

HERITAGE FROM NORTH TO SOUTH

You can identify former sugar plantations by the tall, volcanic-brick chimney stacks peeking out from behind palm trees – these belong to the sugar-processing factories on the grounds. Today the plantations' elegant colonial-style châteaux (as they're known locally) have been revamped and repurposed. Among them are Eureka (p111) in Moka and Les Aubineaux (p72) in Curepipe.

Just outside the hot, busy northern town of **Goodlands**, the evocative **Demeure St-Antoine** is full of colonial charm. Three rooms with period furniture offer a comfortable stay, and the restaurant (open lunch and dinner) has tables on an expansive veranda looking onto lush gardens.

In **Mapou**, the lovingly restored 1830s **Château de Labourdonnais**, with wraparound veranda and breezy rooms, acts as a museum tracing Mauritian history. Join a tour (9.30am, 11.30am and 2.30pm) to get the most out of the experience. The visit ends with a taste of the château's rum in the bar adjoining the restaurant. **Le Quartier des Serres**, on the grounds, hosts a well-priced cafe in a leafy greenhouse courtyard and a handful of shops, such as a cool little stationery store and Must (beloved by locals), stocking womenswear from around the world.

In the 'deep south' – as it's often referred to for that off-the-grid feeling – is the impressive **Château de Bel Ombre** (p96), now a fine-dining restaurant with an impressive wine list. A short drive away, take a look at **Domaine de St-Aubin**, a whitewashed French colonial house with two turrets. A vanilla plantation, a rum distillery and a greenhouse punctuate its grounds.

Other mansion houses of note include the enchanting **Mon Désir**, north of Port Louis, now a top-end restaurant. **Mon Plaisir**, built on the site of Mahé de Labourdonnais' residence in 1823, is in Sir Seewoosagur Ramgoolam Botanical Garden (p69). While it isn't open to the public, the president's home, **Chateau Réduit**, in Moka, is another example of typical Mauritian colonial architecture.

Before exports began, the plantations' sugar-cane was exclusively intended to produce the spirit arrack, which was sold to passing ships. By the 1940s there were an impressive 300 sugar mills in operation across Mauritius, the sweet, slightly acrid smell of ground sugar cane wafting through the air across roads snaking through the fields. Since then the sugar industry has been steadily declining, and today, while a fair few plantations remain, only three cooperatives

---

ALL ABOUT MAURITIUS' SUGAR

The **Beauplan plantation** has seen a revolution. Its sugar-processing factory, still with all the original machinery in place, has become **L'Aventure du Sucre**, a museum about the history of Mauritius, including its sugar exporting days, slavery and indentured labour, and rum production. Open Monday to Saturday, it's an excellent choice for an outing with kids.

There's a delightful creative element to the revamped site, with several murals by local artists, artist residencies, and various venues hosting events such as concerts, talks and art shows.

The museum's **Le Fangourin** restaurant has an expansive menu including Mauritian specialities and a selection of kids' choices.

L'Aventure du Sucre
Explores the island's history as a sugar exporter.

Île aux Aigrettes
The team on the island, home to giant tortoises, helps conserve endemic fauna and flora. (p116)

Curious Corner of Chamarel
This mini-museum of illusions will take you by surprise. (curiouschamarel.com)

actually mill. The 2006 EU sugar regime reform saw a price drop of more than a third in just four years, crushing the island's industry.

You'll find exquisite colonial houses all over the island, hiding behind bamboo hedges or garden walls, so keep your eyes peeled.

Mauritius Through Artists' Eyes
A NEW PICTURE OF THE ISLAND

Mauritius is a hotbed of creative expression, but its art scene is still tricky for newcomers to navigate because of a lack of venues and other support for developing local talent. However, the artists and galleries mentioned here are starting to change all that.

Award-winning artist and architect **Salim Currimjee**, previously on the committee of London's Tate Modern, is the founder of the Institute of Contemporary Art Indian Ocean (ICAIO) in Port Louis (p65). He's known for his big, bright abstract paintings questioning the notion of visual space and our constructed experience of it.

Internationally renowned Mauritian painters include **Malcom de Chazal** (1901–1981), who painted joyful naive works that are a window onto Mauritius' colourful environment and vibrant flower and bird species. **Vaco Baissac** (1940–2023) began by taking inspiration from de Chazal but found his own style as his paintings came to resemble stained-glass scenes. Like de Chazal's, his works are odes to an abundant, buoyant nature and depict everyday life in fruit-tree plantations, fields and markets. You can make an appointment to view his work at his Pereybere gallery in Grand Baie. Socialist and activist for Mauritian independence **Henri Masson** (1919–1990) is known for his avant-garde works depicting the stories of enslaved people and indentured labourers.

Among the younger generation of established artists is **Evan Sohun**, whose character Toudim (*toudimoun* means 'all people' in Creole) appears in many of his colourful everyday scenes. A wolf with a human body, Toudim seeks his identity in a complex and diverse world. Sohun says that 'through my practice I want to bring Mauritian culture, including the Creole language, to the forefront as something to be proud of'. Evan has also brought Toudim out of his paintings and made him into resin sculptures in various sizes and a range of colours, but most commonly black.

Raymond Levantard (also known as RYMD) is known for his wonderfully poetic abstract figures twisting and turn-

---

EXPLORING, ONE CUP OF TEA AT A TIME

The **Route du Thé** allows you to delve into the island's past as you visit three beautiful mansion houses. Begin at **Les Aubineaux** (p72), then move on to the dark-green **Bois Chéri**, close to sacred Hindu site Grand Bassin, and finish in the **Domaine de St-Aubin** (p73), built in 1819 on the south coast. The old sugar estate is now a rum distillery with restaurant, accommodation and lush gardens.

Die-hard tea fans should extend their trip by starting at the 5-hectare **Corson** tea plantation above Curepipe, next to **La Potinière** restaurant (p75). Auguste Jules Corson is credited with introducing vanilla tea to Mauritius in 1919, and it's still a very popular beverage today.

ART SPACES IN MAURITIUS

ICAIO
Founded by leading local artist and designer Salim Currimjee, ICAIO in Port Louis promotes regional art.

Bactory
At this artists' residence north of Quatre Bornes, meet prominent local talents in their workshops.

Lakaz d'Art
Founded by art events expert Kim Siew, Lakaz d'Art in Port Louis helps develop Mauritian talent.

Les Aubineaux

ing, full of movement. See his work online at Saatchi Art. Drop in on Bactory founder **Gaël Froget**, whose work has been shown in Singapore and Paris, to see his female portraits and scribbled flowers. **Skizofan**'s bright paintings fall between pop and tribal art. His work, like Froget's, shows the influence of American artist Jean-Michel Basquiat. Also prominent is young multidisciplinary artist **Kim Yip Tong**, whose paintings and digital installations are steeped in vibrant colour and often infused with an awareness of nature. She's very active in the local scene, and her work has been shown in London and Barcelona.

BEST FINE DINING IN CUREPIPE

La Potinière
Huge windows look onto the Corson tea plantation at this smart spot serving local dishes such as palm-heart salad and octopus, and green-papaya curry. €€

Clé des Champs
Jacqueline Dalais has rustled gourmet dishes for government officials for years. Now her children are keeping her passion alive. €€€

Les Aubineaux
Serving local Creole dishes, this restaurant in a former plantation house is the perfect setting to sit back and soak up the ambience of this fabulous colonial abode. €€

Imaaya Gallery
Based in Vacoas-Phoenix; founder Charlotte d'Hotman has curated exhibitions by Mauritian artists since 2008.

EDITH
Buzzing gallery and events space with restaurant; housed in an 18th-century Port Louis storage facility.

Caudan Arts Centre
Inside Port Louis' waterfront mall, this contemporary centre hosts exhibitions and cultural events year-round.

Le Morne

TOP EXPERIENCE

Mauritius' Best Hikes

The island has a peak for every level of fitness, and hikers reap the rewards of resplendent views of coastal plains and sugar-cane fields. It's possible to do most hikes on your own, but it's safer to go with a local guide, who will also offer insights into the region and the country.

BEST FOR...

A challenge:
Lion Mountain

Expert hikers:
Black River Gorges

Sea views:
Le Morne

Panoramic views:
Deux Mamelles

Gentle slopes:
Le Pouce

Sunrise:
Corps de Garde

Le Pouce

The gentle jungly slopes you see from Port Louis are those of Le Pouce and Pieter Both. Le Pouce, at 812m, is shaped like a thumb and is one of the easiest hikes with maximum reward: 360-degree views of the island. Pieter Both has a little round rock at its peak that looks like a head.

The trail: 4.5km (2.8 miles) round trip; two to three hours

Black River Gorges

The longest and most challenging hike on the island, this trail (p90) takes you through the gorges' jaw-droppingly beautiful vegetation. Scattered with waterfalls, the route includes the 826m Piton de la Petits Rivière Noire, Mauritius' highest peak, which alone takes about two hours. A guide is highly recommended here – while the itineraries are clearly marked, the terrain is challenging.

The trail: 19.5km (12 miles) round trip; 6½ hours; easy to strenuous (includes several hikes in one).

Lion Mountain

Shaped like a lion lying down with its back sloping towards the ground, this is another tough hike requiring a good level of fitness and some knowledge of the area, as paths aren't always clearly marked. A guide is strongly recommended. Several viewpoints look out over Mahébourg, and from the 590m peak you can spot several islands such as Île aux Aigrettes nearby and even Lighthouse Island in the distance. The views are well worth the scramble up.

The trail: 5km (3 miles) return; four to five hours; strenuous

Deux Mamelles

A fairly easy hike that takes no longer than two hours, this route begins in the sugar-cane fields near Beau Bois in Moka and affords great views of the surrounding mountain ranges (Le Pouce and Pieter Both), as well as Long Mountain.

The trail: 2.4km (1.5 miles) return; two hours; easy

Le Morne

A Unesco World Heritage Site with a sombre backstory of enslaved people hiding here and later jumping to their deaths, Le Morne is a multifaceted spot. The hike is a challenging climb through arid landscape, and there's some scrambling as you reach the top, but the views of the turquoise ocean are worth breaking a sweat for.

The trail: 7km (4.3 miles) return; three to five hours; moderate

Corps de Garde

This one is particularly scenic at sunrise, which is when it's advisable to reach the 719m peak in any case: there isn't much shade along the trail and once the sun is up it can get quite hot. It's not necessary to have a guide with you, but hikers will need a good level of fitness.

The trail: 4km (2.5 miles), four hours return; moderate

VOLCANIC ORIGINS

The island of Mauritius is a massive shield volcano that was active from 7.8 million years until about 30,000 years ago. The **Trou aux Cerfs** (605m) on the plateau in Floréal is the site of the volcano's most recent eruption around 700,000 years ago.

Thought to have created the island, that eruption left a crater 350m across and 80m deep that you can still see today. Three other points in Mauritius are thought to have shown recent volcanic activity: Trou Kanaka, Bassin Blanc (p95) and Grand Bassin (p92).

TOP TIPS

- Try local company Yanature if you want to arrange a guide.
- The Fitsy (fitsy.com) and Explore Mauritius (exploremauritius.org) websites have some useful maps and GPS coordinates.
- The best time for hiking is from September until December, when it's the driest and coolest.
- Hiking when it's been raining isn't recommended, as trails can be slippery.
- Stay hydrated by bringing adequate water with you – bear in mind that you can dehydrate quickly in tropical humidity.
- Wear mosquito repellent and SPF50 sunscreen, and be sure to cover your head and shoulders as the sun can be very intense throughout the year.

View from Le Pouce

BEST ART EVENTS

Salon de Mai
Events venue the Mahatma Gandhi Institute in Moka hosts various shows, including the annual Salon de Mai art fair in May.

Laguna Art Prize
A key venue on the art scene, Port Louis' Caudan Art Center hosts several shows and prizes throughout the year, including the Mauritius edition of the international Laguna Art Prize.

Lakaz d'Art
An art venue and hub for the island's creative clan, Lakaz often hosts exhibitions and takes part in various artistic projects across Mauritius.

Le Morne (p78)

You can see many local artists' work in murals around Port Louis (see walking tour, p60). Go to online artist platform **The Third Dot** (thethirddot.net) to read more about these artists and many others.

GETTING AROUND

A car is almost mandatory for exploring the central plateau as buses take much longer to get from place to place – though the network is generally good at covering most of the island.

FLIC EN FLAC

With one of the best beaches in the country and located close to the island's corridor of cities, Flic en Flac is wildly popular with locals, who flock to the long stretch of fine white sand for picnics in the shade of the filao pines. At weekends, don't be surprised to see whole families arriving in minivans and laying out huge spreads of food as music blasts from portable radios. Across the road, the beachfront is lined with a cluster of budget holiday rentals, restaurants, cafes, bars and night-clubs that have built up over the years. A window onto local life, a stay here isn't necessarily an unpleasant experience, but if you're in need of some proper peace and quiet, choose a spot closer to Wolmar's five-star hotels, just south of Flic en Flac proper. Flic en Flac is also a top diving and snorkelling spot.

TOP TIP

As Flic en Flac beach can get quite overrun at weekends and on puplic holidays, aim to visit on a weekday if you can, when the beach is quieter and there's a better chance of having it all to yourself.

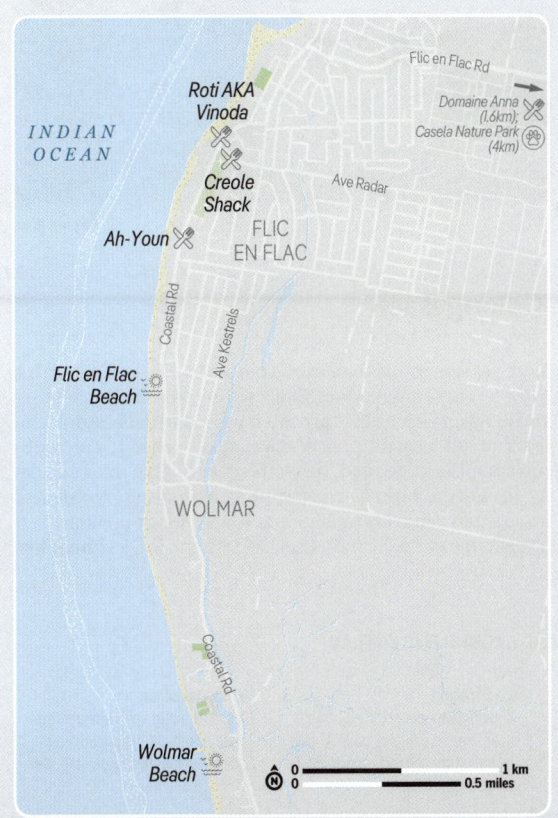

Flic en Flac

Kicking Back

BEACH LIFE THE LOCAL WAY

More seaside resort than exotic paradise, Flic en Flac makes a low-key first impression. Shops selling splashy beach attire and blow-up beach rings are interspersed with bars and nondescript but bargain-priced rental apartments. It's not until you cross the main road, reach the rows of pine trees and descend onto the long ribbon of white sand fronting crystal-clear waters that you truly understand Flic en Flac's popularity. It has got one of the island's best, widest and longest **beaches**

LOCAL FOOD

Creole Shack
Beachside shack dishing up authentic Creole food. Order a rougail (fish or meat in a tomato-based sauce). €

Roti AKA Vinoda
Delicious roti and farata flatbreads piled with lip-smacking fillings. Look out for the little blue shack. €

Domaine Anna
Well-priced fine-dining Chinese restaurant serving excellent seafood and Peking duck. €€

Ah Youn
Try the bol renversé (tipped-over bowl), a Sino-Mauritian dish of rice, vegetables, a fried egg and usually meat stacked in a bowl served tipped upside down. €€

WHERE TO STAY IN AND AROUND FLIC EN FLAC

Sugar Beach
On Wolmar beach, this lively resort has comfortable seafront rooms and a waterside restaurant. €€€

La Pirogue
Among the island's first five-star hotels, soulful La Pirogue has thatch-roofed rooms and a beach bar. €€€

Villa Caroline
A small hotel with simple, sea-view rooms, plus a couple of pools and a diving centre. €€

and a wide range of accommodation, from cheap studios and small hotels to five-star beachfront resorts. **Wolmar**, south of Flic en Flac, is where the beach gets even better, with even finer sand and more translucent waters. It's been somewhat colonised by luxury resorts, but the beach remains public. Don't miss sundowners at La Pirogue's **beach bar** – sunset here is magical.

At night, especially on weekends, Mauritians come to party in the town's **bars and nightclubs**. It's a fantastic opportunity to mingle with locals and see top performers such as prominent seggae (a blend of local séga music and reggae) artist Blakkayo. For daytime activities with the kids, **Casela Nature Park** – with safaris, rides and activities – is less than 10 minutes' drive away. (Tip: get there early.) All in all, Flic en Flac is a handy place to stay if you don't have a car and want to do a little exploring and a lot of sunbathing or diving.

Under the Sea
MAURITIUS' UNDERWATER GEMS

Mauritius is a diving paradise. The island is almost completely surrounded by a barrier reef, so its waters are usually calm, affording great visibility. Marine life is abundant, seascapes are dramatic and there's a handful of atmospheric wrecks to explore. Flic en Flac ranks among the best dive sites in the country as it's sheltered from the wind, leading to excellent visibility and optimal conditions year-round. Diving centres are clustered on and near the beach.

Qualified divers can explore **La Cathédrale**, the star of the show due to its scenic stone arches and cavern housing abundant soft and black corals. Just next to it on the same part of the reef is **Colline Bambous**, popular for its changing colourful scenery and fish. **Rempart Serpent** (Snake Reef), named after the winding, snake-like rock formation you can see here at 25m, attracts plentiful lionfish, scorpion fish, stonefish, groupers and eels, as well as butterflyfish and angelfish. A little further north along the reef is the deeply atmospheric **Manioc**. Still further north and out to sea is **Kei Sei 113**, named after the wreck you can explore here. The ship was sunk in 1988 at 35m to create a reef and today harbours vibrant underwater life such as lionfish and blue-striped red snapper. Off the coast of the old Medine sugar estate, close to the beach-side suburb of Albion, south of Port Louis, **Tug II** is a small tugboat that was flooded to make an artificial reef. Now home to brilliant sea life, it makes for great diving.

BEST PARTY SPOTS IN FLIC EN FLAC

Shotz
Across the road from the beach, popular bar and nightclub Shotz hosts top local performers. Find event details on its social-media pages.

Lakaz Cascavelle
Located inside a mall, this concert venue and restaurant serves up burgers as well as gigs by local artists. Book in advance, as events are popular.

Kenzi
A laid-back bar and grill with rural African decor, Kenzi hosts live music including jazz most weekends and holidays. Open until midnight.

GETTING AROUND

If you have time, the best way to get around is on foot. In Flic en Flac you're never far from a restaurant, bar, supermarket or beach. That said, it's a long stretch of beach, so if you're going from one end to the other regularly, hire a bike and use the coastal road. Taxis are available if you are travelling outside of the town.

Beyond Flic en Flac

A short drive from Flic en Flac lie quiet townships with great surfing and beaches.

Clustered in a palm-fringed bay that's home to dolphins and even a few whales on the other side of the reef, Tamarin has the island's best surf break. It's also the jumping-off point for hiking the spectacular, seven-tiered Tamarind Falls, cocooned in thick forest. Beyond residential Rivière Noire with its beachy coves is sleepy La Gaulette, with a laid-back surf vibe and lots of good places to eat – possibly because it's en route to the dazzling heights of hilltop village Chamarel and its gorges. Further on, Le Morne's postcard-perfect beaches are the island's best. Also here is the peak after which the area is named, which is ideal for hikers who like a challenge.

TOP TIP

Tamarin and Rivière Noire are residential areas, so there aren't many hotels. Book early if you want to stay here.

Dolphins, Tamarin Bay

Tamarin Bay

Surfing the Wave in Tamarin Bay
DOLPHIN SPOTTING AND BEACH TIME

Tamarin is largely residential, with houses clustered around Tamarin Bay and along the beach. Split by a picturesque river, the town has a spectacular backdrop of jungly mountains. Time here ticks to the local pace. Surfers get up at the crack of dawn to paddle out to the **surf break** and catch some waves, often with dolphins zipping past. From the beach, you can sometimes see **dolphins** in the early morning, usually at the northern end of the bay. A slew of companies offer dolphin swimming excursions, which means scores of speedboats roaring through the water, encircling the dolphins and chasing them at full throttle, which distresses them and is an unpleasant experience for visitors. Avoid these tours.

If you want to get out on the water, go **kayaking** on the river with a guide from local company Yanature. Note that the tide here and in the bay can be extremely strong, so be cautious. Alternatively, Tamarin Bay Surf School offers **surfing lessons** and **catamaran day trips**, where you can admire the island's coastline and enjoy an onboard barbecue set to

WHERE TO EAT & DRINK IN TAMARIN

Cosa Nostra
A diverse crowd likely comes here for the excellent pizza – you'll hear at least five languages spoken around you. €€

La Bonne Chute
Has a pretty outdoor patio where you can enjoy some of the best Creole food around. €€

Boulette Stand
Warning: these boulettes (dumplings) in flavoursome broth are addictive. Grab a bowlful from the roadside stand near Tamarin beach. €

Big Willy's
Lively bar that shows sports games, and hosts DJ nights and live performances by local musicians.

WHERE TO STAY CLOSE TO THE BAY

Riverhouse – Le Barachois
Cosy B&B with scenic river views, garden and pool. A path leads straight to the beach. €

Tamarina Golf & Spa
Has a bar-restaurant and 18-hole golf course. Reached by a long drive along a quiet road. €€

Veranda Tamarin Hotel
Lively hotel across from the beach with nightly music performances and thumping weekend club nights. €€

WHERE TO EAT IN RIVIÈRE NOIRE

Hidden Garden
Charming spot perfect for cocktails and tapas. It even has a small pool to cool off in. €€

Nomad
Modern cafe inside a small warehouse with an outdoor area. Locals come for the burgers and lively evening atmosphere. €€

Frenchie Café
Smart covered outdoor cafe with Western bites and fairly tame local food. Does a good breakfast and brunch, though, and has weekend DJ nights. €€

Ousaporn Thai
Charming restaurant with a leafy garden and tasty dishes. €€

Martello Tower

séga music. A fun team of skippers will point out any whales that might be in the area. Catamarans also go to the island of Bénitiers, which used to have a castaway feel but now bristles with souvenir stands lining the entire landing beach. Another popular attraction is a visit to the **salt pans** you can see from the road across from Cosa Nostra restaurant.

Beach Life in Rivière Noire

GET SOME SHORE TIME

South of Tamarin, a long stretch of houses hiding behind walls and fences runs south along the main artery as the area becomes Rivière Noire township (the larger district of Rivière Noire runs from Albion to Le Morne). The area is mainly residential, home to the Franco-Mauritian community. You'll find a stretch of beach coves interspersed with rocky areas all the way to **La Preneuse**, one of the area's best beaches. Right on the beach are relics of Mauritius' naval past, such as a **cannon** aimed at the open water and **Martello Tower**, one of five towers built by the British to protect their colony from invaders – namely the French, whom the British suspected of

WHERE TO STAY IN RIVIÈRE NOIRE

Bay Hotel
North of La Preneuse beach; an attractive boutique hotel with sea views, pool and beachfront restaurant. €€€

Shanti Gar Guesthouse
Mishmash of Mauritian city interiors and boutique design; the sleek-looking pool has smart cabanas. €

La Mariposa
Modern, gay-friendly complex of contemporary rooms with dashes of sea greens; on La Preneuse beach. €€€

supporting a rebellion by enslaved people. Martello is now a museum highlighting the ingenious tower design: 3m-thick walls crowned by a copper cannon that is said to be able to destroy a target 2km away.

There are also a few shops to check out – though, like most worthwhile spots in Mauritius, they're tucked away and tricky to find. Beautiful homeware store **Tutti Frutti** will give you inspiration for your domestic decor. Don't miss Séverine Tyack's **ceramics workshop**, where you can pick up one of her beautiful handmade ocean-inspired creations. Contact her via Instagram at @myceramicadventure. Also check out locally made **Océano Pearls** jewellery, odes to Mauritian sea life, at the Ruisseau Créole shopping arcade. The boutique **My Pop-Up Store** (inside Vanilla Village hotel) brings together beautiful products from clothing to bags, all made locally.

Seven-Waterfall Hike
A DAZZLING, UNMISSABLE SIGHT

If you have one day to spare, you're in good shape but not a die-hard hiker, and you're not keen on seeing the sights of Port Louis (or you've already seen them), make **Tamarind Falls** your day trip of choice. It's about a 40-minute drive from Tamarin or Rivière Noire.

One of the most spectacular sights on the island, the seven-tier waterfall is surrounded by steep, rocky slopes and nothing but jungle as far as the eye can see. Cool, crystal-clear pools just beg you to take a dip. If it weren't so easily accessible (and it weren't for the other hikers), this would feel completely off the grid. While the trail is easy to follow, the slopes leading down to the lower tiers are extremely steep – having a guide with you will definitely help as they can pick out the safest route. **Jay Tannoo**, who works with his son Meetan, is a passionate guide who's a fount of knowledge about the history of the island. Along the route he'll also point out notable trees and birds, such as the rare pink pigeon, the kestrel (emblem of Mauritius' national airline) and the echo parakeet. For ultimate wow-factor, start at the bottom waterfall and ascend to the top.

Be sure to wear sturdy footwear and plenty of mosquito repellent. Although most of the walk is shaded, the waterfall pools are exposed, so make sure you've put on your sunscreen. This hike takes about five hours, including photo and swimming stops.

WATERFALL HOPPING

To hike one of Mauritius' many waterfalls, hire a guide with Yanature or Lokal Adventure. Afterwards, enjoy a cool swim.

Alexandra Falls
In Black River Gorges National Park (p90), this whitewater waterfall affords some of the best viewpoints on the way up.

Cascade de 500 Pieds
Also in Black River Gorges, this moderate hike offers panoramic views across the valley.

Chamarel
Mauritius' tallest single-drop waterfall has some of the island's oldest exposed volcanic rock.

Rochester
Iconic for its black rock face, this wide, 10m-high fall is surrounded by luxuriant vegetation (p121).

WHERE TO STAY AROUND LE MORNE

Lux* Le Morne
Stellar location on one of Mauritius' best beaches with ominous Le Morne as backdrop. €€€

Villas
Well-maintained villas, such as Kozy, Ma Vie La and Villa Ayapana, offer great accommodation. €€

Paradis Beachcomber Golf & Spa
Secluded resort with all the trimmings, plus beach access. €€

Heavenly Beaches

WHITE SAND, IRIDESCENT WATERS

Driving south from Rivière Noire, you'll come to the small roadside village of **La Gaulette**, with a laid-back, surfy vibe and good restaurants. Keep driving south and you'll reach **Le Morne**.

If all you want is a picture-perfect holiday, look no further. Le Morne is among the best places to stay on the island due to its excellent beach of fine white sand and sparkling waters (even on a dull day), set off dramatically by **Le Morne mountain** as backdrop.

A Unesco World Heritage site, the mountain has a tragic history. It's said enslaved people hid out here and later jumped to their deaths when police approached. Slavery had been abolished by then, which is why Le Morne means 'the mournful ones'. The mountain remains a symbol of enslaved people's fight for freedom. Mauritius, an important stopover in the eastern trade in human beings, came to be known as the 'maroon republic' because large numbers of fugitive enslaved people lived on Le Morne mountain.

In recognition of this history, **Nou Le Morne art and music festival** celebrates freedom of movement and mind. The event is usually held at the eco-friendly **Green Village**, an outdoor space at the foot of the peak that also hosts events such as Dance Under the Stars.

From the top of Le Morne mountain you'll be able to see the **underwater waterfall**, an optical illusion that makes it look as though there's a drop below the ocean that's about to suck in the land mass and Le Morne peak with it. Lagoon Flights can fly you above the area to get a good glimpse.

The **Passe St Jacques** in the Baie du Cap is an excellent drift-dive site, with 3m to 30m depths.

Le Morne

WHERE TO EAT IN LE MORNE

Walapalam Island Eatery
Great all-rounder with good atmosphere, attractive decor and local food. Has a sister restaurant in Port Louis. €€

Emba Filao
A local favourite, this beachfront shack with tables serves grilled seafood and other local delights. Arrive early to avoid the queues. €

East at the Lux* Morne
Thai chef Suksan Supprasert's dishes would give any high-end Thai restaurant in Bangkok a run for its money. €€€

GETTING AROUND

It's essential to hire a car if you want to explore the area. Taxis are extremely expensive (especially when booked through a hotel).

CHAMAREL

Perched atop a mountain peak close to the canyons of Black River Gorges National Park, Chamarel is a window onto a different side of Mauritius that sits in appealing contrast to the images in the beachy postcards. Getting there is half the fun. As you wind your way up or down the mountain, the spectacular views of the surrounding peaks and the fields that run all the way to the bright blue ocean will have you gasping in awe. In the cool mountain hamlet of Chamarel itself, the attractions are many. The delightful food is a delicious local twist on Creole cuisine and there are world-class boutique rum distilleries. Capping things off is the island's number-one sight: the spectacular Black River Gorges, with volcanic-rock canyons and waterfalls. Explore by hiking or take in park panoramas from the various viewpoints, such as the Terre des 7 Couleurs.

TOP TIP

Buses can take you to the village, but if you want to do a bit of exploring it's best to rent a car once you arrive because the distances are significant and the terrain is hilly.

Terre des 7 Couleurs (p88)

WHERE TO EAT IN CHAMAREL

Le Palais de Barbizon
In this low-key place Marie-Ange rustles up feasts from her family's cookbook. Choose from a set menu of rice, vegetables, meat and fish. €

Varangue sur Morne
This old hunting lodge has some of the best views in town. Star dishes are braised wild boar and prawns flambéed with Chamarel rum. €€

Le Chamarel
With views all the way to the coastal plains, this huge place is popular with tour groups. Taste local specialities such as palm-heart salad and wild-boar salami. €€

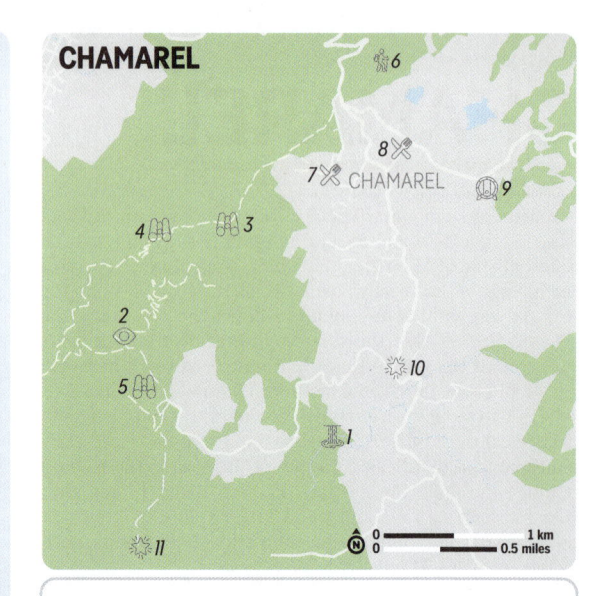

CHAMAREL

SIGHTS
1 Chamarel Waterfall
2 Ebony Forest
3 Piton Canot
4 Sublime Point
5 Terres de 7 Couleurs

ACTIVITIES
6 Black River Gorges National Park
9 Rhumerie de Chamarel
10 Curious Corner

EATING & DRINKING
7 Lakaz Chamarel
8 Palais de Barbizon

ENTERTAINMENT
11 Lavilléon Adventure Park

Rainforest Peaks

MOUNTAIN VILLAGE AND DEEP CANYONS

At **Terre des 7 Couleurs** (Earth of Seven Colours), you can see the various hues of a patch of earth laid bare and take in views of the **Chamarel Waterfall**. The viewpoint is accessible by car via Chamarel Park (an entrance fee applies).

Another way to explore the area is to zip-line across a valley at **Lavilléon Adventure Park**.

Make time for the fascinating indigenous **Ebony Forest** wildlife conservation area, whose admission fee supports an ongoing reforestation project. The conservation area is home to endemic species of bird such as the pink pigeon and echo parakeet. Linked by raised walkways that climb into the canopy, the park's 7km of trails offer heart-lifting views from **Sublime Point** and **Piton Canot** lookouts. The vistas are a glimpse of what Mauritius looked like 250 years ago.

WHERE TO STAY IN CHAMAREL

Lakaz Chamarel
Spectacular lodge on an old pineapple and banana plantation. The best rooms have private pools. €€

Cham Gaia
Private eco-lodge with three smart wooden villas on stilts overlooking the sea and Le Morne mountain. €€€

La Vieille Cheminée
Rustic lodge on a farm with six self-catering rooms; offers horse riding and nature walks. €

Across the road from the park's main entrance, **Curious Corner** is an interactive museum of illusions that's more fun than you might expect and great to visit with children.

Chamarel is known for its flavoursome cuisine, so trying the local dishes is a must. Local favourites include the family-run **Palais de Barbizon** and the wonderful **Lakaz Chamarel** eco-lodge.

Locals also come to the area for the **Rhumerie de Chamarel**, which offers an enjoyable tour rounded off by a tasting at the lovely bar. Visit the gift shop to pick up some of the distillery's best tipples, from spiced rum to its prestigious 2010 golden single barrel.

Eat Your Heart Out
CURRY AND ROUGAIL GALORE

Mauritius has terrific home-cooked Creole dishes you can't leave without tasting. If you try only one dish, make it *briani*. Served at weddings and family get-togethers, it's a saffron rice dish made by the Muslim community spiced with each chef's secret blend of cloves, crushed cardamom, cinnamon and star anise. Slow-cooked potatoes and braised beef or chicken are added into a huge steel pot, and then all the flavours are allowed to simmer together. You have to place a special order with the families who make *briani* and collect the huge pot by car. Don't forget the condiments of grated carrot and cucumber salad, *achar* (pickled vegetables or fruit) and chilli.

Also essential is a trip to a *snack* (small cafe) to try mouth-watering **rougail poisson salé** (dried salted fish cooked in a thick tomato sauce), served with rice and lentils or broad beans in a thyme broth.

Another favourite island dish is **vindaye**, a dry curry made with fried chunks of fish or octopus coated in a mixture of turmeric, mustard seeds, ginger and chilli. It's best enjoyed with **pain maison**, a local round white crusty bread, or roti flatbread.

Cari poule (with chicken) and **cari ourite** (with octopus) are staples. They're curries cooked with a blend of local herbs and spices, and served with rice, lentils and **brèdes songe**, a green leafy vegetable.

Last but not least, beef or chicken **kalia** should also be on your to-try list. Ground meat with spices and herbs is shaped into a ball around a hard-boiled egg, and the meatballs are then slow-cooked and served with roti.

BOUTIQUE RUM

Over the last decade Mauritius has established itself as one of the world's leading producers of quality rum, building on a history of production that dates back to the 19th century.

There are three types of rum in Mauritius: traditional (made in older distilleries), agricultural (made in new distilleries) and *rum arrangé* (spiced rum). Rums tend to be smooth and slightly sweet, with a good finish. Distilleries to try include the top-of-the-range Rhumerie de Chamarel, the 100% craft New Grove, Labourdonnais in Mapou, St-Aubin in the deep south, and the premium Penny Blue and Pink Pigeon by Medine, the island's oldest still-active distillery.

For a simple craft *rum arrangé*, head to Lolita Marie (p109) in Trou d'Eau Douce.

GETTING AROUND

Chamarel is up in the hills and the sights are quite far apart, so having a car is very handy. If you're keen to hike and don't want to loop back to where you started, consider a taxi pick-up at the end.

TOP EXPERIENCE

Black River Gorges

Spectacular canyons and waterfalls lie amid rainforest in Mauritius' biggest national park. Covering roughly 2% of the island's surface, Black River Gorges National Park is home to hundreds of animal and plant species. Hiking its many trails with a guide is a delightful way to experience the 'other' Mauritius.

Macchabée Trail

Start at the Pétrin visitor centre and hike along the plateau to the stunning Macchabée Viewpoint, one of the best places to take in views of the undulating forested hills that slope into the canyon. After you've soaked up the vista from there, head down to the Black River Gorges visitor centre. Along the way, keep an eye out for a host of tropical birds, such as the pink pigeon and echo parakeet. One of the few remaining endemic birds on the island, the pink pigeon nearly became extinct in the '70s but is faring better today, though it's still fairly rare. Also endemic to Mauritius, the echo parakeet is the island's only remaining native parrot.

The trail: 10km one way; four hours; strenuous

THE FIRST NATIONAL PARK

Declared in June 1994, Black River Gorges was Mauritius' first national park. Its 6754 hectares preserve vestiges of pre-colonisation native forest and shelter 163 of the country's 311 endemic flora species and its remaining 28 endemic bird species. With a focus on saving the Mauritius kestrel, pink pigeon and echo parakeet, Black River Gorges is one of the world's most successful conservation programmes.

Macchabée Loop

An easier and shorter hike than the full Macchabée Trail, this trip starts at the Pétrin visitor centre and takes you through the plateau to the Macchabée Viewpoint before returning to the visitor centre.

The trail: 8km return; three hours; moderate

Parakeet Trail

Begin at the Plaine Champagne Police Station and follow a ridge down into the canyon and along the river to the Black River Gorges visitor centre. As the name suggests, parakeets are a top draw along this route.

The trail: 8km one way; three hours; strenuous

Black River Peak

This is a tough hike up the country's highest peak (828m), also known as Piton de la Petite Rivière Noire. Compensating you for all your effort are some of the most magnificent views obtainable on the island. The trail starts on Chamarel Rd. About 300m from the car park, you'll see a sign for the Gorges Viewpoint. It's worth making your way to it: from the viewpoint it's possible to see across the gorges all the way to the coastal plains.

The trail: 6km return; three hours; strenuous

Macchabée Forest Trail

Pétrin visitor centre is the starting point for this trail, which takes you across the plateau in a loop through some of the park's most beautiful rainforest, scattered with black-trunked ebony trees. Endemic to Mauritius, ebony was used to make durable furniture and other items.

The trail: 8km return; three hours; moderate

Mare Longue Reservoir

This hike loops from and back to the Pétrin visitor centre by way of rainforest and a large reservoir you'll find at the northern tip of the park. This part of the park is one of its least visited sites. As you make your way through the forest, look out for flying foxes. The largest endemic mammal on the island, these fruit bats with golden fur can have a wingspan of 80cm (31in).

The trail: 12km return; four hours; moderate

DON'T MISS

Gorges Viewpoint

Macchabée Viewpoint

Pink pigeon

Echo parakeet

Ebony tree

Flying fox

Mauritius kestrel

TOP TIPS

- A guide will help you get the most out of the experience. Yanature and Lokal Adventure are enthusiastic and knowledgeable.
- Your guide will take you to the trailheads; otherwise, you'll need your own vehicle. A taxi to drop you off and collect you at the end is another option.
- Fitzy (fitsy.com) has a wealth of hiking information and helpful GPS coordinates.
- Take plenty of food and water, as there's nowhere to stock up in the park.
- Be sure to bring sunscreen and mosquito repellent.
- It can get quite humid, so a rain jacket and nonslip shoes are essential.

Beyond Chamarel

Beaches, nature reserves and golf

Once you leave the heights of luxuriant rainforest in Chamarel, there's more scenic landscape to be had. Spectacular views span the whole coastal plain as you wind down the mountain. First you'll come to Grand Bassin (Ganga Talao), Mauritius' most sacred Hindu site, with little temples scattered around a lake. Next, the Bois Chéri tea plantations run all the way to the south coast, also known as the 'deep south' for its undeveloped natural beauty. Finally, you'll reach the east coast. Its southern stretch is quieter, with plenty of terrain for hiking, and to the north are the beautiful beaches of Bel Ombre and its handful of luxury resorts. There's also plenty here to keep avid golfers happy.

TOP TIP

If you decide to rent a car halfway through your holiday, it's better to get one from the airport and pay the fee for someone to drive it across to you than to rely on expensive taxis.

Grand Bassin

Heritage le Telfair, Bel Ombre

The Deep South

HISTORIC ESTATE WITH BIOSPHERE RESERVE

A pocket of beautiful scenery and good beaches in quiet inlets, such as **Jacotet Bay**, the deep south is known for its secluded location between fishing villages and countryside. Some locals joke that it's total 'DND' (do not disturb) territory. If real downtime is what you need, then this is the place.

This part of the island has been an important agricultural area since the 18th century, and in 1807 the first foundations of a sugar estate were laid. These were later sold to Charles Telfair, a vital character in the story of **Bel Ombre** whose innovative agricultural methods revolutionised the industry. After 200 years of sugar production, the factory closed, but a hotel group has recently revitalised a large part of the Bel Ombre area. You can still see the vestiges of the sugar plant, but there's now also a bubble of two hotels, a B&B, two **golf courses** and the **Unesco Biosphere Reserve – Bel Ombre**.

A must-visit, the beautiful 36-sq-km reserve is a hiker's paradise with luxuriant plant life. Within the reserve, **L'Abattis des Cipayes** is where nature and history converge. Once serving as an important plantation area for crops, the site has been reclaimed by nature and now has an abundance of

THE STORY OF THE DODO

A super-sized pigeon that grew up to 1m tall and weighed about 20kg, the dodo is the most famous extinct bird. It's been gone for more than 300 years, with last sighting thought to have been around 1660. Dodo meat was apparently tasteless, so what pushed the dodo to extinction wasn't human predators but the rats that ate its eggs. Because it was flightless, the dodo laid its eggs on the ground. There are a few dodo bones at the Mahébourg Museum and the Natural History Museum in Port Louis, where you can also see two impressive fully mounted skeletons – though it's unlikely the bones all came from the same bird.

WHERE TO STAY IN BEL OMBRE

Heritage Le Telfair Golf & Wellness Resort
Chic hotel in a white colonial building with restaurant and huge range of activities. €€€

Kaz'alala B&B
Three-star countryside escape minutes from the beaches of the south, with pretty rooms, restaurant and pool. €

Shanti
Low-key tropical resort with palm-fringed beach, huge pool and traditional all-wood interiors. Close to Souillac. €€

ROAD TRIP

South Coast Road Trip

The most beautiful drive in Mauritius is the descent from the forested hills of Chamarel to the south coast. This drive takes you through the natural park, around the mountains – with sweeping views all the way to the ocean – across a sacred Hindu lake and through tea plantations before reaching the coast, where you'll turn off for the windy cliffs of Gris Gris before continuing to the quiet beaches of Bel Ombre.

1 Gorges Viewpoint
Don't leave Chamarel without visiting this viewpoint for one last look at its dazzling canyons. On a clear day, the spectacular views are punctuated by 828m Piton de la Petite Rivière Noire, the country's highest peak.

The Drive: Drive 2km until you reach the Plaine Champagne Police Station. Turn off the main road at the sign for Alexandra Falls.

2 Alexandra Falls
A smaller road runs to the viewpoint, where you can see 771m Mt Cocotte.

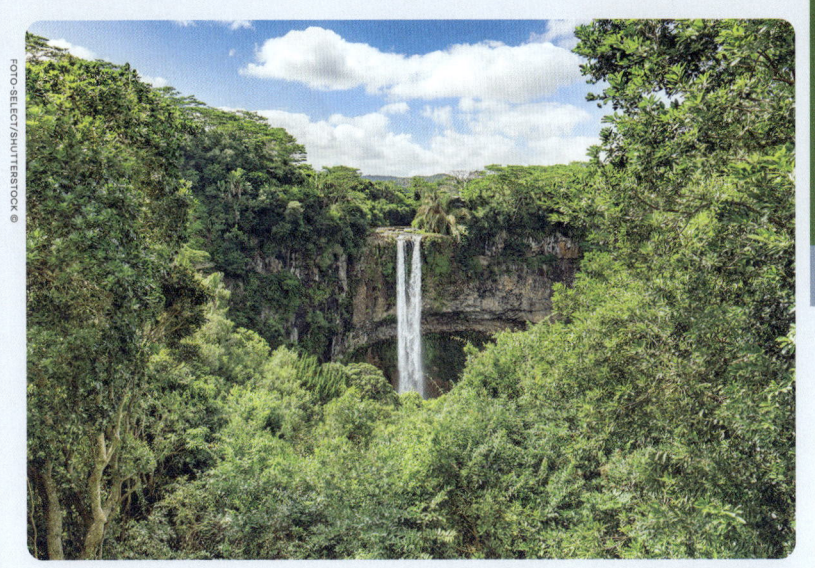

Alexandra Falls

The Drive: Back on the main road, turn right towards Chamouny and follow the road down the hill. Around 3km on you'll see an unpaved parking area on the right.

3 Bassin Blanc

Look for the low ridge of rock – from there you'll great views into Bassin Blanc (White Lake), created by a now-dormant volcano that helped form the island.

The Drive: Returning to the main road, follow signs to Grand Bassin at the roundabout.

4 Grand Bassin

You'll be greeted by two 33m figures of Shiva and Durga before reaching sacred Grand Bassin (Big Lake). It's also called Ganga Talao for its connection to the Ganges after a Brahmin dreamt of a holy lake, set out to find it and felt this was the one. Temples are scattered all around its banks, and thousands of pilgrims flock here during February's Maha Shivaratri festival. The area is best visited at sunset, as it's very quiet, except for the regular chants.

The Drive: Continue on the road that leads out of Grand Bassin and follow signs to Bois Chéri.

5 Bois Chéri & St-Aubin

You'll know you've reached the Bois Chéri tea plantations when you see low, dense hedges of small leaves. The old St-Aubin sugar mill has one of the island's last remaining colonial mansion houses.

The Drive: Continuing towards the coast, you'll come across a turnoff for Souillac. Turn right for Gris Gris.

6 Gris Gris Beach

At the bottom of tall black cliffs, Gris Gris is a windy beach where pounding waves signal a break in the reef. Legend has it a pair of star-crossed lovers marked their names on the rock face here before jumping to their deaths.

The Drive: Continue along the coastal road to Bel Ombre.

7 Bel Ombre

Former sugar plantation Bel Ombre is now a beachy destination. Continue along the coast to Baie du Cap, Macondé viewpoint and Le Morne for a scenic route taking in roadside villages looking out to sea.

LITCHI WINE PIONEER

After long hours of research, Alexander Oxenham, winemaker at the local Oxenham beverages group, has pushed the boundaries of his craft by using sweet Mauritian litchi fruit.

Located in Mare aux Vacoas, just east of Tamarind Falls, **Takamaka Boutique Winery** is the place to try and buy litchi wine.

Takamaka currently makes four whites and a rosé infused with fresh tropical-fruit notes – and all of them free of pesticides and herbicides.

Whether you're looking for a pairing with fish, spicy dishes or cheese, there's a litchi wine to fill the bill.

You can taste the wines at the bistro, which serves everything from hearty fresh salads to local Creole curries.

---

beautiful Latan palm groves. The **Jacotet River** that runs through the area makes for a picturesque two-hour hike. There's also a wildlife sanctuary on the site of the former **Federica sugar plantation**, whose chimney you can still glimpse peeping through the trees.

Stop at **Enba Pié** (meaning 'under a tree' in Creole), set in the shade of a 138-year-old banyan tree, for a taste of local cuisine. Choose from the likes of *arouille* (taro) fritters, octopus salad and *vindaye* (dry curry) and enjoy your meal inside the colonial governor's summer residence, one of the oldest buildings in the area.

Chateau de Bel Ombre

The whole of Bel Ombre biosphere reserve is ripe for exploration. You can hike to get up close to the surroundings or take a 4WD tour with a local guide.

The **Château de Bel Ombre** is now an excellent fine-dining restaurant with upstairs accommodation. Stay overnight to immerse yourself in the mansion's history once all the other diners have left and wake up to the sun rising above the gorgeous gardens. The house was commissioned in the late 1800s by a wealthy Indian patron, but he never visited Mauritius and so never saw the marvel that's now a national historic landmark. The restaurant's delicious dishes are a blend of regional and French styles, using local produce such as wild boar and deer from the reserve. Jimmy, the personable maître d'hôtel, will point you in the right direction if you're looking to try local produce. Buoyant director Jérôme, a trained sommelier, has stocked the beautiful wine cellar – all wood panelling from floor to ceiling – with premium bottles from all over the globe.

The estate also includes two **golf courses** at the Heritage Golf Club: the award-winning Le Château, with incredible views of the coast, and new links golf course La Reserve (named for its views of the nature reserve), created with South African professional golfer and British Open winner Louis Oosthuizen. There's also a beautiful museum, **World of Seashells**, which has the largest seashell collection on the African continent.

GETTING AROUND

The undeniable advantage of staying on the south coast is it's not en route to Port Louis, meaning you're less likely to run into the horrendous rush-hour traffic.

Less than an hour away from the airport, the area is easily reached by taxi, car or – if time is no object – bus.

GRAND BAIE

Grand Baie (Big Bay) is the island's leading tourist resort, offering accommodation from luxury hotels to cheap studios, plus a slew of boutiques, supermarkets, malls and places to eat. At the weekend, Mauritians like to party and see their favourite performers in the town's handful of nightclubs and bars. Locals call everything north of Trou-aux-Biches *le nord*, and this wider Grand Baie region encompasses the beaches of Mont Choisy, Pointe aux Canonniers, La Cuvette, Pereybere and Bain Boeuf. Grand Baie town is quite built up, but look beyond the cars and concrete and you'll find the spots locals come to *le nord* for. The water offers diving and great beaches, and on land there are galleries featuring work by some of the island's top artists. A happy confluence of island microclimates also means Grand Baie tends to have the most sun in Mauritius, always a plus for visitors who relish fine weather.

TOP TIP

Grand Baie is a great place to stay if you love nightlife. If you'd prefer a break from the town's evening bustle, though, choose accommodation in more secluded Mont Choisy or Pointe aux Canonniers.

Mont Choisy (p100) 97

GRAND BAIE

SIGHTS
1 Mont Choisy
2 Pereybere
3 Pointe aux Canonniers
4 Pointe d'Azur

ACTIVITIES
5 Trou-aux-Biches

ENTERTAINMENT
6 Cloud Rooftop
7 N'Joy
8 Safari Bar

SHOPPING
9 Le Rendez-Vous
10 Papyrus
11 Sunset Boulevard

Beach Life in the North

BEACH HOPPING, BARS AND BOUTIQUES

The north brims with great beaches set quite close together, so if you're an aficionado of all things sun and sand you'll enjoy hopping from one to the next to take a dip and soak up the atmosphere.

Clinging to the sides of the coast, Grand Baie town has a mix of accommodation, including a couple of the island's most exclusive hotels, hidden behind garden walls. Away from the hotel oases, it's all shops and restaurants around the bay. Lining the town's main

WHERE TO EAT IN & AROUND GRAND BAIE

Bloom
Attractive contemporary place in Pereybere serving smoothies and dishes such as avocado toast. €€

Onya
In a leafy garden on the sand, colourful Onya serves Mediterranean-style *carpaccio* and octopus salad. €€

Ti Kouloir
The Corridor may not be very large, but it serves excellent *mine bouilli* (noodles) and *boulettes* (dumplings). €

Grand Baie

road, Chemin Vingt Pieds, are restaurants, boutiques and art galleries (p101) worth seeking out if you're staying in the area. **Le Rendez-Vous** is a colourful concept store of all things made sustainably and by hand in Mauritius, from beach bags to fashion brands such as **Goyave** (whose showroom is close to Le Vale roundabout, nearby) and Libertie. There's also a good bookshop, **Papyrus**, in case you run out of beach reads. Closer to the water in the bay, **Sunset Boulevard** shopping area has local brands such as Océano Pearls and Cocosun.

Driving north from Port Louis towards Grand Baie along the coast, you'll come across the small townships of Baie du Tombeau, Balaclava, Pointe aux Piments and Pointe aux Biches. They're all lined up facing the sea and usually have a smaller hub inland. The scenery is more unspoilt here than in the far north, but if you're looking for somewhere to swim, the rocky beaches aren't the best. The exception is **Trou-aux-Biches**, whose beaches (Pereybere, La Cuvette) have returned to postcard perfection. Sadly, the town is otherwise a victim of its own success. It used to be seen as the 'quieter' Grand Baie, but developers have long since capitalised on its spectacular location. It's still from here that diving boats (p101) leave, and all the staples of a beach holiday are present and correct: powder-white shores and spectacular blue

WHERE TO PARTY IN GRAND BAIE

N'Joy
More bar than club, N'Joy puts on live music shows featuring some of the island's best artists. Across the road from pretty La Cuvette beach.

Safari Bar
The biggest nightclub on the island, Safari plays wide-ranging music and hosts live gigs. Check social media for what's on.

Cloud Rooftop
This smart bar is perched atop a pretty white colonial-style house under a huge banyan tree. A local favourite for sundowners, it has great sea views.

Island Babe
Breakfast and brunch spot with a hippie vibe serving fresh salads and juices in a garden. €€

Royal Grill
Enjoy a Thursday-night beach-barbecue feast at the Royal Palm hotel. €€€

Aslam Choychoo
Food shack on La Cuvette beach rustling up tasty Sino-Mauritian specialities. €

Trou-aux-Biches

STAR BEACHES

Pereybere
This popular long beach with fine white sand is great for swimming. It gets busy at weekends.

La Cuvette
The small, beachy cove of La Cuvette is tucked away north of Grand Baie. A few shacks close by serve local food at tables set along the water.

Trou-aux-Biches
Located south of Mont Choisy; the town's getting quite built up, but the beach remains beautiful.

waters with soft sand at the bottom that makes the seawater look like one long natural saltwater pool. However, in recent years the area has suffered from beach erosion.

Quieter **Mont Choisy** has a narrower beach, but its views of the bright blue water fully make up for it. It also offers great-value places to stay.

Pointe aux Canonniers, with top-notch resorts, is another great alternative to staying slap-bang in the Grand Baie action. The town is named for all the heavy iron cannons lined up along the shore, poised to attack invaders and pirates. Perhaps more pertinently for (friendly) visitors, there's also a couple of pretty sunset viewpoints here.

North of the bay, in the beach coves from **Pereybere** to **Bain Boeuf**, things get quieter again and the beaches and swimming are great. Note that things ramp up at weekends, though. However, it's worth braving the crowds to soak up the beauty, especially in Pereybere. Bain Boeuf has a great view of **Coin de Mire** island, also called Gunner's Quoin, which has a wing of rock jutting out that looks like a giant shark's fin.

Pointe d'Azur lives up to its name: it's a great viewpoint for panoramas of sea blues.

WHERE TO STAY IN & AROUND GRAND BAIE

Royal Palm
One of the island's first hotels; bespoke service, great beach, and huge spa and gym. €€€

Seapoint
Attractive small hotel on a palm-fringed beach; its restaurant opens onto a pool with sea views. €€

20 Degrès Sud
Secluded seafront hotel in Pointe aux Canonniers; with tasteful rooms, great pool and a small beach. €€€

Deep-sea Wonders
THE NORTH'S DIVE SITES

The north has an excellent combination of easy dives, wrecks, drop-offs and thrilling undersea adventures. The islands off the coast, such as Île Plate and Coin de Mire, are the main highlights, with splendid sites and marine life, and a real sense of wildness. Trou-aux-Biches is the main jumping-off point for a variety of superb dive trips. Around Coin de Mire are **La Fosse aux Requins** (Shark Pool), an iconic site for its congregation of black-tip reef sharks; **The Wall**, a favourite for its dramatic underwater cliff; and **Djaeba** for its atmospheric wreck dive. Closer to Pointe aux Canonniers on the reef and around the point are **Holt's Rock**, great for underwater domes and boulders; **Tombant de la Pointe aux Canonniers**, with its exhilarating drop-off to 60m; and **Kingfish**, offering drift diving to 28m. Both **Stella Maru**, a must-see wreck 25m deep, and the **Waterlily & Emily wreck** are found south off the coast in Trou-aux-Biches and Pointe aux Piments.

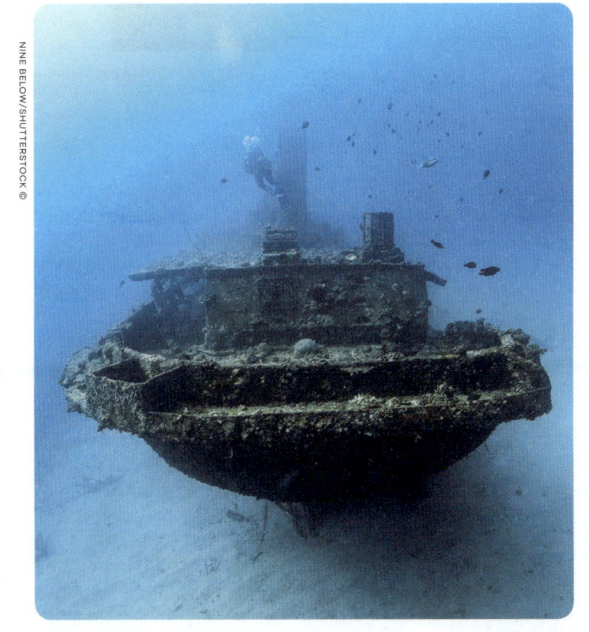

Stella Maru

GALLERY VISITS

The late Vaco Baissac (p74) is one of Mauritius' most famous artists and a visit to his Grand Baie studio is a must. (Note that visits are by appointment only.) **Pop Gallery** and **Shay Hewett's Fine Arts** showroom have works ranging from pop art to abstract paintings by Mauritian and international artists. Smaller spots include **Galerie Raphael**, showing a wide range of regional work; **Toile d'Art**, with figurative beach scenes; **Ilha do Cirne**, showing a mix of tribal and abstract pieces from around the world; the galley of local painter **Amrita Dyalah**, known for her abstract female figures; **Blue Anytime**, with seascapes and depictions of flowering flamboyant trees; and local artist **Françoise Vrot's** studio.

Casuarina
Inviting rooms close to the beach, with pool and cosy local atmosphere. €

Coin de Mire Attitude
Bright, comfortable rooms with pretty dashes of colour right on small Bain Boeuf beach. €

Lux* Grand Baie
New beachfront hotel that's perfect for a young crowd that likes things sleek. €€€

MUSIC FESTIVALS

Mingle with locals at the island's diverse music festivals.

Donn Sa reggae festival
Held in July, Donn Sa features local and international reggae artists.

Mama Jaz
Every April the jazz festival takes place over three days in various venues.

LA ISLA 2068
Every May, LA ISLA features artists from Mauritius and Réunion.

Kafe Kiltir
This annual festival focuses on Mauritian culture in all its diversity.

Also look out for **All Waves**, **Anba Pie**, **Nou le Morne**, **Momix** and the **Underground Rock Festival**.

Linzy Bacbotte performing

Island Sounds
MAURITIUS' RICH MUSICAL CULTURE

A young generation of extremely talented musical artists is putting Mauritius on the map and bringing the local dialect of Creole out of any remaining colonial shadows. You'll hear the sounds of local séga music by the likes of **Désiré François (Cassiya)**, celebrating 30 years in the business, who's one of the most influential artists on the island and in Réunion for his messages of hope and strength for less fortunate members of the community. Several of his songs are still banned in Mauritius because of the political critique they make.

Seggae, séga sounds blended with reggae, was created by the late, beloved **Kaya**. He died in police custody at the age of 38 and his death remains shrouded in mystery. A number of artists were influenced by him, including **Blakkayo**, one of the most prolific seggae artists, who plays all over the island most weeks. **The Prophecy**, a young reggae band from Grand Port in the east, writes heartfelt songs full of humility and spirituality. **Babani Sound System** offers up a unique mix of local music and electro from abroad. In a more spiritual register, the group **Patyattan** plays creative fusion music with traditional instruments. Group member Sarasvati leads cosmic full-moon *ravanne* (traditional drum) group singing sessions in the Daruty woods, a 10-minute drive from Grand Baie. **Emlyn** performs harmonious, infectious and completely uplifting Creole séga music, and **Zulu**'s hit single 'La Métisse' has brought him renown locally and abroad. Talented seggae-soul artist **Linzy Bacbotte** is also an ambassador for women.

Some local artists, such as Avneesh, electronic-music DJ, visual artist and founder of the collective Electrococaïne, put out an eclectic underground sound at home and overseas from Singapore to France. DJ **GREG** serves up a mix of techno Afro, disco and drum'n'bass. His first gig abroad was at none other than Lollapalooza Paris and he's resident DJ at La Creole nights in Paris.

Pop music is also extremely widespread on the island. Wildly popular singer and composer **AnneGa** takes her cues from such artists as Coldplay and Amy Winehouse and sings in Creole. Based in Australia, singer and drummer **Jason Heerah** saw his cover of Pharrell Williams' 'Happy' go viral. He's played with bands from NYC to Australia and is still very successful in Mauritius.

Above all, Mauritian music, like Mauritian cuisine, draws from a broad, diverse heritage. Singer and guitarist **Christophe** is working on an EP of songs about love, identity and equality that celebrate his Mauritian roots. He says, 'I'm a political artist even if my aim through my songs isn't to cause a revolution but maybe to get people who listen to my music to see things in a fresh light. My main aim, though, is to broaden the audience for so-called "black" music – my music is a real mix of influences, from reggae to séga and from pop to Réunionnais maloya sounds.'

MORE ON MUSIC

Read more about Mauritian musical heritage on p282.

TABLE D'HÔTES

Get a taste for local life by booking a meal in the home of a local at a *table d'hôte* (casual eateries set up inside local homes), – these are becoming rare finds. A 10-minute drive from Trou d'Eau Douce, **Mamie Sophie** dishes up beloved local favourites such as fritters, palm-heart salad and *cari poisson* (fish curry). At **Mama Hélène So Lakwizine**, close to Flic en Flac, Hélène serves Creole dishes at a handful of tables on her manicured lawn. She also gives cooking lessons. If you're not staying near Trou d'Eau Douce or Flic en Flac, ask your hotel or host for a *table d'hôte* recommendation for the local area.

GETTING AROUND

Everything in the area is reachable on foot or by bike, but if you want to explore from the beaches of Trou-aux-Biches all the way to the north of the bay, you can hop on a bus. To explore further than *le nord*, a car is a good idea, as it can take a while to get from one place to another on the frequently stopping buses.

Beyond Grand Baie

Peaceful beaches and islands belie a history of shipwrecks and military invasion

Beyond Bain Boeuf, Grand Baie's northernmost beach, lies the 'real' north coast. The first village you'll come to is Cap Malheureux (literally, 'Unhappy Cape'), named for the many shipwrecks that have happened here and the 1810 defeat of the French by the British. Today the north coast is one of the quietest parts of the island, with beaches ranging from narrow, rocky stretches to wider, palm-fringed strands. There's a good choice of accommodation, yet development feels minimal. Further around the coast is Grand Gaube, immortalised in Jacques-Henri de Saint-Pierre's 18th-century novel *Paul et Virginie*, which recounts the shipwreck of the *Saint Géran*. This is also the jumping-off point for exploring Amber Island and Îlot Bernache.

TOP TIP

Choose your hotel wisely if you're after a good beach: sadly, due to erosion many beaches have shrunk to rocky coves.

Cap Malheureux

Auxiliatrice de Cap Malheureux

Exploring the 'Unhappy Cape'
BEACH HOPPING AND HINDU FESTIVALS

Once you leave tourist-thronged Grand Baie and pull into **Cap Malheureux** – to be greeted by the small Notre-Dame **Auxiliatrice de Cap Malheureux** church with its iconic bright-red gabled roof – the pace of life slows almost to halt. Aside from hopping from one bit of coast to the next as you hunt for the best beach, there's very little to do but relax and enjoy the tranquillity. It's so quiet it's hard to imagine this was the place where the British invaded the island, triumphing over the French in 1810. Before you continue along the coast, make a 10-minute detour to the mysterious **Daruty Forest**, where you can walk along a red-earth path in the shade of a thick canopy of trees. Mauritians believe the forest is haunted with all kinds of whispering spirits, especially at night. A word of caution: don't go by yourself, as attacks on lone walkers or joggers have been known to happen.

Nearby in **Petit Raffray**, ceramics artist Hélène de Senneville – credited with opening Mauritius' first art gallery in the Grand Baie area in 1987 – has a colourful gallery of island-themed crockery. Continue east and inland to the town of **Goodlands**, a major Hindu area with a market and an array

PAUL ET VIRGINIE

Jacques-Henri Bernardin de Saint-Pierre's 1788 novel *Paul et Virginie* might have been published centuries ago, but it has left an indelible mark on Mauritian minds.

Set on the island when it was under French rule (at that time was called Île de France), the novel tells the tragic tale of two young people, friends since birth, who fall in love.

Paul et Virginie has inspired numerous pictures, sculptures and paintings – if you visit a local home you're almost certain to see an image of the young lovers.

The story is so deeply ingrained in the culture that it's hard to believe it's a work of fiction.

WHERE TO STAY FROM CAP MALHEUREUX TO GRAND GAUBE

Paradise Cove
Gorgeous, loosely Creole-style hotel with a wonderful infinity-edge pool right on the water. €€€

The Good Life
Well-appointed, laid-back hotel a block from the sea with great gardens and healthy food options. €€

Lux* Grand Gaube
Stunning beach, beautiful rooms, big pool; the town's a little built up but has great facilities. €€

HINDU FESTIVALS

Hindu celebrations are a feature of the Mauritian calendar.

Cavadee
(January–February)
Devotees may have their cheeks and tongues pierced with needles before carrying offerings on their backs.

Maha Shivaratree
(February–March)
In honour of Shiva; Hindus throng to Grand Bassin to sanctify themselves in the water of the holy lake.

Holi
(March)
Celebrated by throwing brightly coloured powders.

Ganesh Chaturthi
(August–September)
Small replicas of elephant god Ganesh are immersed in water.

Diwali
(October–November)
The festival of light. Hindus decorate their homes with oil lamps and candles.

Siva Soopramaniar Kovil, Goodlands (p105)

of shops. It comes into its own during the religious festivals of Ganesh Chaturthi and Diwali, when everyone wears their best clothes, women's hair is adorned with jasmine flowers, and deities are paraded through the streets to the beats of music. There isn't much to see outside festival times, but just beyond Goodlands is the atmospheric colonial mansion of Demeure St-Antoine (p73), offering food and accommodation.

From here you can head back up to beachy **Grand Gaube**, where the **LUX*** hotel has a smart seafront bar, the **Bodrum Blue**, and the **Creole Smokehouse** restaurant, set under a huge banyan tree on the beach. The public beach in Grand Gaube is great for a swim or a spot of kitesurfing with **Kite at North**. From Grand Gaube you can also go on a day trip to wild, uninhabited Amber Island and Îlot Bernache, with pristine white-sand beaches and turquoise waters.

As you curve around the eastern edge of the island you'll reach the site of the *Saint-Géran* shipwreck: in 1744 a flute ship belonging to the French East India Company capsized at Amber Island with 110 crew and settlers on board. The quiet agricultural village of **Poudre d'Or** has a small stone monument to those who were lost in the wreck.

WHERE TO STAY IN GRAND GAUBE

Mythic Suites & Villas
Sleek serviced and fully equipped white-and-wood villas with pool and spacious rooms. €€

Lagoon Attitude Hotel
Cool open-plan hotel with lots of outdoor nooks, lovely gardens, and a stunning bit of sea to swim in. €€

Seaview Calodyne
One- or two-storey rooms, some with kitchens, plus a restaurant and small, pretty beach. €

Island Hopping

UNINHABITED ISLANDS, RUINS AND RESTAURANTS

Several small islands are dotted about the pristine waters off Mauritius' coast. Near Grand Gaube is the embarkation point for **Amber Island**, untouched save for the ruins of buildings dating back to French colonisation. Hop over to **Îlot Bernache**, just offshore, for a swim. The locals' favourite island remains **Île aux Cerfs**, even though it's overrun with weekend visitors, who come for the lovely beaches and great swimming. There are (pricey) restaurants here as well as a hidden, very exclusive golf course that you need to sign up for before you arrive. Île aux Cerfs can be visited by day trip from Trou d'Eau Douce (p108). You can get good-value deals that include a feast of barbecued seafood on a nearby island as well as a visit to a waterfall, but if you don't want to run from boat to boat, just opt out and relax on Île aux Cerfs. If you follow the sandbar linking Île aux Cerfs to **Îlot Mangénie**, you can also enjoy the more isolated beach there. In the southwest, off Mahébourg, **Île de la Passe** is known for the remains of fortifications and a wall etched with soldiers' names from the 1800s. It isn't quite a tropical paradise, but it's an interesting reminder of Mauritius' naval past. You can also enjoy the island's secluded beaches and have lunch at an old ruin.

In the north of the island, off Grand Baie, visit **Flat Island & Gabriel Islet** for spectacular beaches and lunch at the **Governor's House**, inside a 19th-century ruin. **Coin de Mire** (Gunner's Quoin) is another must-see, but from the mainland at Bain Boeuf: locals love the island's striking wedge shape, an emblem on the Mauritian skyline.

Flat Island & Gabriel Islet

WHERE TO EAT ON THE NORTH COAST

Amigo
Slightly inland from Cap Malheureux' church, this well-loved local favourite serves delicious seafood dishes in a very simple dining room. €€

Linda's Place
Always wanted to know how to pair rum with fried rice? Find out at Linda's, where Sino-Mauritian favourites are served with the local tipple. €

La Friandise Village
On a road leading away from the ocean, this eatery serves fresh grilled fish daily at good-value rates. There are several other snack-style joints on the same road. €

GETTING AROUND

A car is necessary here, unless you want to pay through the nose for taxis. To hop around the different islands, it's best to look online or enquire at your hotel about available excursions as no single operator serves all the islands.

TROU D'EAU DOUCE

If you want to experience local island life and also log plenty of time on gorgeous, secluded beaches, then the east coast of Mauritius is the place to stay. Base yourself in the small town of Trou d'Eau Douce with its casual, fun places to eat. Sandy beaches with great swimming run almost the entire length of the east coast, meaning you'll be spoilt for choice when it comes to setting yourself up for some R&R. Hotels are scattered all along the coast, and some are among the island's best, but the town's vibe is a far cry from the bustle of Grand Baie or Flic en Flac. Trou d'Eau Douce is also the jumping-off point for the popular Île aux Cerfs day trip. Known as the 'windy coast', it's cooler than other coastlines and the wind is extremely strong in the winter months (May to October). In summer, though, conditions are just right.

TOP TIP

Aim to be town on a weekday if you're planning to join a boat trip to Île aux Cerfs, as the island gets very crowded at weekends. Take a picnic with you if you want to avoid eating at one of the island's overpriced restaurants.

Fishers, Trou d'Eau Douce

EATING
1 Café des Arts
2 Chez Tino
3 Green Island Beach
4 L'Assiette Longtemps
5 Lacaz Poisson
6 Les Alizés

DRINKING & NIGHTLIFE
7 Lolita Marie

Keeping it Local

FOOD AND A SECRET RUM BAR

Trou d'Eau Douce has some great restaurants and handful of *snacks* (small cafes), such as **L'Assiette Longtemps** for Creole food and **Les Alizés** for *mine bouilli* and *boulettes* – be prepared to queue at lunchtime. **Lacaz Poisson** is another great, low-key spot serving up grilled fish. The town itself doesn't see many visitors, so you may be something of an object of curiosity to locals.

For rum, head to **Lolita Marie**. Drive through a tangle of residential streets and you'll get to a white house with a sign on the gate. Beep and the rum-maker will let you in and slide back her house's garage door to reveal a secret bar where you can try to buy all sorts of *rum arrangé* in recyclable bottles. Passion fruit is a favourite flavour, but there are also vanilla, coffee and even chilli. Lolita Marie makes her rum in small batches and sells it to some of the island's most exclusive hotels, as well as the visitors who venture out here.

The other notable reason to come to the area is Île aux Cerfs (p107), an uninhabited island with great swimming and a castaway vibe. For beach time, choose a spot past the sun loungers and facing the open sea. A sandbar now links the island with neighbouring Îlot Mangénie, which has a terrific stretch of sand that feels even more secluded. Note that the rest of the islet belongs to luxury hotel Le Touessrok.

GETTING AROUND

There are two embarkation points for Île aux Cerfs: the *débarcadère* south of town and the jetty. The speedboat ride takes about 10 minutes. The last boats leave the island around 4pm in winter and 5pm in summer.

Beyond Trou d'Eau Douce

The wild, windy east coast has gorgeous beaches, luxury hotels and pockets of nature to explore.

Along the untamed east coast north of Trou d'Eau Douce the quiet beaches, fringed with palms or filao trees, are among the best in Mauritius. Coastal towns Palmar, Belle Mare, Poste Flacq, Poste Lafayette and Roches Noires are home to some of the island's most exclusive hotels, tucked behind big gates. There's also the Shiv Mandir Hindu temple and wild Bras d'Eau National Park to explore, and don't miss the fantastic market in the small, inland town of Central Flacq. Adventurers can make the trip to see dried lava tubes near Roches Noires, and if you're planning to pick up some local vanilla pods, the spice gardens in St Julien d'Hotman are a must-visit.

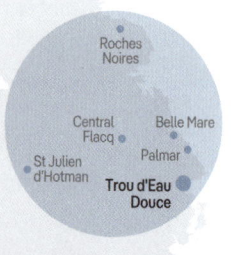

TOP TIP

Alongside the top hotels, there's some really well-priced accommodation on some of the area's best beaches, so it's worth shopping around.

Belle Mare

DRIVING TO THE HEART OF THE ISLAND

You can't visit Mauritius without exploring its scenic forested interior, with peaks jutting from sugar-cane plantations and stretching to the sky. If you're staying on the eastern side of the island, you can get a taste of Mauritius' mountain ranges by driving westwards towards the central plateau. Pick up the A6 between Rivière du Rempart and Roches Noires and follow it to colonial mansion house and events venue **1 Château de Ville Bague**. Next, drive south to Ville Bague and take the B49 until you reach the picturesque **2 La Nicolière Reservoir**, a favourite with hikers. There's a viewpoint where you can stop along the road.

Keep on B49 southwards through sugar plantations to a township called Nouvelle Découverte and on to Ripailles, where the views of the various mountains are worth the drive. You'll see **3 Calebasses** (632m); **4 Pieter Both** (823m), with a small round rock on the top; **5 Grand Peak** (326m); and **6 Le Pouce** (812m), named for its thumb-like shape. Just after the roundabout, you'll find the trailhead for **7 Deux Mamelles**, named after dog teats due to their shape, which you'll see rise above to the right. Continue straight, then turn right onto B34 at L'Avenir Shivam Mandir temple and drive up to the **8 Avenir viewpoint** between Pieter Both and Deux Mamelles mountains. Many of the mountain trailheads are here – have a look on Fitsy for details. All these views surely work up an appetite. Swing by colonial mansion **9 Eureka** (p71) in Moka (15 minutes away) to dig into Creole food at the restaurant. Finish by returning east via **10 Long Mountain** (307m) and then looping back to La Nicolière.

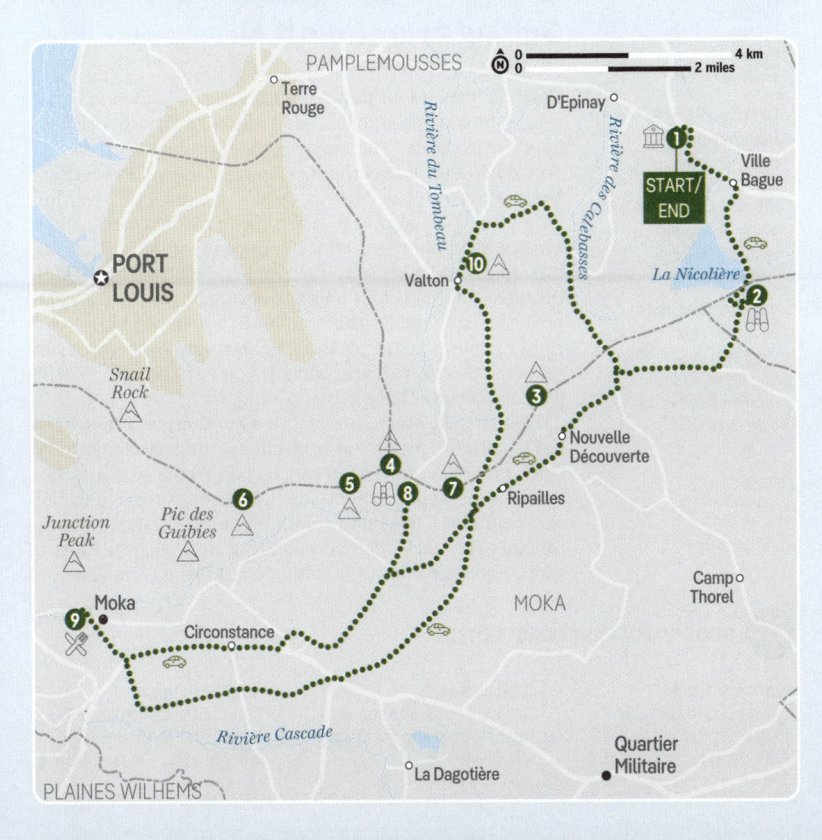

EAST-COAST LUXURY STAYS

Shangri-La Le Touessrok
Excellent service and direct access to sublime beaches. €€€

One & Only Le Saint Géran
Very exclusive, but surprisingly unstuffy. Great diving. €€€

Constance Le Prince Maurice
With orange touches that acknowledge Dutch settlers. The Barachois bar, surrounded by mangrove islands, is accessed via elevated walkway. €€€

La Maison d'Eté
Boutique hotel with beachy white-clapboard rooms offering stunning sea views. Acclaimed restaurant. €€

L'ilôt (Muse Villas)
It doesn't get more exclusive than renting your own island. This private villa of four rooms even has its own chef. €€€

Shangri-La Le Touessrok, Trou d'Eau Douce

Getting Away from It All
RESORTS, BEACHES AND MARKET BUSTLE

North of Trou d'Eau Douce, along a scenic lagoon of iridescent waters and fine golden sand, the island's most exclusive hotels congregate. The best beaches are found just beyond Trou d'Eau Douce after the cemetery and then in **Palmar** and **Belle Mare**. In Belle Mare, stop at an abandoned sugar mill for a spot of island urbex (exploring abandoned sites) and at **Poivre d'Or** boutique, which sells made-in-Mauritius candles, spices and other souvenirs. Red-and-white **Shiv Mandir temple** is an important holy site devoted to Shiva. It used to float on a large rock in the water until a road was built to run right up to it. The temple is particularly atmospheric at sunset when there's no one around. If you visit, be sure to bring a sarong to cover bare legs or shoulders.

When in Belle Mare, turn off inland to **Central Flacq Market** to get a feel for its laid-back but bustling namesake town. Open every day (and at full capacity on Wednesday and Sunday), the market's centrepiece is a large expanse selling fruit and vegetables, but there's clothing and other knick-knacks towards the back. The surrounding area also has lots of shops and roadside stalls selling everything from delicious

GOOD-VALUE EAST-COAST HOTELS

Sunrise Attitude
This simple, fun hotel has a good palm-fringed beach that's great for swimming. €

Solana Beach
Intimate hotel with stairs leading right into the crystal-clear water. €

SALT of Palmar
A fun, colourful adults-only hotel with a Moorish design influence and a great beach. €

dhal puri to colourful woven baskets. It's also in Flacq that artist Mohammad Asraf Sowdayer has his gallery, where he shows his colourful depictions of everyday life on a Mauritius sugar and fruit plantation as well as fishing boats, beaches and Mauritius' beautiful flowers.

Beyond the Beaches

VANILLA GARDENS
AND A NATIONAL PARK

Mascarene paradise flycatcher

Inland from Central Flacq, beyond Riche Fond, look for signs indicating the **Vanilla and Spice Gardens** as you approach the village of St Julien d'Hotman. Back on the coast, near Poste Flacq, you'll come across a small British cemetery with a commemorative **chapel** to British soldiers who died on the island. The chapel was built in 1864 out of volcanic stone.

From Poste Flacq, drive north along the coast and follow signs to turn down the jungly access road to **Bras d'Eau National Park**, named for the arm-shaped patch of ground it occupies (*bras* means 'arm'). One of three national parks on the island, together with Black River Gorges and The Islets, Bras d'Eau is a forest of mahogany, tecoma, eucalyptus and araucaria trees, as well as ebony, the remains of a plantation of non-indigenous trees. The park covers an area of just 5 sq km, and an easy and very pleasant hiking trail takes you through the forest to a lake and the sea and back again. It's also possible to cycle through. The simple visitor centre has lots of pictures to help you identify flowers, trees and birds.

Further north, in Roches Noires, you can explore a trail through **La Cave Madame**, with rock that slopes into the darkness below ground. The site holds great significance for locals as enslaved people formerly used it as a hiding place. Nearby, the intriguing **Roche Noire Lava Tubes** look like caves. On the coast is the **studio** of South African ceramics artist Sharon Thompson, who makes vivid starfish bowls and speckled plates. Stop when you see a small gate with two mosaic cats on each post just before you come to the Radisson hotel.

BEST RESTAURANTS IN TROU D'EAU DOUCE

Chez Tino
A visitor hub for good reason, welcoming Chez Tino serves seafood and dishes such as rougail saucisses (sausage in tomato sauce with rice). €€

Green Island Beach
Often packed with visitors as well as locals, especially at weekends. Be sure to order the crab soup – it's delicious. €€

Café des Arts
Inside an 1840 sugar mill that became a spectacular gallery for the works of Yvette Maniglier, who spent a year as Henri Matisse's student. Her son now serves French-meets-local cuisine here. €€€

GETTING AROUND

The sights stretch out all along the east coast and few buses cover the area frequently, so a car is essential for exploring.

BLUE BAY

Part of a protected marine park, the calm, shallow, crystal-clear waters of beautiful Blue Bay glisten in the sunshine like a swimming pool. Lovely as the bay is, the larger area offers lots more. Just north of the bay is Pointe d'Esny, which has fantastic diving and is near the jumping-off place for trips to Île aux Aigrettes conservation island, where the Mauritius Wildlife Foundation is working to replant endemic trees. Further north is the peaceful town of Mahébourg, which was Mauritius' first port before French colonial governor Mahé de Labourdonnais moved it to Port Louis. It's in these waters that the great naval Battle of Vieux Grand Port took place in 1810. In that conflict the French defeated the British, who wanted to fold Mauritius into their portfolio of islands for its resources and its strategic location on the trade route between Africa and India.

TOP TIP

Blue Bay has some great accommodation options, so it makes an ideal base. Hire a car here to explore the south coast for its quiet hikes and the coast north of Blue Bay to gain a deeper sense of Mauritius by visiting Mahébourg and Vieux Grand Port.

Île aux Aigrettes

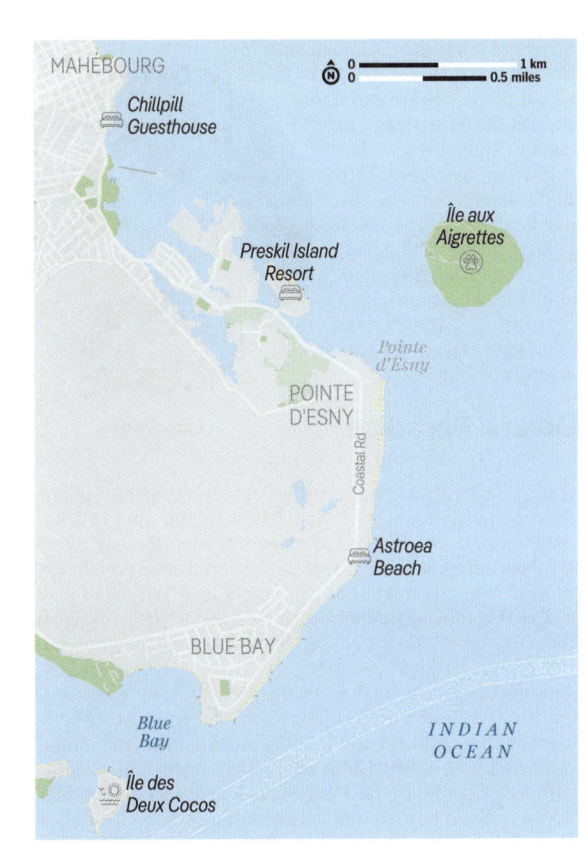

EXPLORING ÎLE AUX AIGRETTES

Managed by the Mauritian Wildlife Foundation (MWF), the tiny 26-hectare nature reserve of Île aux Aigrettes lies less than 1km off Pointe d'Esny.

For a glimpse of what Mauritius looked like before development, book a tour (1½ hours or 2½ hours) on the MWF website. You'll see giant land tortoises in the wild (the only place in Mauritius you can see them), endemic trees such as ebony and vacoa, and birds such as the pink pigeon.

There's quite a lot of walking on the tour, but none of it is difficult and all of it is in the shade; just be sure to wear comfortable shoes and bring mosquito repellent.

The Bay & Beyond

BEACHES, DIVING AND HISTORY

No speedboats are permitted within Blue Bay Marine Park, to protect the underwater forest of rare corals. There are no tours of the park, but its waters offer wonderful **snorkelling**. You can explore with your own mask and tube from the beach in the bay, or go on a boat trip: several tour companies stop for snorkelling en route to the open sea. Jean-Caude Farla and his son (+230 54 23 13 22) offer an authentic experience aboard a wooden pirogue (fishing boat) and One Love runs a fun, lively tour with music. There are lots of islands to explore in the area, including Île de la Passe (p107), off the coast of Mahébourg, with

WHERE TO STAY IN BLUE BAY

Preskil Island Resort
Has a great little beach, but the high points are the mountain views and diving. €€

Chillpill Guest House
Good-value, very simple spot by the sea; its restaurant has water views. Great for sunsets. €

Astroea Beach
Pretty, well-priced boutique hotel set across a lovely beach, with a good restaurant. €

historical naval sites. As you paddle in the bay, you'll see the nearby leafy island of **Île des Deux Cocos** right at the edge of the azure lagoon. Once used to host British governor Sir Hesketh Bell's lively parties, today it serves to give Lux* resort guests a taste of castaway life. You can stay on the island in a revamped 1920s villa that is big enough for two or a family of four.

Sea anemone

Divers' Paradise

SHIPWRECKS AND UNDERWATER MOUNTAINS

If you're a diver and you can only get under the water in one part of the island, make it Blue Bay. A unique spot in Mauritius because it's protected from currents, the bay offers good diving conditions year-round. There are several diving centres near the town, but Christophe and Daveena's club at **Preskil Island Resort** beach (accessible via a side road that runs along the water – at the gate, ask the hotel's security guards to show you the way) is among the area's best and most experienced. Part of the French Underwater Federation, they have a fully equipped PADI centre with five divers. You can explore a 400m underwater canyon and mountains at a spot called **Colorado**, with places that look like towns fit for human life. Close by is **Roches Zozo**, another five-star dive site with tunnels and more canyons. There are stunning anemone gardens as well as a multitude of fish and turtles in the lagoon and along the barrier reef further out to sea. Highlights include the **Trou Moutou** site and **Grotte Langouste**, a cave filled with lobsters. The most impressive, spine-tingling dive is an exploration of the **Sirius**, a shipwreck that dates back to the 1810 Battle of Vieux Grand Port between the British and the French. You can still see parts of the burnt ship, a few cannons and even bones that could be of animal or human origin.

THE BATTLE OF VIEUX GRAND PORT

The British moved in on Mauritius in 1810 as part of their grand plan to control the Indian Ocean. However, their lack of knowledge of the territory around Mahébourg and the shallow sandbanks that line the coast saw their ships founder as they attempted to land during the Battle of Vieux Grand Port.

You can still see one of the sunken ships, the *Sirius*, on dives from Blue Bay or Pointe d'Esny.

A few months later the British took control of the island from the north via Cap Malheureux. It wasn't until 1968 that Mauritius became independent from Britain.

GETTING AROUND

As in most parts of Mauritius, you're best off with your own wheels here. Attractions in the area are clearly signposted.

Beyond Blue Bay

Blue Bay is the gateway to the southeastern area of Mauritius, which has some of the island's least developed terrain.

Once you've explored Blue Bay's underwater treasures and beaches, push north to Mahébourg, Mauritius' old port, and Vieux Grand Port, for subtle but significant historical landmarks and a market town with great foodie pockets. It's here that the island's story began: the Dutch first landed at what is now Vieux Grand Port, and you can still see the ruins of the fort they built, which was called Frederik Hendrik. In the hills inland is Ferney, one of the most beautiful conservation areas in Mauritius. Head south, and you're in for a complete change of scene. Here you can hike to waterfalls and other natural features, stop at rocky beaches and enjoy the quiet, deep-south seclusion.

TOP TIP

If you're hiking, book a guide through Yanature or Lokal Aventure. Local sites can be tricky to find.

Ferney Valley

SUSTAINABLE DINING AT FALAISE ROUGE

Mauritian Gerald Richard, the new chef at **Falaise Rouge** restaurant, is making a historic part of the coast a beacon of sustainable cuisine.

Up on the *falaise rouge* (red cliffs) where the great Battle of Grand Port took place, the restaurant benefits from the fresh produce, deer and wild boar cultivated in neighbouring Ferney Valley conservation area (p122).

Dishes are refined, creative and full of local flavour (try the taro ice cream). Richard's goal is to source 100% of his produce locally. He's not far off, because he rarely uses anything imported, and he's the first chef on the island to make this commitment. Book lunch here and take in the stellar sea views.

Frederik Hendrik fort ruins

Tracing Origins at Frederik Hendrik Museum

THE BEGINNINGS OF MAURITIUS

Records show that Arab traders stopped over in Mauritius as early as the 10th century and that the Portuguese came by in 1507, but neither group settled on the island. It wasn't until 9 September 1598, under the command of Wybrand van Warwyck, that a Dutch colony was established. The arrival spot is marked by a modest brick tower called **Dutch Landing**. However, what is now called Vieux Grand Port, 3km north, is where the colony actually settled, building a fort as the headquarters for the Dutch East India Company. The settlers named the island Mauritius, after the Dutch Stadtholder Maurits (also known as Maurice of Nassau, the Prince of Orange).

In 1710 the Dutch abandoned the island for several reasons, including rat infestations and widespread illness. There's a small museum, the **Frederik Hendrik Museum** (free), close to the remaining ruins of the fort, church, bakery, prison, forge, powder magazine and dispensary, although it's hard to make out the various buildings today. A few artefacts such as clay pots and weapons are on display at the museum, but

Continued on p122

WHERE TO STAY IN VIEUX GRAND PORT

Ferney Lodge
Four beautiful lodges looking out to lush green hills, with restaurant and relaxing pool. €€

La Case du Pêcheur
Rustic rooms on the water with spectacular views of Lion Mountain. €

Hacienda
Simple rooms, some with kitchens, up in the hills with great sea and mountain views. €

EAT YOUR WAY AROUND HISTORIC MAHÉBOURG

A wander around Mahébourg takes in a market, a museum, seafood specialities and relics from the island's early days. Start on the **1 waterfront promenade**. Hidden in the shadow of a huge banyan tree is an abandoned **2 train station**, a remnant of the island's 1860s railway. Close by is a stall selling *merveilles*, a sweet crispy cracker doused in tamarind, tomato and coriander chutney. Sunita's been making these for 20 years and sells them with her husband and daughter, who's a master at chopping coconuts with a machete. Walk along the pier to the lively, open-air **3 market**, with street-food stalls at the back. You can try mangouak, a purple shellfish similar to an oyster, shelled and seasoned or fried and thrown into *mine bouilli* and other local specialties at **4 Le Basilic** or **5 Chez François**. Don't miss pocket-sized **6 Café de Labourdonnais**, whose owner makes the best *gâteaux banane* (banana fritters).

Take a boat to explore La Chaux River, lined with picturesque mangroves and the homes of families who make their living by fishing. At the end you'll reach **7 Nativ Lodge & Spa**, a guesthouse run by the charismatic Nicolas. Its laid-back restaurant has live music at weekends. Take the road to **8 Mahébourg Museum**, where the three main periods of Mauritian history – Dutch, French and British rule – are brought to life through artefacts, paintings and explanatory panels. Plan to spend at least an hour here. On the other side of town, across **9 Cavendish Bridge**, the **10 Rault biscuit factory** still makes manioc biscuits almost entirely by hand according to a secret family recipe handed down since 1870. You'll get to sample them if you join the 20-minute tour.

HIKING & ROAD TRIP

Hike & Drive the Deep South

Scattered with waterfalls, unusual rock formations and small, secluded beaches, the southeast coast makes for great hiking territory. Consider hiring a car and driver for the day, so you don't have to do a loop to collect your car from the starting point. A guide is also a great idea to help you get the most out of your hike. Contact local companies Yanature or Lokal Adventure.

1 La Cambuse Beach

Starting from Blue Bay, drive to the quiet rocky stretch of La Cambuse beach. Stop at the coconut sellers on the side of the road for a quick, refreshing drink of coconut water before continuing on to the Palm Forest. It's accessible via small, winding roads that begin at the southern end of the beach. A beautiful area of very tall palms draped in jungly vegetation, the forest feels like the Mauritius of old.

The Walk: Walk along the narrow lanes close to the coast and you'll reach Le Bouchon public beach. *Camaron* (shrimp) fishers used to leave from here before *camaron* numbers declined. Facing the shore is the private Brocus islet, with mangrove forests and pools of shallow blue water. The walk takes about 40 minutes.

2 Pont Naturel

Keep going along the sea and look out for Pont Naturel (Natural Bridge), a rock formation that indeed looks like a bridge. Continuing, you'll come across Le

Cascade Mamzelle

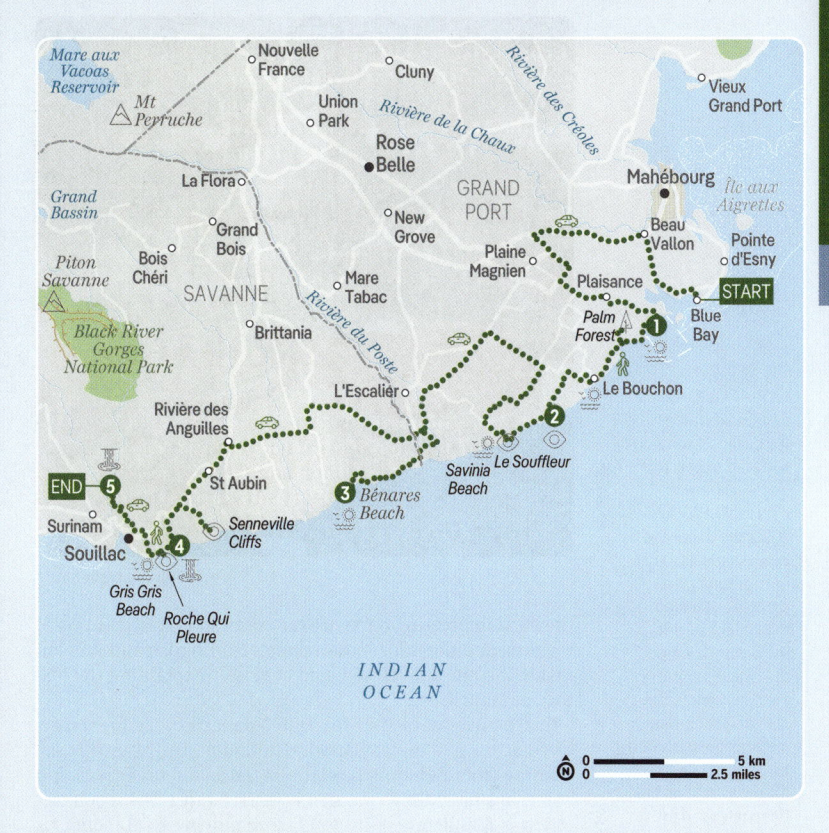

Souffleur (The Blower), a half-formed grotto that spouts a geyser-like fountain of water up to 20m in the air when the sea is rough. The hike here is a little challenging and can be slippery, so avoid coming on rainy days. Stop at Savinia beach to catch your breath.

The Drive or Walk: Ideally, you'd have your own car or a taxi waiting for you to take you to the next stop, Bénares Beach. If not, the beach is a 2½-hour walk away. Unfortunately, it's not a very picturesque route and you have to spend part of the time on main roads before getting back to the coast.

3 Bénares Beach
Lined with volcanic rock cliffs, this part of the island has a lonely atmosphere that's heightened by the rough water and windy conditions. There are small beachy coves where you can have a dip, but you wouldn't come here for a beach day.

The Drive: Continue to Senneville Cliffs and the viewpoint close by. Some parts can be hiked, but you'll need a car for at least part of this route.

4 Cascade V & Cascade Mamzelle
From the viewpoint you can hike to two waterfalls: Cascade Ow En and Kins Ley. From Senneville Cliffs you can also walk to Cascade V and Cascade Mamzelle, the most scenic falls in the area, perfect for a cooling dip.

The Walk: It's then a 10-minute walk to Roche Qui Pleure (Crying Rock), which looks as though it's shedding tears when the water sprays through it, and Gris Gris Beach, with waves crashing against a cliff face.

5 Rochester Falls
Push on for Rochester Falls, a small but wide waterfall that's a local favourite. Drive to the trailhead from Gris Gris, then it's an hour on foot to the falls.

Market, Mahébourg

THE WAKASHIO OIL SPILL

As the COVID-19 pandemic was in full swing, Mauritius suffered a blow from quite a different quarter. On 25 July 2020, the Japanese *Wakashio* bulk carrier ran aground on a coral reef, spilling thick black oil into the ocean. It was the island's worst ever environmental disaster, according to media reports shared by Greenpeace. Very little information has been released by the government, and the area hasn't been made accessible to NGOs, scientists or the media, so very little is publicly known about the real impact of the spill. For now, all that's clear is that the shores of the island and immediate surrounding waters look clean.

the most interesting parts are the ruins and reconstitution of the area and the information panels (in English and French) inside the museum clearly and concisely explaining the history of Mauritius.

In 1715, five years after the Dutch departed, the French arrived at the site under Captain Guillaume Dufresne d'Arsel. Coming from Réunion, he claimed the island for France and – perhaps inevitably – named it Île de France. A French colony was founded here in 1721 before moving to Mahébourg, Port Louis and beyond.

Peace & Hiking at Ferney Valley

EXPLORING AN ENDEMIC FOREST

One of the most beautiful spots on the island, Ferney Valley (ferney.mu) is home to an important conservation area protecting a stand of endemic forest. Today these forests cover less than 3% of Mauritius. The conservation area was created in 2006 after the government teamed up with a Chinese construction company and planned to bulldoze the area to build a road network. Locals rose up in protest – and won. Ever since, the **Mauritian Wildlife Foundation** has been leading efforts to grow the forest and shelter

WHERE TO EAT IN VIEUX GRAND PORT

Falaise Rouge
Great views and delicious local cuisine using produce from the area. €€

Le Grand Vent
Casual bamboo eatery on the roadside that's great for a quick bite or drink. €

La Case du Pêcheur
This guesthouse is known for its weekend seafood dinners. €€

its birds, such as the pink pigeon, echo parakeet and rare kestrel, as well as the flying fox (a kind of fruit bat). The protected area now extends to 200 hectares, while the whole estate covers 3100 hectares.

When driving from Mahébourg, follow the signs to Ferney Valley and park behind the recently renovated white colonial house. Beyond the alluring spice garden, which often hosts school children on trips to learn about the island's wealth of plants, you can glimpse the corrugated-iron roof of the old **Ferney sugar mill** peeping through the trees. Here you'll also find what is said to be the island's oldest **coffee tree**. The story goes that Pierre Poivre (p68), Mauritius' famed botanist, brought coffee from here to French writer Voltaire, who didn't like the taste of the 'murky water'. Ferney was named after Voltaire's hometown in France, Ferney-Voltaire.

Give yourself time to soak up the peaceful surroundings by staying at **Ferney Lodge**, overlooking the rolling Ferney hills and the ocean beyond. You can explore the estate by 4WD or on foot with a guide, choosing from three **hiking trails**: 5km (one hour), 13km (three to four hours) and 20km (four to five hours). Keen hikers might also tackle the demanding **Ferney Trail**, which opens to participants in the first half of September. Mauritius has more than 700 indigenous plants, and many of them can easily be found here. Guides are compulsory and the cost is included in the valley entrance fee (€13). Nearby, other hikes include Lion Mountain (p77).

North of the mountain is **Kestrel Valley** nature reserve, also known as the Domaine du Chasseur (Hunter's Estate), where the rare kestrel is often sighted. Covering more than 10 sq km and running up to the hills looking out to the coastal plain, the valley offers wonderful views. Note that, as of mid-2023, the estate had yet to reopen to the public.

Vacoa-tree baskets

HANDMADE VACOA-TREE BASKETS

Introduced to Mauritius by African enslaved people, baskets woven with dried vacoa-tree leaves are a rare find these days. However, look out for the group of women drying the leaves in the sun at a house in Vieux Grand Port, just before you reach the Frederik Hendrick Museum as you come from Mahébourg. Here you can see the whole process, from gathering the leaves to the final product. Baskets have been made by a local women's association overseen by Fabiola for the last three decades. You can order any number of them, but the association will need at least a week's notice, so drop in ahead of time to place your order.

GETTING AROUND

Even though it's only a 15-minute drive from the airport, the southeast coast is the least developed part of Mauritius. To get around independently, it's best to hire a car.

RODRIGUES

Named after the Portuguese navigator Don Diégo Rodriguez, who discovered the island in 1528, the tiny volcanic outcrop of Rodrigues is made up of fishing villages whose population is mainly Creole. The culture is celebrated each December in the three-day Kréol Festival. Just an hour's flight from Mauritius, Rodrigues is surrounded by a turquoise lagoon and has a mountainous interior – its terrain is very similar to that of its big sister. The island has some great low-key accommodation and places to eat, as well as hiking trails you're likely to have all to yourself. There's also great diving in the island's waters, which are dotted with 17 offshore islets. Rodrigues' beautiful, secluded virgin beaches and islands will give you a glimpse of what Mauritius' coastline might have looked like before it became built up with hotels. The capital, Port Mathurin, has a market and laid-back, island-style urban life.

TOP TIP

Be sure to book your flights, accommodation and restaurants at least a couple of weeks ahead. There aren't many options, so everything tends to fill up. This is especially true at weekends: Rodrigues is a popular local choice for a weekend away.

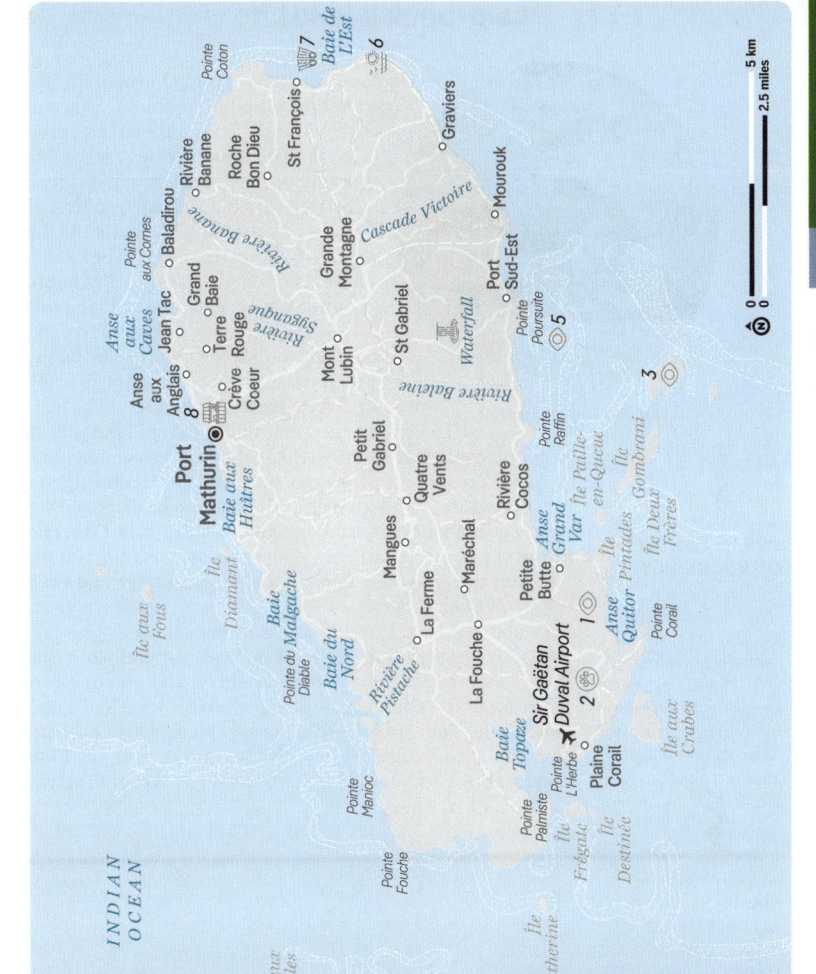

SIGHTS
1 Caverne Patate
2 François Leguat Reserve
3 Île aux Chats
4 Île aux Cocos
5 Île Hermitage
6 Trou d'Argent

ACTIVITIES
7 La Passe St François

EATING
8 Port Mathurin Market

Rodrigues

Laid-back Island Life

BOAT TRIPS AND LOCAL FOOD

Once you've been to Port Mathurin's Saturday **market** for a dip into urban life, you can settle in for some relaxation on a beach such as **Trou d'Argent** cove, accessible on foot via the northern coastal trail (between St François and Graviers). If you're lucky, you might stumble on the pirate treasure that's said to be hidden here. Don't miss a trip to **François Leguat Reserve** to see giant land tortoises. Those looking to keep active can hike along the island's best beaches on the northeast coastern and dive in the pristine waters at **La Passe St François**.

Francois Leguat Reserve

To explore the surrounding seas, take a boat trip to **Île aux Cocos** to see the seabird colonies, or go on a half-day excursion to **Île aux Chats** and **Île Hermitage** to see Rodrigues' southern coast. All trips can be arranged via your accommodation. Back on land, you can visit **Caverne Patate**, an impressive cave system whose rock formations are said to resemble a dodo, Buckingham Palace and even Winston Churchill.

Sample the local cooking at the island's *table d'hôtes* (casual eateries set up inside local homes), especially octopus dishes such as *cari ourite* (octopus curry) and *vindaye ourite* (octopus dry curry), plus *saucisses creole* (dried and cured meats) and *Rodrigues torte,* a papaya, pineapple or coconut jam tart. If you can, time your visit to coincide with the **Fish Festival** (first week of March). December's **Kréol Festival** is also a great time to visit.

WHERE TO STAY ON RODRIGUES

Tekoma Boutik Hotel
Possibly the most beautiful place to stay in Rodrigues, Tekoma Boutik has a handful of freestanding rooms on a rocky headland. There's a great beach, too. €€

Bakwa Lodge
A smart, all-white handful of rooms with a beachy vibe, plus a wooden deck looking out onto pristine sands. €€

Origine Eco-Chalet
A sustainably built cluster of four chalets whose terraces offer views over the spectacular surroundings. €€

GETTING AROUND

Flights land at Sir Gaëtan Duval Airport in the southwest of Rodrigues. There's a public bus service, but the most efficient way to get around is to organise transport through your accommodation before you arrive.

Octopuses drying on the beach, Rodrigues

Arriving

Most people arrive at Sir Seewoosagur Ramgoolam International Airport, in the southeast of the island, near Mahébourg. While the airport has been transformed into a larger hub, it's still deemed a small airport. There are car-hire, hotel and tour booths at the exit.

Sir Seewoosagur Ramgoolam International Airport

Visas
Residents of most nations won't need a visa for a stay under three months. To save time, fill in your immigration papers before arrival – ask at check-in for a QR code with the paperwork.

ATMs
There's an ATM inside the airport (to the right of the only duty-free shop in the baggage hall) and a couple outside around the back of the building. There's often an Rs10,000 withdrawal limit.

Rush Hour
If you can, plan to arrive outside rush hour (7.30am to 9.30am and 3.30pm to 5pm) or you'll risk being stuck in traffic on your first day.

Car Hire
You can arrange your hire car before you arrive. Alternatively, head to the concrete block in the airport car park, where all the rental agencies are lined up.

BAGGAGE CLAIM

Here's a tip that might save you a tense few minutes after you land. Once you're in the baggage hall and have found your flight's conveyor belt, you might not see your luggage. Some suitcases are taken off the conveyor belt as they arrive and stacked just nearby to avoid cluttering up the belt. If you don't see your suitcase at first, check the stacks of luggage around your flight's conveyor belt. All bulky pieces of luggage, such as strollers and surfboards, are stacked in a different corner of the baggage-claim hall.

TRANSPORT FROM THE AIRPORT

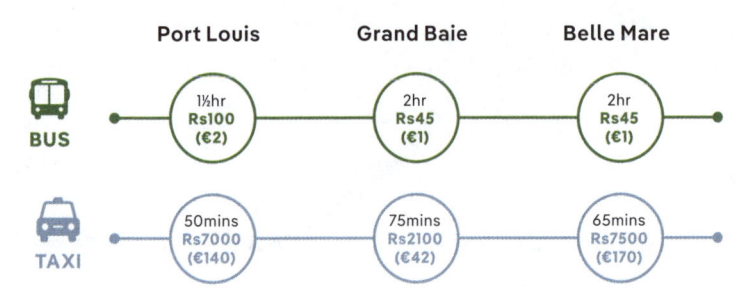

	Port Louis	Grand Baie	Belle Mare
BUS	1½hr, Rs100 (€2)	2hr, Rs45 (€1)	2hr, Rs45 (€1)
TAXI	50mins, Rs7000 (€140)	75mins, Rs2100 (€42)	65mins, Rs7500 (€170)

Getting Around

Mauritius has a good bus network and trams between Port Louis and the plateau cities. Taxis are eye-wateringly expensive (Rs2000 for a 30-minute trip), so it's best to hire your own car.

CHECK YOUR TYRES
Be sure to check the tyres of your hire car and ensure you have a spare as well.

HIRING A CAR
You can hire a car at the airport (the cheaper option) or once you're at your hotel. Rental companies can drop off a car at your accommodation.

HIRING A DRIVER
Hiring a driver gives you the freedom to enjoy the island without having to do any driving or navigating. It's about Rs4000 a day, including petrol, for a driver with their own car. Make sure your travel insurance covers you for injury and damage to the car.

TRAVEL COSTS

- Car hire **From €45/day**
- Petrol **RS74 (€1.48)/litre**
- Tram ticket **Rs35 (75c)**
- Bicycle rental **€12/day**
- Scooter rental **€18/day**

ROAD CONDITIONS
Roads are generally very good. Mauritius operates under a British administration system, so driving is on the left. Locals can be a bit unruly behind the wheel, so drive slowly and take extra care. Keep your distance with public buses, which spew black fumes every time they stop.

METRO & BUS
The bus network covers most of the island. However, journeys take a long time due to the speed of the old metal buses. There's an excellent tram service between Port Louis and the plateau cities. See the Metro Express Light Rail website (mauritiusmetroexpress.mu) for schedules.

PARKING
There aren't many official car parks in Mauritius outside the cities. Even then, try to find enclosed open-air car parks with their own security guards. Parking costs about Rs50 an hour – give the fee directly to the guard. Otherwise, people park wherever they can.

DRIVING ESSENTIALS

Drive on the left.

110
Speed limits: town and city 40km/h; open roads 80km/h; motorways 110 km/h

0.02
Drink drive limit is 0.02 mg/L.

EXTRA CAUTION
Driving in Mauritius is fine overall, but be extra careful at night, as many areas don't have street lighting, and at the weekends, when there's a higher chance you'll encounter drivers who've been drinking. Don't leave anything visible in the car seats when you leave your vehicle unattended.

Stay extra cautious by anticipating other drivers' errors – small knocks and bumps are common on the road.

Above: Piton de la Fournaise (p198); Right: Red cardinal bird

THE MAIN AREAS

ST-DENIS
Historic and economic capital.
p136

ST-PAUL
Sea life, beaches and leisure.
p147

ST-PIERRE
Arts, culture and a wild coastline.
p159

ST-ANDRÉ
History, water sports and volcanic lands.
p176

RÉUNION
VOLCANIC DRAMA AND VIBRANT MULTICULTURALISM

A Unesco World Heritage Site, Réunion island is home to stunning landscapes, and is also at the crossroads of African, Asian and European cultures.

Born from two volcanoes, Réunion is firstly defined by its relief. Steep and wild, it is somewhat chaotic and not easy to conquer. It's made up of mountains, ravines and waterfalls. Yet, on such a small territory – only 2,500 sq km! – this unique geological configuration has allowed a formidable natural sanctuary to grow. Today, the Cirques, plains and coastal areas are home to about 300 protected flora and fauna species.

Among the most unique features of the island are its 200 microclimates. You can hike under a cloudy sky in a rainforest in the afternoon before driving an hour later to the west coast, where you'll find clear skies and sunset. This also means you'll tread on one of the richest lands in the Indian Ocean. Thanks to the Piton de la Fournaise volcano, one of the most active in the world, the island continues to expand.

Immigration waves – voluntary and forced – from three different continents over the past three and a half centuries have created a contemporary melting pot on the island. 'Mixed' is a concept embedded in the population, from European, African, Malagasy, East Asian and Indian descent. Across the island today, the arts, architecture, cuisine, and religious landmarks testify to a complex history and heritage.

Welcome to Réunion, land of diversity and natural treasures.

SALAZIE
Culture at the heart of green mountains.
p186

CILAOS
Trails and hikes in spectacular mountains.
p190

MAFATE
Mountain hikes accessible only by foot.
p194

PITON DE LA FOURNAISE & THE PLAINS
One of Earth's most active volcanoes.
p198

Find Your Way

Réunion is mostly urbanised on the coast. The inland Cirques have created a steep indented terrain, referred to as 'the heights'. Volcanic eruptions still occasionally expand the island in the southeast.

St-Denis, p136
The capital of Réunion is home to major historic and architectural landmarks. Its lively cultural scene gives a sense of Réunion's heritage.

St-Paul, p147
The biggest city on the island is home to historic sites and opens up on the beach area of Réunion, along the west coast.

Mafate, p194
One of the only remaining regions in the world with no roads or cars, it offers some of the most spectacular and remote hikes on the island.

St-Pierre, p159
The most vibrant city in the south, and a gateway to the Wild South and the volcano, St-Pierre is a perfect mix of culture and nature.

ST-DENIS
Ste Clotild
La Possession
Le Port
Dos d'Ane
St-Paul
Boucan Canot
St-Gilles-les-Bains
L'Hermitage-les-Bains
La Saline-les-Bains
La Petite France
Cirque de Mafate
Haut Mafa
Trois-Bassins
Piton de Neiges
Pointe des Châteaux
Cilaos
Cirque de Cilaos
St-Leu
Le Tévelave
Les Makes
Piton St-Leu
Entre-Deux
Étang-Salé-les-Bains
St-Louis
Saint-Pierre-Pierrefonds International Airport
St-Pierre

INDIAN OCEAN

CAR

A car will allow you to reach the heights and remote areas more easily. The road network is mostly new and well-maintained. As every family drives their own car, beware of traffic at rush hour. Patience is a virtue on Réunionnais roads.

BUS

Travelling by bus can be a good means of transportation when you're not in a hurry – a way to enjoy the landscapes stress-free, though routes do not cover the whole island. Some express buses run between main cities.

BICYCLE

Cycling around the island has become more and more popular among locals but remains tricky if you're not an experienced cyclist: car traffic is heavy and the roads are not always geared towards cyclists.

Salazie, p186

The most accessible Cirque, Salazie is home to lovely mountain villages amidst luxuriant vegetation and waterfalls.

Piton de la Fournaise & The Plains, p198

A fiery desert surrounded by humid plateaus, the volcano is a land where earth and lava seem to meet the sky.

THE GUIDE

RÉUNION

Plan Your Time

Explore the various facets of Réunion's natural heritage from the coast to inland mountains and the volcano. Get a sense of the island's multicultural background and history by visiting its museums and religious places.

Hell-bourg (p187)

A Short Stay

- If you have only five to seven days to spend in Réunion, start in **St-Pierre** (p159). It will be a good base to explore **Piton de la Fournaise** (p198) and the Wild South (p174), or the rugged mountains of **Cilaos** (p190).

- Drive north via the east coast to experience the luxuriant green side of the island, up to **Salazie** (p186), where you can stay overnight in the charming Creole village of **Hell-Bourg** (pictured left, p187).

- You may have time for a quick hike through **Mafate** (p194), or head to **St-Gilles-les-Bains** (p154) to enjoy a day by the sea before flying home.

Seasonal Highlights

A year in Réunion is punctuated by the religious celebrations of different communities and the agricultural calendar. Watch out for tropical storms in the rainy season (December to July).

JANUARY
Fire-walking rituals for the **Fête de Pandialé** (p178) take place in January among the Hindu community, mainly in the east.

FEBRUARY
The **Spring Festival** is celebrated by the Chinese community at the Guandi temples in the north and south.

JUNE
The start of the **whale migration season** off the west coast, which lasts until October.

Two Weeks to Explore

- With ten to fifteen days, you will be able to drive around the island and explore inland Réunion more deeply. Stop in **St-Denis** (p136) to visit its historic museums before enjoying the panoramas of **Le Maïdo** (p152) and the lagoons between **St-Gilles-les-Bains** (p154) and **St-Leu** (p156).

- There will be time for an overnight stay in **Mafate** (p194) for hikers, or in **Cilaos** (p190) for a thermal bath.

- You may be able to fit in a day or two around **St-André** (p176) to experience more of the local culture and religions, or even to see **Le Grand Brûlé** (p184) volcanic area.

If You Have More Time

- With more time, you'll be able to drive less, spend more time in each of the highlighted places, and plan for longer hikes.

- Add an evening in **Les Makes** (p167) and a hike to **Camp Dimitile** (p170), and take your time to discover local products and spices around **St-Joseph** and **St-Philippe** (p172). You could even fit in visits to **Hindu temples** (p177).

- Extend your stay in Salazie to hike up to **Forêt de Bébour-Bélouve** (p189), and in **Cilaos** (p190).

- Finally, spend some time in **Plaine des Cafres** (p199) to find out more about the volcanic plateaus.

JULY
The start of the **sugar-cane harvest** and transition into the southern hemisphere winter is slightly drier and fresher.

OCTOBER
The **Madmen's Diagonal race** (p162), part of the Grand Raid trail, kicks off in St-Pierre.

NOVEMBER
The lunar month of Ashvina in the Hindu calendar, when **Diwali** (p177) is celebrated in and around Hindu temples.

DECEMBER
On 20 December, festivities all around Réunion celebrate the **abolition of slavery**. It's also the start of the fruit season.

ST-DENIS

Tucked between mountains and a roaming ocean, the capital city is an interesting contrast between its Creole villas, cultural and religious landmarks, and its institutions, commercial streets, offices and social housing. St-Denis – the largest and most urbanised city on the island – is multi-faceted, attracting a fair share of workers and students.

The old city centre holds undeniable interest for architecture and history lovers, who will enjoy the many historic buildings, museums and art venues. The food scene is also vibrant and diverse, boosted by the daily influx of office workers.

However, the residential areas in the heights (Le Brûlé, La Montagne, Bois de Nèfles…), and the districts to the east (Ste-Clotilde, Le Chaudron, Moufia) make St-Denis a city to live in rather than visit. It is a great base or starting point to not only prepare for the rest of your journey, but also to learn more about Réunion from documented archives.

TOP TIP

Mainly a daytime city, St-Denis is a lively hub until 6pm. After this time, shops and services are closed, although some restaurants and bars near the seafront stay open in the evenings.

Le Barachois (p139)

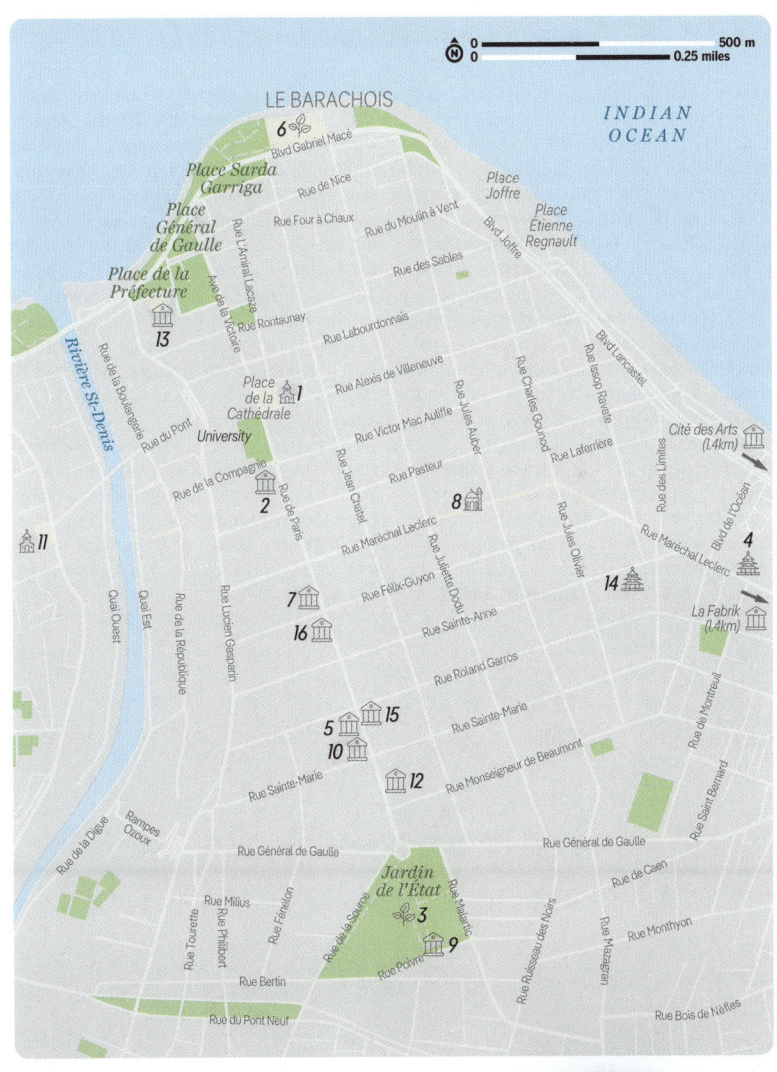

SIGHTS

1 Cathédrale de St-Denis
2 Former Hôtel de Ville
3 Jardin de l'État
4 Kalikambal Temple
5 L'Artothèque
6 Le Barachois
7 Maison Carrère
8 Mosquée Noor E Islam
9 Musée d'Histoire Naturelle
10 Musée Léon Dierx
11 Notre-Dame de la Délivrance
12 Number 49
13 Préfecture
14 Temple Chane and Temple Lisi Tong
15 Villa Angélique
16 Villa du Département

Notre-Dame de la Délivrance (p139)

CREOLE ARCHITECTURE & HISTORY

Head to Rue de Paris to admire its Creole villas. Rich landowners, administrators and their families used to stay in these sumptuous houses sometimes concealed behind lush gardens. Throughout the city centre, information plates have been set up in front of listed historic buildings, with archive pictures used instead when they no longer exist.

At **1 Number 49**, the first remarkable house belongs to the regional office. Its symmetrical architecture, with front columns around a *varangue* (veranda) and rectilinear windows with traditional mantling, makes it characteristically Creole.

Further down, the **2 Musée Léon Dierx** and **3 L'Artothèque** are great spots for art lovers, and they also offer a chance to see traditional buildings from the inside. Across the street, take a look at the superb **4 Villa Angélique hotel**, in particular at the glasswork on the windows.

At Number 18, the **5 Villa du Département** is the headquarters of the Conseil Général de la Réunion. On the corner, note the *guétali*: an elevated kiosk where residents could observe passersby without being seen. Stop then at the restored **6 Maison Carrère**, hosting the North Tourist Office, to learn more about the stories behind the town's heritage houses through a short exhibition. Don't hesitate to slightly stray from the itinerary to take a peek at other villas scattered in the northern part of town.

The closer you get to the sea, the more you come across imposing administrative buildings, displaying architectural styles common in French colonies at the time: the **7 Ancien Hôtel de Ville** with its yellow walls, and the grand **8 Préfecture**, facing the ocean.

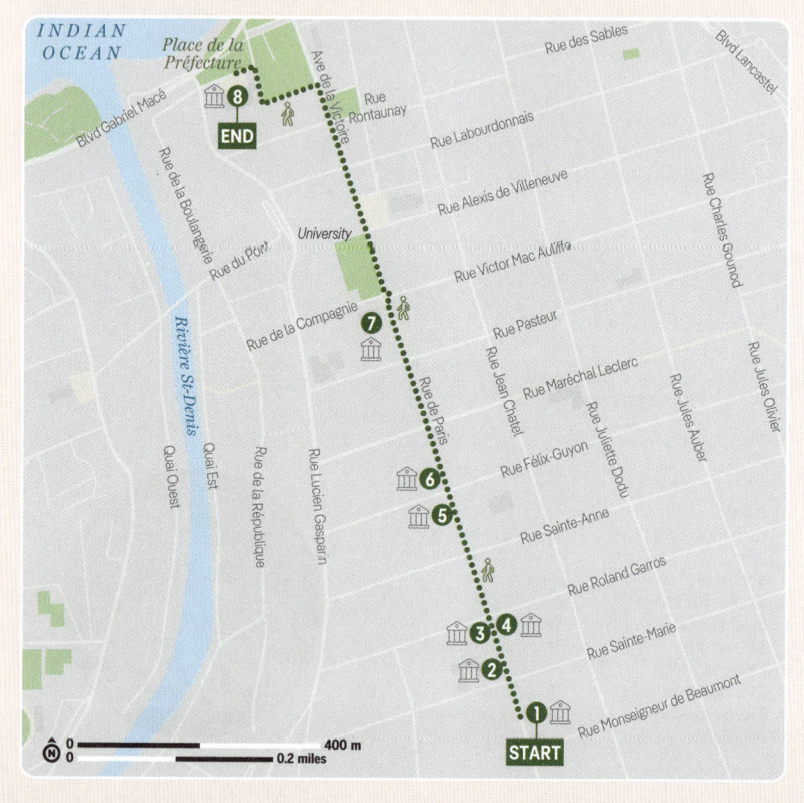

Cathedrals, Mosques & Temples

WHERE RELIGIONS LIVE SIDE BY SIDE

With a mix of populations comes a mix of religions.

Close to the seafront stands the neoclassical Cathédrale de St-Denis. A listed historic monument, it was built in 1743 to meet the needs of a growing population. It is now at the centre of the only animated area in the evenings: the Carré KTdral, made of bars and restaurants.

A few streets away, the **Mosquée Noor E Islam** is not only the oldest mosque in Réunion (1898), but also the first Islamic building ever built on French territory. It is open to the public outside of prayer times, with guided tours available on request (ask the gatekeeper).

A dozen metres away from the mosque sits the **Kalikambal Temple**, the city's main Tamil temple. Although smaller than some, its impressively sculpted *gopura* (front porch) and colourful statues of Hindu gods and goddesses are worth seeing. Visits are possible for a limited number of people at a time.

A bit further down to the east, two Chinese temples face each other: the **Temple Chane** and **Temple Lisi Tong**, both dedicated to Guandi, a warrior turned god.

Among notable catholic churches, **Notre-Dame de la Délivrance**, with its colourful facade overlooking the Rivière St-Denis, is also worth a visit.

When you visit religious places, be discreet and make sure your legs and shoulders are covered.

Breaking Down Chains

A PARADE TO CELEBRATE FREEDOM

On 20 December, festivities and parades take place everywhere on the island to commemorate the 1848 Abolition of Slavery declared by Commissioner of the Republic Sarda Garriga on Le Barachois (now Place Sarda Garriga). It's a major popular event, so much so that it's a bank holiday in Réunion.

Cultural associations, schools and bands of the city and beyond gather in the streets to sing, dance and celebrate freedom. Many see it as a moment to not only recognise

HAPPY BIRTHDAY GUANDI!

A general turned god, Guandi is a deity worshipped by a large part of the Chinese diaspora, for his courage and loyalty. He is often represented with a red face, long moustache and beard.

Every other year in July or August (depending on the Lunar calendar), the Guandi Festival celebrates the deity's birthday. Festivities and activities such as dragon and lion dances, demonstrations of martial arts, conferences on Chinese culture and a food court are set up in the area around the Chinese temples of St-Denis. The festival includes people from other communities, but also involves and attracts younger Réunionnais from Chinese descent, eager to learn more about their roots.

MORE ABOUT GUANDI

The **Temple Guan Di de Terre-Sainte** (p161) is not only the largest on the island, but also in the Indian Ocean. It's a place where the Chinese community gathers, and where all are welcome to learn more about this culture.

WHERE TO TAKE A LOCAL BREAK

Mafate Café
A Creole coffee shop, serving breakfast and brunch with a touch of Réunionnais flavours. €

Bar Dalons
Dalons means 'friends like brothers' in Creole: a friendly invitation to this bar belonging to a local brewery. €

Majik Glaces
An ice-cream shop with a variety of local flavours, from tamarind-chilli to guava. €

139

OUR PERFECT DAY IN ST-DENIS

Lucie Dégut
Réunionnais graphic designer
@luciedegut
and Jose Morel
Developer from NYC
@jsemrl

Lucy and Jose share their recommendations for a day out in St-Denis.

Have breakfast at L'Oiseau du Jardin before visiting the Musée d'Histoire Naturelle.

Then, stop by the contemporary art gallery 12 La Galerie before lunch at Bois la Tasse, a vegetarian coffee shop.

Stroll on Le Barachois towards the smaller market, to have fresh fruit juice at La Kaz à Jus.

Head back via Maréchal Leclerc shopping street. Graphic novel fans should stop at Les Bulles dans l'Océan bookstore before dinner at Crêperie Saint-Georges. Finally, enjoy a well-deserved sleep at Villa Marie Lucie.

Jardin de L'Etat

the suffering and courage of their ancestors, but also to acknowledge Réunion's slavery past. The main streets of the capital are filled with a festive crowd, who follow the parade like a moving *kabar*.

Typically, a *kabar* is a gathering with talks, dance and music, originating from Madagascar. Musicians play maloya, the music of enslaved people – similar to singing the blues – on traditional instruments.

At the end of the parade, concerts usually take place on the seafront. Even during the rest of the year, it's a great sunset spot, and a popular place among locals to grab a snack or 'American' sandwich (a type of local sandwich with meat and fries in a baguette, and grated cheese on top) at one of Le Barachois food trucks.

Nature, Past & Present

FLORA AND FAUNA OF THE INDIAN OCEAN

In the shade of camphor and coconut trees, **Jardin de l'Etat** is a garden where locals take shelter from the heat. It used to be a laboratory for new species introduced in the 18th-century colony, at a time when few endemic plants and trees were edible. Many species, now completely integrated in

WHERE TO EAT CREOLE FOOD

Le Reflet des Îles
An old benchmark for locals: its traditional cuisine is consistent, authentic and generous. €€

Pépé do Fé
A small venue in a hidden courtyard, with traditional recipes served in colourful enamel dishes. €

Snack Chez Yann
Takeaway only, with generous portions. A popular place among locals with no time to sit down. €

Kalikambal Temple (p139)

RESIDENCES TURNED MUSEUMS

Musée Léon Dierx
One of the best-preserved neoclassical buildings in the capital. Not only are its collections diverse but the museum also boasts a few impressionist masterpieces, and pieces selected by art seller Ambroise Vollard, who was born in Réunion.

L'Artothèque
'A window to contemporary art.' The contrast between the traditional wooden building and the modern pieces, from photography to sculpture, is what makes the experience interesting and somewhat unusual here.

Maison Carrère
This small permanent exhibition retraces the history and lifestyle of the former house owners. It now hosts the North Tourist Office, so stop by to gather information for your trip too.

Réunionnais gardens and cuisine, were introduced there: breadfruit, lychee, cocoa, mangosteen, black pepper, nutmeg trees...

At its centre, the **Musée d'Histoire Naturelle** shows not only the current and past fauna of the island, but also stuffed animals of the Mascarene Islands and Madagascar. The fascinating second floor displays extinct species such as the dodo bird, in an effort to echo today's preoccupation for environmental preservation.

Art on Walls

TRACK RÉUNIONNAIS STREET ART

The work of Réunionnais graffiti artists like Jace Ticot (the creator of the Gouzou characters: round beige little men scattered across the island, like local Space Invaders), Eko, Floe, Kid Kreol & Boogie, Vincent Box and others, can be identified on CartoGraff, an interactive leaflet that gives the location of hundreds of wall artwork and graffiti across the city. Pick it up at the North Tourist Office and use QR codes to access street-art circuits, as well as interviews and local recommendations from the artists themselves. A personalised Google map also helps to locate the murals. Your search will lead you across the whole city, up to art venues such as **La Fabrik** and **Cité des Arts**, an artistic haven located in a rehabilitated industrial site.

Musée d'Histoire Naturelle

GETTING AROUND

Close to the airport, St-Denis is a convenient starting point for your trip, and the best place to deal with administrative or business issues (plane tickets, passport...)

The historic city centre is easily visited on foot. It's preferable to avoid driving in the centre as its maze of one-way streets is generally congested from 7am to 10 am, and 4pm to 6pm.

The city's bus service, Citalis, is reliable during the day and is useful for getting from the centre to the heights. Head to the Océan bus terminal to catch a bus to other major towns. An express bus, Car Zeclair, connects St-Denis to St-Pierre in about one hour.

Beyond St-Denis

The area beyond St-Denis, down to Ste-Suzanne, used to be called 'The Beautiful Land' by the first settlers – with good reason.

Beyond the capital city, from the Route du Littoral (the road over the ocean connecting St-Denis to the western cities) to the north of Ste-Suzanne, with Ste-Marie and the airport in between, up to the villages on the external sides of the northern cirques, this area is what most Réunionnais consider 'north'.

Very urbanised and industrialised in the immediate surroundings of St-Denis, the area becomes more agricultural outside the city centres. More than just residential areas, the heights offer popular hikes and stunning panoramas. As you go east, sugar-cane fields soon start to cover the gentle mountain slopes. That's where your journey can easily lead you to beautiful waterfalls, lesser-known temples and historic landmarks.

TOP TIP

Avoid rush hour (7am to 10am, and 4pm to 6pm) if you're driving around towns on the periphery of St-Denis.

Niagara Waterfall, Ste-Suzanne (p144)

The Other Niagara
THE BIGGEST WATERFALL IN THE NORTH

Don't take the road across the river in the rainy season, when driving to Niagara. Instead opt for the road from **Ste-Suzanne**. The waterfall appears at the end of a narrow way bordered by dense sugar-cane fields, and is a surprise sight. The gush of water is deafening, especially in the rainy season. Needless to say, it doesn't compare to the Canadian Falls, but it does impress when the curtain of water rushes down the mountain.

This is a very popular spot for picnics as it's very accessible compared to other waterfalls on the island. Avoid swimming in the main pond, as the water flow can be very strong and drag you down in seconds.

From Sugar to Vanilla
A SUGAR ESTATE TURNED VANILLA PRODUCER

The 140m-long alley of coconut trees leading to La Vanilleraie, about 3km southwest of Ste-Suzanne, is already visible from the expressway. **Domaine du Grand Hazier**, a former sugar estate, now hosts this vanilla production site in its ren-

WATERFALL WALKS IN STE-SUZANNE

Bassins Boeuf, Nicole and Grondin
Well upstream of the Niagara waterfall, this trio of water ponds is accessible after a short hike. To access Bassin Boeuf, where the biggest waterfall flows, walk down first to the quieter Bassin Nicole, which offers a nice picnic area on the rocks. Continue upstream to reach the waterfalls.

Cascade des Délices
There's a short walk through the jungle and a bamboo forest by the river before reaching this small waterfall, popular among locals, who come to foot-bathe, grab a bite or take pictures on the rocks.

Avoid crossing rivers and swimming in ponds in case of heavy rain, however tempting the sights may be.

La Vanilleraie

WHERE TO STAY BEYOND ST-DENIS

Les Terrasses de Niagara
With a direct view of the Niagara waterfall, these three bungalows are a gem in Ste Suzanne! €€

La Maison d'Edith
A traditional Creole villa with garden in La Montagne, with a beautiful ocean view. €€

L'Escapade Bellepierre
Very close to the centre of St-Denis, this guesthouse offers a calm family-friendly break. €€

ovated stables. The owner, Mr Come, believes in introducing the notion of *terroir* in the vanilla industry, hoping to single out tastes and flavours according to lands, climates and the know-how of each local producer he works with. A guided tour available in English, French and Spanish takes you through the fascinating vanilla-production process.

The Path by the Sea

A PATH ALONG THE NORTHERN COASTLINE

A pedestrian and cycling path, **Sentier Littoral Nord** stretches over 22km. This recently built path is loved by locals who can now enjoy the coastline, which had been considered hostile, stuck between jungle and violent waves.

It starts in Ste-Suzanne at the **Bel-Air Lighthouse**, the last one standing on the island, and partly follows the ancient train tracks that used to connect the eastern towns to the capital. Only a few vestiges from that time remain, such as a photogenic tunnel invaded by vines.

From time to time, sideway paths lead to discreet picnic areas and rock beaches. A few Hindu temples are also scattered along the shore. One of the most popular, **Temple du Front de Mer**, is concealed behind lush vegetation but visible from afar.

Bel-Air Lighthouse

A Walk Back in Time

THE OLDEST ROAD ON THE ISLAND

In 1810, English troops arrived in the north and took over the island for five years. They used a rather large paved road going from La Possession to La Montagne. Hence the name **Chemin des Anglais** (Road of the Englishmen).

Its original purpose was to facilitate the passage of cowcarts. Entirely paved with basalt rocks in 1775, it became the first road on the island. It's now an interesting hike between **La Grande Chaloupe** and **St-Bernard**.

In La Grand Chaloupe, you can see the **old train station** dating back to the 1870s, and **Le Lazaret**, a building where freshly disembarked workers used to be quarantined.

The station is one of the only remains of the railway, which

HISTORIC CREOLE GARDENS

For botanists, Creole gardens are a way to travel back in time. Initially, almost nothing was naturally edible or useful among the vegetation of the island. Over the centuries, this led settlers and immigrants to bring their own seeds and cultivars.

In the heights of St-Denis, in Le Brûlé, Madame Boyer-Vidal cultivates and takes care of a vast Creole garden dating back to the 19th century, inherited from her grandfather. La Vallée Heureuse is even listed as a historic monument.

She welcomes the public for guided tours (in French), by reservation through the North Tourist Office.

PANORAMAS BEYOND ST-DENIS

La Vigie
On the road to La Montagne, a viewpoint over the whole city of St-Denis.

Pic Adam
A panoramic view over the northern coast, on one of the most popular hiking loops.

Sentier des Cordistes
Vertiginous viewpoints over the coastal viaduct over the ocean. Very discreet entrance path.

OCEAN DRIVE

Everybody has an opinion about the titanic construction that has been going on for almost 12 years. The **Nouvelle Route du Littoral** (new coastal road) is now in service between St-Denis and La Grande Chaloupe. It is supposed to go all the way to La Possession eventually.

It is a stunning achievement considering the challenges in terms of architecture, engineering and environmental protection.

What an impressive experience it is to drive 8.5km above the Indian Ocean! The black somber cliffs that have caused so many lethal accidents in the past 50 years seem almost harmless from afar. However, many questions still remain as to the follow-up and end of the construction.

---

used to go over almost three quarters of the coastline. Until recently, a group of enthusiasts was still able to run the last locomotive engine. Nearby, one remaining lazaret is occasionally used for cultural events, as a reminder of the time when thousands of workers were indentured from India, China, Africa, Madagascar and the Comoros to work on Réunion's fields.

At the higher end of the hike, another historic landmark is worth a detour: the old leprosarium. Now a social centre, it hosts one of the best Creole restaurants in La Montagne: **Le Saint-Bernard**. Ask for a *rhum arrangé* (flavoured rum) before or after your hike in the footsteps of English soldiers.

La Roche Écrite

THE MOST POPULAR PEAK IN THE NORTH

No less than nine different paths lead to **La Roche Écrite**, the intersection where the Cirque de Salazie and the Cirque de Mafate meet.

Most hikes to this 2,276m-high peak require good physical fitness. They are rarely shorter than six hours there and back when starting from Le Brûlé or Pic Adam.

Consider spending the night at the Plaine des Chicots refuge for a better chance of getting an early clear view at the top, since it tends to get cloudy here from 9am.

La Roche Écrite

GETTING AROUND

You will find the road network particularly well-maintained between St-Denis, Ste-Marie and Ste-Suzanne. Although cars are the most convenient way to get around, cities beyond St-Denis in the north are mostly well-connected by bus as they benefit from their proximity to the capital.

Residential areas in the heights are well-connected by buses during the day, provided you're flexible with timings, but you will definitely need a car to reach the mountain trails starting beyond the highest villages.

It is also possible to cycle from Ste-Suzanne to St-Denis thanks to the Sentier Littoral Nord, but avoid doing this in the middle of the day because of the heat.

ST-PAUL

Although the historic city centre of St-Paul only consists of a few blocks along a 3km stretch of the shoreline, the conurbation is nevertheless the most populated and extended city on the west coast. It includes the seaside resort town of St-Gilles-les-Bains, legally speaking. It's also a large industrial area, with major commercial activity for locals.

The first group of men to ever set foot on the island arrived in the area of St-Paul Bay in 1663. Two years later, the Compagnie des Indes ordered the first official settlements. So historically, St-Paul can be considered the 'cradle of the island'. Although only a few colonial buildings remain in the centre, the area bears traces of these first settlements.

Beyond historic landmarks, St-Paul is also home to an exceptional biodiversity, particularly around L'Étang St-Paul, a nature reserve stretching over nearly 200 hectares next to the city.

TOP TIP

St-Paul is a good place to stop at briefly for a day of culture on your way to the western coast. Travel by car and it's advisable to book your accommodation outside of the city centre, as there is a wider choice near the beach or in the heights.

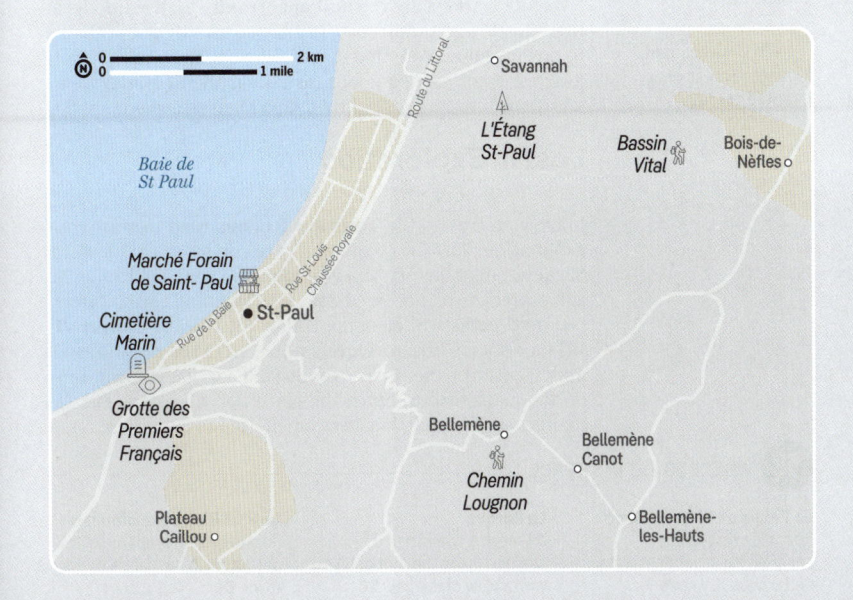

In the Steps of the First Settlers
A LANDMARK IN HISTORY

In 1663, Louis Payen, with another Frenchman and ten Malagasies, disembarked in St-Paul Bay. Legend has it that they took shelter in a natural cave nearby, now known as **Grotte des Premiers Français**. Within this first group of people, a baby girl of Malagasy origin was born: Anne Mousse. She is considered the first child of Île Bourbon. For safety reasons, the cave itself is not currently accessible, but its surroundings have been turned into a picnic park with promenades.

Just across the road, don't miss another mythical landmark: the Cimetière Marin (built in 1788). The cemetery is a listed historic site and the last home of illustrious Réunionnais: the Panon-Debassayns, poets Eugene Dayot and Leconte De Lisle...and the pirate Olivier Le Vasseur, better known as 'La Buse' (The Buzzard).

In the 2000s, a graveyard of enslaved people below the official cemetery was unearthed by the ocean. The sunset light gets a bit eerie over the tombs, as many local legends whisper of ghosts in the area.

Samosas, Seaside & Souvenirs
SHOPPING FOR SNACKS AND CRAFTS

On Friday and Saturday mornings, a wide variety of snacks, crafted goods, fresh fruit and vegetables are available at the **Marché Forain de Saint-Paul**. Don't miss Bruno's stall for fresh coconut juice. Take some away to the nearby black-sand beach with a bag of fresh samosas.

Weekly markets are the best opportunity to dive into local ingredients and try all sorts of snacks, usually not available to buy in shops. Note that due to the popularity of this market, prices for crafted goods (usually made in Madagascar) and souvenirs can be slightly higher than elsewhere.

Lost in Exploration
REMAINS AROUND A NATURAL RESERVE

Make your way to the **Tour des Roches** road to start your exploration. Past the commercial area and former site of the Savanna sugar factory, you will soon find yourself driving on a lush green road, bordered with reed beds and coconut trees.

Several paths will open up. Follow the road to **Bassin Vital** for a sporty hike to a lovely waterfall in the rainy season, and beautiful panoramas over St-Paul. Or you can continue on the main road to reach the old water wheel, the last remains of an old mill. Washerwomen used to come here regu-

---

BEST LOCAL MARKET SNACKS

Samosa
A fried Indian pastry traditionally stuffed with beef or lamb, in a triangular shape.

Bonbon piment
A fried chickpea ball with spices.

Piment farci
A fried green chilli stuffed with a savoury filling (meat or fish).

Candied papaya
Called 'jam' by locals, and usually presented in long strips.

Gâteau patate
A sweet cake made of white sweet potato – this is a local's favourite!

Galette manioc
A sort of sweet fried pancake made of grated cassava.

WHERE TO EAT IN ST-PAUL

Le Palais de l'Eau de Coco
Roadside restaurant specialising in coconut water and dishes. Try coconut samosas and nougat. €

La Barque
A French-style fish and seafood menu (but not only) with a view of the bay. €€

Le P'tit Bistro Réunionnais
Fusion cuisine prepared with care, right in the centre of the town. €€

Fruitstand, St-Paul

larly before the pool was downsized and became a small natural swimming pool for families.

Further on, towards Grande Fontaine, you will come across **Chemin Lougnon**, a former paved road built to support the development of coffee culture. It was rehabilitated with care by a local association a few years ago and often welcomes grazing goats. Take a peek at the traditional village recreated at the end of the hike.

Last but not least, at the far end of Tour des Roches (you will be back in a residential area at this point) sits an old powder house, a listed historic site built as part of the first defence system of the city in 1723.

L'ÉTANG ST-PAUL

This nature reserve is home to many protected species.

Waterhen
Dark with a red beak. It nests in the humid vegetation. You may hear it chuckle rather than see it.

L'endormi (chameleon)
This symbol of Réunion used to only live around the pond, but has since invaded the island.

Papangue (Circus maillardi)
If you look up, you might see the only endemic bird of prey in Réunion hunting over the pond.

Papyrus reed
Not protected. Scientists don't know where this hairy reed comes from. But it's the real deal: the same papyrus used by Egyptians to make paper.

GETTING AROUND

The city centre of St-Paul is well-served by buses, and well-connected to St-Denis and St-Pierre via the main bus station. While buses run to the Tour des Roches road, connecting various residential areas, you will need a car to explore the surroundings and make the most of the heights in particular.

Note that the N1 road passing by St-Paul, which connects the area of St-Paul-Savannah to the Route des Tamarins expressway, is often congested, every day and at any time.

Beyond St-Paul

The area beyond St-Paul holds an incredible variety of landscapes, from dense humid forests to sun-kissed beaches and lagoons.

Beyond the city of St-Paul lies the coast 'under the wind': the overall drier part of the island. But from La Possession to St-Leu, across St-Gilles-les-Hauts, up to the impressive Belvédère du Maïdo viewpoint, the diversity in landscapes and microclimates can be disconcerting. There are savanna plains, tamarind forests, and a dry bush overlooking the sea. Along the coast lies a protected blue lagoon.

Once a dynamic economic area thanks to coffee and then sugar, the west coast is now more popular for beaches and nautical activities. With the democratisation of surfing and scuba diving in more recent years, more and more people have turned to the west for sports and seaside holidays.

TOP TIP

Don't take the Route des Tamarins expressway, unless you're in a rush. Choose the scenic coastal road between St-Paul and L'Étang-Salé.

Belvédère du Maïdo

Cap Noir

Hike to Cap Noir

PANORAMIC VIEWS OVER LA POSSESSION

The Roche Verre Bouteille loop is an easy way to get panoramic views over Mafate, provided you are not scared of heights and a few ladders. Often recommended to travellers who don't have much time (the loop can be completed in less than two hours) but still want to be impressed with the island's rugged terrain, the hike to **Cap Noir** and around Roche Verre Bouteille is a locals' favourite. The trail owes its name to a peak that looks like a glass shard, serving as a landmark in the northern part of Mafate. It can be busy but the views over the Cirque de Mafate are worth it.

To the Belvédère du Maïdo

A DAY OF ACTIVITIES AND BIRD'S EYE VIEWS

The Belvédère du Maïdo, a 2190m-high natural balcony, is one of the Réunionnais' favourite viewpoints in the west. No wonder: on clear days, you face the Piton des Neiges peak, the highest summit on the island, majestically overlooking the whole Cirque.

ROADS WITH VIEWS

Route Forestière des Hauts (RF6)
The road from Le Maïdo to the Tévelave village stretches over 30km. It goes through a dense forest of tamarinds, with many popular picnic spots.

Route Hubert Delisle (D3)
Created in the mid-19th century, this road crosses many villages in the western heights. It's a rural alternative to the Route des Tamarins expressway.

Route des Tamarins
Opened in 2009, this expressway going from St-Paul to L'Étang-Salé in the south has made the coast less congested and changed the lives of many Réunionnais.

WHERE TO STAY IN THE HEIGHTS OF ST-PAUL

Villa Laurina
A warm Creole villa overlooking the bay, with a large park and plantation of local coffee. €€

High Hub Hostel
A hostel on the high forest road, and a great starting point for hikes. €

Le Ruisseau
A charming B&B in the countryside, with a panoramic view over St-Paul. €

Plage de L'Hermitage

THE RÉUNIONNAIS ART OF PICNICS

In Réunion, picnic is an art. The first rule is to pick the right spot: you need a view, a kiosk, a place to barbecue and some shade. On weekends, finding a good picnic spot can be a real headache!

Once everybody has arrived, the show can begin: large pots full of *cari* (a traditional Creole dish with meat cooked in sauce) are put on the fire. Aubergines are shoved into the burning coal and tarps are fastened around trees to create more shade. With tables and chairs unfolded, music turned on and occasionally hammocks hung, the picnic is ready to begin. It will last until the sun goes down!

The road from St-Paul is easy to drive despite a few curves, and leads you through multiple microclimates: leaving behind the coastal savanna, a few hydrangea shrubs start to appear and the landscape changes into a humid forest, turning again into drier bush further up. It's like going through several worlds in no more than 30 minutes.

Don't be surprised to see locals 'booking' their picnic kiosks on the road from the crack of dawn on weekends. The spots are that good. Some people will also come to watch the sunrise with a coffee thermos in hand. Even if you're not an early bird, still make sure you get to the viewpoint before 9am, as the clouds come in quite quickly. But if you haven't planned for a picnic, stop at the iconic restaurant on the Maïdo road: **Chez Doudou**. The owner has been working to develop and preserve a traditional lifestyle in the area for years.

Along the way, several family-friendly activities are worth a stop. Try the fun **jungle sledge** (Parc de La Luge) which slides through, above and below ferns and forest, or go for a horse ride through the tamarind forest with **Les Chevaux du Maïdo**.

Once at the Belvédère du Maïdo, note that this is the starting point for several hikes over the ridge, with stunning views across Mafate: for a short walk, head to Piton des Orangers (45 minutes). For longer trails, go either left to Îlet Alcide, or right

SHORT WALKS NEAR LE MAÏDO

Sentier de la Tamarineraie
A short forest walk to learn more about the endemic tamarin des Hauts tree.

La Glacière
A path leading to what used to be a frozen pool, from which slaves extracted ice.

The King of Tamarind Trees
Walk up to Îlet Alcide from the Sans-Souci forest to see this 400-year-old tree.

to Le Grand Bénare. This peak will offer a double view over Mafate and Cilaos. After a four-hour hike, it won't disappoint.

Sea, Snorkel & Sun

SUNBATHE AND SWIM IN THE LAGOON

Filaos trees dancing in a warm breeze, white sand and a turquoise lagoon: welcome to Plage de L'Hermitage, one of the longest beaches on the island, where tourists, families and groups of teenagers gather to enjoy the sunset – and the richness of the coral reef. To the south of St-Gilles-les-Bains, this lagoon is a privileged spot for snorkelling.

Be careful to stay in the authorised zones, as this beach is part of the Natural Marine Reserve. Some areas completely forbid any sort of activity to help accelerate the redevelopment of marine fauna. Maps are set up across the beach to locate the different areas.

For a pedagogical experience, contact the Natural Marine Reserve. They organise free snorkelling tours with a specialised guide to better understand the biodiversity of the coral reef. You must bring your own equipment.

To the south of **L'Hermitage-des-Bains**, Plage de La Saline-les-Bains and Plage de Trou d'Eau have become local favourite beaches in recent years, especially because of the risk of sharks on some beaches located further north. Plage de Boucan Canot and Plage des Roches Noires are the only two other authorised swimming spots protected by anti-shark nets. For your safety, always strictly follow the flags and instructions.

Giants of the Ocean

COLLABORATIVE WHALE WATCHING

From June to October, humpback whales come back to the Indian Ocean from Antarctica. It's a formidable oceanic show, which can be observed from the entire west coast of the island. Some of the best spots to see the whales include **Cap La Houssaye**, **Boucan Canot** and **Cap Homard** beaches, all the way down to St-Leu's Pointe au Sel.

Whale watching in Réunion can be a collaborative activity: you can help recognise whales and track their way across the ocean. This way, Globice, the NGO in charge of cetacean observation and protection in the Indian Ocean, can count and follow the evolution of the whale population. By taking a picture and sending data to Globice, you take part in the KODAL programme. Send your pictures directly by email or download the ObsEnMer mobile app to do so. If you're the first to identify a whale, you will even get to name it!

LOCAL ADVICE: BEST PLACES TO EAT BEYOND ST-PAUL

Roxane, *writer and photographer behind the food blog* Avis d'Assiette *@studiohappei*

Roxane shares her recommendations for the best places to eat beyond St-Paul.

Copacabana
A quiet bar-restaurant where food is served all day. Relax with your feet in the sand.

Madame Glaces
The owner of this ice-cream shop works with fresh local fruit to create original colourful desserts.

Le Demeter
This place brews craft beer with local flavours (passionfruit, coconut stout) during the day and opens as a bar in the evening. It's a family business: the son brews the beer while his parents host the bar.

🍸 **WHERE TO HAVE A SUNSET DRINK**

Les Balançoires
This beach bar is popular among locals for its cocktails and brunches by the sea. €

Le Choka Bleu
Near Plage de Trou d'Eau, sit on this terrace to enjoy a cocktail or a Creole dinner. €€

LUX*
St-Gilles-les-Bains' 5-star hotel, where you can have a sip between the pool and white-sand beach. €€

BEST WAYS TO ENJOY THE SEA

Sea Kayaking
You don't have to dive or swim to enjoy the ocean or admire the coral reef. With or without a glass floor, kayaking is allowed at Plage de Trou d'Eau and Plage de L'Hermitage. You can also rent stand-up paddleboards for a swift glide over the lagoon.

Surfing
While Réunion offers world-ranking surf spots, the only places in the west where you can practise safely are Plage de Boucan Canot and Plage des Roches Noires. Strictly follow the coast guards' recommendations.

Sunset on a Catamaran
Offered by many companies in St-Gilles-les-Bains harbour, this is a quieter, but not less beautiful way to spend a moment off the coast.

In terms of approaching whales in high seas, boat companies are required to respect a policy of responsible approach that has been recognised and rated by the French government: no more than five boats should be around the animals and it is strictly forbidden to surround, let alone swim, towards them.

Some companies organise underwater encounters. These are also highly regulated and not recommended by NGOs for animal well-being. If you're tempted to swim with dolphins, one question you can ask providers is whether there is a briefing and first dive without cetaceans, so your group can prepare in advance and behave in the least intrusive way possible when meeting the animals.

Under the Sea

SCUBA DIVE OFF THE COAST

Réunion may not be listed among the most impressive scuba diving spots in the world but some places along the west coast can be of interest to autonomous and novice divers. Among the most accessible ones, with a rich coral reef, are Cap La Houssaye, where most first experiences take place, Maharani and La Passe de L'Hermitage. More experienced divers will enjoy the shipwrecks between **St-Gilles-les-Bains** and St-

St-Gilles-les-Bains

WHERE TO STAY NEAR BEACHES

Hôtel les Bougainvilliers
Hotel with a pool, cosy rooms and an excellent location by Plage de L'Hermitage. €€

Coco Island
Near L'Hermitage, a welcoming and convenient rental. Some rooms are equipped with a small kitchen. €€

Senteur Vanille
Luxury bungalows and small Creole villas with either a garden or ocean view near Boucan Canot. €€€

Leu. However, it's always best to discuss with local divers before heading to any of these sites.

Your trip to Réunion may be an opportunity to try diving for the first time. In this case, contact the West Tourist Office or go directly to St-Gilles-les-Bains harbour where many scuba diving clubs are based.

Underground Culture

EXPLORE A 400,000-YEAR-OLD LAVA TUNNEL

The crossing of the **Tunnel du Bassin Bleu** in **St-Gilles-les-Hauts** can be done only with a caving guide.

Once inside, you'll discover one of the oldest lava tunnels on the island and the only one in the west. During your underground walk, not only will you observe solidified lava at close quarters, but you may even have the chance to see a few salanganes (endemic birds similar to sparrows), which nest inside these tunnels. You can experience pitch black here; a darkness that is free from any light pollution and only possible underground.

Some caving guides, such as **Bazaltik Réunion**, organise special tours to enhance the special underground atmosphere, and offer underground meditation sessions or traditional music experiences in the dark.

FOR TUNNEL LOVERS

On the opposite side of the island, visit **one of the world's youngest lava tunnels** (p185), created by a volcanic eruption at Piton de la Fournaise.

SHOP UNTIL YOU DROP!

You may fall for the charming restored craft village of **L'Éperon**, in St-Gilles-les-Hauts.

Located on the site of a former sugar factory, it is now a welcoming market where you can buy local crafted goods. The trendy village is full of concept stores, handmade clothing accessories and pottery workshops, to mention only a few. Don't miss the Creole house with blue shutters hosting craft shop L'Atelier des Margouillats and cafe-bookshop Zou, which specialises in Réunionnais literature.

The items in L'Éperon village tend to be more original than the crafted goods found at weekly markets, which often come from Madagascar, but their prices are higher too.

Myths & Controversies

VISIT THE DOMAIN OF MADAME DESBASSAYNS

If there is one historic character every Réunionnais knows, it's Madame Desbassayns, who was perceived during her lifetime as both a providential saviour – she supposedly kept the English at bay in 1809 – and a cruel enslaver. She managed a huge estate and hundreds of enslaved people during her exceptionally long life: 85 years.

Word-of-mouth and oral tradition were enough to build all sorts of myths about her. Over the centuries, she was described at times as a well-educated businesswoman, or as a demon master, depending on the political needs of those who used her image. In local tales, she is even sometimes depicted

WHERE TO EAT IN ST-GILLES-LES-BAINS

Le Bistrot de Pépé Gentil
French cuisine served artfully alongside a good wine selection, one minute away from Boucan Canot. €€

Le D.C.P.
A restaurant by the harbour where you eat fresh fish only, directly from the boat. €€

L'Arc-En-Ciel
A local snack with traditional dishes to take away. Two steps away from Plage de L'Hermitage. €

Paragliders, Les Colimaçons

THE ISLAND FROM ABOVE

From a helicopter, you can see the island from a totally different perspective. It's the only way to glimpse some inaccessible sites, such as the spectacular Trou de Fer.

Worthy of a film scene, the flight above Réunion has been recognised as one of the most spectacular in the world. Hold your breath as the Cirques suddenly appear between massive cliffs in front of your panoramic cabin!

Book with Corail Hélicoptères for a group of four to six, and take off from St-Gilles-les-Hauts for a complete island tour or shorter more affordable flights over the lagoons or Cirques only.

as the most maleficent witch on the island, Grand-Mère Kal.

The **Musée de Villèle in St-Gilles-les-Hauts**, located in one of her former estates, retraces her life as well as the history of slavery in Réunion. Legend has it that in 1866, when her ashes were transferred to Chapelle Pointue (the Pointed Chapel) across the road, a huge thunderbolt almost cracked the building.

Spread Your Wings

PARAGLIDING ABOVE THE WEST COAST

Locals are used to seeing paraglider wings dot the sky with colours above Les Colimaçons hills in **St-Leu**. With good air conditions and easy access, the area is a great spot for a first experience.

You'll always be paired with an instructor for your first flight. People often say the takeoff is the shakiest moment. The rest of the flight is usually calm, leaving plenty of time to enjoy the absolutely breathtaking views over the coastline. From over 1km high, you can almost see the curve of the earth (or at least have that impression!)

Paragliding schools such as **Parapente Réunion** offer a wide choice of flights, for all levels, throughout the year.

WHERE TO EAT IN ST-LEU

Le Blue Margouillat
The hotel hosts one of the most praised gastronomical restaurants on the island. €€€

Le Vieux Pressoir
French-style restaurant in the calm setting of the botanical garden. Access by paying the garden fee. €€

Le Mascarin
French-Creole and Moroccan dishes are served on this small terrace overlooking the sea. €€

Réunion's Flora Treasure Chest
STROLL THROUGH A BOTANICAL GARDEN

In an old area overlooking the sea above St-Leu, the **Mascarin Jardin Botanique de La Réunion** opens its rich collections to plant lovers.

In a peaceful atmosphere, a long basalt stairway leads you to a traditional Creole residence surrounded by artfully arranged tropical flowers. It's only a shop. Walk around a park of endemic and ancient plants, orchard trees, a vast palm grove, and orchid gardens. The visit can last for a couple of hours if you're interested in local plants and their origins.

Although they are two separate entities, the garden also hosts the Conservatoire Botanique National de Mascarin, where researchers work to protect threatened flora species in Réunion, Mayotte and the Scattered Islands.

Meet the Rescue Turtles
GET TO KNOW SEA TURTLES BETTER

What is it like to be a sea turtle? How many species are there? Who is this small turtle with a shorter leg, rescued off the Réunionnais shores? All of these questions will find answers at **Kelonia marine observatory**, about 2km north of St-Leu.

The background story of this marine centre and museum is quite fascinating as it used to be a turtle meat farm in the 1970s! Now the conservatory leads a number of research and protection programmes around Réunion and the Scattered Islands.

You will meet several rescue turtles, learn about them and observe them from below and above, in giant pools by the ocean. Don't miss the panoramic view over St-Leu's coastline.

> **EXTEND THE TURTLE EXPERIENCE**
>
> You can meet (and even feed) the sea turtles' tortoise cousins at **Le Jardin des Tortues** (p167) in Les Avirons.

A FULL COCONUT HOUSE

Common in many tropical countries, coconut culture hasn't developed that much in Réunion. Apart from drinking its juice, coconut flesh is not often used in Réunionnais cuisine. Only the Tamils occasionally use it in religious ceremonies.

Yet, in St-Leu, the Maison du Coco (House of Coconut) wants to show how versatile the fruit is. Have you ever tried grating a fresh coconut or weaving coconut leaves? You can learn to do this at daily workshops.

Maison du Coco is located on the larger farm of Domaine de la Pointe des Châteaux, alongside a public orchard and garden. If you visit in December, it's even possible to harvest mangoes from the trees!

WHERE TO STAY IN ST-LEU

Villa Moaï
A pretty guesthouse nested behind Stella Matutina museum, with a cosy terrace and swimming pool. €€

Iloha Seaview Hotel
A conveniently located seaside resort with a panoramic view over the cove of St-Leu. €€

Cases Couleurs
A traditional Creole house surrounded by palm trees, with an outdoor pool and a sea view. €€

A PINCH OF SALT

Head to St-Leu's **Pointe au Sel** for a panoramic view over the ocean cove. The contrast in landscapes is striking, from dry savanna to green slopes, with roaming waves crashing on a black shoreline.

The salt flats were active until WWII, but are now only an educational site. The small Musée du Sel retraces the history of salt flats in the Indian Ocean.

This part of the coast is also renowned for its basalt grottoes, ponds, and *souffleurs*, where high pressure blows sea water out through a hole in the rocks, in a strong water jet. Stop along the road to watch this phenomenon, especially in the southern hemisphere winter.

Stella Matutina Museum

Once Upon a Time in the Sugar-Cane Industry

A HISTORY OF INDENTURED WORKERS

In the early 19th century, sugar canes started to replace coffee trees in Bourbon. Until 1817, there were only three factories on the island but more than two hundred were active at the peak of the sugar trade. Located in one of the former factories built in the 1860s, **Stella Matutina museum** spreads over 3,700 sq m and is about 4km south of St-Leu.

From the beginning, it was meant to show the technical and scientific aspects of the industry, especially as the factory equipment was still present on-site. During your visit, you will see cogs and wheels, tanks and instruments, and learn about the different products of sugar cane. But the museum also pays tribute to Piton St-Leu's sugar-cane workers, mainly indentured people and descendants of slaves.

It presents a complete picture of an agricultural lifestyle almost gone today: you can discover items from *Réunion lontan* (old-time Réunion) such as cow carts, cane cleavers, no-window buses…A real journey back in time!

GETTING AROUND

If you stay only within the beach area and along the coastline, you will be able to hop from one beach to the other by bus or by foot for the closest ones. However, if pressed for time, it's better to drive a car. Outside of the beach areas, a car is necessary to reach the beginning of trails and hikes, often located in the heights, where buses are less frequent and convenient.

The fastest way to get around is the Route des Tamarins expressway, but watch out for exits as some places are accessible only when coming from one direction and not the other, so check beforehand on GPS or a map. If you choose the more scenic route along the coast, avoid rush hour.

Parking can be challenging near beaches over the weekends, and around popular picnic areas (for instance in Le Maïdo and on the forest road), so plan your time carefully and be patient on the road.

ST-PIERRE

The main city in the south, St-Pierre has been on the rise in the past few years, thanks to its vibrant seafront and lively commercial streets, especially at weekends. It has become a convenient and pleasant city, more and more prized by younger Réunionnais and tourists, who appreciate its pulsing rhythm and energy. It also offers easy access to beaches and a lagoon where you can swim near the city centre, although it tends to be less popular than the western spots.

Over recent years, St-Pierre has been gradually reviving its industrial and agricultural heritage, slowly transforming old villages such as Terre-Sainte into tourist-friendly areas. And although it doesn't compete with the economic, political and cultural vibrance of the capital, it hosts two major international events: the international Sakifo music festival and the start of the Madmen's Diagonal race, one of the world-renowned Grand Raid trails.

TOP TIP

St-Pierre is great as a base to explore the south, from L'Étang-Salé to the volcano plains. It's also a gateway to the Wild South. But be aware of constant traffic jams at the various entrances to the city: patience is a key word here.

Fruit stand, St-Pierre (p162)

ST-PIERRE

SIGHTS
1. Attyaboul Massadjid Mosque
2. Croix des Pêcheurs
3. Église du Bon Pasteur
4. L'Usine à Gouzous
5. Market
6. Notre-Dame-de-Lourdes
7. Shri Maha Badra Karli
8. St-Pierre Cemetery
9. Temple Guan Di de Terre-Sainte
10. Temple Tamoul Narassingua Péroumal
11. Terre Sainte

ACTIVITIES, COURSES & TOURS
12. La Ravine Blanche

ENTERTAINMENT
see 12 Sakifo

Port of St-Pierre

Waterfront, St-Pierre (p159)

Unmissable Religious Diversity

FROM ONE PLACE OF RELIGIOUS WORSHIP TO THE NEXT

In the west of the city, start at the two Hindu temples: **Temple Tamoul Narassingua Péroumal** and **Shri Maha Badra Karli**, which are separated by a couple of streets. One reason why Tamil temples are so common in Réunion is that they were encouraged by employers, so that indentured workers from India wouldn't waste time going to faraway places to pray. Many have been privately funded by the workers' families themselves.

Nearby, the **Église du Bon Pasteur** Catholic church is worth a detour, if only to admire its glasswork facade made by the main master glassmaker in Réunion. After a 20-minute walk, you will reach the **Attyaboul Massadjid Mosque** and its garden haven.

Continue east to reach the beautiful yet unusual **Notre-Dame-de-Lourdes** by the Rivière d'Abord. In her grotto, the Virgin stands side by side with St-Expedit, the most worshipped and adored Catholic saint in Réunion.

A final walk or drive will take you to **Temple Guan Di de Terre-Sainte**, the biggest Guandi temple, not only in Réunion but in the Indian Ocean. In the centre of an immense park,

THE VAMPIRE OF RÉUNION

The most famous sorcerer on the island is buried in **St-Pierre Cemetery**. Simicoudza Simicourba, called 'Sitarane', has been the object of a black magic cult ever since his death in 1911.

He was the executioner in a gang of three villains, known for house invasion and violent crimes in the early 20th century. Their reputation as vampires and sorcerers developed as it was reported by the press that they performed black magic rituals to put their victims to sleep before drinking their blood.

Although never a guru in his lifetime, Sitarane has followers now who come asking for help in their dark deeds.

WHERE TO STAY IN ST-PIERRE

Les Baroudeurs
One of the few hostels, with dormitories and private rooms, just outside the city. €

Le Battant des Lames
On the seafront, this big hotel has a pool with a sea view and a private beach corner. €€

Le Terre Sainte
A city-centre hotel ideally located two minutes from the beach. €€

WHERE DO GOUZOUS COME FROM?

Gouzous are like the local Space Invaders. If you're not familiar with those chubby faceless figures yet, you will be after your trip:

Jace Ticot's creations are everywhere, from the side of a building opposite St-Pierre's main bus station to the back of an electrical transformer on the volcano road... Gouzous have even travelled internationally and been painted on walls on every continent!

To discover Jace's work, head to his gallery, **L'Usine à Gouzous**. Don't miss the Very Yes Art Gallery, located at the back of the factory in a set of rehabilitated containers. It showcases local street art and more.

this imposing building regularly welcomes community events.

All of the places mentioned here can be visited. Book your tours either through the South Tourist Office or directly on social media for the mosque and Guandi temple.

For Early Birds
MAKE THE MOST OF THE MARKET

Wake up early to shop like locals at the weekly market on St-Pierre seafront. Every Saturday morning, it becomes crowded with vegetable and craft stalls, but also snack vendors. This is more organised than St-Paul's market in that the same types of goods are located in dedicated corners, and it's also bigger.

Full of colours, it's been ranked the third best market in France. It's a good place to learn about local fruits and vegetables, see live chickens, and buy cheap souvenirs and handmade baskets, mostly from Madagascar. It is advisable to arrive here no later than 9am as the best goods are always sold first!

Ready, Steady, Go!
KICK OFF THE DIAGONAL WITH THE MADMEN

Around October 20th, St-Pierre kicks off the **Madmen's Diagonal race**. The whole seafront is filled with a supportive crowd, street performances and vendors. The Diagonal is the most famous race of the Grand Raid, so much so that it is often mistaken to be the Grand Raid itself (it is only one of four races). The Diagonal is a three-day ultra-trail over 165km, from **La Ravine Blanche** to La Redoute in St-Denis.

The trailers start by climbing Piton de la Fournaise and continue across the Cirques, over the ridges and through Réunion National Park. What makes this race particularly famous is the crossing of the island's demanding slopes: on top of the monumental physical effort necessary, the landscapes trailed are among the most impressive in the world.

When selected for the trail, competitors from around the world flock to Réunion, and some train all year long for the chance to finish the Diagonal. It is not rare to see them when hiking on mountain paths.

FOR STREET-ART HUNTERS

Spend some time tracking down local **street art and graffiti in St-Denis** (p142) thanks to CartoGraff, an interactive leaflet.

WHERE TO EAT IN ST-PIERRE

Le Caritologue
A buffet of traditional dishes served in a backyard, directly from iron pots on the fire. €€

Kaz à Léa
French and Creole dishes served on the terrace of a traditional house with a charming decor. €€

A la Table de Lyne
A family restaurant serving Creole dishes made with love, right in the city centre. €

The Music You Need

RÉUNION'S BIGGEST MUSIC FESTIVAL

For the past twenty years, the **Sakifo** music festival has earned an international reputation, with artists coming from the Indian Ocean and beyond every year. Born in the small seaside town of St-Leu, the festival relocated to St-Pierre in 2009. It now takes place over three days in June, usually on several stages around Ravine Blanche.

Sakifo means 'What you need' in Réunionnais Creole. With an eclectic programme, it has aimed since its creation to bring international music to the Réunionnais public. Every year, the Sakifo weekend fills the city with a festive crowd from all corners of the island. Book tickets and accommodation well in advance.

Madmen's Diagonal race

RÉUNIONNAIS RHYTHMS

A slow three-beat rhythm, with reflective melodies, maloya is somewhat like New Orleans blues. Said to be born from the complaints of slaves around the fire, it was considered a political threat and banned by the colonial administration until the 1980s. But since then, this musical style has been recognised as one of the two main local genres.

The second genre is séga, a more joyful two-beat rhythm, which usually expresses love. Many Réunionnais artists create their work using these roots, mixing the two with wider musical genres.

Among the artists who have contributed to Réunionnais music are Ziskakan, Baster, Danyel Waro, Ousanousava, Davy Sicard, Alain Peters... They generally sing in Réunionnais Creole.

🍽 WHERE TO EAT IN ST-PIERRE

Chez Philippe
A wooden house across the beachfront, renowned for its 'American' sandwiches. €

Guinguette Aux Gens Heureux
A discreet place in the style of a cabaret bar, serving French dishes near Rivière d'Abord. €

La Terrasse
A restaurant with a boho look, with a view over the beach and the banyans of Terre-Sainte. €€

WHY I LOVE ST-PIERRE

Fabienne Fong Yan, *writer*

I was born in the North, but I spent most of my weekends in St-Pierre as a child. For the Réunion-born and raised, North and South are like two different countries. It may be only one hour-drive away, but the vibe is totally different. Even our Creoles sound different!

So to me, St-Pierre has always been a city made for the holiday. First because of the drive along the whole west coast between mountain and ocean, then because of sunsets on the beach, ice creams on the seashore, and late walks on the jetty to listen to the sea rolling...It's always hard to leave when I come back.

For Evening Owls
GRAB A SANDWICH ON THE SEAFRONT

Along the beach is where the evening activity takes place in St-Pierre. All year long, food trucks and seaside restaurants serve French fries and sandwiches to passersby and late swimmers. The 'American' sandwich, supposedly a Réunionnais creation, is said to have been invented on St-Pierre's seafront – although it's likely many food trucks in Réunion claim the same story.

Among locals' favourites is the *Americain Bouchons*: a baguette with chicken or pork dumplings (inherited from a Chinese recipe now totally integrated into Réunionnais cuisine) with fries and grated cheese. You'll have a wide choice of sauces but a recommended one is *piment siave* (chilli and soy sauce).

Under the Banyan Trees
AN OLD FISHERMEN'S VILLAGE

The village of **Terre-Sainte** is becoming a trendy district of St-Pierre, with more and more tourist accommodation and even a few concept stores. The winding narrow streets and small houses built almost on top of one another, with their hidden terraces and balconies, offer some picturesque corners. It's very popular among tourists for the calmness and immediate proximity of Terre-Sainte beach, although this is much smaller than the main one.

From the fishermen's time remain the **Croix des Pêcheurs**, a tiny chapel lost in the labyrinth of houses, and the traditional canoes pulled under the old banyan trees bordering the beach. In the afternoon, locals come to have a chat in the shadow of these centenary trees and their impressive root network.

Banyans can be admired in various locations on the island (one of them in Le Port was ranked second at the 'Most Beautiful Tree in France' contest). But they are particularly charming in Terre-Sainte, looming over a small white sand beach, with the silhouette of the harbour's jetty in the background. This tree is a symbol of strength and longevity for the Indian community, and is believed to bear all sorts of magical powers.

GETTING AROUND

Avoid driving in the city centre as it becomes easily congested, especially near the beachfront at night and because of the many one-way streets. It's also not easy to park here. The roads leading into the city are congested most of the day, but avoid rush hour in particular.

St-Pierre's city centre is well-connected by bus to its various districts, including Terre-Sainte and Grand Bois. So if you're staying in St-Pierre, it is easy to get around. But note that buses are much slower than cars and they can't always be relied on.

Beyond St-Pierre

From L'Étang-Salé up to the remote heights of St-Joseph, the area beyond St-Pierre to the south impresses with its diverse landscapes.

The area beyond St-Pierre to Les Avirons is mostly urbanised, marked by agriculture and the heritage of sugar-cane industry, and the landscape starts to change as soon as you pass Grand Bois, towards the south. The coastline becomes more rugged and the ocean stronger. No more lagoon: the broken volcanic coast meets the waves in a rough encounter under the *vacoa* (screw pine) trees. Only a few natural sea ponds are scattered along the coast from Grand Anse to St-Philippe as you approach the part of the island that is formed by the latest volcanic eruptions. More deeply sunk in nature, at the gates of the volcano, spreads the well-named Wild South.

TOP TIP

Past St-Pierre, the roads become more winding. You'll need a car and time to discover all the hidden spots in the Wild South.

Cascade de Grand Galet, St-Joseph (p172)

RÉUNION — THE GUIDE

≈ A LOVE-HATE RELATIONSHIP WITH THE OCEAN

The Réunionnais have long been scared of the power of the ocean and regard their coasts in awe. Apart from high-sea fishing or the occasional coastal rod-fishing, nautical activities were not that developed on the island until recently. Réunionnais historically trust the mountains more than the ocean: haven't they sheltered and brought protection to people running away from slavery?

But there is also a geological explanation. The seafloor drops abruptly very close to the shore, leaving little space for safe human activities. However, with the growing popularity of surfing and other sports, more and more locals are daring to enjoy the sea differently today.

Le Gouffre de l'Étang-Salé

From the Blower to the Devil's Tip

CYCLE DOWN THE SOUTHWEST COAST

In the southwest, the sea rushes towards the coast into a series of volcanic pits and abysses, transforming them into *souffleurs*. The most popular one, in St-Leu, can be exceptional, especially in winter. Avoid swimming or going near the ocean in case of strong wind: the waves can be treacherous. They have taken more than one life along these shores – hence the scary place names, such as the Abyss and Tip of the Devil.

A path, popular among cyclists despite the absence of shade, follows the coastline down the black-sand Plage de l'Étang-Salé. It continues down to **Le Gouffre de l'Étang-Salé**, one of the largest basalt pits. Now arranged as a viewpoint, this is a safe place to experience the powerful battling sea. A few metres down, a hidden pond continues to attract young swimmers regardless of the danger of the waves.

If you're not into cycling, Ze Trott Run offers electric scooters for rent and guided tours as an alternative.

🍴 WHERE TO EAT IN THE SOUTHWEST

Le P'tit Resto
In the centre of Les Avirons, French-Creole cuisine is served in a vintage traditional house. €

Le Nomeolvides
A refreshing break in St-Louis, under a covered terrace, with elaborate French dishes. €€

Restaurant de la Plage
On the St-Louis seafront, a hidden Creole restaurant, with a hall opening on the ocean. €

Gentle Giants

FEED GIANT TORTOISES

In the heights of **Les Avirons**, an old schoolmaster with a passion for tortoises has created a park to take care of them on his own lands, **Le Jardin des Tortues**. In the garden with unexpectedly splendid views over the southwest coast, a dozen species (land tortoises and water turtles) are cared for.

It all started when a few of them were rescued from animal trafficking. The place is now a protection centre and a small park where you can see the tortoises at close quarters and even feed the giant ones yourself. Never stand in front of them, and watch your fingers! Expert guides stay in the pen to teach you how to interact with these gentle, yet powerful, giants.

Reach for the Stars

NIGHT AND DAY IN LES MAKES

At about 1km high, with little light and atmospheric pollution, the small village of **Les Makes** above St-Louis is a perfect stargazing spot. That's why after the passing of Halley's Comet in 1986, a group of enthusiasts set up the Observatoire

Aldabra giant tortoise

FLY AWAY ULTRALIGHT

This is another way to reach for the sky, and see Réunion's incredible slopes from above.

From Pierrefonds airport, board a microlight aircraft and fly over the western lagoons, the Cirques and even the volcano (check if the company is authorised to fly over the zone beforehand).

It is an incredible feeling to be close to mountain summits and edges...in an aircraft almost all to yourself, next to your pilot instructor. You can even take your first flight as a pilot in Réunion if the company or school offers this.

Ask for information at the South Tourist Office or Pierrefonds airport, where staff can recommend ULM providers and schools.

ORIGINAL PLACES TO SLEEP

Les Bungalows des Makes
Four bungalows and a bubble are available at this glamping site, five minutes from the observatory. €€

Entre 2 Songes
Sleep under the trees in your tent, or literally in the trees, in perched treehouses! €

Îlet Boulon
In Bras de la Plaine, this hidden guesthouse is accessible only by hiking or by helicopter. €

SHAPED BY SUGAR

St-Louis has been shaped by the sugar industry. With one of the only two active sugar factories remaining on the island (Sucrerie du Gol), it has become a town with an important group of 'Malbars': Tamil families mainly descending from indentured workers who were brought here from India to work in sugar-cane fields in the second half of the 19th century.

The community settled, building temples and perpetuating their traditions. In January/February, the **Cavadee** festival takes place in the streets of St-Louis, along with fire-walking ceremonies at some temples to honour the Hindu goddess Pandialé. The **House of India**, a famous ashram belonging to the guru Amma, is also based near the sugar-cane factory.

Astronomique at the heart of the mountains to observe the formidable show of constellations.

Today, during open nights, the observatory team invites the public to discover the southern hemisphere constellations and learn about the principles of astronomy. Several times a month, through gigantic telescopes, you can see various star formations and even the moon at close quarters. Book way in advance on the observatory's website to take part in an open night (in French only). Alternatively, the company Makes Astro also offers stargazing nights, sometimes at hotels or guesthouses in the west or the south. Check online for events.

Many travellers spend the night in the village after a night of stargazing, as Les Makes also offers a few interesting daytime activities: take a walk on the botanical path of Bon Accueil forest or hike up to the spectacular viewpoint at La Fenêtre, with an amazing panorama over the Cirque de Cilaos. Tree-climbers will enjoy spending an afternoon at Makes Aventures park, which has no less than seven different circuits up in a high cryptomeria forest.

Art on Coffee Grounds

A MUSEUM ON AN OLD COFFEE ESTATE

In the heights of **St-Louis**, the stables of the former Maison Rouge estate host the **Musée des Arts Décoratifs de l'Océan Indien** (Museum of Decorative Arts of the Indian Ocean). Parts of the collection are shown to the public every year through thematic exhibitions. Their objective is to shed light on arts and cultures of the historic communities who have lived in and around Réunion.

The place can be visited. It dates back to the 18th century, when coffee was the main culture on the island. Although the master house is yet to be renovated, it is one of the last remaining estates of that time. Behind the museum's terrace, you can still see the *argamasses*, flat areas where coffee beans used to dry in the sun.

> ### FOR CREOLE HOUSES LOVERS
>
> The village of **Hell-Bourg** (p187) in Salazie is another beloved stop to admire the traditional architecture of mountain village houses, often concealed behind luxuriant tropical gardens.

WHERE TO HIKE IN THE SOUTH

Entre-Deux's Stone Arch
Get a glimpse of Bras de la Plaine's surprising basalt formation. Avoid after heavy rains.

Camp Dimitile via Boeuf-La Chapelle
Reach one of Dimitile's viewpoints over Cilaos. The former base camp of runaway slaves is nearby.

Bras de Pontho
A hike in a riverbed with impressive basalt rock formations. Avoid after heavy rains.

Entre-Deux

The Village of Choka

CREOLE LIFESTYLE AND HERITAGE IN ENTRE-DEUX

In the heights of St-Pierre, dozens of Creole houses were preserved thanks to the remote location of their village. The peaceful, traditional character of **Entre-Deux** is noticeable from the first houses you see, with their walls covered by shingles and colourful shutters.

Surrounded by mountains and in the shade of longan trees, the small centre seems to be frozen in time. Yet, tourists in search of authenticity and nostalgic locals like to drive to the village at weekends. A guided tour of the houses, organised by the Entre-Deux Tourist Office, takes you through architectural anecdotes. You can also ask for a map of the houses for a self-guided visit.

The village hosts the **Fête du Choca** every July. The *choka* tree is an agave species. Many grow on mountainsides across the island. The blue *choka* used to be woven into ropes, and the fruit used for cooking. This know-how has been disappearing and is now considered a part of Réunionnais heritage.

A TIME MACHINE

On the grounds of a former coffee estate dating from 1802, the **Vieux Domaine** was rehabilitated by a local association. It's open to visitors who are curious to discover what life used to be like in 19th-century Réunion. You'll be moved by the village where families of indentured workers from Malagasy used to live when their workforce was needed in coffee plantations, and then sugar-cane fields.

It's a visit back in time, during which you can discover old-time occupations and tools. With the guided tour (in French), you can also see a vast orchard filled with local species used by the *tisaneur*, the traditional plant healer present in most Creole communities at the time.

WHERE TO EAT IN THE SOUTH

L'Arbre à Palabres
This gastronomic restaurant in Entre-Deux knows how to pair Creole food and good wine. €€

L'Ambéric
At the heart of a tropical garden, this restaurant serves traditional, sometimes rare, Creole dishes. €€

Chez Ti Fred
In Petite-Île, this family canteen serves traditional dishes in a simple, somewhat old-style atmosphere. €

A FORGOTTEN BEAN

In 1711, an Arabica coffee bean, of the Laurina variety, was discovered in Réunion. Bourbon Pointu is a natural mutation of the Arabic coffee plant: its beans are slightly more pointed than the classic Bourbon variety, hence the name.

As coffee culture declined on the island and was completely replaced by sugar cane, this variety remained under the radar for decades. It was rediscovered by visitors from a Japanese coffee company traveling to Réunion in 1999. Their excitement led a few local producers to work again with this bean to create a luxury product. Today, Bourbon Pointu is one of the most expensive and rarest coffees in the world.

Back to the History of Slavery

A MOUNTAIN CAMP OF RUNAWAY SLAVES

After the period of slavery in Réunion came the period of *marronage*, when enslaved people fled their masters' properties to escape from their condition. The recreated **Camp Dimitile**, at the top of Le Dimitile mountain, aims to remind visitor of the time when *marrons* (runaway slaves) hid in the mountains to escape slave hunters.

The local association Capitaine Dimitile pays a tribute here to the former runaway chief Dimitile (in Malagasy, 'Watchman of the South') who led dozens of people and established survival plans at this base camp. Today, visitors can see reconstructed wooden sheds and picture how the runaways organised their lives so they were ready to flee again at any time.

A very moving historic place, the camp is reachable after a two-hour hike from Entre-Deux, or by booking a 4x4 through the South Tourist Office. At the top, a viewpoint offers impressive panoramas over Cilaos.

Hanging lobster claw, Domaine du Café Grillé

TASTY VISITS

Sucrerie du Gol
Visits to this sugar factory are only possible July to December. Tasting sessions are at the shop.

La Saga du Rhum
On the historic site of the Isautier distillery, this museum is dedicated to the rum industry.

The Bean-to-Bar Factory
In Grand Bois, this young chocolate factory sells its locally made products under 'Les Cabosses Ailées'.

History Told by Trees
VISIT AN ETHNOBOTANICAL GARDEN

The **Domaine du Café Grillé** will appeal to those who are eager to learn more about Réunionnais flora. Surprisingly located in the middle of an industrial zone in **Pierrefonds**, it's a green oasis with endemic, indigenous and exotic species. Although the 'grilled coffee' reference in the name doesn't reflect what's in the garden (there are not many coffee trees around), a tour guide will take you through the history of Réunion via more than ten different areas with decorative and fragrant plants, local bush, palm trees and a few emblematic species of the island such as flamboyant, kapok, papaya and tamarind trees. Self-guided tours are also possible. Despite not seeing coffee fields, coffee enthusiasts can taste Bourbon Pointu coffee, which is endemic to Réunion.

A Creative Sanctuary
CONTEMPORARY ART IN AN OPEN-AIR MUSEUM

In the residential neighbourhood of **Le Tampon** lies a fantastic garden paved with contemporary sculptures. The LAC or Lieu d'Art Contemporain (Place of Contemporary Art) was designed and created by the artist Vincent Mengin-Lecreulx and his wife Roselyne. For almost forty years, they have invited dozens of international contemporary artists to exhibit here, from street artist JonOne to Nils Udo. Painters, photographers and sculptors have all gathered and left their mark in this open-air museum, making it a cultural and art sanctuary that is renowned beyond the island's boundaries.

The garden is a park of sculptures – the most impressive piece is a gigantic life-size Noah's Ark covered in black matter. Don't miss the Mengin Chapel, an excellent art gallery where visitors are shown into a parallel universe made of collages, surrealist photographs and sculptures, all of which tell intimate stories of the artists who have worked in residence here.

Visits are possible only by reservation, in French, for groups of eight minimum.

Haven by the Shore
THE CHARMING PARADISE OF MANAPANY-LES-BAINS

Manapany-les-Bains is a favourite spot of travellers and locals alike, with its natural pool and arches of basalt. Originally, it was a docking station for canoes restocking the ships in the bay with merchandise from the southern

---

TEATIME IN THE HEIGHTS

It's a winding road to Grand Coude, the last village at the end of a land strip caught in the middle of two vertiginous valleys. The narrowest part of the road is less than 100m wide. With clear skies, the panorama on either side is breathtaking.

At the edge of a humid forest, you will find Le Labyrinthe En-Champ-Thé (a pun meaning 'the enchanted labyrinth'). This is the only tea plantation in Réunion. Take a guided tour (in French only) to learn more about tea on the island. They produce a range of teas, some paired with other local plants such as geranium rosat, which is also cultivated on the property.

WHERE TO STAY NEAR ST-JOSEPH

Les Grands Monts
This guesthouse with a pool and covered terrace has kept an old-style charm. €€

L'Arbre de Vie
A welcoming guesthouse in Vincendo, and cosy base for the Wild South. Don't miss the homemade breakfast. €

Terre Rouge
An original B&B concept with open bungalows (literally) looking at the property's lush garden. €€

factories. Its transformation into a natural swimming pool has contributed to the popularity of the little cove.

Although this spot is covered by nature – so much so that it's become the home of the endemic Green Gecko of Manapany – remains of its industrial past, such as the lime kiln, are still visible.

Walk from the tourist office based near Grand Cap, at the easternmost tip of the cove, to see both the ancient kiln's tower and the dark rock formations plunging into the ocean. Do so with care as the waves can be unexpectedly strong and high.

On the Wet Rocks
RÉUNION'S MOST PHOTOGENIC WATERFALL

The narrow road to the spectacular **Cascade de Grand Galet** – often congested due to the site's popularity – paves the way to a postcard landscape. Born from the resurgence of underground water, an ensemble of waterfalls rushes down a circular cliff to drop into a vast pond below.

Along the steep road, which is accessible by foot once you've parked your car a few metres further down, a couple of viewpoints have been set up so you can admire the show. Although many people look for paths downstream to reach the pond, note that it's dangerous to swim below the waterfalls.

A Tour of Flavours & Spices
SMALL AGRICULTURAL MUSEUMS AND GARDENS

With high humidity and volcanic soils, the heights of **St-Joseph** and **St-Philippe** provide fertile lands for produce to flourish: turmeric, geranium, vanilla, vetiver...these renowned local products all grow well in the area. If you're up for a rural tour and are looking for typical Réunionnais products, several places will be of interest. Call for opening and visiting times (it's preferable to speak French for guided tours).

Look for the **House of Turmeric**, a tiny museum where you can learn more about this rhizome, and **Far Far de Bézaves**, a farm where you can find out about planting and harvesting vetiver. Plant connoisseurs will love visiting **Le Jardin des Parfums**

Geranium

A MINI-GUIDE TO LOCAL FRAGRANCES

Geranium Rosat
One of four varieties of geranium on the island. Its essence is extracted from the leaves and used in pastries or perfumery.

Vetiver
Its long leaves hide a fragrant root, from which a subtle essence is extracted and used in perfumes. Its leaves can be woven into traditional hats.

Faham
An orchid endemic to the Mascarene Islands. Its use in *rhums arrangés* (flavoured rums) has resurfaced in recent years.

Turmeric
Falsely called 'safran' by locals, it has nothing to do with actual saffron. Ground in a powder, this orange rhizome is commonly used to perfume rice or sauces.

WHERE TO EAT WITH A VIEW

Le Nirvana
Traditional dishes served on a hidden terrace overlooking the small creek of La Marine Langevin. €

Le Cap Méchant
The very first restaurant of a renowned chain, near the spectacular site with the same name. €

Les Embruns du Baril
Ask for a table on the terrace by the sea at Côté Mer, the hotel's restaurant. €€

et des Épices (Garden of Perfumes and Spices), where a thousand plant species grow freely. Note that there are no information boards in the garden, which adds to the wildness of the place.

An Endemic Tree Cathedral

THROUGH A PROTECTED PRIMARY FOREST

A nature reserve, **Forêt de Mare Longue** (St-Philippe) is a vestige of the initial tropical forest present on the island at low altitude. Growing on lava soil, it's home to dozens of endemic plant species, but is in danger of extinction as the ecosystem which is necessary to its development has been slowly disappearing. To fight for its preservation, Mare Longue has become one of the most researched places in Réunion.

A botanical path with informative panels guides the hiker through this cathedral of trees, which are frozen in time. On a two-hour walk, an attentive eye will detect trees that have been part of the Réunionnais pharmacopoeia and cuisine for centuries.

Walk on Lava Sculptures

ON A 40-YEAR-OLD LAVA FLOW

In June 1986, a tremendous volcanic eruption at **Piton de la Fournaise** sent huge lava flows down the Takamaka slope in the southeast. In only a few hours, the lava reached and crossed the N2 road. As a result, the island expanded by 30 sq km into the ocean, engulfing trees and other rock layers on its journey, and creating the Pointe de la Table site.

The solidification of burning lava when it made contact with the sea created fantastic volcanic sculptures and stone arches, which are now beaten by the southern waves. From Puits Arabe to Pointe de la Table, a path was set up with informative panels to explain the origin of these curious dark formations, sculpted by the encounter of fire, air and water.

Check if the discovery path is open either with the tourist office or when you get there, as there have been unexpected closures recently. Wear hiking boots, as the terrain can be sharp and irregular.

FANTASTIC FILMS IN THE WILD

Réunion is a land of legends and superstitions, it makes perfect sense that it would hold a festival of fantastic cinema. What is surprising, though, is the choice of location: not the capital or one of the major cities. The festival takes place in the town of St-Philippe, deep in the Wild South.

With the objective to show films that would be difficult to watch elsewhere because of their unconventionality, the **MEME PAS PEUR** (Not Even Scared) festival presents an international selection of short and long films every February in a local cinema.

GETTING AROUND

A car is recommended to make the most of the south, and is absolutely necessary in the Wild South area. To navigate the area without getting too lost along winding roads, look carefully at signs and online maps, but you shouldn't trust the latter entirely. Roads and streets change regularly and may be mapped differently online, or not mapped at all.

Locals drive fast on these roads they know well, so be extra careful when going up narrow roads in the heights, especially in rainy weather.

Avoid getting close to the ocean in case of tropical storms or strong winds, especially near volcanic rock formations, jetties and hidden pools. Ocean waves can swell briskly and surprise hikers and swimmers. This safety recommendation should be followed at all times.

ROAD TRIP

The Road to the Wild South

This road trip takes you through a succession of popular and lesser-known viewpoints along the shore. Although the road follows the coast, only side tracks lead to the discovery of coves and panoramic sights over the ocean. The route can be driven in only 30 minutes from Grand Anse to Le Baril, but it's way more enjoyable to spread the journey over two days to soak in the special atmosphere of the Wild South's nature.

1 Grand Anse

Begin with the exceptional white-sand Plage de Grand Anse, although the strong tide makes it dangerous to swim here. Prepare a picnic to enjoy in the shade of coconut trees. Climb up to Piton Grand Anse for a panoramic view: a path starts at the eastern end of the beach.

The Drive: Take road D30 towards St-Joseph and park after Ravine Petite-Île bridge.

2 Petite-Île Viewpoint

This 150m-long rock emerging 30m above the ocean is home to a few indigenous birds only. On the track though the fields, turn right as soon as you can (the viewpoint sign is difficult to see). Head towards the ocean. Don't cross private properties.

The Drive: From D30, head back to the main road (N2) and to St-Joseph city centre. Find a parking spot around the church.

3 St-Joseph

The town was founded by a botanist, to encourage the poorest settlers to live off the culture of spices. Walk from the church to the running track and head to Piton Babet's viewpoint, from where you can enjoy panoramic views. Have lunch at gourmet restaurant Le Ti Comptoir.

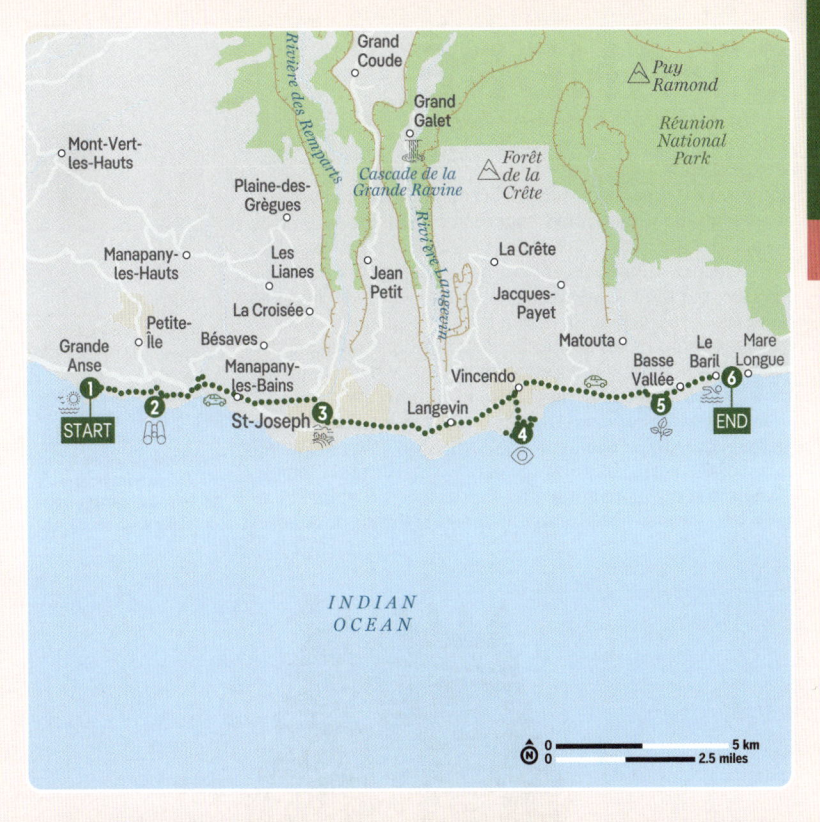

The Drive: Leave St-Joseph and head in the direction of St-Philippe. Drive to Vincendo and follow the 'La Marine' road signs.

4 Sentier Cap Jaune

The path to reach Cap Jaune is about one hour long following the coastline. This surprising orange-yellowish geological curiosity results from the formation of volcanic glass inside layers of lava when magma comes into contact with the cold sea and cools rapidly. Beware of the very steep path going down the cliff.

The Drive: Take the N2 towards St-Philippe. Follow the signs to Cap Méchant and park near the restaurant.

5 Cap Méchant

This cape owes its name to the crashing waves battling its shore. Turn right towards the sea to reach it. Another path goes through a forest of vacoa (screw pine) trees. At the end, you'll reach a beautiful view over a natural stone arch in the ocean.

The Drive: Back on the N2 road towards St-Philippe, drive past the old sugar-cane weighing scale. Your final stop is at the Baril-les-Bains car park.

6 Le Baril

Reopened in 2022, this well-loved swimming pool made headlines due to its construction directly on the volcanic shore, facing the ocean – note that it may be closed during rough seas. End this trip with a quick walk to the Souffleur d'Arbonne stone arch, which spouts vertical water jets when winds are strong.

ST-ANDRÉ

A city with a strong agricultural heritage, St-André has been shaped by the 19th-century sugar-cane industry. From this period, the still-active Sucrerie de Bois-Rouge sugar-cane factory remains, and there is also a large community descending from the Indian indentured labourers who were brought from India to work in the sugar-cane fields. Hindu celebrations are more frequent and important in St-André and its surroundings than in the rest of the island, which has made the city a cultural heart for the Tamil community.

On the eastern coast, St-André is the largest residential town as well as an active economic city, benefiting from the dynamism of the north. It is also the gateway to the more remote – and some say more authentic – eastern coast, with waterfalls, hikes, water-based activities, and the Cirque de Salazie.

TOP TIP

St-André and the eastern coast are more difficult to 'crack' on your own. With more outdoor activities and cultural attractions than the rest of the island, it's easier to discover with local guides or friends who can share stories and lesser-known spots with you.

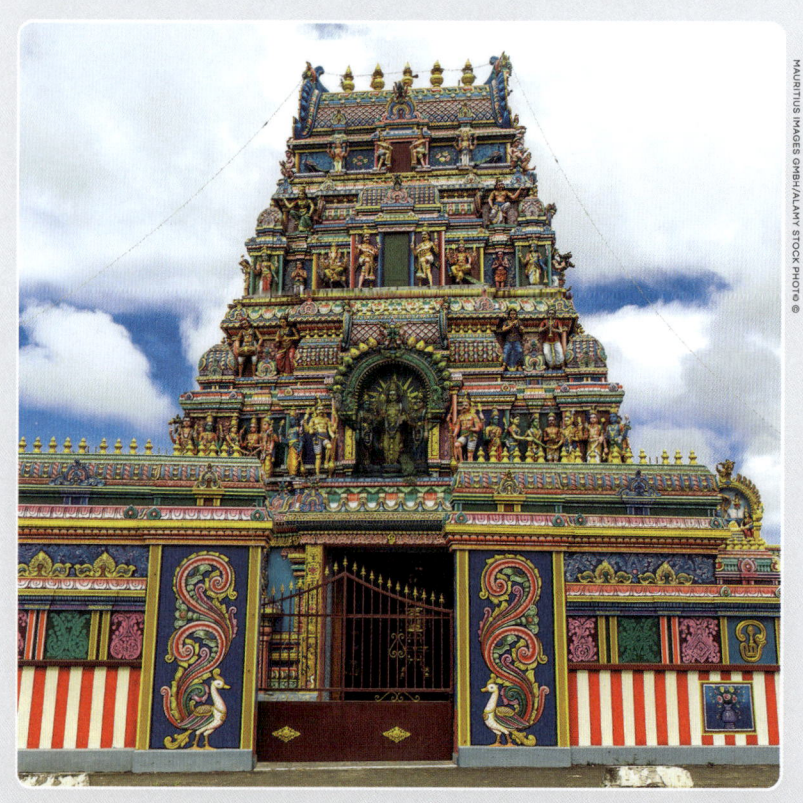

Temple du Petit Bazar

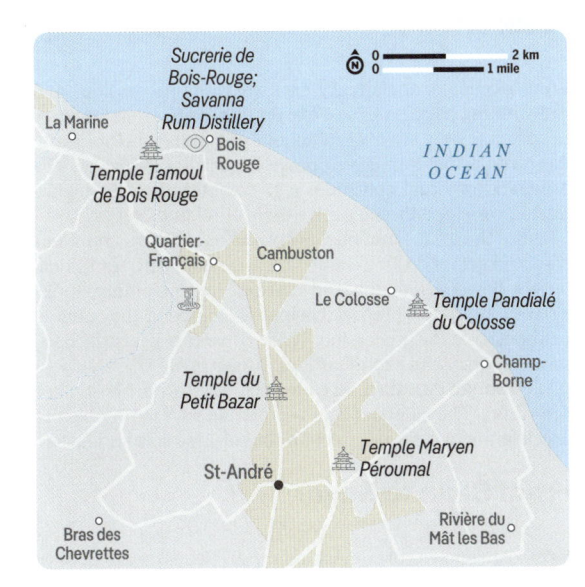

A City of Light & Fire

CELEBRATE DIWALI WITH THE TAMILS

Diwali or Dipavali, the Festival of Light, is one of the most important religious celebrations in the Indian world, and for the Tamil diaspora in Réunion. It generally takes place between the end of October and mid-November, and symbolises the triumph of light over darkness...of good over evil.

For several days every year, a festival is organised in St-André and all are welcome to come and learn more about Indian culture and traditions through shows and workshops – dancers, fire artists, musicians and craftsmen gather in a 'Tamil village' that is set up for the occasion. Fireworks and an illuminated parade are usually the highlight of the celebration, filling the streets with light!

The programme of festivities is usually available online on the tourist office website.

REMARKABLE HINDU TEMPLES

Many temples are private, but some welcome visitors. Be discreet and respectful when entering religious places.

Temple Maryen Péroumal
One of the rare temples you can visit with a guide. Book through the East Tourist Office.

Temple du Petit Bazar
Its front is richly decorated with the Hindu pantheon. Visits are not allowed. Temple Pandialé du Colosse Only for the community, except during the Pandialé festival when hundreds of visitors come for the fire-walking.

Temple Tamoul de Bois Rouge
Near the sugar factory, this beautiful temple is closed to the public, but some ceremonies welcome visitors.

WHERE TO EAT IN ST-ANDRÉ

Velli
Just behind Le Colosse. Serves traditional dishes, sometimes with unusual ingredient combinations. €

La Terrasse Kréol
A simple yet welcoming restaurant serving Creole dishes. Across from Musée Dan Tan Lontan. €

Jam Rose
On the road to Salazie, this traditional Creole restaurant serves dishes cooked over the wood fire. €

SUGAR ELECTRICITY

'Nothing is wasted in sugar cane!' That's what people say when they talk about the advantages of sugar production from the cane.

Indeed, a sugar cane doesn't produce only sugar. When the canes are first brought in, they are pressed for juice extraction. The dry stems are then put in boilers to produce electricity, and this energy is used by the factory.

The extracted juice is heated and centrifuged several times to encourage the creation of sugar crystals. The last step is to transfer the treacle to the rum distillery where it is fermented to produce industrial rum.

At the end of the process, all parts of the sugar cane have been used – nothing was wasted indeed!

Walk on Fire

WATCH THE PANDIALÉ FIRE-WALKS

From December to January each year, the processions and fire-walking rituals of the **Fête de Pandialé** are impressive to witness. They are held in honour of Pandial, a Hindu goddess who walked on fire to prove her faith and loyalty. The fire-walking ritual concludes a 17-day period of abstinence during which penitents purify their mind and bodies.

Before the final ceremony, people who follow this religious tradition get ready for a colourful procession, with traditional outfits, flower art, drums and chariots. In front of the temple, a *tikouli* (firepit) is prepared, which is crossed by the barefoot penitent after the procession. These rituals are generally open to the public, who should attend respectfully.

The **Temple Pandialé du Colosse** in Saint-André hosts such fire-walks. The calendar and venues can vary, so it's best to check online, ask locals...or enjoy the surprise on your journey.

From Cane to Sugar

SUGAR-CANE INDUSTRY IN A WORKING FACTORY

Sugar-cane fields cover most mountain slopes on the eastern coast. From July to December, early birds may see cane-cutters working in the fields from 5am, before the midday heat. About 6,000 manual workers cut canes in the fields in Réunion.

It may not look like it at first, considering only two sugar factories remain today – out of the 200 in the 19th century – but this is still a prominent sector in the island's economy. And the process also leads to electricity production and rum distillation. Everything is transformed by a sugar cane!

During the harvest season, book a guided tour of the **Sucrerie de Bois-Rouge** and experience the transformation of canes into crystal sugar from the inside, through a labyrinth of chimneys and tanks. Adjacent to the factory, the **Savanna rum distillery** is open all year long to visitors, who can taste local rum, fresh from the barrel. Contact the Tafia & Galabé shop to book your visit.

MORE ABOUT SUGAR-CANE HISTORY

In a former factory in the heights of St-Leu, the **Stella Matutina museum** (p158) holds 3,700 sq m of installations and exhibits to further explore the history of cane and sugar.

GETTING AROUND

It's easy to drive around St-André, which is a rather small city. It is well connected to both the north and the east by the main road network, and buses run regularly between the main cities. However, you will definitely need a car to make the most of the smaller roads in the heights around the city. The road to Salazie starts in St-André.

Beyond St-André

Where water meets fire: beyond St-André, the rainiest coast turns into volcanic lands as you progress south.

More rural and humid, with lush vegetation but no beaches, the area beyond St-André to the east is called 'the coast in the wind'. This part of the island tends to be overlooked by travellers, maybe because its sights are less accessible and not often talked about compared to other areas on the island. But it is also more preserved and calmer. From St-André to Ste-Rose, at the gates of Grand Brûlé's volcanic lands where eruptions continue to expand the island, the eastern coast abounds with natural sights. With constant wet weather, it's a fertile country – and the water tank of the island – where everything grows easily. It's also a real paradise for water and outdoor sports enthusiasts!

TOP TIP

Be prepared to drive in the rain and don't forget your raincoat as the weather can change rapidly.

St-Benoit (p181)

Bassin La Paix

The Real Bourbon Vanilla
A TOUR OF VANILLA PRODUCERS

It takes almost two years for a vanilla pod to reach market stalls after the flower is fertilised. From harvesting the vines to monitoring the beans for signs of rotting before they're put out to dry, they are then matured for several months, and sorted by size – everything must be done by hand.

First, go for a vanilla tour at the **Plantation de Vanille Roulof** in St-André to see the rows of vanilla vines, and learn about the different production steps. Continue with a bigger spot, **ProVanille**, the Cooperative of Vanilla Producers in **Bras-Panon**, about 4km south of St-André. Note that there are more plantations located further east, down to St-Philippe, due to ideal weather conditions in the area.

The Secrets of Creole Cooks
INSIDE TRADITIONAL RÉUNIONNAIS KITCHENS

You are welcomed by a *risofé* (heated rice) traditional breakfast, as soon as you arrive at Philippe Morel's, in the heights

---

THE STORY OF EDMOND ALBIUS

Vanilla was already used by the Aztecs before the conquistadors came to South America. But it was introduced in the Mascarene Islands in the 18th century, with hopes of cultivating the fragrant spice. However, none of the plants bloomed, as its natural fertilisers were absent.

In 1841, Edmond Albius, a 12-year-old Réunionnais slave, discovered how to fertilise the vanilla flower by hand pollination. Adopted by botanist Fereol Bellier Beaumont, he had been assisting his master in his research. With his young sense of observation and astuteness, the young boy invented the artificial process that would revolutionise vanilla culture and lead to its worldwide industrialisation.

WHERE TO EAT AROUND ST-BENOÎT

Ferme-Auberge d'Eva Hannibal
The mother of vanilla duck! Eva's table is constantly booked because of her special dish. €

Les Letchis
Enjoy fresh products and traditional cuisine on a terrace by the river, under the lychee trees. €€

Le Saint-Benoît
Above the centre's covered market, this comfortable restaurant offers Creole and French cuisine. €€

of **St-Benoît**. In his outdoor kitchen, the *caris* have been simmering slowly in cast-iron pots. Don't worry, you will get to taste everything after a tour of his farm, during which he will tell you more about the close relationship the Réunionnais maintain with nature, and what old-time lifestyle is like. Monsieur Morel holds his workshops on weekends.

For a full cooking experience, starting from market shopping to putting the ingredients in the pot, go with Far Far Kréol. With Jacky, you will learn about local fruits and vegetables on the stalls, and discover the village of Bagatelle, in the middle of dense sugar-cane fields. Cook together and learn about all the secrets behind Reunion's Creole dishes and local cakes. Jacky holds workshops almost every day.

Both activities can be booked through the East Tourist Office. For a similar experience, look for La Sirandane, and La Ferme du Piton Rouge (this one is on the west coast).

Marine Sunrise

EARLY MORNING WITH THE FISHERMEN

It's a discreet little spot down the coast of St-Benoît where fishermen come and go all day long according to the time of the tides. The view over the roaming ocean at the small beach at **Pointe du Bourbier** (where swimming is not allowed), with the slopes of the volcano in the background, can be spectacular.

Early birds will love watching the sunrise at this oriental viewpoint under the *vacoa* (screw pine) trees. From there, when the tide is low, you can take a morning walk following the old train tracks which were in use until the 1960s, transporting sugar canes along the coast. Or else, drive back to one of the neighbouring cities to grab breakfast on market days: Thursdays in Bras-Panon, Fridays in St-André and Saturdays in St-Benoît.

Get Your Feet Wet

A HIKE BETWEEN WATERFALLS

Bassin La Paix & Bassin La Mer are among the most popular (and beautiful!) ponds in the east. The multiple rock columns around the ponds, formed by lava contraction, seem suspended in the air. They surround the water in the shape of a basalt amphitheatre, creating natural pools where swimming is possible when the water is calm.

LOCAL TIPS: WHAT TO DO IN THE EAST

Carole Hoareau
Multimedia creator of La Petite Créole *blog,* *@lapetitecreole.re*

Carole shares her top recommendations to get a taste of the east.

La Sirandane
Take a cooking class at La Sirandane – Daniel will show you the secrets behind Creole *caris*. After cooking and eating together, enjoy the pool!

Temple Maryen Péroumal
Take a guided tour of this familial temple – the guides are also believers, so it's a unique chance to learn about Tamil culture and Hindu traditions from them.

Salazie & La Rondavelle d'Adeline
Head to Salazie, the lush green northern Cirque. If it's not too late, grab a bite at La Rondavelle d'Adeline on your way.

WHERE TO STAY AROUND ST-BENOÎT

Poivre & Citronelle
In a lush tropical garden, this guesthouse offers a quiet break with pool and Jacuzzi. €€

Le Saint Alexandre
Just next to Grand Étang; a good base camp to navigate between the plains and the east. €

Diana Dea Lodge
This 5-star hotel offers luxurious rooms with a panorama over the ocean. €€€

PICNIC BY THE RIVER

Join Geoffrey, from Les Aventuriers de l'Est, for a hike that includes cultural discovery, adventures in nature and a tasty finale. Along Rivière des Marsouins, your guide will lead you through the lychee trees to reach Îlet Bethléem, a village with a strong religious presence, of which only ruins remains today.

The highlight of this family-friendly walk is local fruit and snacks by the river, where you can (re)discover the art of the Réunionnais picnic: a feast at the heart of nature! You may even be able to take a dive to complete the afternoon.

The walk to reach the ponds takes place among sugar-cane fields – there are occasionally a few roots to keep an eye out for (wear closed shoes), but overall it is easy. Watch out for the steep paths going down to the ponds, though.

The Power of Water

A ROAD TRIP TO THE WATER DAMS

This is one of the rainiest areas on the island, with an average of 1m of rainfall per year. It has become a power source: the **Takamaka** hydroelectric power plant provides electricity to the equivalent of 35,000 homes. The plant is located underground, and is therefore not visible. Two water dams process the water in the mountains, upstream of Rivière des Marsouins: Takamaka I and II.

The road leading to the Takamaka viewpoint over the first water dam (Barrage Gingembre) is a real journey through the island's lush nature. The power plant is built among a succession of abundant waterfalls that have become emblematic of the island – they repeatedly feature on tourist office posters. Some are visible on the difficult hike by the river, but the whole site can only be fully seen from the air. It's one of the highlights of helicopter trips!

Aquatic Fun

RIVER RAFTING AND CANYONING

With record rainfalls, the eastern part of the island is a paradise for those with an interest in river sports. If you're not afraid to get wet, board a rafting boat and head off for a sensational trip along Rivière des Marsouins or Rivière des Roches. If you'd rather give up your boat and slide on the rocks instead, opt for canyoning. Two ways to enjoy lush Réunionnais nature from a totally different perspective…and not for the faint-hearted!

Rando Aqua Réunion, specialising in water sports, offers half-day activities with a guide. Never practise these activities on your own in case of stormy weather.

Rafting, Rivière des Roches

PANORAMAS

Dioré Forest
After the Dioré picnic area, this viewpoint looks over Salazie and Piton des Neiges.

Belvédère de l'Eden
Overlooking former tea plantations, with fabulous views of the east coast. The path can be slippery.

Waterfall of the Dog
Visible only from the road. It's impossible to get to the bottom of this waterfall.

Papangue

Around a Volcanic Lake

GRAND ÉTANG BY FOOT OR ON HORSEBACK

The only mountain lake on the island lies 500m above sea level. Lava flow from an eruption 6000 years ago blocked the Bras d'Annette river and a lake formed. Grand Étang is now an accessible, quiet body of water entirely surrounded by emerald mountains. It's particularly appreciated by locals during weekends.

Although not suitable for swimming, it offers both easy and more challenging hikes near a picnic area. After a short 20-minute walk, you reach a panoramic viewpoint between tree ferns. The lake colour is a mesmerising deep blue on clear days. The water level, depending on the volume of recent rainfall, can vary from one season to the next.

Take the most popular path around the lake for a 2-hour-long walk, or alternatively, book a horse-riding tour with the nearby club, Ferme Equestre du Grand-Étang. Don't forget your bag if you are travelling from April to August, as you may be able to harvest some *goyaviers* (little red sour guavas), adored by the Réunionnais!

PAPANGUE: A CREOLE BIRD OF PREY

The only endemic bird of prey on the island, the *papangue* (Circus maillardi) can be seen over ravines, forests and water ponds, such as the Grand Étang mountain lake. It can reach a wingspan of 1.3m. For a long time before it became protected, the *papangue* was regularly poached. The estimated number of *papangues* today is between 100 and 200 couples, which makes it one of the rarest birds of prey in the world. The popular and recognisable *papangue is* often used as a symbol of the island by brands or individuals, as a token of Réunionnais identity.

OCEAN VIEWS

La Cayenne
A picnic spot under the *vacoa* trees, overlooking the roaming waves of the wild east.

Ste-Rose Marina
The small harbour in Ste-Rose is the starting point of the coastal Path of the Fishermen.

1977 Lava Flow
Beyond Notre-Dame-des-Laves, towards the ocean, stand on a legendary lava flow.

A VIRGIN TO SHELTER US ALL

In the beginning of the 20th century, a landowner established right on the volcano's slopes kept having his vanilla cultures destroyed by recurring eruptions. To try and prevent this from happening, he had a statue of the Virgin Mary erected.

Supposed to protect his fields, the Virgin with an Umbrella stood at the end of his plantations. Legend has it that lava crossed his lands but spared the Virgin.

Many still believe that the statue remained intact and survived all eruptions for a century. But the truth is it was moved several times, sometimes in extremis, as it was threatened too closely by the eruptions.

Now located near Notre-Dame-des-Laves, it is still a pilgrimage site for many Catholic believers.

Where the Ocean Meets Waterfalls

A ROMANTIC STOP AT ANSE DES CASCADES

There's something magical about this oceanic cove, overlooked by cliffs bordered by dozens of trickling waterfalls on one side and hundreds of palm trees on the other. Anse des Cascades, about 3km south of Ste-Rose, is like a hidden piece of paradise, marking the end – or the beginning – of volcanic lands.

Couples and families come to this tranquil spot for picnics in the shade of *vacoa* (screw pine) and palm trees, or under the kiosks lining the ocean. Stop here before entering the Grand Brûlé area, or after a drive across the lava slopes on Route des Laves.

A Pilgrimage Across Burnt Lands

DRIVE THROUGH SOLIDIFIED LAVA

You're walking on volcanic grounds. For hundreds of thousands of years, lava layers have shaped Réunion. The area called **Le Grand Brûlé** ('the great burnt land') refers to the part formed by the most recent eruptions, down the slopes of Piton de la Fournaise towards the ocean.

This zone accounts for the extraordinary power of the volcano: a blackened mountain made of visible lava flows, solidified year after year, on both sides of the road. Following some eruptions, vapours and gases can be seen coming from fumaroles on the burnt grounds. Here, nature commands and humans must adapt their way of life. Information plates with the dates of the eruptions are visible on the side of the road.

There's only one way through this fiery land: the N2 road between Piton Ste-Rose and St-Philippe, called the 'Lava Road'. It can be drowned in smoke during eruptions, or even completely cut off when lava bursts outside of the volcanic pen. Thankfully, this doesn't happen too often, considering the high volcanic activity of Piton de la Fournaise.

This eerie part of the island is full of legends and superstitions. Notre-Dame-des-Laves in Piton Ste-Rose, is a Catholic church revered for its supernatural force. In 1977, lava was heading straight towards the village and had already overflowed

Le Grand Brûlé

WHERE TO EAT NEAR THE LAVA ROAD

L'Anse des Cascades
Creole cuisine served at the heart of the magical site of the same name. €

L'Atelier du Palmiste Rouge
The core of red palm tree (a Réunionnais special) is the culinary speciality of this restaurant. €€

La Case Volcan
This traditional restaurant lets you try the dishes in small bites before you order. €

a part of it. But right in front of the church, the flow miraculously stopped, sparing the religious building. The dark rock wall is still visible in front of the church today.

Lava from the Inside

ONE OF THE WORLD'S YOUNGEST LAVA TUNNELS

In **Ste-Rose**, the walk to the entrance of the tunnel, a hole in the ground, is a chance to see how the first lichens, orchids and small trees grow on cold lava, years after an eruption. In a few minutes, you will be able to see their roots from down under.

The tunnel formed in 2004 is the most visited in the east, and is suitable for all ages from six years old. With a certified caving guide, you will observe unique lava formations, only visible in this kind of tunnel where lava has cooled down quickly. Such tunnels are formed when lava meets colder air. The surface of the flow solidifies into a crust while the burning core inside continues to run towards the ocean, thus forming a cavity.

It is definitely not advisable to enter lava tunnels on your own. Ask for experienced speleology guides at the South Tourist Office. Bazaltik Reunion works with English-speaking guides.

Caving, Ste-Rose

THE BEACH OF THE CENTURY

In April 2007, following several eruptions in previous months, the volcano showed seismic signs, alerting volcanologists that the upcoming eruption would be particularly intense.

On 2 April, a crack opened on the southeast side of the great slopes. The lava reached the ocean in less than twelve hours, blocked the N2 road, and a huge cloud of smoke rose in the sky. Unprecedented, this was the 'eruption of the century', the most intense eruption recorded on the island since it had been inhabited.

The small fishing village of Le Tremblet was evacuated and nearly destroyed. And a new beach, Le Tremblet, was born and became the youngest accessible beach on Earth.

GETTING AROUND

Although there are buses serving the eastern coast, this is not the most convenient way to get around. You will need a car to explore and reach the different points of interest, starts of hikes and spots for outdoor activities.

Windier and rainier than other areas of the island, the roads require more patience. Although it's easy overall to drive on the well-maintained N2 road, don't rely on GPS only for directions. It is smart to combine careful reading of road signs and online maps.

SALAZIE

The most accessible of the three Cirques, Salazie is also said to be greener, and more full of fruit and vegetables. The *chouchou* – a small waterlogged pear-shaped vegetable that's very loved by locals – has become its emblem! Abundant rainfall also makes this a waterfall haven, and the Voile de la Mariée (Bride's Veil) is one of the most famous waterfalls of the island.

Historically a refuge for people escaping slavery, like other Cirques, Salazie was only colonised by smaller landowners from the 1820s. Until the mid-19th century, it remained a popular holiday destination for people from the coast, who came for fresh air and to use the thermal baths.

It is now regularly visited both by travellers in search of peace in a preserved Creole village, and by hikers eager to reach deeper in the island. Salazie is a convenient gateway to exceptional hikes such as the Forêt de Bébour-Bélouve and the Trou de Fer.

TOP TIP

Spend at least a night in Hell-Bourg to make the most of your stay in Salazie. Get there early to enjoy the panoramas, as the mountain tops get cloudy from 9am. Always bring your umbrella and raincoat as the weather can turn quickly.

Creole house, Hell-Bourg

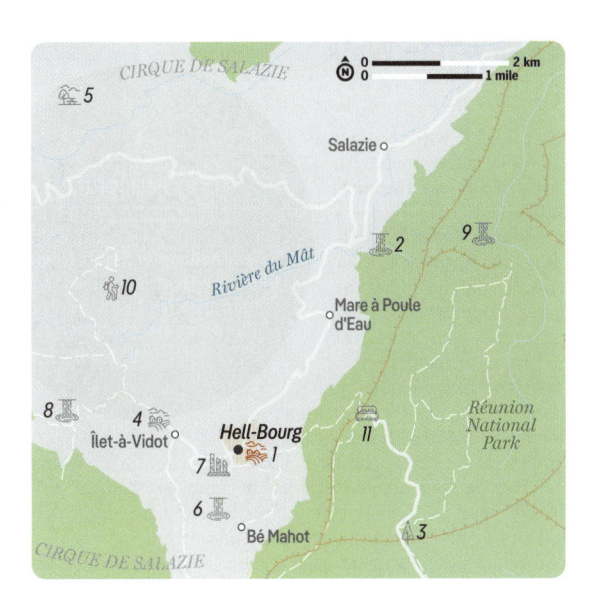

HIGHLIGHTS
1 Hell-Bourg

SIGHTS
2 Cascade du Voile de la Mariée (Bridal Veil Falls)
3 Forêt de Bélouve
4 Îlet-à-Vidot
see 1 Maison Folio
see 1 Maison Morange
5 Mare à Martin
6 The Virgin with her Feet in the Water
7 Thermal Baths
8 Trou Blanc
9 Trou de Fer

TOURS
10 Piton d'Anchaing

SLEEPING
11 Gîte de Bélouve

The Prettiest Houses of All

A TOUR OF HELL-BOURG'S CREOLE HOUSES

At the heart of Salazie, after a few winding road turns, you will reach one of the most beautiful villages in France. With some of the highest mountain peaks all around, almost hidden in the characteristic vegetation of the greenest Cirque, **Hell-Bourg** could have been forgotten. Yet, thanks to the devotion of a few inhabitants who couldn't give up the architectural heritage of their pretty mountain village, it made it to the top of the list of unmissable spots in Réunion in recent years.

Start your walking tour on the main street, from the tourist office, where you can either book a tour guide – it's preferable to book English tours in advance by phone or online – or ask for printed information about the village. Head to **Maison Morange**, where the panorama over the surrounding mountains is beautiful. After a visit to see the collection of musical instruments from the Indian Ocean displayed in the house, continue back on to the main street to see some of the private Creole houses, until you come to a small stairway on your left. Go up for a view over the village, before heading to **Maison Folio**, one of the loveliest houses in the village. With its small fountain and reading kiosk hidden behind a tropical garden, it's a great chance to see a Creole house at close quarters.

BEST PLACES TO EAT IN HELL-BOURG

Chez Alice
There's a rich choice of Creole *caris*, and this is also your chance to taste Hell-Bourg's trout: the local fish farm is only a few minutes away. €

Villa Marthe
The garden of this restaurant is so lush, it feels like having lunch under a canopy. Try *bol renversé royall*, a Chinese-inspired dish found only in Réunion. €€

Ti Chouchou
Under the covered terrace of this typical Creole house, sample *chouchou* – Salazie's emblematic vegetable – in all its forms! Try the delicious gratin. €

A Fairy-Tale Walk

A LEISURELY HIKE THROUGH THERMAL BATH REMAINS

It's a quick walk from the village's centre down to the ruins of the old **thermal baths**. Until 1948 the baths were eagerly used by well-off people wanting to take a break from the heat of the coast. After the passing of a strong tropical storm, they unfortunately collapsed.

The way to the current site is easy and has been well arranged down the cliff. In about ten minutes, you reach the ruins. Nature has taken over and it's become a charming spot covered in grass and flowers. You can figure out what used to be the main pools near a stream, which adds a fairytale-like atmosphere to the setting.

More athletic hikers can pass by the spot and continue on to take a loop through the forest, up to **Îlet-à-Vidot** and possibly to **Piton d'Anchaing** (1350m).

Sensational River

CANYONING DOWN TROU BLANC

Upstream from Rivière du Mât, the fast-flowing waters have carved an amazing site in the rocks, at **Trou Blanc**. For fans of waterslides, this spot is one of the most well-loved on the island, as you can plunge down all year round and none of the sections require any particular technical knowledge – the site includes slides, jumps and even a zip line! It's also a great opportunity for a hike with views, since the approach (a 30-minute hike) leads to a fantastic viewpoint overlooking Cirque de Salazie and the Piton des Neiges. To go with a guide who will reveal the rock cathedral's secrets to you, book online with the tourist office or directly with specialised outdoor companies such as Envergure Réunion.

Among Mystical Trees

HIKE IN FORÊT DE BÉLOUVE

This is yet another fairytale-like site to discover in Salazie. With high ferns and intertwined trees hovering way over your

---

LOVE BEYOND SLAVERY & DEATH

The **Piton d'Anchaing** peak visible from Hell-Bourg takes its name from the story of Heva and Anchaing, both runaway slaves who became an iconic couple in the fight for liberty.

After escaping slavery, it is said they led a simple hidden way of life and raised their children right there, at the heart of the island. Only passed down by oral tradition, it is hard to tell where the real story ends and the myth begins.

In most versions, Anchaing is captured, and chooses suicide rather than returning to slavery. Heva gets to live but is taken back to her master. They are later reunited after Anchaing's death thanks to the strength of their love.

FLY BY HELICOPTER

Several **helicopter flights from St-Gilles-les-Hauts** (p156) – and some from St-Pierre – fly tourists over the island to enjoy otherwise impossible-to-access sights.

WATER SPOTS IN SALAZIE

Cascade du Voile de la Mariée (Bridal Veil Falls)
A waterfall of tears shed by a father after his daughter fell off a precipice on her wedding day.

The Virgin with her Feet in the Water
Among the Trois Cascades waterfalls, this oratory is a pilgrimage site close to Hell-Bourg.

Mare à Martin
A charming picnic spot in Grand Îlet overlooking Piton des Neiges.

head, the humid **Forêt de Bélouve** on the southern slopes of Cirque de Salazie is almost otherworldly. On misty days, this impression is even stronger.

From Hell-Bourg, a hike up to the **Gîte de Bélouve** leads directly into the forest and is on the way to Trou de Fer. You can either go back to the village straight away, or spend the night at the *gîte* (walkers' lodge) to enjoy the dense vegetation of the forest the next day.

Note that Bélouve is also accessible by car, but only from Plaine des Palmistes. As it touches the Forêt de Bébour, this vast ensemble is often referred to as 'Forêt de Bébour-Bélouve'. So an alternative to reach the *gîte* and hike the many paths in both forests is to drive via the plains.

Forêt de Bélouve

THE FALLS OF TROU DE FER

Trou de Fer is one of Réunion's most wonderful natural sights, and also one of its most inaccessible. It was successfully explored only at the end of the 20th century, but has since become an emblematic spot on the island.

A large circular hole on the slopes of Piton des Neiges, this is an abyss towards which various rivers flow and converge. With a drop of about 700m, the Trou de Fou waterfalls are the highest in France, and some of the highest in the world.

The falls can be reached from the Gîte de Bélouve, but the view at the end of the path is limited compared to the view from the air – it is really only possible to fully enjoy this incredible sight by helicopter.

GETTING AROUND

Salazie is the easternmost Cirque. It is easily reached by car from St-André. The road is overall good and not too winding, but be careful in case of heavy rain as it becomes slippery and visibility on the bends in the road can be low. Before heading to Salazie, it is advisable to check the state of the road with your accommodation or on the tourist office website. Occasional landslides may block the way.

The road goes first through Salazie, where very few people stop, and then splits into two branches: one goes to Hell-Bourg and the other goes through Grand Îlet to Col des Boeufs, where you can enter the Cirque de Mafate on foot. There are generally parking spaces near tourist sites, the start of hikes and trails, and picnic areas.

CILAOS

It supposedly takes 400 bends in the road to reach Cilaos town, at the heart of the Cirque of the same name. Like the two other Cirques born from the collapse of Piton des Neiges, Cirque de Cilaos was a shelter for runaway slaves for a long time. But in the 19th century, it started to gain the attention of people from coastal cities because of its hot springs, which are still active today – these have been transformed into thermal baths and even bottled as delicious sparkling drinking water.

Today Cilaos is way more than a thermal resort town: beyond the popular 'change of air', it's also a collection of sharp peaks and deep valleys, which offer, some would argue, the most impressive panoramas on the island. The name, from the Malagasy word *Tsilaosa*, means 'the place where you're safe', referring to the rugged slopes that provided the runaways with the hideouts they needed to escape those who were hunting them.

TOP TIP

Brace yourself for the winding road! It takes about an hour to drive up to Cilaos from St-Louis, but plan for more. Staying overnight is advisable to make the drive worth it and so you can enjoy the landscapes early in the day.

Cirque de Cilaos

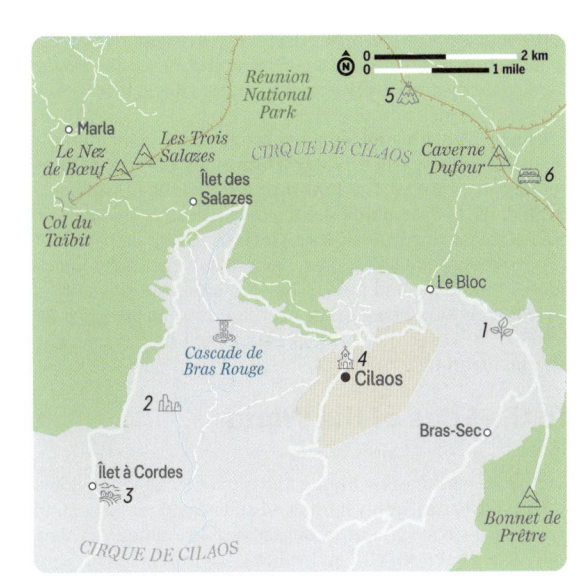

SIGHTS
1 Cilaosa Parc Aventure
2 Fleur Jaune
3 Îlet-à-Cordes
4 Notre-Dame-des-Neiges
5 Piton des Neiges

ACTIVITIES & TOURS
see 4 Thermes de Cilaos

SLEEPING
6 Caverne Dufour

EATING
see 4 Kaz Métisse
see 4 Le Cottage

Take the Scenic Road

EPIC LANDSCAPES ON YOUR DRIVE

Listed as one of the most beautiful tourist roads on the island, the way to the heart of the southern Cirque is nothing less than spectacular. It's an experience on its own to discover the dense lush mountains, as they appear turn after turn, peak after peak.

The ancestor of the famous road with 400 turns started to be used only at the beginning of the 1930s. Before then, you could reach the Cirque only by a narrow cliffside path. Some Réunionnais elders – there are few of them left now – still remember a time when they had to deliver goods all the way up to Hell-Bourg, by foot, sometimes with their ox. Talk about an adventure!

Today's drive, way easier in comparison, feels like entering a mythical valley. All that's left to spot would be a couple of dinosaurs!

A Change of Air

OVERNIGHT IN A THERMAL TOWN

Cilaos

Imagine how attractive the thermal springs must have been for people to decide to go up there on foot! The **Thermes de Cilaos** are still popular today: you can book relaxing hydromassages and even thermal health treatments, and enjoy the high mineralisation rate (due to the rock's volcanic origin) of Cilaos' natural springs.

Cilaos itself is a pleasant stop. After your bath, have lunch at **Le Cottage**, a restaurant located on the large water pond at the centre of the town, Mare à Joncs. On bright days, it becomes a mirror reflecting the surrounding mountain crown, like an ode to earth and water. Then take a pedal boat across the pond for an afternoon ride.

If you prefer going for a walk through town, don't miss the beautiful whitewashed **Notre-Dame-des-Neiges** church, looking defiantly at the hovering dark peaks in the background. After a shopping session at the local crafts market, grab a homemade cake at **Kaz Métisse** pastry shop.

For a good night's rest, head to a one of the many guesthouses in and around town. They are often set in beautiful typical mountain houses. The next day, you can either go for a hike or discover the three specialties of Cilaos: wine, lentils and embroidery.

To the Edge of the World
A VISIT TO REMOTE ÎLET-À-CORDES

There's an even more winding and narrow road going down to **Îlet-à-Cordes**, a tiny hamlet on an isolated plateau, 11km from Cilaos. It's a couple of houses beside a unique driving road, stuck between cliff and valley.

The road ends after a couple of kilometres in the middle of vegetable crops. The extreme quietness almost inspires respect. The *îlet* (Réunion's isolated mountain hamlet) seems suspended in time and space.

Îlet-à-Cordes is the starting point for several trails that lets you enjoy the casuarina trees (*filaos*) with beautiful viewpoints on the surrounding slopes. Note that it's possible to spend the night in one of the few guesthouses. Driving, you will get the chance to admire a couple of panoramas over Cilaos and waterfalls flowing down to the Bras de Cilaos river.

Mother of Mountains
HIKE THE HIGHEST SUMMIT

At the centre of the three Cirques, the **Piton des Neiges** rises to a height of 3069m. Not only is it the highest mountain in Réunion, but it's also the highest in the Indian Ocean. Emerging from the ocean about 3 million years ago, its eruptions gave birth to more than two thirds of the island. Major collapses of its slopes created the deep valleys and cliffs of Salazie, Cilaos and Mafate.

It's possible to start the climb up to the summit from Salazie, but hikers generally prefer starting from Cilaos, as this

---

THE THREE TREASURES OF CILAOS

Lentils of Cilaos
These make delicious side dishes in the typical Réunionnais meal (rice, beans and *cari*), but are much more expensive than ordinary lentils.

Embroidery
This art was brought to the village in the early 20th century by the daughter of the doctor who popularised the baths. Now, Cilaos embroidery is renowned beyond Réunion's borders.

Wine
The mountain wine produced in the village has started to make a name for itself in recent years. Head to the Chai de Cilaos to discover what it's made of.

OUTDOOR ACTIVITIES IN CILAOS

Canyoning in Fleur Jaune
Sunny, technically accessible, it's a local's favourite on the island. Book a guide.

Tree-Climbing at Cilaosa Parc Aventure
Family-friendly circuits in the dense cryptomeria forest, 12m above ground!

Cycling with Tof Bike
The mountain bike is a surprising way to explore the spectacular Cirque. E-bikes are also available.

Hiker, Cilaos

> **BEST HIKES IN CILAOS**
>
> **La Roche Merveilleuse**
> A forest path with a picnic area and a botanical trail offering panoramic views over Cilaos.
>
> **La Chapelle**
> A locals' favourite. This path leads to the entrance of a canyon, 'the Chapel'.
>
> **Cap Noir Waterfall**
> This path follows the ancient road, which used to be taken by tourists coming to the baths on foot or in sedan chairs.
>
> **Les 3 Salazes**
> This difficult hike is only possible with a mountain guide. Ask for one at the tourist office. Don't take any risks.

is the shortest way to get to the top. Generally done with a mountain guide, the most common hike goes overnight, as watching the sunrise from the top is a highlight.

The first day is spent walking from Le Bloc. After an evening stop at the only refuge, **Caverne Dufour**, the most difficult part of the climb starts in the middle of the night to reach the summit at dawn.

The volcano has been dormant for over 120 centuries but it is still monitored by scientists for potential awakening. On the planet's geological scale, it's only been a short time!

GETTING AROUND

Cilaos is the southernmost Cirque. Its main town, also called Cilaos, is accessible only via a winding mountain road (but the views are worth it!). The road splits into several branches, one leading to Îlet-à-Cordes and another to the village of Bras Sec. It is advisable not to take the road in case of heavy rainfall, especially if you are not familiar with the area.

It is possible to take a bus from St-Louis to Cilaos. But most people prefer driving their own car to explore the *îlets* (hamlets) and reach the start of hiking trails more easily.

MAFATE

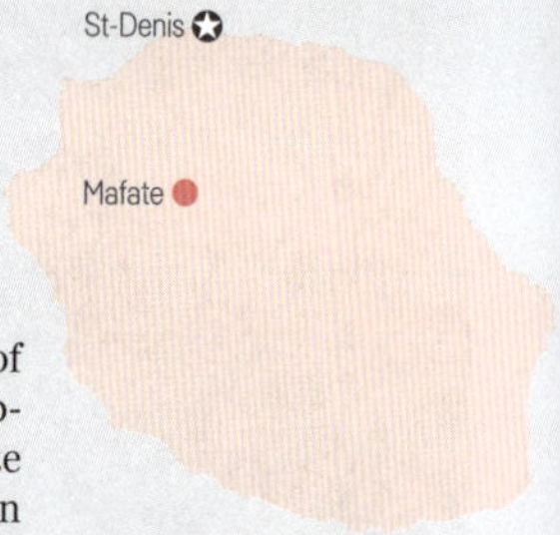

The Cirque de Mafate could be called the best-kept secret of Réunion. It's only accessible by foot, and by service helicopters which deliver goods and fly teachers to the few remote schools nested in the mountains. It's one of the last places in the world with no road or car, and yet it is inhabited. Overnight hikers will have no problem finding lodgings in one of the various *îlets*: those isolated hamlets with a few houses and limited cultures, born from the former camps of runaway slaves.

The name 'Mafate' may come from the Malagasy word *mahafaty*, meaning 'lethal' or 'dangerous', referring to the terrain of the Cirque. But it could also be named after runaway chief Maffack, who was reportedly killed by slave hunter Mussard in 1751. Either way, the etymology reflects both the history and geography of this impressive site, which is praised today by hikers.

TOP TIP

Plan your hiking trips carefully before heading to Mafate, and don't forget maps as you may not be able to get online everywhere in the Cirque. Book your accommodation and a mountain guide (if necessary) in advance at the tourist office.

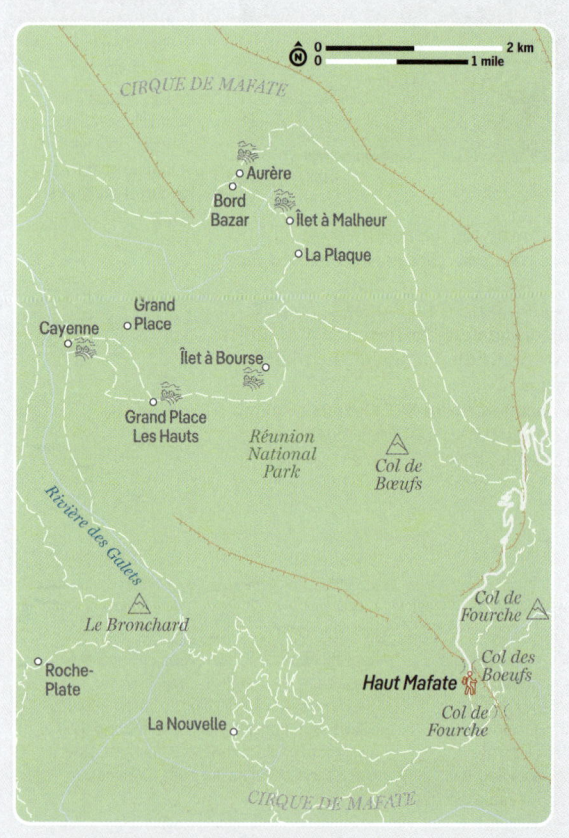

Stay with the Mafatis

A HIKING LOOP AROUND THE ÎLETS

Visiting the remote villages of Mafate to get a taste of the lifestyle far from urbanisation is possible on a challenging loop hike over two or three days. With a total population of about 800 hundred people, Mafate lets you experience a very traditional way of life: most houses have their own vegetables growing in the garden, a few farm animals (mainly chickens), and some offer accommodation.

First, you'll need to cross the Rivière des Galets riverbed, either on foot (about 2½ hours) or by 4WD. You can book a lift through the West Tourist Office. It's also possible to prepare for your hiking trip with them.

You will pass **Cayenne**, **Grand Place** (historically among the most populated *îlets*), **Îlet à Bourse**, **Îlet à Malheur** and **Aurère**. They all used to be homes to runaway slaves, and some names bear traces of this history. *Orera* means 'the good land' and *Îlet à Malheur* refers to a confrontation with slave hunters. Spending several days in the Cirque is a great opportunity to learn about the lives of Mafatis and to hear their stories, sitting next to the fire on a terrace overlooking the mountains. You may even see, one morning when you wake up, a helicopter fly by.

Grand Place

THE MAFATE POSTMAN

Without any roads to travel and deliver letters to the inhabitants of Mafate, the postman has always been a central figure of communication between the *îlets* and the rest of the world. Of course, that was before the phone and the digital age, but the postman is still a mythical figure in the Cirque.

Yet, this is a flesh-and-bones person who remains in recent memories: Yvrin Pausé was the Mafate postman for 40 years after his father. In his lifetime, hiking from one *îlet* to the other, he walked the equivalent of five times around Earth! A statue pays tribute to him in Grand Place, at the heart of his beloved Cirque.

GETTING AROUND

Mafate can be entered at several points, but they don't all lead to the same part of the Cirque. It is divided into three main parts, separated by impassable mountain ranges.

The easiest way in is from Col des Boeufs (through Salazie), but it's also possible from the west via Rivière des Galets by 4WD ('Deux Bras'), the Maïdo (via Roche Plate *îlet*) and the path named 'Canalisation des Orangers'. The final way to enter is via the Taïbit ridge (Cilaos), which requires a particularly steep hike.

Inside the Cirque, trails usually connect the *îlets*, making it possible for hikers to stop for food (although that can be limited) or lodgings. Keep an eye on the forecast to prepare for weather changes, which can happen fast in the Cirques. It's advisable to plan your hikes in advance as some guesthouses may be fully booked. Going with a mountain guide is also a great way to discover all the trails safely.

HIKING TOUR

Hiking the Haut Mafate

This popular overnight hiking loop takes in the rich natural environment of the Haut Mafate, and is a chance to spend a night in a unique area that is entirely free of cars. You will walk among tree ferns and cryptomerias, through a tamarind forest, and across remote îlets via cliffside paths and river valleys. All of this to be able to awake to sunrise in the middle of a mountain crown.

1 Col des Boeufs

The path to enter Mafate is easy to find, at the end of the Col des Boeufs car park. It's best to arrive early, as clouds come in pretty quickly in the morning. Entering the Cirque can be a moving experience, as majestic mountains reveal themselves gradually through dense, humid vegetation.

The Hike: Go down the steep path from Col des Boeufs. You'll soon reach a plateau, then go up the path to reach La Nouvelle (about 2 hours).

2 La Nouvelle

Most hikers choose to have lunch or a snack in this village at 1400m. La Nouvelle is the most easily reached and populated îlet in the Cirque de Mafate, with about a hundred inhabitants. It also has the most accommodation options. Grab pastries at the small bakery or have a drink at Le Bistrot des Songes.

The Hike: Hike down the path to Marla. The path splits into two after about 30 minutes.

Cirque de Mafate

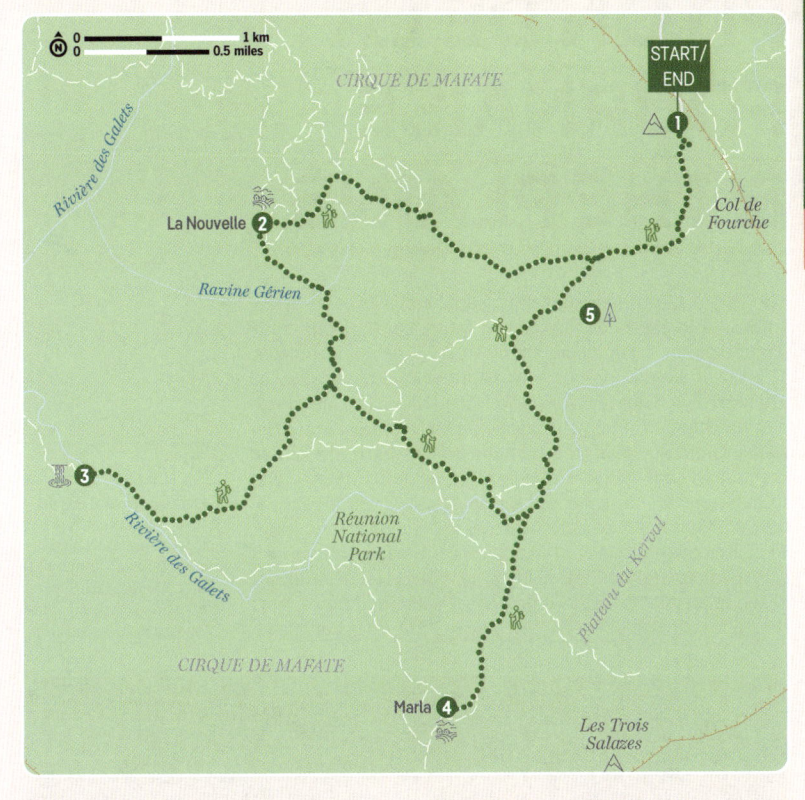

One branch goes down the riverbed; the other continues through the mountain. Both lead to Marla.

3 Les Trois Roches (optional)

Just before the fork in the path between La Nouvelle and Marla, there's an option for experienced fast hikers to go back and forth on the same day to Les Trois Roches via La Plaine des Sables, which leads to high waterfalls falling into a rock abyss. Hikers usually return to spend the night in La Nouvelle rather than staying in Marla.

The Hike: This is a very steep there-and-back hike. The trip down and up again takes about 4 hours, and the path back can be particularly demanding.

4 Marla

Coming directly from La Nouvelle, you can reach Marla in about 2 hours. After the school, you'll pass the îlet's few houses. Yolande Hoareau's guesthouse offers a comfortable stay. Be sure to look at the stars, free of any light pollution, before going to bed.

The Hike: The end of the loop from Marla is shorter and less steep than the way there. It takes about 2 hours to reach the tamarind forest.

5 La Plaine des Tamarins

Just before starting the climb back to Col des Boeufs, you will cross a plateau with a tamarind forest. Sometimes covered in mist, it's a rather eerie part of the hike. You may come across local oxen among the trees – they are not aggressive, and will just watch you go your own way.

The Hike: The hike back to Col des Boeufs takes about 45 minutes, depending on your pace.

PITON DE LA FOURNAISE & THE PLAINS

THE GUIDE

RÉUNION

St-Denis

Piton de la Fournaise & The Plains

The southeastern quarter of the island consists of its active volcano and the plateaus formed on its slopes (commonly named 'plains'): Plaine des Cafres and Plaine des Palmistes. The varied landscapes are much appreciated by locals, who often drive here for picnics and weekend trips. The area's vegetation changes quickly: from the tamarind forest and drier zone around Bourg-Murat in Plaine des Cafres, to the humid Forêt de Bébour-Bélouve in cloudy Plaine des Palmistes. Not to mention the immense red scoria desert of Plaine des Sables, which is made of ashes and looks like a lunar landscape. This area of about 225 sq km is a concentration of Réunion's rarest microclimates. All of them are gathered around one of the most active volcanos on Earth, with sometimes more than one eruption per year. Welcome to Piton de la Fournaise.

TOP TIP

Be sure to arrive at Pas de Bellecombe before 9am to admire the views over the volcano and its outer crater. It is very rare to get clear skies in this part of the island if you come too late.

Formica Leo, Piton de la Fournaise

HIGHLIGHTS
1 Piton de la Fournaise

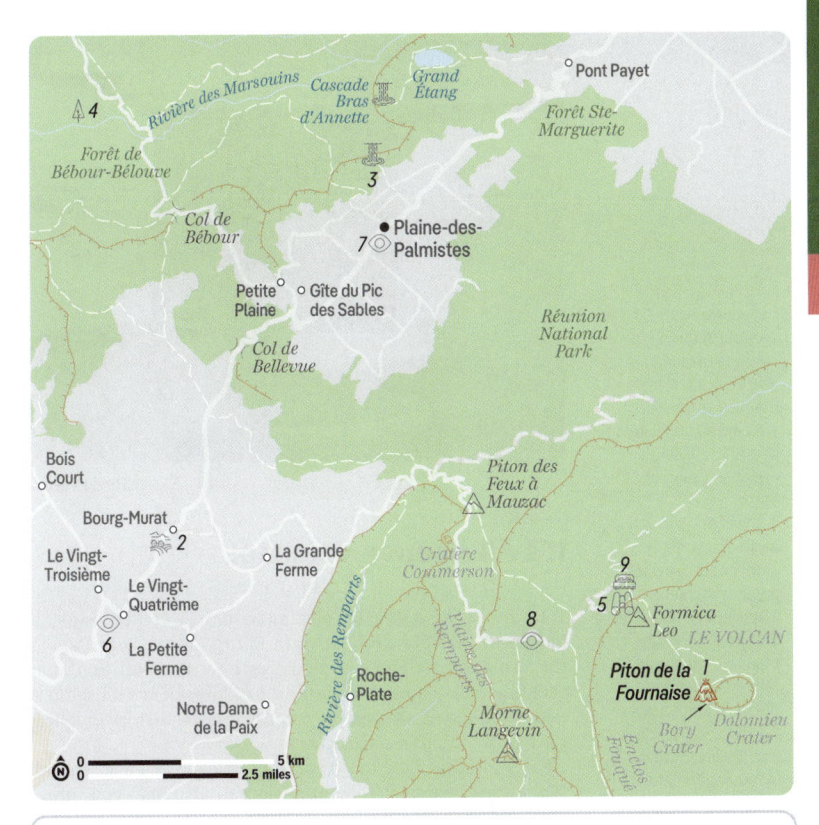

SIGHTS
2 Bourg-Murat
3 Cascade Biberon
see 2 Cité du Volcan
see 7 Domaine des Tourelles
4 Forêt de Bébour
5 Pas de Bellecombe
6 Plaine des Cafres
7 Plaine des Palmistes
8 Plaine des Sables

SLEEPING
9 Gîte du Volcan

A Trip to Mars

ACROSS A RED DESERT

Just before reaching **Pas de Bellecombe**, the road to the volcano opens up onto a vast desert of scorias, as you leave the heathland landscape of the plateaus.

Scientists think that **Plaine des Sables** (the Sand Plain) was born about 65,000 years ago from a gigantic collapse. The red scorias covering the entire area were blown out from Piton Chisny, one of the three volcanos located in this area, to the west of the Enclos Fouqué (outer crater). They don't erupt anymore.

The way down to Plaine des Sables, from **Plaine des Cafres**, is a winding road from which you can admire this martian desert. It's also possible to hike from Pas de Bellecombe, with the option of spending a night at the **Gîte du Volcan** on your way.

Plaine des Sables

Cité du Volcán

It's All About a Volcano!
A VISIT TO THE VOLCANOLOGY MUSEUM

You can stay for half a day playing with the interactive installations at the **Cité du Volcán** in Bourg-Murat. Learn about the formation of those lava monsters, how they work and what ecosystems are born from eruptions. This science museum is dedicated to volcanology in general and the history of volcanoes in Réunion in particular.

It's the right place to go through volcano science, and all the stories behind it. The archives can also help you to understand the relationship that the Réunionnais have had with Piton de la Fournaise, from fright to awe.

A Botanical Lesson
LEARN ABOUT TREES IN FORÊT DE BÉBOUR

You are about to head into one of the most dense primary rainforests on the island. **Forêt de Bébour** is home to an extraordinary biodiversity: trees covered with epiphytes and orchids, ferns flanking sinuous paths, and huge roots sometimes barring your way. The forest gets darker in some places, with branches and leaves blocking the sun…but you won't get lost: you can wander among the plants and trees of this mystical primary forest thanks to a well-marked path around Piton Bébour. Note that although this is an easy path overall, it can be muddy.

A CREOLE CABARET

Pat'Jaune was created in the 1990s by three brothers (the Gonthiers) from Plaine des Cafres, who were soon joined by a unique female member, Claudine Tarby.

It was originally more of a comedy club, but they added music and dance, inspired by the Creole culture of the high plains. Their shows talk with humour about Réunionnais lifestyle, in French and Creole, bringing in music and dance influenced both by local culture and French chanson.

They sometimes tour internationally. When not touring, they host cabarets in their hometown. Check online for cabaret evenings in Plaine des Cafres, and book by phone.

WHERE TO EAT ON THE VOLCANO ROAD

Chez Guilaine
This Creole restaurant is always full on the weekends. Warm and welcoming, it's a treat. €

La Kaz
At the centre of Bourg-Murat, this restaurant serves traditional meals, on the terrace on sunny days. €

Les Sens Ciel
One of the only bistro restaurants in the area. French dishes with a Creole touch await! €€

Ride in the Plains
PLAINE DES PALMISTES ON HORSEBACK

At the edge of Forêt de Bébour, with one of the highest humidity rates in Réunion, the **Plaine des Palmistes** plateau has always been a favourite place for a 'change of air'. But with only two small villages and no major tourist landmark, it is not an easy part to explore if you don't have a guide.

And what if your guide has a horse? François from La Porte des Cascades takes you on tailored tours around the area on his Irish Cobs. He guides you through the lush Forêt de Bébour, to the nearby **Cascade Biberon** waterfall, and to other secret spots that only locals like him know about. It's preferable to know how to ride a horse for half-day and day trips. Book by phone.

Cascade Biberon

MEET THE LOCAL CRAFTSPEOPLE

A vast sight stands at the centre of Plaine des Palmistes: with its imposing white facade and two turrets, **Domaine des Tourelles** is a beautiful example of Creole architecture.

Originally built by a rich landowner, La Maison de Villeneuve was restored in the 1990s and arranged into a small market promoting local craftsmanship. Around the main house, small shops introduce the work of local artisans: you can take workshops with a painter, or visit a brewery and a distillery producing local spirits.

A 'heritage trail' leaflet, available at the main house, relates the history of the sight and the villages on the plateau.

GETTING AROUND

The Route des Plaines road runs across the island, from St-Pierre/Le Tampon in the south to St-Benoît on the east coast. The only way to the volcano is from Bourg-Murat, in Plaine des Cafres. The road is good (although winding) until you reach Plaine des Sables. This section just before you head up to Pas de Bellecombe can be quite rocky, so it's advisable not to go with a small car.

It is possible to arrange a bus tour to the volcano with the South Tourist Office if you don't want to drive there.

PRACTICALITIES
Scan this QR code for prices and opening hours.

TOP EXPERIENCE

Piton de la Fournaise

One of the most active volcanoes on the planet, Piton de la Fournaise is both a place of great interest to scientists and a unique tourist sight. Listed among the 'cirques, peaks and mountain walls' by Unesco World Heritage, it has become a symbol and pride of Réunion.

Réunion's Volcano

With eruptions occurring every eight months on average, the Piton de la Fournaise volcano has become a proud symbol for the Réunionnais – it's even on Réunion's flag! Yet, this volcano wasn't the one that gave birth to the island: the original one, Volcan des Alizés, is now buried below La Fournaise. Formed 500,000 years ago, the Fournaise mountain massif is constantly growing and evolving, with eruptions producing layer after layer of lava.

Pas de Bellecombe Viewpoint

The Enclos Fouqué, the volcano's outer crater, is where 98% of eruptions take place. It is very rare to see eruptions beyond its rim, which is why threats to the population are unusual. The last time this happened was in 2007, with the 'eruption of the century' that gave birth to Le Tremblet beach. From the Pas de Bellecombe viewpoint (pictured), you can see the central cone of the Fournaise volcano, made up of the main active craters: Dolomieu and Bory. Other craters, not necessarily active at the moment, are also visible, such as Formica Leo and Chapelle Rosemont.

> **DON'T MISS**
>
> Pas de Bellecombe viewpoint
>
> The ramparts crater walk
>
> The hike to the smaller Formica Leo crater
>
> An eruption, if it happens during your visit!

Around the Ramparts

Leave Pas de Bellecombe to hike around the crater. These walks are mainly flat, but are very exposed to the sun, so don't forget your sunscreen and water! The darker flows visible on the slopes of the Dolomieu and Bory craters mark the most recent eruptions. On the northwest face, traces are less significant than on the other side, where the lava flows have created the Grand Brûlé burnt slopes, and can potentially reach the ocean.

Inside the Outer Crater

Outside of eruption periods, it is possible to enter the outer crater and hike to the edge of the Dolomieu crater. The hike is otherworldly: surrounded by brownish-red earth, you walk for several hours in a desert landscape close to what we imagine the planet Mars may look like. Note that you are walking on the slopes of an active volcano: for your own safety, never stray from the white marks on the ground and always make sure you have checked live information beforehand.

During an Eruption

Scientists at the Piton de la Fournaise volcano observatory monitor seismic activity closely. They work with the authorities to decide when to close the outer rim and raise alerts. The risk posed by the volcano is low as lava movements are generally predictable and slow. It is always an exciting event among the Réunionnais when the first flows emerge. 'Volcan la pété!' is the Creole sentence you hear everywhere: 'The volcano exploded!'. Strictly speaking, it's not an explosion but rather the opening of a crack in one of the craters. If you're lucky to be on the island during an eruption, don't miss the show: head to Plaine des Cafres and the Volcano Road to find a viewpoint – traffic jams await though! Herds of curious tourists flock to the Enclos Fouqué at the first signs of seismic activity: it is often more of a beautiful show than a danger to the population.

Volcanic eruption, Piton de la Fournaise

AT THE HEART OF RÉUNIONNAIS LEGENDS

More than a natural phenomenon, the volcano is like a mythical character in Réunionnais folklore. It is said to be the home of the devil, but also the den of Grand-Mère Kal, a witch – or sometimes a sorceress, cursed bird or ogre – who all Creole children are scared of, as she comes to take children who refuse to go to bed!

TOP TIPS

- The earlier, the better: arrive by 9 am for clear skies, and during eruptions in particular, try to make it early to avoid crowds and traffic.
- Check for information about eruptions. In general, you will know from speaking to the locals, but stay tuned for volcanic activity if you intend to visit.
- Stay overnight at the Gîte du Volcan if you plan to hike inside the outer crater or take a long trail around it.
- There's no shade in the desert area, so make sure you bring sun protection and enough water.

Arriving

You can only arrive in Réunion by plane, from Mauritius or Paris. There are up to four daily flights between Réunion and Mauritius, and three daily flights between mainland France and Réunion. Prices go up during the high season, in December and January in particular, and flights between Paris and Réunion are generally full, all year round.

Roland Garros Airport, St-Denis

Visas

Réunion is a French territory. If you are an EU passport holder, you don't need a visa. For any other passports, the same conditions as entering France apply.

Airports

There are two airports in Réunion. Most national and international flights land in Roland Garros in the north. Some rare flights from Mauritius land in Pierrefonds in the south.

Money

Réunion's currency is the Euro. There is an ATM and an exchange counter in the arrivals hall. Good to know: luggage trolleys require a Euro coin to work!

Wi-Fi & Roaming

Although there are more and more wi-fi hotspots, they remain rare. French and European SIM card users will generally not incur additional costs, but it is advisable to check with operators beforehand.

Transport from Roland Garros International Airport to

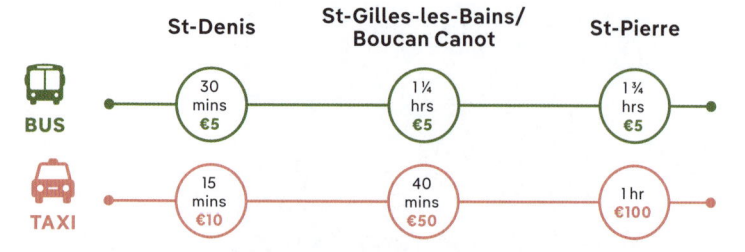

	St-Denis	St-Gilles-les-Bains/Boucan Canot	St-Pierre
BUS	30 mins €5	1 ¼ hrs €5	1 ¾ hrs €5
TAXI	15 mins €10	40 mins €50	1 hr €100

ENTERING A NATURE RESERVE

Most of Réunion is part of a protected nature reserve. It is therefore strictly forbidden to import or export any type of animal (except for pets abiding by health regulations) or vegetation, unless previously cleared by customs. This includes any sort of plant, flower or seed, as they can be a major risk to endemic flora and fauna. This also applies during your hikes across the island: some species growing in one area can become invasive in another! By being mindful of this, you can help to preserve the unique ecosystem.

Getting Around

Cars are the most common transportation means in Réunion and the best way to get around as a tourist. The island has one of the best-maintained road networks in France and the surrounding area.

BEST WAY TO GET AROUND

Despite the investment in public transport, the easiest way to explore Réunion remains a private car. But if you don't have your own car, taking a bus will be a lot cheaper than a taxi!

HIRING A CAR

It is strongly recommended that you book your rental car in advance of your arrival on the island. Car-rental services can be found at airports. Manual and automatic cars are both available for hire.

ROAD CONDITIONS

It's easy to drive from north to south thanks to the Nouvelle Route du Littoral and the expressway (Route des Tamarins). Getting inland can be trickier because of road turns and occasional landslides. GPS is not always accurate, so combine this with careful reading of road signs.

DRIVING ESSENTIALS

Drive on the right.

Legal driving age is 18 years old.

.43
Drink drive limit is 0.43 mg/L.

TRAVEL COSTS

Car hire
From €30/day

Petrol
±€1.72/litre

City bus ticket
From €1.30

Express bus ticket
€5

EXPRESS BUSES

'Car Zeclair' express buses O1 and O2, operated by the Car Jaune company, run between St-Pierre and St-Denis several times a day. The journey takes about one hour, and connects both airports too. Check the Car Jaune network for information.

BUS NETWORK & TICKETS

Major cities and some inland areas are well-connected by the 'Car Jaune' bus network. It can be a good way to see the main sights, provided you are not in a rush. A non-express ticket costs €1.30 to €2, regardless of your destination.

TAKE IT EASY

Traffic jams have unfortunately become emblematic of the island, and they can be really crazy in and around cities at rush hour or, in worst-case scenario, road accidents. As there as generally no alternative roads, patience is a key virtue when driving in Réunion. Thankfully, most drivers are understanding and polite in these situations and they generally know when to make way and wait for their turn to go.

TIP

Tune in to Freedom 2 for live traffic info

- 94.5 FM in St-Denis
- Around 102.5 FM for the west/south)
- French language

Above: Anse Patates (p245), La Digue; Right: Grilled fish

SEYCHELLES

ISLAND HOPPING AND WORLD-CLASS BEACHES

Seychelles is a fascinating evolutionary isolate, a veritable modern-day Jurassic Park that also harbours a unique Creole culture that blends African, European, Indian and Asian influences.

Situated in the middle of the Indian Ocean, 1000 miles north of Mauritius and east of the African coast, Seychelles is an ancient archipelago of 115 islands that splintered off the supercontinent Gondwana 75 million years ago. This ancient separation made it an evolutionary isolate with no indigenous mammals (the islands' flying foxes migrated later) where reptiles reign supreme across the world's only oceanic granitic islands.

While many travellers are content to flop on the fine beaches, Seychelles has so much more to offer. Its wonderful biota include a *Sooglossus* frog smaller than a fingernail, a crab so big it can climb a palm tree and cut a coconut free with its pincer, a quarter-ton (225kg) tortoise that lives for two centuries, and a 20kg nut – the coco de mer – once worth its weight in gold and still so coveted that rangers guard the prehistoric forest where it grows.

This natural richness is matched by the country's diverse character. The Seychellois blend African, Malagasy, Indian, Arab, Chinese, French and British heritage in a distinct and harmonious Creole culture that has emerged from a difficult history of slavery. This culture is something Seychellois are justifiably proud of and work hard to celebrate (the kreol language received national status in 1978). It's also Seychelles' hidden secret, and those who seek it out will be rewarded with surprising flavours, fascinating musical hybrids and an interesting emerging art scene.

THE MAIN AREAS

MAHÉ
The main island and cultural hub.
p212

PRASLIN
Home to a prehistoric palm forest.
p233

LA DIGUE
Cycling haven with glorious beaches.
p242

OUTER ISLANDS
Marine marvel full of pelagic megafauna.
p249

Outer Islands, p249

A true marine wilderness. The Outer Islands are coral atolls – reefs and islets that trace the rims of ancient volcanoes and teem with megafish, sharks, rays and turtles.

Inner Islands See Main Map

Bird Island
Denis Island
Praslin
Mahé

AMIRANTES GROUP
Desroches Island
Île Platte
Alphonse Island
ALPHONSE GROUP
Coëtivy Island

OUTER ISLANDS

ALDABRA GROUP
Aldabra Atoll
Cosmoledo Atoll
Assumption Island
Astove Island

FARQUHAR GROUP
St Pierre Island
Providence Atoll
Farquhar Atoll

INDIAN OCEAN

North Island

INDIAN OCEAN

La Passe
Silhouette Island

Las Mamelles
Brissare Rocks
Îlot
Ste Anne Marine National Park
Beau Vallon
VICTORIA
Ste Anne Island
Morne Seychellois National Park
Cerf Island
Conception Island
Mahé
Thérèse Island
Seychelles International Airport

Mahé, p212

The largest Seychelles island, and home to the capital, Victoria. It's covered in luxurious tropical forest, surrounded by great diving and supplied with good restaurants.

AIR

Air Seychelles operates an extensive network of inter-island flights. Scheduled services operate only between Mahé and Praslin (a 20-minute hop), with around 25 flights per day. The luggage limit is 20kg. Charter flights or Zil Air helicopters service other private islands' resorts.

BOAT

Inter-island boat travel is easy and efficient. Ferries run regularly between Mahé, Praslin and La Digue. In high season it's advisable to book tickets a few days in advance at seychellesbookings.com. A ferry operated by Hilton Labriz resort serves Silhouette from Mahé.

CAR

If you're resort-based, you can probably rely on taxis for the odd outing on Mahé and Praslin. However, taxis are expensive with short trips costing Rs150 to Rs200, so if you want to explore more you'll need to hire a car. There is no car hire on La Digue, just bikes.

Praslin, p233

Laid-back Praslin is the site of the World Heritage-listed Vallée de Mai. Beautiful beaches fringe the shoreline looking out at offshore islands that make for easy excursions.

La Digue, p242

Quaint La Digue steals everyone's heart with its laid-back vibe, local guesthouses and car-free quietude. Its beaches are regularly voted the best in the world.

Find Your Way

Travel times between islands are short (20 to 90 minutes); modes include fast ferries, catamarans, yachts, cruise ships, prop-planes, twin-otters and helicopters. On land, buses and bicycles get you most places, although taxis are plentiful and car hire easy.

Plan Your Time

Seychelles' languid climate insists you slow down and enjoy your incredible good luck at landing here. But there's also tons to explore, including forest hiking, world-class diving, stunning spas, great food and island-hopping.

Arul Mihu Navasakthi Vinayagar Hindu Temple (p216)

A Quick Week

● With just a week, stick to Mahé for this island-nation's best hits. Base yourself near **Beau Vallon** beach (p213) where restaurants and bars concentrate.

● Spend a day hiking in the **Morne Seychellois National Park** (p224), another day snorkelling or diving at **Baie Ternay** (p217) or **Ste Anne Marine National Park** (p230) and a third day exploring the capital, **Victoria** (p213).

● Beyond that, you can go horse riding at **Barbarons** (p228), visit art galleries on **Cap Lazare** (p228), or dine at the spice plantation **Jardin du Roi** (p221).

● Whatever you do, leave time to enjoy whatever spectacular beach you're based beside.

Seasonal Highlights

Seychelles has a glorious climate with temperatures rarely falling below 24°C or rising above 32°C. The wind (and sea) is calmest between October and March, during the northwest trade wind.

JANUARY
This month and February are traditionally Seychelles' **rainy season** when you can expect short-lived tropical downpours.

APRIL
The southeasterly trade winds prevail (10–20 knots) bringing **drier weather** and more agitated seas on south-eastern coasts.

MAY
Fewer tourists make this a great month to visit along with the **Fet Arik** African heritage festival.

A Leisurely Fortnight

- Consider an island-hopping itinerary between Mahé, Praslin and La Digue.

- Explore Mahé as described in A Quick Week, then take the ferry to Praslin. Once there visit the **Vallée de Mai** (p235) and take an excursion to **Curieuse** and **Cousin** islands (p240) to meet giant tortoises and thousands of sea birds.

- Just spend time snorkelling and swimming off **Anse Lazio** (p235), **Anse Volbert** (p235) or **Anse Georgette** (p238).

- Finally, head to **La Digue** (p242) for a few days spent on the world's most stunning beaches and don't forget to order seafood curry lunch at the local beach shacks.

If You Have More Time...

- With additional time, you can really dig into this beautiful island nation. Plan ahead on Mahé and book in two nights at **Hilton Labriz** (p232) or some dive time in the marine reserve around **Silhouette Island** (p231).

- From either Mahé or Praslin, fly to **Bird Island** (p231) or **Aride Island** (p240), where tens of thousands of endemic seabirds nest.

- And, from **La Digue** (p242), get out and explore the dive sites and surrounding islands.

- Or simply book an additional one-week trip of a lifetime with Blue Safari to the stunning **Outer Islands** (p249).

AUGUST
Great weather, but European holidays push prices up. La Digue celebrates the **Feast of the Assumption** in grand style.

SEPTEMBER
The Hindu **Vinayagar Chathurthi Festival** is celebrated with a colourful chariot procession from the Hindu temple in Victoria.

OCTOBER
Dry, calm weather and good underwater visibility. The island-wide **Festival Kreol** is celebrated with an explosion of cultural experiences.

NOVEMBER
Shoulder-season prices entice travellers keen to avoid Christmas. Seychelles' **Ocean Festival** hosts film screenings and dive centre events.

MAHÉ

Mahé is Seychelles largest island (157 sq km) and the location of the capital, Victoria. As such it's as busy as Seychelles gets, and has the widest selection of resorts and restaurants. The Morne Seychellois National Park blankets the island in tropical forest. It cascades luxuriantly down the steep hillsides and frames the 60 sugar-white beaches that encircle the island.

With 90% of Seychelles' population living here, Mahé is also the repository of the country's history and its cultural hub. It is named after a French governor of Isle de France (modern-day Mauritius), who placed the Stone of Possession here in 1756. You can see it in the National Museum and then visit the spice farms on which the archipelago's economy was originally built. The legacy of that plantation system, which blended African, French, British, Indian, Malagasy and Cantonese influences, now forms the Creole culture that gives Seychelles its multicultural character.

TOP TIP

The capital city (Victoria), the busiest beach (Beau Vallon) and the majority of resorts, restaurants and guesthouses are concentrated in the north of the island. The southwest is scenic, rural and quiet, while the southern tip is completely undeveloped. The ferry port and airport are on the eastern side.

Beau Vallon (p213)

Beach Life on Beau Vallon

BEACH LIFE, SOCIAL HUB

Nestled in Mahé's northwest corner and largely sheltered from the trade winds, Beau Vallon beach (pictured opposite page) is the island's longest and most glorious. It is bookended picturesquely by large granite boulders and backed by a thicket of mature takamaka trees and lovely leaning palms.

Hotels with 70s-sounding names like Fisherman's Cove, Sunset Beach and Coral Strand sit nestled beneath their branches alongside popular restaurants, such as **La Plage** and **Beach Shack**. And although locals comment on the beach's 'busyness' there's only ever a pleasant smattering of snoozing tourists, football-playing teenagers and relaxing locals who sit gazing out to sea on the beach wall.

Behind the beach you'll find food and juice stalls, and a string of dive outfits where you can arrange excursions to Baie Ternay, Port Launey or the marine park around Silhouette Island. The **Dive Seychelles Underwater Centre** at the Berjaya Resort also runs courses and whale-shark-spotting trips in September and October. Other excursions take divers to the **Twin Barges** wreck, the granite outcrop of **Îlot**, iconic **Shark Bank** or the granite pinnacle of **Brissare Rocks**, all of which are thick with an incredible array of fish.

The swimming is also lovely here and very family-friendly as the beach slopes gently beneath the waves. There's pleasant snorkelling around the boulders at the northern end and, being northwest-facing, it is a prime spot for viewing electric sunsets. Head to the Beach Shack bar early to enjoy the fabulous scenery of catamarans bobbing in the foreground and the cloud-covered cone of Silhouette Island set against the prettiest baby-pink sky.

HEADING TO BAIE TERNAY?

Behind the beach at Beau Vallon are a number of boat and dive outfits that organise snorkelling and dive excursions to the marine reserves of **Baie Ternay** and **Port Launey** (p217).

BEST DIVE OUTFITS

Dive Seychelles Underwater Centre
The excellent dive centre at the Berjaya Resort offers certification courses, great dive packages, snorkelling and whale-shark spotting.

Blue Sea Divers
A super-professional outfit offering diving adventures, certification courses and various dive and snorkelling packages. It also runs cruises around the Seychelles.

Big Blue Divers
This experienced, Mare Anglaise PADI outfit has introductory dives, single dives, dive packages and certification courses.

Teddy's Glass Bottom Boat
Glass-bottom trips to Baie Ternay and Ste Anne Marine National Park include swimming and snorkelling stops.

Discovering Victoria

THE WORLD'S SMALLEST CAPITAL

Victoria, Seychelles tiny capital, tumbles down the granite slopes of the northeastern coast, overlooking a deep bay. It's

WHERE TO EAT IN BEAU VALLON

Baobab
A popular beachside pizzeria where you can sip cold Seybrews and gobble wood-baked pizzas. €

Boat House
A local favourite serving coconut curries and barbecued fish. There's live music at the weekend. €€

La Perle Noir
The Black Pearl serves a largely fish-based menu with an Italian twist. Book a table on the patio. €€€

MAHÉ

SIGHTS
1 Anse du Riz
2 Anse Intendance
3 Anse Royale
4 Anse Takamaka
5 Arul Mihu Navasakthi Vinayagar Hindu Temple
6 Beau Vallon Beach
7 Botanical Garden
8 Cathedral of the Immaculate Conception
9 Clock Tower
10 Domaine de Val des Près
11 Domus
12 Eden Art Gallery
13 Jardin du Roi
14 Kaz Zanana
15 Kenwyn House
16 Michael Adams Gallery
17 National Museum of History
18 Port Launay Beach
19 Quatres Bornes
20 St Paul's Anglican Cathedral

ACTIVITIES, COURSES & TOURS
21 Anse Major Trekking Trail
22 Baie Lazare
23 Baie Ternay
24 Big Blue Divers
see 6 Blue Sea Divers
25 Brissare Rocks
26 Dive Seychelles Underwater Centre

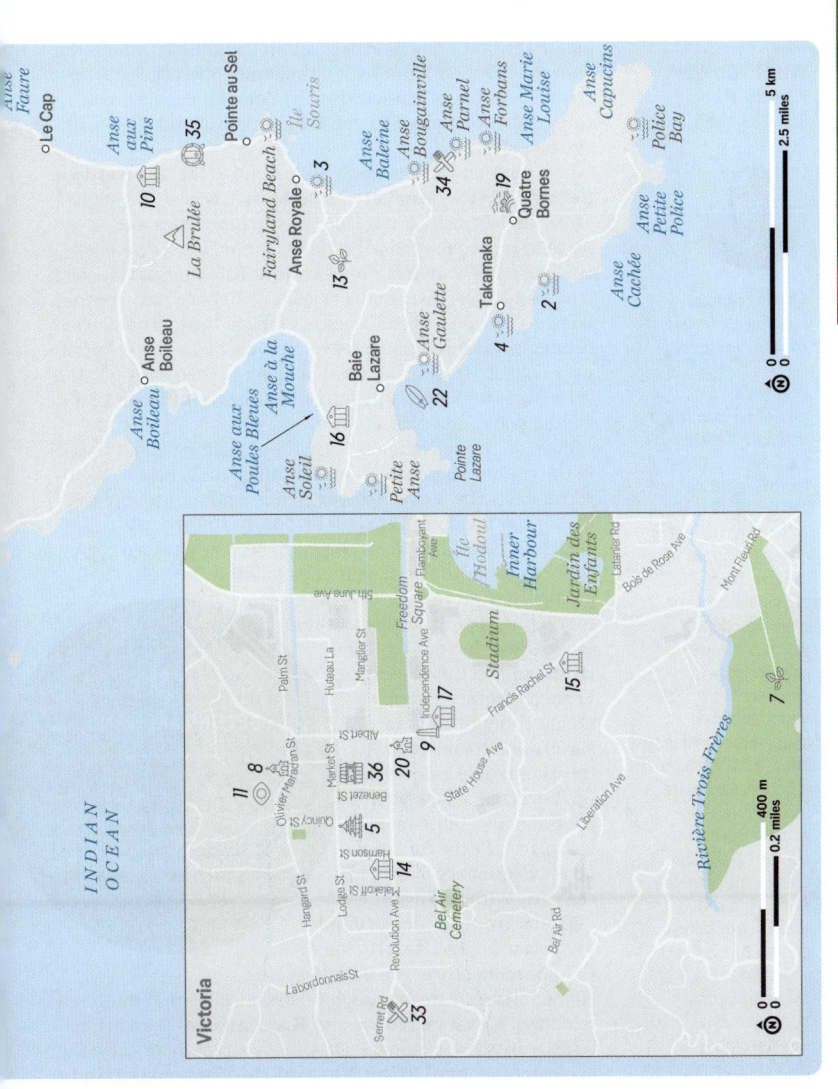

27 Îlot
28 Matoopa Point
29 Port Launay
30 Shark Bank
see 24 Teddy's Glass Bottom Boat
31 Twin Barges

EATING
32 Beach Shack
see 4 Chez Batista
see 6 La Plage
33 Marie-Antoinette
34 Surfers Beach Restaurant

DRINKING & NIGHTLIFE
35 La Plaine St André

SHOPPING
36 Sir Selwyn Selwyn-Clarke Market

THE GUIDE

SEYCHELLES

WHAT TOURISM MEANS TO SEYCHELLES

Sherin Francis, *Principal Secretary at Tourism Seychelles*

Seychelles is renowned worldwide for its sustainable tourism, but I believe there is more we can do, particularly with the challenge of climate change.

We're mindful of the capacity of our beautiful islands which is why we manage growth carefully. We're now focused on improving community engagement, which is critical to climate adaptation, and helping travellers connect with local cultural initiatives, whether that is through exploring our cuisine, music or art.

Tourism is the bedrock of our economy – as the global pandemic painfully demonstrated. Sustainability here isn't a buzz word – it's the foundation of our survival.

---

where the first French settlers set up L'Etablissement du Roi (Royal Settlement) in 1778, later renamed Victoria by British colonists in 1841. Characterised by Colonial-Creole architecture, it's a great place to get to grips with Seychelles history and culture.

The distinct blue pagoda that houses the **Sir Selwyn Selwyn-Clarke Market** sits on Market Street. It's named after the last British governor of the Seychelles and is the place to get acquainted with the key ingredients of Seychelles cuisine, namely an incredible array of fish, unusual tropical fruits and specialist products such as banana and coconut jam and bilimbi and chilli sauce. Come in the morning when fishmongers set out giant glistening tuna, black-spotted groupers, jobfish, trevally and red snappers. Then seek out the spice stalls and stock up on fresh nutmeg, cinnamon quills, vanilla pods and essence.

Move on to the National Museum of History. You'll find it in the restored Supreme Court building (1885) next to Victoria's focal point, a **clock tower** that is a miniature replica of the one on London's Vauxhall Bridge. It was brought to Seychelles in 1903 when the archipelago became a Crown colony.

The museum's didactic exhibition tells the archipelago's dramatic 300-year history, from its initial ties to the Mascarene Islands of Mauritius and Réunion (still a French overseas department) through the era of slavery and colonialism to the islands' role as a haven for liberated slaves post-abolition and subsequently a place of exile for royal and revolutionary figures in the early 20th century.

GETTING ART SMART

If you'd like to know more about the Seychelles art scene and familiarise yourself with emerging talent before you visit **Kenwyn House and Kaz Zanana**, turn to page 226.

Afterwards wander around Victoria to appreciate its Colonial-Creole architecture. The buildings are characterised by steep roofs, 1st-floor balconies and shuttered windows. **Kenwyn House** and **Kaz Zanana** – two art galleries – are great examples. On Quincy street there's also the eye-catching **Arul Mihu Navasakthi Vinayagar Hindu Temple**, which you can visit. **St Paul's Anglican Cathedral** is on Albert Street. It is a modern interpretation of the oldest chapel in Victoria, which was consecrated here in 1859.

The granite Catholic **Cathedral of the Immaculate Conception** sits on Maradan Street framed by frangipani trees.

WHERE TO EAT IN VICTORIA

Papagalo
A wildly popular takeaway serving Creole staples like pineapple chicken, lentils or chow mein. €

News Café
A good spot for a casual breakfast or lunch. There are wraps, paninis and seafood brochettes. €

Le Rendezvous Café
This cafe serves smoothies, good coffee, vanilla tea and light meals such as wraps and sandwiches. €

National Museum of History

Next door is the Spanish-style **Domus** (or Capuchin House), a beautiful seminary built by Brother Gélase between 1930 and 1934 to house capuchin missionaries. It's now the Roman Catholic priests' residence and a national monument.

Another heritage site is the lovely **Botanical Garden** located on Mont Fleuri Road. It was created in 1901 by Mauritian agronomist Paul Rivaltz Du Pont. Streams trickle down the lush gardens and there's a huge pond afloat with lilies. It's also the only place on Mahé where you can see the prehistoric coco de mer palm tree and a very rare cannonball tree, which bears fruit that look like cannonballs.

Snorkelling & Diving Cap Ternay

MARINE PARK, SHARKS, BEACH BARBECUES

Baie Ternay and **Port Launay** are adjacent marine parks on either side of Cap Ternay at the western tip of Mahé. They're characterised by their clear turquoise water, diverse fringing coral reefs and plentiful fish life, including parrot, lion and Napoleon fish, eagle rays and sting rays, lemon sharks and blacktip sharks, and turtles, which you often see just scooting along on the surface. Whale sharks also visit between August and October.

MARIE ANTOINETTE

With its high red roof, wide verandas and shuttered windows, the Marie Antoinette restaurant is a traditional Creole-style house. It's said that American explorer and journalist HM Stanley stayed here while waiting for the French mail steamer to take him back to Europe after visiting David Livingstone.

While the sense of history in the lovely weathered house is real, the fame of Marie Antoinette is due to its fabulous Creole cooking.

Created by Kathleen Fonseka in 1972, the restaurant showcases a panoply of Creole dishes including fish fried in turmeric-hued batter, grilled fish with sweet-and-spicy Creole sauce, mango salad and chicken coconut curry. Bring an empty stomach and order the set menu for the full experience.

WHERE TO SHOP IN VICTORIA

Jivan Jetha Imports
The oldest trade emporium in Victoria (c 1860). It's full of colourful textiles and home furnishings.

Camion Hall
Victoria's shopping arcade is full of souvenir shops; the best are Artisan des Iles and Kreolor jewellery.

Kaz Zanana
The art gallery of George Camille, one of Seychelles' best-loved artists. There's a nice cafe on-site.

WHAT TO DO IN BAIE TERNAY

Paul Levigne
Tuna fisherman-turned-park patrol officer

Paul gives his top tips on Baie Ternay.

Anse Major Trekking Trail
One of the most beautiful coastal trails through the forest ending at Anse Major beach.

Shark-spotting
A hot spot for lemon sharks, black-tip and white-tip sharks, especially during the October to December breeding season.

Matoopa Point
The northwestern tip of Mahé is one of the best dive sites on the island – you'll see huge groupers, Napoleon fish and grey sharks.

Anse du Riz
The secluded beach in Baie Ternay. If you plan an excursion here, book one with a beach barbecue.

It's possible to reach the marine park via the Anse Major Trekking Trail (p218) from Bel Ombre-Danzil, or more easily from **Port Launay Beach**. But it's best to visit on a glass-bottom boat or snorkelling tour, which you can arrange easily in Beau Vallon with any dive outlet. Check the tides when arranging your trip as the beautiful beaches of Anse du Riz and Baie Ternay disappear almost completely at high tide. Dive excursions also head out here though to deeper water at the edge of the reef.

Once anchored in the calm bay, you simply hop overboard and snorkel away. The water is crystal clear in the sunlight and you can easily spot rays sunning themselves on the bottom as fish glide by. The water is only about 1m to 1.5m deep and is lovely and calm, so even less confident swimmers and kids will be happy. The Port Launay bay is similar although the beach is even better. The **Constance Ephélia Resort** occupies much of the beach. If you come independently, book lunch at their beachside restaurant.

Boat excursions typically include the park entry free (Sr100), barbecue lunch and snorkelling gear. A group of four to six people is required. April to May, and October and November are best for visibility.

BOOKING EXCURSIONS

For a list of reliable boat operators and dive outlets running snorkelling, diving and glass-bottom boat trips to **Baie Ternay**, see page 217.

Grandma's Savoir Faire

PLANTATION HISTORY, NATIVE KNOW-HOW

To understand Seychellois history and culture you'll want to visit some of Mahé's heritage plantation homes, such as the **Domaine de Val des Près**, which is managed by Seychelles Heritage Foundation. Originally the Roch Estate, it was built in 1870 during the British Colonial era when coconut and spice plantations covered much of Mahé. For a century, the plantation was owned by the Irish-English Bradley, then Bailey (through marriage), family who originally farmed coconuts, cinnamon and patchouli.

Although too small to be a primary player in the Colonial plantation economy, Seychelles was critical to facilitating the Mascarene slave trade in the 19th century. It was an essential 'refreshment station' for ships travelling from

---

WHERE TO STAY IN BEAU VALLON & GLACIS

Georgina's Cottage
Bright, comfortable rooms a stone's throw from the beach. The manager is a fount of information. €

Carana Hilltop Villa
Above Carana beach are 11 well-priced rooms, a large garden and a pool. You'll need a car. €€

STORY Seychelles
The best hotel on Beau Vallon beach with suites and villas, plus multiple restaurants and a spa. €€€

the East African coast to the plantations of Mauritius and Réunion. Ships typically spent a month in Seychelles en route conducting repairs and allowing their captives time to recuperate. Seychelles' plantations supplied provisions and some enslaved people were sold here to cover expenses. At the peak of the plantation economy in 1818 there were some 7000 enslaved people in Seychelles, but it's estimated around 115,200 people were trafficked through here to Mauritius and Réunion between 1770 and 1810.

The Domaine's plantation house is typical of its era, built of hardwood on coral blocks with a tall pitched roof and dormer windows, a deep wraparound veranda, and shuttered windows on all sides. The main building consists of dining, living and sleeping quarters that are furnished in sparse period style, while various ancillary structures house the kitchen and bathroom. Also on the property is **Lakaz Rosa**, a reconstructed servant's house from the 1960s.

Although you can visit any day (except Sunday), on Tuesday and Thursday a group of senior Seychellois women descend on the Domaine to host the brilliant Grandma Savoir Faire experience. It involves a tour of the plantation, as well as craft and cooking workshops where they demonstrate how

BEST CREOLE RESTAURANTS

Maison Marengo
Seafood with exotic Creole sauces. The black-spotted grouper cooked on banana leaf is sensational. €€

Jardin du Roi
Spice-plantation dining serving specialities such as soursop juice and spice-sprinkled crepe. €€

Le Gaulette
Fish straight from the sea out the front. The red snapper with green papaya is a house favourite. €€€

Chez Plume
A west-coast favourite serving Creole black pudding, smoked swordfish and *capitaine blanc* (fish fillet) with passion-fruit sauce. €€

La Reduit
A family-run affair serving bat, squid and crab coconut curry. €€€

Domaine de Val des Près

WHERE TO STAY IN BEL OMBRE

Casadani Hotel
A good deal with 25 well-appointed utilitarian rooms with fantastic sea-view balconies. €

Treasure Cove Hotel
Named after the pirate treasure that is said to be buried here. Offers top Seychellois hospitality. €€

Le Meridien Fisherman's Cover
Seventy stylish, sea-facing rooms buffered by tropical gardens overlooking the beach. €€€

Domaine de Val des Près (p218)

PIONEERING TAKAMAKA RUM

In 2002 the d'Offay family dreamed of making their *rhum arrangé* (a sailor's rum made with fruits and spices) into a distinctive Seychellois spirit. But Seychelles had no sugar-cane industry, due to a historically onerous tax. So they had to reach out to farmers and convince them to plant cane. They supplied free rainwater tanks and advice on planting and harvesting, and they returned the crushed cane for animal feed. Their ingenuity paid off and today Takamaka rum is the nation's signature spirit.

You can visit the distillery in the historic structure of **La Plaine St André**, which dates back to 1792. At the end, there's a tasting of six rums.

to make traditional local items such as the kapatia baskets woven out of coconut fronds, or lavann baskets used for winnowing rice. Other groups head up cookery demonstrations in the primitive plantation kitchen, whipping up breadfruit chips and coconut curries in a traditional *marmit* (cast iron cooking pot), then serving guests at a shared table.

These Seychellois seniors are full of verve and the project has a beneficial social element; the women come from different communities and the day at the Domaine provides them with a social get-together. In the course of nattering with tourists about the 'old ways' they trade gossip and roar with laughter at private jokes. After lunch there's a session of traditional music and dance, showcasing the *sega* and *moutya,* both dances introduced to Seychelles by enslaved people. The *moutya,* a call-and-response dance accompanied by African frame drums, was added to Unesco's list of intangible heritage in 2021.

The tour and demonstrations – which could easily come off as phoney performances for tourists – feel authentic and are genuinely good fun. They also illustrate the deep integration that Seychelles has achieved since independence (1976) between its once severely segregated communities. Before leaving, browse the craft kiosks dotted around the front lawn,

---

WHERE TO STAY ON THE EAST COAST

Pied dans L'Eau
Great apartments located practically on Anse Royale beach with shops and restaurants nearby. €

Hilltop Boutique Hotel
Comfortable rooms with Victoria city views; the excellent Marie Antoinette restaurant is next door. €€

L'Escale Resort Marina & Spa
L'Escale is backed by forest and overlooks the marina, with yacht masts bobbing in front of the pool. €€€

which sell Seychellois crafts. The most fascinating is Monsieur Marchesseau's workshop where he makes exquisite historically accurate model boats.

Jardin du Roi's Spice Trail
SPICE GARDENS, ISLAND FLAVOURS

While coconut palms are indigenous to Seychelles, cinnamon, vanilla, pepper and patchouli – for which the islands were once famous – are not. They were introduced to Seychelles by rogue French pirate-botanist Pierre Poivre, who stole nutmeg, cloves and other spices, including what we now call pepper, from Indonesia and elsewhere in Asia. He smuggled them to the islands of Mauritius and Réunion in the late 18th century in the hope of breaking the Dutch monopoly on the spice trade. He also brought them to Seychelles where he planted them in the 1770s near the beach of Anse Royale in the garden of Jardin du Roi.

The original garden was deliberately burnt down by the French who mistakenly thought they were under attack from the British. Nowadays it sits uphill in the mountains above Anse Royale, where it was re-established in 1854 by the great grandfather of 82-year-old Micheline Georges, the fifth-generation family owner. The gorgeous 30-hectare estate with its romantic sea views is open to the public and you can take a guided, or self-guided (pick up a map at the restaurant), tour of the old plantation house and the spice garden if you book ahead. More than 120 different species of spices and fruit trees grow here.

Meandering around the trails you'll see nutmeg and cinnamon trees, as well as vanilla vines alongside breadfruit, mango, guava, soursop, golden apples and Indian plums. In its time, the estate was active in the production of cinnamon, vanilla (the second most expensive spice after saffron, which was stamped to prevent theft), cloves, pepper and patchouli. You can buy small packets of the spices on your way out. Before leaving, be sure to have lunch in the open-air dining room (p219).
Continued on p226.

Achiote, Le Jardin du Roi

UNIQUE FLAVOURS

Soursop
Annona muricata belongs to the custard apple family, is high in vitamin C, and tastes somewhere between a mango and pineapple.

Golden apple
Spondias dulcis is a pear-shaped apple used as a flavouring agent or for pickles. It tastes sweet, spicy and sour.

Bilimbi
Averrhoa bilimbi has small, waxy fruit that are crisp and acidic. They give a tangy flavour to sauce and soup.

Breadfruit
Artocarpus altilis is one of the world's highest-yielding food plants and is a substitute for potatoes or bread.

WHERE TO STAY IN ANSE ROYALE

Chalets d'Anse Forbans
A hotel with 12 bungalows sleeping two or four to six people. They monitor turtle nests on Anse Forbans. €

La Nautique Mahé
A smart collection of eight self-catering chalets with spectacular sea views. €€

Laïla Hotel
The Marriott's hotel hopes to connect with the community through its smart cultural programme. €€€

AN ISLAND CIRCUIT

Start in Victoria with a visit to the **1 Sir Selwyn Selwyn-Clarke market** (p216). If you have the time, you can also check out the **2 National Museum** and **3 Kenwyn House** (p216) art gallery. After this, take off into the hills on the Chemin Sans Souci. This scenic road wends its way through the **4 Morne Seychellois National Park** (p224) and is lined with takamaka trees, bwa rouz, mahogany and albizia trees. At the summit stop at **5 Mission Lodge** (p225) to take in the spectacular view.

As you descend to Port Glaud you'll pass the **6 SeyTé tea factory** (p225). Turn south along the coast road, swooping past the glorious bay of **7 Grand Anse** (p238). Beyond, you'll see a sign for the **8 National Biodiversity Centre (p222)**. Drop in here for fascinating tours that describe the medicinal properties of the island flora, including tips on how hibiscus petals clean your shoes and Asiatic pennywort helps arrest dementia. It's pretty wild!

Then, push on southwards – you may want to make a pit stop at lovely **9 Anse à la Mouche** (p222) for a swim, before turning left again onto **10 Chemin les Canelles**. This road takes you back into the mountains where you'll find the **11 Jardin du Roi** (p221) spice garden (book ahead for lunch).

Descend to the town of **12 Anse Royale** (p228) and turn left to head back north. En route you'll pass the **13 Takamaka Rum Distillery** (p220). Then scoot back to Victoria and over the headland on the **14 St Louis Road** to finish at **15 Beau Vallon beach** (p213) for a picture-perfect sunset and pina colada at Beach Shack.

Beau Vallon beach (p213)

SEYCHELLES | THE GUIDE

PRACTICALITIES
Scan this QR code for prices and opening hours.

TOP EXPERIENCE
Hiking Morne Seychellois National Park

Mahé's dramatic mountainous interior is characterised by the three peaks of Trois Frères (Three Brothers), the highest of which is 905m. They were named by Vasco da Gama in 1502, who mapped them on his return voyage to India – the first European sighting. Now they sit at the centre of Morne Seychellois National Park, a tropical forest crisscrossed with 15km of hiking trails.

DON'T MISS

- Mission Lodge
- The carnivorous pitcher plant at the summit
- A beach barbecue lunch at Anse Major
- Spotting blue pigeons along the Trois Frères trail
- The summit views over Ste Anne Marine National Park

Bel Ombre-Danzil to Anse Major

Beginning at Danzil-Bel Ombre, this easy trail to the Anse Major beach hugs the western edge of the park. Before independence, vanilla, cinnamon oil, copra, citrus fruit and patchouli were cultivated here. The walk is easy, climbing just 100m before flattening out and offering sensational views out to sea where white-tailed tropic birds coast on the breeze. After an hour, you reach Anse Major. Most people stop here for a swim and barbecue lunch served at the beach shack.

The hike: Three hours return; elevation 206m

Les Trois Frères

Save this hike for a sunny day to best enjoy the summit views of the Ste Anne Marine National Park – the trailhead is near the Sans Souci Forestry Station. The path winds between cinnamon trees, palms, screw pines and koko maron. In the canopy you can sometimes spot endemic birds like the blue pigeon and the Seychelles kestrel. The 'summit' is at the base of the three peaks and the steep path beyond here is inadvisable unless you're with a guide. Still, the views are spectacular. The point is marked by a cross, as this is an important pilgrimage site for Catholics on Good Friday.

The hike: 40 minutes; elevation 699m

Copolia

The park's most popular trail is this moderate 1.4km hike. It rises 500m from the San Soucis Rd kiosk (where you pay the Rs100 entrance fee) to the summit from where there are panoramic views of the Trois Frères peaks and the offshore islands of Ste Anne and Cerf. It takes roughly an hour to climb through the luxuriant forest of endemic palms interspersed with cinnamon and takamaka trees. The final section involves a short climb up a ladder onto the flat-topped inselberg where you'll find the rare carnivorous pitcher plant.

The hike: One hour; elevation 497m

Morne Blanc

Mahé's most iconic peak is the sheer cliff face of Morne Blanc. The trailhead is 250m uphill from the tea factory on the San Soucis Road. Although moderate in difficulty, the trail heads straight up for 800m and is unshaded, so its best tackled in the morning. However, it is a fabulous hike through lush mist forest. The palms and ferns are intensely green and the granite boulders swathed in moss. You'll also hear the loud chirruping of the Gardiner's Seychelles frog, a tiny endemic frog the size of your fingernail. At the summit you're rewarded with sweeping views of Mahé's west coast. Note: clouds gather in the afternoon.

The hike: 1½ hours; elevation 667m

Mission Lodge

For non-hikers, the highest point in Mahé reachable by road is Mission Lodge (450m). It is the ruins of an old town (called Venn's Town) where the London Missionary Society once had a school dedicated to educating the children of liberated slaves who arrived in Seychelles following the abolition of slave trading in 1807. There's little left except foundations, a small cemetery and a shaded gazebo – where Queen Elizabeth II once enjoyed a cup of tea – but it's a beautiful site that invites reflection. It's a 6km drive from Victoria.

SeyTé Factory

At the southern edge of the national park about 3km above Port Glaud is Seychelles' only tea factory, SeyTé. It enjoys a nice location on the slopes of Morne Blanc with fine west-coast views. The factory offers brief 20-minute tours that take you through the tea-making process. On the way out you can purchase packs of vanilla tea and citronnelle as a nice souvenir.

TOP TIPS

- Most hiking trails are free, except the Copolia Trail that costs non-residents Rs100.
- Copolia Trail tickets can be bought at the Sans Souci roadside ticket stall.
- Trails are open 8am to 4pm. Note the sun sets fast around 6pm to 6.30pm.
- Trek early in the morning; it starts to get hot around midday.
- Carry plenty of water and a hat (there is no shade at the summits).
- Wear suitable hiking shoes or river runners that you don't mind getting wet.
- Spray yourself with insect repellent or wear light trousers.
- Other than the Copolia and Anse Major trail, a guide is advisable.

Digging into the Art Scene

ART HISTORY, CONTEMPORARY TALENT

Until recently, it was generally held that there was no art in Seychelles prior to the late 20th century when the first gallery opened on Mahé in 1972. That is other than the botanical studies and watercolours produced by Victorian botanical artist, Marianne North.

The daughter of an English parliamentarian, North travelled to Seychelles between 1883 and 1885. While there she painted a huge number of works detailing the islands' flora and landscapes, many of which fill a small gallery at Kew Gardens, London. North was friends with Charles Darwin and her paintings and plant studies were taken seriously by the artistic and scientific communities of the day. She even had a local tree, *Northea seychellana*, named after her.

Less well-known is the work of Billy no.37, an enslaved person who arrived on Mahé as a child in October 1867 on the gun vessel HMS *Penguin*. Supposedly 'liberated', he was sent to work for Mr W Warren where he was renamed Billy 'King'. He is known to have produced a number of autobiographical drawings recording his capture and extradition to Seychelles. His descendants still live in Seychelles today.

These two artists, creating at the same time, exemplify the different faces of Seychelles that challenge contemporary artists. There's no doubt that North, painting in the idealised landscape tradition of John Constable, is an important influence. Many artists, such as Michael, Alyssa and Tristan Adams, Nigel Henri, Donald Adelaide and Jude Barallon follow in this tradition. Their aesthetically pleasing work isn't simply an effective way of securing sales, but also reflects a genuine desire to celebrate, understand and capture the beauty around them.

But for some, the overwhelming focus of Seychelles art on the island's Eden-like qualities is problematic when it inhibits intellectual exploration of social and cultural issues that reverberate from the island's slave-based history. Scholar Deryck Scarr, who authored *Seychelles Since 1770*, describes Marianne North as a primitivist whose work reflects a 'malevolent innocence'.

Artists working to challenge this utopian vision of Seychelles and enquire more deeply include Léon Radegonde, who creates collages and sculptures in the Arte Povera style. He was one of the first Seychellois artists to exhibit at the 2016 Venice Biennale, alongside George Camille whose work focuses on the details of Creole life. Egbert Marday, who unveiled his *Liberated Slave* sculpture at Mission Lodge in 2021, is another artist whose work explores challenging social and environmental issues.

GALLERIES TO KNOW

Kenwyn House
This 1868 Creole house in Victoria displays rotating exhibits from established and emerging Seychellois artists.

Kaz Zanana
George Camille's gallery in Victoria displays original artworks in a lovely 1915 Colonial Creole house.

Michael Adams Gallery
The gallery of Seychelles' most famous artist is located at his charming traditional home, where the work of Alyssa and Tristan Adams are also shown.

Eden Art Gallery
The largest contemporary art space in Seychelles promoting emerging talent.

WHERE TO STAY IN BAIE LAZARE

Villa Chez Batista
A vintage villa connected to the excellent restaurant Chez Batista. There are 11 large, retro rooms. €

Anse Soleil Resort Beachcomber
Set on secluded bay is this family-run hotel with modern rooms with private terraces. €€

Pineapple Beach Villas
An impeccable self-catering resort set right on the beach with eight well-equipped apartments. €€€

Kenwyn House

There's no doubt that sustaining an artistic career in Seychelles is difficult when the market is dominated by the tastes and perspectives of visitors. However, a new generation of Seychellois artists, such as Ryan Chetty, Rino Joubert, Daniel Dodin and Michel Denousse, are pushing the boundaries. Working with a variety of media they interrogate historical and social issues in works with significant emotional and psychological depth.

Furthermore, national institutions are now waking up to the fact that the local art scene needs support to flourish. In 2019, two young artists – Zoe Chong Seng (@zozofromseychelles) and Juliette Zelime (@brandedbyjadez) – were sponsored to attend the Venice Biennale alongside the curator of the Seychelles pavilion and the development officer of the National Arts Council.

From Where the Wind Comes

WILD BEACHES, SURFING, PIRATE COVES

The southern tip of Mahé – south of Anse Royale and Cap Lazare – is wild and undeveloped. Creole's call it 'Owan', which translates as 'from where the wind comes' and currents around here are strong during the southeast trade winds (May to September). But the beaches are beautiful and there's seldom a soul in sight other than a few picnicking locals at the weekend.

BEST ARTISANAL CRAFTS

Alyssa Adams silk textiles
Alyssa's hand-silk-screened pareos, kaftans, bags and scarves are works of art. @alyssa.adams.designs

Seyramic jewellery
Artist Zara Albert's hand-painted ceramic jewellery and homewares are inspired by flora and marine fauna. seyramics.com

Payet painted coconuts
Roland Payet is the brains behind the painted coconut fish and wooden keepsakes you see around Seychelles.

Later Rouz ceramics
Mickey Arnephy creates homewares and hand-painted keepsakes from local red clay. facebook.com/laterrouzceramic

Belliche
Plant-based beauty, skin and hair care products created from Seychelles abundant natural larder. @bellicheseychelles

WHERE TO PARTY IN MAHÉ

Beach Shak
The most popular bar on Beau Vallon. Serves great cocktails and has a prime sunset spot.

Barrel Night Club
Seychelles longest-running nightclub is known for its good reggae, zouk and sega.

Katiolo
A fashionable beach disco with diverse music from rock, pop and reggae to international hits.

BEACH & FOREST RIDING

Damien and Tamara Dreyer are the owners of **Turquoise Horse Trails** and seven friendly Appaloosa horses. They lead fantastic one- and two-hour hacks along either Barbarons Beach or from Barbarons through the forest to Grand Anse. The one-hour experience is done at a walk and is best for less-experienced riders. Otherwise, opt for the two-hour trek, which is full of variety and takes you through an aqua-coloured lagoon and up into the forest, affording scenic views out to sea.

Advanced bookings are essential and treks are planned around tides. Riders must be over 15 years old, be comfortable on a horse, and wear long trousers and close-toed shoes that won't slip off.

Although **Anse Royale** is Mahé's second largest town and the location of the university, it is a sleepy place on a long curved bay. The **Laïla Hotel** hopes to jazz things up with an open-house programme of cultural events, including live music, guest writers and artists. **St Joseph's Church** stands photogenically jutting out to sea at the town's southern edge and beyond it a wild tropical landscape beckons.

St. Joseph's Church, Anse Royal

South of here, the beaches become increasingly deserted. First you'll pass **Anse Baleine**, then **Anse Bougainville** and **Anse Parnel**, where surfers park-up at the Surfers Beach Restaurant and head out to tackle the waves. Next is **Anse Forbans** and **Anse Marie-Louise**, identified on old maps as Pirate's Bay. There's nothing here except the small self-catering Chalets d'Anse Forbans.

Then the road sweeps west across the peninsula to the village of **Quatres Bornes**. The fork to the left leads to **Anse Intendense** – Mahé's second largest beach after Beau Vallon. In the 1970s, ex-Beatle George Harrison and actor Peter Sellers bought a plot here, which is now the lush location of the Banyan Tree Resort. The road peters out nearby at Anse Corail and Pointe Police, where an old police building once commandeered the steep forested hillsides and the unprotected beach of Police Bay.

If you turn right at Quatres Bornes instead of left, the road returns north along the western coast via **Anse Takamaka**. It's an equally fine broad beach that is more protected from the wind and waves most of the year. Lined with takamaka trees and framed with granite boulders, it's a great place to land for the day thanks to the beachside restaurant, **Chez Batista**, which serves great grilled fish and a Sunday Creole buffet. Once you round Pointe Maravi you'll drop into **Baie Lazare**, another good surf spot and where you'll find a cluster of local art studios on **Cap Lazare**.

GETTING AROUND

Hiring a car is by far the easiest and most efficient way to get around. They can be hired at the airport, or arranged through your accommodation and delivered to you. Taxis services are good but expensive, and you need to book ahead at peak times as they get busy. The bus network is extensive, but buses are busy.

All scheduled and charter inter-island flights (and helicopters) depart from the Seychelles International Airport, 8km south of Victoria. Likewise, all ferries depart the Port of Victoria. Boat excursions to marine parks can be arranged through your accommodation, on Beau Vallon beach or at travel agents in Victoria.

Beyond Mahé

Mahé is surrounded by smaller granite islands covered in forest and encircled by shallow reefs, placid lagoons and fantastic dive sites.

Around the northern end of Mahé is a handful of small granite islands that make for great day-trip excursions. Six of them sit in Ste Anne Marine National Park, just 5km offshore. The park covers 15 sq km and showcases a range of marine habitats. Daily boats depart for snorkelling and on Ste Anne, Round and Cerf there are a couple of small resorts.

On the west side of Mahé is uninhabited Thérèse with its fabulous reef, while further north rises the cone of Mont Dauban on Silhouette Island. It is Seychelles' third largest granitic island and is covered in pristine forest. In its shadow is North, an exclusive private-island resort favoured by celebrities and royalty.

TOP TIP

Silhouette Island is a conservation haven and home to 75 endemic species of flora and Seychelles' only population of sheath-tailed bats.

Silhouette Island (p231)

BEST MULTIDAY CRUISES

Variety Cruises
Offers jam-packed, three-, four- and seven-day cruises island-hopping between Mahé, Praslin and La Digue aboard small yachts.

Diving Cruises Seychelles
The gorgeous Turkish gulet *Galatea* sleeps 12 on its diving safaris around the inner granitic islands.

Seychelles Cruises
Weekly liveaboard cruises on a couple of 40m yachts that sleep 18 guests. Trips include daily diving, water sports and on-land excursions.

Mason's Travel
Seychelles' biggest travel agency can book liveaboard yachts and catamarans for all manner of short and long itineraries.

Ste Anne Marine National Park

Day-Tripping to Ste Anne

BOATING, SNORKELLING, BEACH WALKS

Sitting in front of Victoria is a collection of six small islands that make up the **Ste Anne Marine National Park**. Established in 1973, it was Seychelles' first marine park and makes for a great half- or full-day snorkelling trip from Mahé. The park has rich seagrass beds and is an important site for nesting turtles.

Ste Anne is the largest island in the park and has long, white-sand beaches. This is where the first settlers set up home in 1770. Since then it's been a whaling station and a WWII gun battery, and is now home to a five-star Club Med. While day-trippers can't land on Ste Anne, you can come ashore on **Moyenne Island**, and the channel between the two is a prime snorkelling spot.

Uninhabited for most of the first half of the 20th century, Moyenne was purchased for £8000 by former UK newspaper editor Brendon Grimshaw in 1971. He spent 50 years replanting more than 16,000 indigenous trees and setting up a breeding programme for Aldabra tortoises. When Grimshaw died in 2012 he was buried here alongside the island's two pirate

---

WHERE TO STAY IN STE ANNE MARINE NATIONAL PARK

Club Med
A five-star, eco-certified resort in a vast tropical garden. The 'Go-team' arranges activities and beach parties. €€€

JA Enchanted Island Resort
A discreet honeymoon retreat with just 10 villas with private pools. You can walk around the island in 40 minutes. €€€

Cerf Island Resort
A private villa resort set in tropical gardens with two pools. Water sports is a big focus. €€€

graves. It takes about an hour to walk the path between the ruins of two old houses.

Otherwise, there's great snorkelling in the vicinity of tiny, private **Round Island**, which now hosts honeymooning couples at JA Enchanted Resort. **Cerf Island** also has a couple of hotels and you can lunch here at the 1756 restaurant at Cerf Island Resort (book ahead).

Cerf Island Explorer runs affordable diving and snorkelling excursions in the park. Excursions can also be arranged with travel agents and boat outfits in Mahé and Beau Vallon run daily trips.

Silhouette Island

BIODIVERSITY HOT SPOT, ACCESSIBLE LUXURY

Dominating the view from northwest Mahé is the cloud-covered mist forest of cone-shaped Silhouette Island. The third largest island in the archipelago, it is a biodiversity hot spot with 93% of its area designated a national park and its surrounding waters a marine reserve. Most of the Seychelles' 75 endemic trees and shrubs can be found in the **Anse Mondon Valley**, while the peak of **Mont Dauban** (740m) harbours rare orchids and the only colony of sheath-tailed bats. There are no roads, no cars and just 200 permanent residents who work in the island's two hotels: La Belle Tortue and Hilton Seychelles Labriz Resort.

Although the crew of the British East India Company vessel *Ascension* came ashore in 1609, it wasn't until the 1860s that Silhouette was settled by the Dauban family from Mauritius. With slave labour they created extensive plantations of coconut, cinnamon, patchouli and fruit trees on the plain, earning Auguste Dauban the nickname 'the Rothschild of the Indian Ocean'. The **Grann Kaz** (Big House) in La Passe was their plantation home and their colonnaded mausoleum, built to replicate the Église de la Madeleine in Paris, remains near Pointe Ramasse Tout. The last Dauban sold the island in the 1950s and the Seychelles government took ownership in 1983.

Inset: Ghost Crab, Silhouette Island

THE ULTIMATE ECO-LODGE

No TV. No air-con. No phones. No pool. Just 24 simple wooden chalets, millions of birds and the inky blue ocean – far-flung **Bird Island Lodge** is the ultimate ecotourism adventure.

Set at the edge of the Seychelles Bank, it is a nesting site for some 1.5 million sooty terns and thousands of fairy terns and common noddies who descend en masse between April and October.

Sit on your veranda and they will literally land on your head. You can also venture out for snorkelling, kayaking, deep-sea fishing (some of the best in Seychelles) and dolphin-spotting. Bird is also one of the most affordable private islands in Seychelles.

Flights depart from Mahé Monday to Friday.

WHERE TO EAT ON SILHOUETTE

La Belle Tortue
An intimate, plantation-style hotel with an excellent French chef, serving fabulous multi-course Creole meals. €€€

Teppanyaki
A lakeside pavilion at Hilton Labriz serving local seafood in the Japanese teppanyaki style. €€€

Grann Kaz
French-Creole fusion food served in the atmospheric, 140-year-old plantation home of the Dauban family. €€

PRIVATE ISLAND HIDEAWAYS

North Island
North is an under-the-radar celebrity magnet and a conservation hero. Barely the size of Monaco, North Island is as exclusive as they come. It has four bone-white beaches and is occupied by a single, 11-villa resort designed in spectacular naturalistic style.

Denis Island
Sitting on the edge of the Seychelles Bank, Denis is a flat coral island edged with white beaches set between an emerald-green interior and intense turquoise sea. The 25 villa-resort, Denis Private Island, is the only accommodation. Diving and fishing are fantastic due to the proximity of the continental drop-off.

The plantation house is now owned by the **Hilton Labriz Resort**, a 111-villa hotel that sits on the silvery beach of Anse La Passe. It's one of the most affordable luxury resorts in Seychelles and is deeply engaged in sustainability and conservation work – it has a grey-water filtration system, water-bottling plant and organic vegetable gardens. It also regularly teams with the Island Conservation Society (island-conservationseychelles.com), which has an office on the island, for beach clean-ups and wildlife-monitoring programmes; and hosts it for talks and films in the hotel's cinema suite.

If you want to visit Silhouette for hiking or diving, you can do so through Labriz. Its Eco Centre dive outfit offers a full range of certification courses and runs dives to the rocky reef at Anse Mondon, which has a good diversity of butterfly, angel and devil scorpion fish amid colourful nudibranchs, anemones and soft corals. It's a great spot for beginner divers and photographers, while more experienced divers should opt for the Grande Barbe or Turtle Rocks, which have impressive rock formations, swim-throughs and large pelagic fish. The best dive site, however, is Sprat City, off nearby **North Island**, which is a deep carbonate reef with great coral diversity.

Otherwise, get out into that pristine forest with one of the guides from ICS (take insect repellent). They will help you explore the rich ecosystem of Anse Mondon Valley, pointing out endemic palms, sandalwood, tangled vanilla vines, tiny orchids and palm spiders suspended in shimmering webs. They'll also offer encouragement on the sometimes steep climb up to the **Grande Barbe plateau** where bats hide and migrating seabirds swoop in to rest between November and March. There are five peaks over 500m on the island, so there's plenty of trails to choose from and the views are some of the most dramatic in Seychelles.

Labriz is also a great place for families, with a brilliant kids' club and tailored activities; in addition, there are cookery classes among the eight restaurants and a fabulous spa.

GETTING AROUND

Guests staying at any of the resorts in the Ste Anne Marine National Park will have their transfers arranged through the resort, with boats departing from Eden Island. The fast ferry to Silhouette departs from Bel Ombre jetty on the west coast and takes 45 minutes. Book tickets through Hilton Labriz Resort. Day trips to the Ste Anne and Silhouette marine national parks, and Thérèse Island, can be arranged at any travel agent or dive/boat outlets on Beau Vallon beach. Boats depart for Thérèse Island from Port Glaud. North Island guests typically transfer by Zil Air helicopter, although it's also possible to reach the island by boat, via Silhouette. Denis Island is serviced by charter planes and helicopters from Mahé. There's a 15kg luggage restriction.

PRASLIN

When General Gordon of the ill-fated Khartoum siege took up a post as Commander of Mauritius in 1881, he visited Seychelles as part of an exploration of British bases on the Cape route to India. An ardent Christian cosmologist, he was so moved by the archipelago's beauty, he declared it the literal location of the Garden of Eden. More specifically, he pinpointed the location in Praslin's unique Unesco-listed Vallée de Mai, with its signature palm, the coco de mer, taking a star role as the Tree of Knowledge.

The valley is an extraordinary place that's largely unchanged since prehistoric times and is the centrepiece of Seychelles' second largest island. Like Mahé, which lies 45km southwest, Praslin is a granite island characterised by central mountains (Fond Azore reaches 367m) and is fringed with stunning beaches and reefs, off which sit an array of satellite islands. With only 8662 residents, Praslin has a tranquil rural feel.

TOP TIP

Other than the Vallée de Mai, Praslin's most appealing sites are its world-class beaches. Anse Lazio is the highlight. All beaches in Seychelles are public, including gorgeous Anse Georgette that is within the Constance Lémuria resort. Call ahead to register your visit.

Anse Lazio (p235)

PRASLIN

HIGHLIGHTS
1 Anse Lazio
2 Vallée de Mai

SIGHTS
3 Anse Bateau
4 Anse Boudin
5 Anse Citron
6 Anse Consolation
7 Anse Georgette
8 Anse Gouvernement
9 Anse Marie-Louise
10 Anse St Saveur
11 Anse Takamaka
12 Anse Volbert
13 Café des Arts
see 13 Galerie Passerose
14 Grand Anse
15 Notre Dame des Îles Chapel
16 Pointe Cabris
17 Ravin de Fond Ferdinand Nature Reserve

ACTIVITIES, COURSES & TOURS
18 Black Pearl Seychelles
19 Chauve Souris
see 20 Lémuria Dive Centre

SLEEPING
20 Constance Lémuria Resort

EATING
see 1 Le Chevalier Bay Restaurant
21 Les Rochers Restaurant
see 1 Mabuya Restaurant

Cruising the Golden Coast

PERFECT BEACHES, HOLIDAY HUB

The Côte d'Or (Golden Coast) runs along almost the entire northeastern coast of Praslin's. From **Anse Gouvernement**, a lovely sheltered bay at the southern end, to the boulder strewn **Anse Boudin** at the northern end, its a virtually uninterrupted string of soft white sand facing a placid sea. Seaweed can gather here during the northeast trade winds between May and October, but otherwise the swimming is glorious.

This stretch of coastline is also Praslin's hub, particularly around **Anse Volbert** beach and village. It's great for safe swimming and sunbathing, and is one of the few places in Seychelles where you'll find motorised water-sport activities (you can also skydive here with Fly Seychelles). A small islet – **Chauve Souris** – floats offshore and is good for snorkelling (you can swim to it). There are plenty of facilities here, including Sagittarius Taxi Boat where you can charter a boat to take you island- or beach-hopping to more inaccessible spots. Otherwise, you can just walk the stunning 4km coastline, hopping from Anse Volbert to Anse Petite Cour, Anse Possession and Anse Takamaka.

Behind the beach there are a handful of galleries and artist studios tucked between the restaurants and resorts, including **Galerie Passerose** – the most highly regarded gallery on the island – and the popular **Café des Arts**, which rotates local exhibits. **Le Studio**, the photography studio of Paul Turcotte, is located just before the road descends to **Anse Lazio**. Regularly topping lists of the world's best beaches, Anse Lazio is picture-perfect in every way, with a long deep beach sloping gently beneath lapis-coloured waters, backed by a thick fringe of takamaka trees. There's good snorkelling here and two popular beachside restaurants: **Mabuya Restaurant** and **Le Chevalier Bay Restaurant.**

Unique Unesco-Listed Vallée de Mai

PREHISTORIC PALM FOREST

Nestled in the heart of Praslin's National Park is the smallest Unesco World Heritage Site in the world, the 19.5-hectare Vallée de Mai. This primordial palm forest, where the ancient coco de mer palm (*Lodoicea maldivica*) thrives is unique in the world and remains virtually unchanged since prehistoric times. That the forest survives at all is nothing short of a miracle. A second, smaller indigenous forest on the nearby island of Curieuse succumbed to 18th-century botanical poaching, when the double-nut coconut – worth its weight in gold

BEST NORTH-COAST RESTAURANTS

Les Lauriers
Famous for Edwin's barbecued fish and Creole dinner buffet, which showcases swordfish, jobfish and snapper. €€

Café des Arts
By day, this art filled cafe serves wraps and pasta; at night, it is a romantic, haven serving sophisticated Seychellois seafood. €€€

Le Chevalier
Overlooking Anse Lazio, this popular place serves up fish and octopus curries, garlic prawns and calamari. €€€

Mabuya Restaurant
Mabuya has Creole-Colonial decor and a contemporary menu focused on fish, tropical salads and good cocktails. €€

WHERE TO STAY IN THE NORTHEAST

Jardin Marron
Bright, comfortable self-catering apartments with a mix of modern and vintage wood furnishings. €

L'Hirondelle
Fairly functional but fantastically well-situated and comfortable apartments, all with sea views. €€

Cote d'Or
Eleven charming bungalows near Anse Volbert. You can self-cater but half-board is a good option. €€

> **PRASLIN'S NATURAL UNESCO TREASURE**
>
> **Marc-Jean Baptiste**, Site Manager of Vallée de Mai, shares his passion for the forest.
>
> The Vallée de Mai is a source of pride to Praslin. It's a rare example of an earlier stage of plant evolution. We work hard to share the forest's beautiful symphony – the sound of unusual birdsong, the wind and rain in the palms – while ensuring tourism doesn't impact negatively. This is the green heart of the island. Without the forest there would be no water (it's the main catchment area) and without the coco de mer we would lose unique species. I've worked in conservation for 25 years including on Aldabra, but my true love is this terrestrial wonderland.

at the time – was pillaged by British traders and set on fire to ensure the highest price for their precious cargo.

A walk through the valley is a surreal experience akin to natural time travel. Here everything is supersized and the silence is sepulchral, broken only by the chatter of bulbuls and the calls of rare birds like the blue pigeon and the black parrot, which nest in the hollowed-out trunks of fallen trees. If a breeze blows there's a great creaking and rasping far above, as the giant 20m- to 30m-high palms sway like metronomes, scraping their giant fronds against each other. If it rains, the great corrugated leaves shelter you, amplifying the symphony of water droplets that they channel to their roots down the great gutter in their leaf stems. At times, you almost expect a dinosaur to emerge from the undergrowth.

There are two well-maintained paths in the forest, which are clearly marked. The shorter is a 1km **Circular Route** – part of which has been made accessible to a nice viewpoint – while the **North Path** climbs upwards between giant Precambrian boulders to a rustic shelter, which offers views over the forest. If you take this path and combine it with the circular path, it will take two to three hours to explore the park.

Before heading in, be sure to pause at the entrance gate to pick up one of the nuts on the display table to feel its incredible weight (30kg to 40kg). It is the largest seed in the plant kingdom and famously looks like a woman's hips and thighs, while the male catkin is equally phallic. It's why the tree and nut have generated endless myths about its aphrodisiac qualities and power as an antidote to poison.

Although the coco de mer is the keystone species in the park, all of Seychelles' six endemic palm species (latannyen) can be found including the palmiste *(Deckenia nobilis)*, latannyen fey *(Phoenicophorium borsigianum)*, latannyen lat *(Verschaffeltia splendida)*, latannyen milpat *(Nephrosperma vanhoutteanum)* and latannyen oban *(Roscheria melanochaetes)*. They in turn support the endangered black parrot, blue pigeons, Seychelles sunbirds, the rare bronze gecko, Seychelles skinks, tiger chameleons,

Seychelles sunbird

WHERE TO STAY IN THE NORTHEAST

Les Laurier Eco Hotel
Edwin and Sybille run a sustainably focused hotel with eight bungalows and a good Creole restaurant. €€€

Hotel L'Archipel
An elegant landscaped resort by Anse Gouvernement. It has a pool, two restaurants and a veranda. €€€

Le Duc de Praslin
Le Duc's lovely rooms orbit an alluring pool and they run the excellent Café des Arts. €€€

Vallée de Mai (p235)

caecilians, sooglossus frogs and bright-green tree frogs. It is a living laboratory, exemplifying a major stage in the evolutionary history of the world's flora.

The park is managed by Seychelles Island Foundation (SIF; sif.sc), which also manages the incredible Aldabra Atoll in the Outer Islands. SIF is self-financing and ticket sales go directly to managing the two parks and supporting the staff and scientists who work here. If you're visiting independently, you may want to avoid visiting between 9.30am and 11am when most tour groups arrive.

The Wild Southwest

WORLD-CLASS BEACHES, RESORT LIFE

Take the coastal road south of Baie Ste Anne to traverse some of Praslin's most stunning coastline. As you leave the port the road climbs steeply to **Pointe Cabris** offering commanding views. A handful of guesthouses – Chalets Côte Mer, Le Grand Bleu, Colibri and the luxurious Le Château des Feuilles – cling to the slopes on the headland before the road descends to the beach of **Anse Marie Louise**.

COCO DE MER FACTS

The male palm reaches 30m in height; the female 24m. The palm takes 25 years before it bears fruit. As the nut ripens a white jelly forms inside, which eventually becomes a hard white kernel.

The *coco fesse* (bi-lobed nut) can weigh as much as 20kg. When the nut falls to the ground the husk takes six months to disintegrate before it can begin to root. The tree has a unique 'joint' at its base that allows the palm to sway without breaking.

You can purchase a *coco fesse* for €200 to €400 from Seychelles Island Foundation (SIF), which will issue the required export permit.

WHERE TO STAY IN THE SOUTH

Colibri Guesthouse
René Parmentier's A-framed bungalows are set on a headland with glorious views over La Digue. €€

Hotel Coco de Mer
A combination hotel with the resort-style Coco de Mer adjoining the adults-only Black Parrot Suites. €€€

Le Château des Feuilles
This bijou hideaway commands the headland of Pointe Consolation. There's a hilltop hot tub. €€€

SOUTHWEST FOOD HIGHLIGHTS

Les Rochers
Superb seafood with sophisticated Creole influences overlooking the beach. €€€

Paradisier Restaurant
A Grand Anse eatery with a Creole-Mediterranean menu including black mussels in white wine. Pizza is also available. €€€

Britannia Restaurant
A family-run hotel restaurant serving fantastic Creole cuisine in a wood-panneled dining room. €€

Vero's Takeaway
A popular food truck prepping lamb curry, fish kebabs or roasted spare ribs. €

Capricorn Restaurant
The Islander's restaurant at Anse Kerlan is famous for its 'octopus-Patrick-style', in a saffron sauce. €€

Located here is the **Ravin de Fond Ferdinand Nature Reserve**. It is much quieter than the Vallée de Mai and six times larger with a second healthy population of coco de mer palms. The 2-to 3-hour trek to the summit is also one of the nicest hikes on Praslin (visits are by guided tour only between 9.30am and 1.30pm). The road then swoops around Pointe Consolation and what follows is a delightful stretch of undeveloped coastline dotted with wild beaches, starting with **Anse Consolation** with its scenic configuration of rocks, rock pools and reefs.

At points, you can pull off the road to admire the view as you pass **Anse Takamaka** (lots of shade), **Anse St Saveur** (good for snorkelling), **Anse Bateau** (very photogenic), **Anse Citron** (always quiet) and finally **Fond l'Anse** with its amazing aquamarine water. En route is the excellent **Les Rochers Restaurant** where you may want to make a pit stop.

Next comes Praslin's other main beach hub, **Grand Anse**, from where boat trips to Curieuse and Cousin depart. It is lined with resorts and guesthouses, and backed by a small village with banks, travel agents and a petrol station. At the northern end is **Black Pearl Seychelles**, the only pearl oyster farm in the Indian Ocean. Here you can see the pearl-growing clams in their aquarium and buy raw black pearls and jewellery (made by Linneys of Australia) in the Pearl Gallery.

Finally, at picturesque **Notre Dame des Îles Chapel** you'll near the end of the road and the enormous Relais & Châteaux **Constance Lémuria Resort**. It is the largest hotel on Praslin, replete with an award-winning 18-hole Mark Farry golf course. It also sits on **Anse Georgette**, an indescribably lovely stretch of white sand surrounded by dramatic green hills at the northwestern tip of the island.

While Lémuria is gated, the beach is public– you just need to call ahead and register your visit before guards will let you in. Once inside the property you can get to the beach on foot or via a buggy shuttle. You can also book to dine at one of the resort's three restaurants, squeeze in a spa treatment or pick up a club and play a round of golf amid the coconut palms. The 5.5km course is spectacular, and climbs from a grassy plateau into the hills from where you can enjoy views of the sea.

Also on-site is the professional and well-equipped **Lémuria Dive Centre**, which is open to nonguests (by advance reservation). It runs courses for beginners as well as diving trips to some of the 20 dive sites around Praslin.

GETTING AROUND

Praslin Airport is 3km north of Grand Anse and is serviced by daily Air Seychelles flights to Mahé (20 minutes). Regular Cat Cocos and Inter-Island Ferry fast ferries also connect Praslin with Mahé (one hour) and La Digue (15 minutes). Buy ferry tickets online or at the port. Virtually all resorts and hotels on Praslin rent or offer bikes. However, the island is long and hilly, so if you want to explore use the local buses or car and boat taxis. Sagittarius Taxi Boat is on Anse Volbert. Offshore island excursions can be arranged through hotels or local travel agents at the port, as can car hire. Expect to pay €50 per day for a car.

Beyond Praslin

Praslin is surrounded by great dive sites, island nature reserves and tiny islets, making it a great springboard for island-hopping.

While you can easily spend a week lazing on Praslin's endless beaches, the island is surrounded by 20 fantastic dive sites and other small islands that are definitely worth a visit. One of the most interesting is Curieuse, 1.5km off Praslin's north coast. It's a nature reserve and breeding colony for Aldabra tortoises and makes for a great day trip, often in conjunction with St Pierre Islet and Cousin Island, a breeding ground for thousands of seabirds.

Further afield, Grand Soeurs has one of the most beautiful beaches in Seychelles, while far-flung Aride and Bird host spectacular nesting colonies of tens of thousands of birds. Lovely La Digue is also just 20 minutes away.

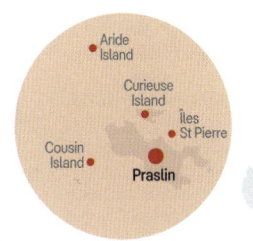

TOP TIP

If visiting independently, park the boat in designated places only. Bring food and drink, and be aware of the landing fee.

Curieuse Island (p240)

ARIDE ISLAND

Aride Island, 10km north of Praslin, supports the greatest concentration of seabirds in Seychelles – roughly 1.25 million to 10 resident conservationists!

Accessible by boat only between October and April, the island is managed by the Island Conservation Society, whose members lead the tours of the island. It's an incredible experience to wander through forests full of nesting noddies, sooty terns and massive frigate birds while fluffy white-tailed tropicbirds huddle in the clefts of tree roots.

This is also the only natural home of the fragrant Wright's gardenia and the view from the island's summit (134m) is sensational.

Excursions usually include a barbecue lunch on the beach.

ICS often needs volunteer support. Use this QR code for more information.

Curieuse Marine National Park

Day-Tripping to Curieuse & Cousin
ISLAND WILDLIFE SAFARIS

Like Praslin, **Curieuse Island** was once entirely covered by palm forest. And, for many years, its designation as a leper colony (1829 to 1965) protected its island ecosystem and hundreds of coco de mer palms. However, that all changed in 1967 when the island suffered a devastating fire that destroyed most of the coco de mer and laid bare its reddish laterite soil.

Following the fire, the government took over management and since 1979 the entire 3-sq-km island has been a nature reserve and the surrounding waters a national marine park. Nowadays, no one lives here except for the rangers who take care of the prehistoric-looking Aldabran tortoises that roam freely among the takamaka trees. There are nearly 300 of them, the largest colony outside of Aldabra Atoll.

Although you can visit the island alone by taxi boat, the full-day tours run by Geoli Charters, Angel Tours and Sagittarius Tours are really excellent. They deposit you at **Anse St José** on the southern side of the island, from where a

WHERE TO BOOK EXCURSIONS

Geoli Charters
A well-organised outfit offering great group and private tours to Curieuse, Cousin, Aride and Félicité.

Angel Tours
Mid-priced private boat charters with group trips to Curieuse and big-game fishing excursions.

Sagittarius Taxi Boat
A boat taxi from Anse Volbert to Praslin's beaches, and tours to Curieuse, Cousin, Aride and Félicité.

guide takes you on a brilliant trek over the headland and through the mangrove swamp, pointing out fascinating features of the island and interesting flora and fauna. En route you'll pass the old colonial doctor's house of the leprosarium before descending to Baie Laraie, where the **Tortoise Breeding Centre** is located.

Here mature tortoises roam around beneath the trees, sidling up to visitors in the hope of a nice neck rub. You can see the tiny babies in the breeding pens and marvel at how they transform into enormous prehistoric-looking creatures. Meanwhile, your boat crew will be prepping a massive barbecue spread for a group lunch at shared tables. Afterwards, everyone collapses on the beach for a snooze or wanders along the sand through the stunning rock formations to snap pictures and have a swim.

Most excursions to Curieuse also include a spot of snorkelling around **Îles St Pierre** or **Cousin Island**. The latter is a Special Reserve for nesting seabirds, which is looked after by Nature Seychelles (natureseychelles.org). At its peak, Cousin's bird population is estimated to exceed 300,000 on an island measuring just 29 hectares. It's an amazing experience to walk through a forest thick with birds seemingly nesting on every branch. Seven species nest here, including fairy terns, white-tailed tropicbirds, Seychelles warblers, Madagascar turtle-doves and the magpie robin, Seychelles' rarest bird. Cousin is also an important nesting site for hawksbill turtles between October and April.

Both Curieuse and Cousin charge a landing fee (included within the cost of excursions), which goes towards conservation programmes on the island. Visits to Cousin are by guided tour only. The two-hour visits are led by a resident conservationist and as the birds are completely unafraid of people, a strict behaviour code is in place for all visitors.

Aldabra tortoise

PRASLIN'S BEST DIVE SITES

Ave Maria
Coral-covered granite boulders 20m below the surface form swim-throughs and overhangs that attract plentiful fish.

Booby Rock
A seamount sizzling with fish action, including parrotfish, moray eels, turtles, eagle rays and nurse sharks.

Coral Garden
This 16m-deep carbonate reef attracts a variety of colourful fish and is great for photographers.

Point Rouge
A 20m dive off Curieuse with pink and purple corals attracting schools of fish and eagle rays.

GETTING AROUND

Half- and full-day excursions to Curieuse, Cousin and Aride can be arranged through all of Praslin's hotels and guesthouses. Full-day excursions include a barbecue lunch. Otherwise, you can arrange a return taxi to Curieuse and Cousin with Sagittarius Taxi Boat on Anse Volbert – Aride Island is too far for a taxi. If arriving by taxi boat, you'll have to pay the landing fees to the park ranger so bring some cash.

LA DIGUE

Little La Digue steals most people's hearts with its natural beauty and laid-back Creole charm. Despite being the third most populated island in Seychelles, only 3000 people live here in four quaint villages: La Passe, La Réunion, Belle Vue and Roche Bois. La Passe is the island's main hub and has a handful of restaurants and shops, a couple of banks, the tourist office and several bike-hire outfits. That's because there are only 60 cars on La Digue, so everyone tools around the island by bike.

Despite its miniature size, La Digue is a microcosm of Seychelles. French navigator Lazare Picault sighted the island in 1742 and plantation owners exiled from Réunion followed in the late 18th century. They established spice plantations, one of which – the L'Union Estate – is preserved as a heritage site. Otherwise, daily activities revolve around beach-hopping, snorkelling, diving and kayaking off some of the world's most beautiful beaches.

TOP TIP

The Tourist Office is at the La Passe roundabout and provides information on all activities on La Digue, plus a map. Otherwise, note that it's dangerous to swim at Grand Anse, Petite Anse and Anse Coco between November and May due to strong currents.

SIGHTS
1 Anse Bonnet Kare
2 Anse Caiman
3 Anse Cocos
4 Anse Marron
5 Anse Patates
6 Anse Sévère
7 Anse Source d'Argent
8 Anse Union
9 Cemetery
10 Grand Anse
11 L'Union Estate
12 Nid d'Aigle
13 Veuve Reserve

EATING
14 Belle Vue Café

Historical Insights at L'Union Estate

COLONIAL HISTORY, PLANTATION SPICES

The tranquil L'Union Estate was originally a large coconut and vanilla plantation. It was active in producing copra (the white flesh of the coconut from which oil is extracted) up until the 1980s, when palm oil decimated the industry.

On entering, stop first at the **cemetery**. La Digue's first settlers – who arrived in 1789 – are buried here, including Rassool and Hossein, two Muslims from Persia (now Iran) who were big Seychelles landowners. Alongside are gravestones marked Mellon, Payet, Camille and Laporte, all émigrés from Réunion whose descendants still live on the island today, most famously the artist George Camille.

CURIEUSE ISLAND

As La Digue is only 20 minutes from Praslin by boat, it's possible to arrange full-day excursions to Curieuse Marine National Park from here. For more information on the island and its tortoise-breeding programme, see p240.

The plantation house is the earliest example of French Colonial architecture in Seychelles, and at the mill you can see how copra was produced: coconut husks had to be broken, the white flesh baked in an old calorifier and then crushed on a stone mill drawn by an oxen. It took two hours to make one pail of coconut oil.

Vanilla vines continue to be cultivated and sold here. This South American spice has no native pollinators in the Indian Ocean so it has to be pollinated by hand with a toothpick (a discovery made by enslaved Edmund Albius on Réunion Island). Such was the reliance on slave labour that in 1807, when slave trading was abolished, 6638 of Seychelles' total population of 7323 were slaves.

Also near the vanilla plantation you'll find an enclosure of giant Aldabra tortoises. It sits in the shade of the giant union rock, a 40m-high monolith of Precambrian granite that is estimated to be 700 million years old.

Scaling the Eagle's Nest
HEAVENLY HIKING, SENSATIONAL VIEWS

La Digue's most challenging hike takes you to the highest point of the island, **Nid d'Aigle** (333m). It's a steep, hot climb, but at the top you'll be rewarded with a spectacular bird's-eye view of the island surrounded by the silvery sea, with Praslin, Félicité, Marianne and even Frégate Island visible in the distance.

It's advisable to hike early in the morning with a guide as the track is not easily visible and, in any case, guides have so much to share about the island's flora, history and culture as you walk. Sunny Trail Guide, Paradise Tours and Coco Trail are all reliable options. The trailhead starts at Belle Vue Café. At the steps, you'll see a sign marked 'To the Mountain'. Within minutes there is an inconspicuous fork in the path; the less-trodden one to the right heads to Nid d'Aigle.

While it's only 300m to the summit, the climb is 100m in elevation. Some of it up slippery paths and some over large boulders. However, when you reach the ridge you'll be rewarded with a phenomenal view. An easier option is to book a sunset dinner at **Belle Vue Café** (Sr550 per person), which includes a taxi pick-up and drop-off. While it is a total tourist experience, the sunset is unforgettable with raptor-size fruit bats riding the thermals down below.

Other beach-hopping hikes are possible on La Digue, the easiest being the coastal trail from Grand Anse to **Anse Cocos**

BEST SOUVENIRS

Vanilla
Stock up on raw vanilla essence and whole pods at L'Union Estate where they grow and extract it.

Coconut oil
Virgin coconut oil has many purposes. It's a low-fat cooking oil, is great for hair and skin care and is rich in immune-boosting lauric acid.

George Camille artwork
George Camille's watercolours, etchings and collages are worthy souvenirs. Camille was raised on La Digue and his gallery is at Anse Banane (georgecamille.com).

Eco-beach bag
Homegrown brand Coco Seychelles (coco.sc) creates sturdy, sustainably sourced cotton beach bags, printed with island-inspired designs.

WHERE TO STAY ON LA DIGUE

Pension Michel
Lovely bungalows, with peaceful verandas, hammocks and vibrant trimmings of yellow and green. €

Calou Guesthouse
A great option in the village for families, with smart rooms and deep verandas. €€

Cabanes des Anges
A peaceful place set around a pool and deck area. Three rooms and six one-bedroom apartments. €€

or **Anse Caiman**. The more challenging hikes between Grand Anse and **Anse Marron** (1½ hours) and from **Anse Source d'Argent** to **Anse Bonnet Kare** (three hours) are more adventurous and better with a guide.

Fun in the Water
BOATING, DIVING, SNORKELLING, SURFING

The crystal-clear waters around La Digue are an open-air aquarium filled with colourful fish, starfish, sting rays, turtles and sharks. You can amuse yourself for hours snorkelling around the rocks on Anse Sévère and Anse Patates, and exploring the reef at **Anse Union**. But there's much to discover offshore as La Digue is well-situated between lots of other islands and islets that are prime snorkelling and diving stops.

Nid d'Aigle

A CULTURAL BIKE TOUR

A cultural bike ride with Josiana Rose of **Pedaler Velo** (2723084; jonathalierose@gmail.com) is a La Digue highlight. Starting in La Passe you'll head to Pointe Cap Barbi, pausing at the cemetery and the shrine of the Virgin Mary, where Josiana will fill you in on local customs and characters. You'll eat her homegrown mangos at Anse Patates, before heading into the 'countryside'. You may stop at her mum's for passion-fruit juice, or have breadfruit with cousins at Calou Guesthouse. You'll visit ancient baobab trees and have a takeaway lunch at popular Rey & Josh. It's fun nipping through the Veuve Reserve and glimpsing local life.

Anse Sévère Beach Villas
Six self-catering apartments in gorgeously designed Creole-style chalets. Great verandas. €€

Domaine Les Rochers
Architect-designed apartments with open-plan living rooms and well-equipped kitchens. €€€

Le Nautique
Occupies a waterfront position and its Creole cottages are beautifully designed. There's also a fun bar. €€€

Anse Marron

TOP EXPERIENCE

La Digue Beaches

Just 5km long and 3km wide, La Digue is surrounded by coral reef, so you can swim and snorkel safely in most of the island's bays. Snorkelling is top-notch and the island's beaches are extravagantly beautiful, lapped by chrysoprase-coloured water and backed by coconut palms. Most of them also feature charming beach shacks serving moreish fruit smoothies, coconuts and seafood.

DON'T MISS

Hiking from Grand Anse to Anse Coco

Sunset at Anse Sévère

Snorkelling around Anse Marron

Kayaking off Anse Source d'Argent

Grilled fish at the Old Pier Café

Anse Source d'Argent

One of the most photographed beaches on the planet, Anse Source d'Argent is a spectacular beach with dazzling white sand bookended by immense eroded boulders and lapped by shallow emerald water. Located inside the L'Union Estate plantation, you'll need to pay the park's entry fee to access the beach (valid for a day). Come early or late to avoid the crowds. During the day, beach shacks beneath the palms sell fruit and refreshment. The **Old Pier Cafe**, also inside L'Union Estate, is an excellent open-air restaurant.

Anse Marron

Anse Marron (pictured) sits tucked behind Gaudíesque granite boulders at the remote southern tip of La Digue.

The tiny inlet is truly a hidden spot with its sheltered, crystal-clear waters providing a memorable location for a swim or snorkel. The beach can only be reached via a somewhat tricky walking trail. A guide is advisable.

Grand Anse

La Digue's longest beach is located on the southeastern side of the island. The water at Grand Anse is deep and the currents strong from April to October, which is why it's a favoured local surfing spot. A walking trail starts from here and heads northeast to the more secluded coves of Petite Anse and Anse Coco. Note, there's little shade on this beach.

Petite Anse

Accessible only by foot from Grand Anse, this dramatic crescent of bleached white sand receives very few visitors, even though the 300m walk over the headland is easy. There isn't much shade here, but vendors on the beach set up some palm-frond shades. Again, currents are strong between April and October. Sunbathers are better off heading on to Anse Coco (900m further north).

Anse Coco

Anse Coco is a gorgeous curving bay of salt-white sand. Unlike other southeast beaches, it's backed by large casuarina trees that shade snoozing sunbathers. There's also a small **beach shack** here that serves coconut and fruit juice and cooks up a storming traditional Creole fish barbecue. Strong currents also prevail here, but there's a sheltered pool at the northern end of the beach that allows for a good wallow. The walk here from Grand Anse is roughly 1.3km and takes about 1½ hours.

Anse Sévère

A short bike ride north of La Passe, west-facing Anse Sévère is a great beach to spend the day on. It's long and deep and shaded by a thick stand of takamaka trees, while the jade waters are shallow and family-friendly due to the protection of a barrier reef. Behind the beach, you'll also find a couple of beach shacks serving snacks and drinks. **Bikini Beach Bar** serves fruit cocktails laced with rum, which are the perfect accompaniment to the spectacular sunset you can enjoy here looking out towards Praslin.

Anse Fourmis

The last beach on the northeastern side of the island. Anse Fourmis has lots of shade and shallow water making it ideal for families. There are few amenities, so bring some water. However, **Chez Jules** is nearby, which serves the best seafood on the island.

CLEAR THE DECKS

It's one thing to kayak around La Digue; it's totally another to do so in a transparent kayak that reveals the aquatic treasures that lurk beneath. Crystal Kayaks offers guided tours of 2½ hours that take in Anse Source d'Argent and Anse Pierrot or Anse Sévère and Anse Patates. Others visit Félicité and Île Cocos. Guests can also hire kayaks for independent paddling.

TOP TIPS

- Pack reef-safe sunscreen without oxybenzone or octinoxate, which cause coral bleaching.
- Southeastern beaches are best visited in the morning when the hike over the headland isn't too hot.
- Conversely, the northwestern beach of Anse Sévère is great in the late afternoon at sunset.
- Kayaks can be hired by the hour at Anse Source d'Argent.
- Consider taking a boat trip around La Digue to enjoy the island from a different perspective.

Nevis Ernesta (excursioinsladigue.com) and Lizzy Boat Charters (lizzyboat.com) run excellent half- and full-day snorkelling tours (€65/125 per person respectively) hopping between **Ave Maria Island**, **Îles Cocos**, **Félicite**, **Petite Soeur** and **Grand Soeur**, where they'll prep a beach barbecue on the full-day tour. It's a great day out. Other sunset cruises and leisurely boat trips around La Digue can be easily arranged through 7°South and Mason's Travel in La Passe.

Divers also have good options around La Digue, including the dive sites of **White Bank**, Ave Maria, **Channel Rock**, **Marianne Island**, **Sister Reef** and **Cayman Rock**. Ave Maria is notable for its shark sightings, while White Bank is an iconic spot with stunning tunnels and arches filled with prolific sea life. Further east, **Marianne Rock** offers a 25m dive to an underwater cathedral of granite peaks and ravines, popular with tuna, barracuda and several shark species. Azzura Pro Dive (based at La Digue Island Lodge) and Trek Divers offer dive excursions, single tanks and a variety of certified courses.

Finally, although Seychelles isn't generally known for surfing (due to the shallow Seychelles shelf and inconsistent waves), Grand Anse beach on La Digue boasts the best waves. Good months to surf are during the southeast winds (April to August) when the waves are waist to shoulder high and bigger swells are less frequent. Nicholas Jeannevol (+248 2588331) is a local surfer and guide who can advise.

Snorkelling, Félicite

BEST PLACES TO EAT

Chez Jules
A roadside shack serving tasty Creole cooking, particularly the octopus curry. Cash only. €€

Old Pier Café
An open-air restaurant at the L'Union Estate serving cold beer and plates of spicy jobfish with papaya salad. €€

Le Nautique
Fine Creole dining on a deck overlooking the ocean makes this one of the most romantic dining spots on La Digue. €€€

Rey & Josh Takeaway
La Digue's best takeaway serving home-cooked meals, including octopus and barnacle curry. €

Ton Greg
The island's most popular, local pizzeria. €

GETTING AROUND

There is no airport on La Digue, but ZilAir offers helicopter services from Mahé and Praslin. Inter-Island Ferry and Cat Cocos run regular services to Praslin and the crossing takes only 15 minutes. Buy tickets online or at the ticket office near the jetty. Transport on La Digue is almost exclusively by bike. Many hotels offer guests bikes for free, otherwise there are loads of bike rentals in La Passe – Tati's Bicycle Rental is one of the biggest. There is no street lighting so a head torch is helpful to navigate in the dark. There are also a handful of taxis, mainly useful for getting up to Belle Vue Restaurant. If you need one, book ahead as they get busy.

THE OUTER ISLANDS

Zil Elwannyen Sesel, as the Outer Islands are known in Creole, are scattered across a vast expanse of ocean 230km to 1150km southwest of Mahé. Barely peeping above sea level, they are mostly coral atolls – rings of reefs and islets that mark the ghostly rim of ancient volcanoes now submerged. It's a place so pristine it provided the location for one of *Blue Planet II*'s most memorable sequences, when giant trevallies leapt from the sea to snatch baby terns in flight, to presenter David Attenborough's astonishment. This is as wild as you can get from a marine point of view.

In a world where biodiversity is being lost at an astonishing rate, Seychelles' Outer Islands are rare, precious and important. They are managed by the parastatal IDC (Island Development Company) and are uninhabited except for a few scientific research stations, two luxury resorts and one pioneering marine safari outfit.

TOP TIP

The only way to visit the Outer Islands is by booking into one of the private resorts (they will arrange air transfers, usually inclusive in your booking), by visiting on a cruise ship, or by private yacht or fishing charter (once permission has been obtained from the IDC).

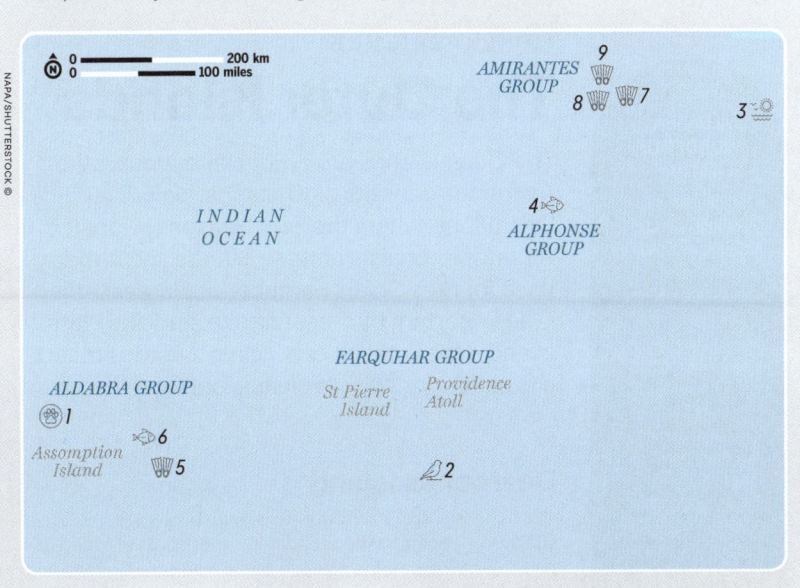

SIGHTS
1 Aldabra
2 Farquhar Atoll
3 Platte Island

ACTIVITIES, COURSES & TOURS
4 Alphonse Island
5 Astove Island
6 Cosmoledo Atoll
7 Desroches Island
8 Poivre
9 Saint Joseph's

Bird colony, Cosmoledo Atoll (p251)

Desroches Island

TOP EXPERIENCE
The Outer Islands

The Outer Islands are divided into groups: the Amirantes consists of 10 islands, including Desroches, where the Four Seasons is located; Alphonse consists of three islands and is the base for Blue Safari; Farquhar, the largest atoll, is an important bird-nesting site; and tiny Platte Island – the location of a Waldorf Astoria resort– sits alone, ringed with pristine barrier reefs.

Desroches Island

The main island of the Amirantes group, Desroches (pictured) sits atop a submerged crater 230km southwest of Mahé. It's just 5.5km long and is covered in a green forest of coconut and hardwood trees, surrounded by 13km of fine-white-sand beaches. The only thing here is the 71-villa Four Seasons Resort, an outlet of the Island Conservation Society and the WiseOcean dive company, which operates diving and fishing excursions to nearby **Poivre** and St Joseph's Atoll. As a nationally important nesting site for green and hawksbill turtles, Desroches is a great place to see them while snorkelling amid the seagrass beds.

ALDABRA: WONDER OF NATURE

Seychelles' most remote island is Aldabra, an island of such environmental value that it forms a baseline for scientists. Here the marine biomass is 5.5 tonnes per hectare (it's less than half a tonne around Mahé) and the island is home to 150,000 giant tortoises. A plaque, installed by Unesco in 1982, states simply: 'Aldabra, wonder of nature given to humanity by the people of the Republic of Seychelles.'

St Joseph's Atoll

St Joseph's, 44km northwest of Desroches, is a spectacular atoll made up of a circle of 16 islands that sit on a wide reef that encloses a 3.5km-wide milky lagoon. Tidal action cuts off the lagoon periodically each day, making this an important breeding ground for blacktip reef and sicklefin lemon sharks. Dozens of other shark species also love the lagoon along with tuna, trevally, snapper, barracuda and bonefish, while huge rays circle the perimeter. Hundreds of hawksbill and green turtles nest here and the coral reefs teem with life.

Platte Island

Sitting separately, 130km south of Mahé, Platte Island is a low wooded sand cay, just 1.4km long. In the 1840s there was so much guano here that it was excavated and sold as fertiliser. It also nurtured the lush palm forest that covers the island today. In 2023, Waldorf Astoria debuted a new 50-villa private resort on Platte, featuring six restaurants, a top-drawer spa and a marine discovery centre, which will help guests explore the incredible 12km-wide lagoon and extensive barrier reefs that surround the island. It's a US$100 million development, so expect it to set a new benchmark for luxury in the Outer Islands.

Alphonse Island

Even more distant Alphonse Island (250km southwest of Mahé) is the main base of Blue Safari, a pioneering experiential travel company with light-food accommodation on three outer islands. On the coral island of Alphonse their charming Creole cottages sit beside pristine beaches overlooking unspoilt sea flats where reef walks are possible with the resident marine biologist. The island is also a magnet for migrating seabirds and nearby St Francois – which the Alphonse Foundation also manages – is considered one of the greatest saltwater fishing spots in the world, home to the almost mythical Giant Trevally.

Astove Island & Cosmoledo Atoll

Blue Safari also operates the fishing and dive base, Coral House, on Astove Island – situated 1042km southwest of Mahé, almost at the tip of Madagascar. Astove is the location of the stunning 'Wall', an underwater coral Grand Canyon that forms one of the best dive sites on the planet. Nearby, on the huge coral atoll of Cosmoledo, there's also a back-to-nature Eco Camp, made up of a handful of container pods and an open-air mess tent. Cosmoledo is another fluctuating lagoon full of fish and turtles. Visiting these wild marine environments and participating in Blue Safari's conservation-focused activities – which includes manta ray monitoring, fly-fishing and tagging, and reef flat walks – is a once-in-a-lifetime experience.

DON'T MISS

Snorkelling to see turtles around Desroches

Diving Astove 'Wall'

Fishing on St Joseph's Atoll

Manta ray monitoring with Blue Safari

Reef walks with a marine biologist on Alphonse

TOP TIPS

- Use reef-safe sunscreen without octinoxate and oxybenzone, which damage coral.
- Pack a hat, saltwater wading boots, a waterproof rucksack, polarised sunglasses, lightweight long-sleeve shirts, gloves and buffs.
- Turtle breeding season is September to March.
- The luggage restriction on flights to the Outer Islands is 15kg (Mahé airport has a left-luggage store).
- 'From Scene of Accident Medevac Insurance' is advised and is mandatory for Blue Safari.
- Astove and Cosmoledo are closed between May and October.
- Visits to Aldabra require a special permit from Seychelles Island Foundation; a few high-end cruise ships stop here.

Arriving

Virtually all travellers – other than those on cruises or large ocean-going yachts (!) – arrive by air at Seychelles International Airport, about 8km south of Victoria. It is the only international airport in Seychelles. Most hotels will offer a pick-up service, otherwise taxis are available outside. There are no boat services between Seychelles and other destinations in the Indian Ocean.

Visas

Entering Seychelles is hassle-free, with no visa required for most nationalities. Before arriving you have to apply for an online Digital Travel Authorisation (seychelles.govtas.com).

Customs Regulations

Seychelles has restrictions on importing plants, seeds and animal products. It is also illegal to export turtle products and a special permit is required to export the coco de mer nut.

SIM Cards

Seychelles has a good mobile phone network on the main islands, but roaming charges are high. Buy pre-paid SIM cards from Cable & Wireless or Airtel at the airport. Passport required.

Wi-Fi

All mid-range and top-end hotels offer wi-fi, as do most self-catering places. Access elsewhere is harder to come by. There are a few internet cafes in Victoria.

Transport from Seychelles International Airport to

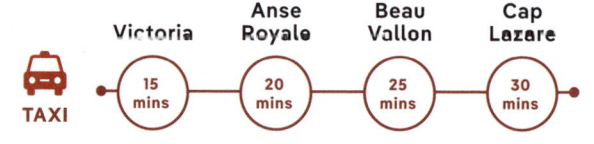

TAXI

Victoria	Anse Royale	Beau Vallon	Cap Lazare
15 mins	20 mins	25 mins	30 mins

Taxi from Praslin Island Airport to

TAXI

Praslin Ferry Terminal	Anse Volbert
15 mins	25 mins

SEASONAL VARIATIONS

Seychelles has a tropical equatorial climate, which means it's between 24°C and 32°C year-round. What seasonal variation there is depends on the trade winds. The northwest trade wind brings warmer, wetter airstreams from October to April. The wettest months are November to February, and Mahé and Silhouette are the most affected islands. From May to September the southeast trade wind ushers in cooler, drier weather, but whips up waves. April to May and October to November are the calmest periods.

Getting Around

Regular Air Seychelles flights run between Mahé and Praslin. Ferries connect Mahe, Praslin and La Digue, and Mahé and Silhouette. Other islands are served by charter flights or helicopter.

TRAVEL COSTS

Flight from Mahé to Praslin
€100–170

Car hire
€45–60 per day

Ferry from Mahé to Praslin
€60–84

Ferry from Praslin to La Digue
€14

TIP
In high summer, book air and ferry tickets a couple of days in advance. Seychellesbookings.com is a useful resource.

AIR
Air Seychelles runs all inter-island flights, whether scheduled or chartered. The only scheduled flights are between Mahé and Praslin (20 minutes). Charters also fly to Bird, Denis, Desroches and Alphonse and must be booked through the resort. La Digue, Silhouette, Félicité and Frégate are reached by helicopter.

CAR & TAXI
Mahé and Praslin are large, hilly islands, so if you want to explore rent a car, either at the airport or through your hotel/guesthouse. Prices drop by 20% if you rent for more than three days. If you're resort-based and just doing a few excursions, use local taxis.

BOAT
Fast Cat Cocos catamarans run regular services between Mahé and Praslin (one hour) and on to La Digue (15 minutes). Inter-Island Ferry also runs services between Praslin and La Digue. Children under 12 travel for half price. For other islands you must charter a boat or take a tour.

BICYCLE
Bicycles are popular throughout the islands, although their use is more restricted on Mahé and Praslin given the hilly terrain. On La Digue and most other small islands, however, they are the main mode of transport as car usage is heavily restricted or, in some cases, nonexistent.

CRUISING
Seychelles is an increasingly popular cruise destination during the October to April cruise season. Many itineraries combine Seychelles with Madagascar, Zanzibar, the Maldives and ports in East or South Africa. Hapag-Lloyd, Silversea's expedition ships, South African Silver Cloud (via Mozambique and Madagascar) and Emerald Cruises are some of the biggest and best operators. Ponant and Variety Cruises also offer year-round cruises; Ponant's itinerary includes the Outer Islands.

BUS
Seychelles Public Transport Corporation (stpc.sc) operates an extensive bus network on Mahé and Praslin. Destinations and routes are shown on the front of buses, and schedules are posted at bus stops. Tickets cost Sr12 regardless of where you're going. Buses get busy during rush hour and when school is out.

DRIVING ESSENTIALS

Drive on the left.

21
Drivers must be over 21 years old and have held a driving licence for at least a year.

.08
Blood alcohol limit is 0.08%.

TOOLKIT

TOOLKIT

The chapters in this section cover the most important topics you'll need to know about in Mauritius, Réunion and Seychelles. They're full of nuts-and-bolts information and valuable insights to help you understand and navigate Mauritius, Réunion and Seychelles and get the most out of your trip.

Money p256

Accommodation p257

Family Travel p258

Health & Safe Travel p259

Food, Drink & Nightlife p260

Responsible Travel p262

LGBTIQ+ Travel p264

Accessible Travel p265

Nuts & Bolts p267

Language p268

Trou-aux-Biches (p99), Mauritius
TB-PHOTOGRAPHY/SHUTTERSTOCK ©

Money

CURRENCY: MAURITIAN RUPEE (RS); RÉUNION EURO (€); SEYCHELLES RUPEE (RS)

HOW MUCH FOR…

a cup of coffee
Mauritius **Rs 20–95**,
Réunion **€2**,
Seychelles **Rs 30–50**

a local curry lunch
Mauritius **Rs 300–600**,
Réunion **€16**,
Seychelles **Rs 400**

a cocktail
Mauritius **Rs 400**,
Réunion **€12**,
Seychelles **Rs 200**

a museum/marine park entry
Mauritius **Rs 1000**,
Réunion **€5–15**,
Seychelles **Rs 150**

ATMs

ATMs are easy to find in towns, airports and ferry terminals. They are scarce in small villages and in the mountains of Réunion, so carry some cash. Euros are the best hard currency to carry and many hotels, excursions and car-hire services quote in euros. Be aware that charges on withdrawals can be high.

Credit Cards

In all three destinations, major credit cards, including Visa and Mastercard, are widely accepted in hotels, restaurants and tourist shops. Amex is only accepted at some luxury hotels. Smaller guesthouses may refuse cards, so check ahead. For small, local restaurants, beach shacks and food stalls, you'll need cash.

Tipping

Tipping is not generally practised in Seychelles and Réunion, although a service charge of 10% to 15% is often automatically included in bills at top-end hotels. Tipping is widely practised in Mauritius in line with European standards.

LOCAL TIP

Bargaining is not part of the culture; prices quoted are fixed. However, in tourist areas and street markets (not food), it's worth asking if the price offered is the final one.

HOW TO… SAVE SOME MONEY

- First, avoid travelling during Easter and European summer holidays.
- Book accommodation in local guesthouses or self-catering apartments – they are plentiful on all islands.
- Eat at food stalls and takeaway places, which are excellent.
- Shop in markets, where a bit of bargaining is possible.
- Buy a local SIM card.
- Bring your own snorkelling gear.
- Réunion is the most affordable of the three islands.

VAT REFUNDS

In Mauritius and Seychelles you can claim a VAT refund on departure. In Mauritius, this applies to goods bought in shops displaying the 'Tax Refund' sticker. You'll need to retain your receipt to show at MCCI Tax Refund Counter at the airport. In Seychelles, VAT can be reclaimed on artisanal items, jewellery, fashion, accessories and toiletries. Again, registered vendors display a VAT sticker. The Seychelles Revenue Commission booth, where you claim your refund, is on the first floor of the airport departure lounge.

Accommodation

Resorts
Mauritius and Seychelles are famous for their dreamy resorts. Booking through travel agents or opting for a hotel-and-flight package usually saves money. Between November and April, book a month ahead. Private-island resorts are all-inclusive. Although the daily price might give you a heart attack, once you price in all the activities included, you may find they aren't that outrageous.

Guesthouses & Chambres d'Hôtes
On Mauritius and Réunion there's an extensive network of well-priced, privately run guesthouses and chambres d'hôtes (B&Bs). It's a fantastic way to enjoy home-cooked meals by booking to eat at the tables d'hôtes (host's table). Options include everything from restored Creole houses to rooms in rural homes set in scenic locations. Breakfast is always included.

Camping
There is little camping culture on any of the islands. There are no campsites in Seychelles and just a handful on Mauritius (in Flic en Flac) and Réunion. The latter has two official campsites, on the southwest coast at Étang-Salé-les-Bains and L'Hermitage-les-Bains. You'll also find a couple of camping chez l'habitant (informal, privately run camping grounds) in Îlet-à-Vidot and Bébour-Bélouve.

TOOLKIT

HOW MUCH FOR A NIGHT IN...

a double room in a B&B
€100

a one-bedroom self-catering apartment
€160–180

a double room in a high-end resort
€350–1500

Gîtes de Montagne
These basic mountain cabins are a feature of Réunion's mountainous interior. Operated by the local authorities, they are bookable through explorereunion.com. Most are in good shape with solar power, bunk beds and kitchens. They must be paid in advance. On arrival and departure you must 'book' in and out with the manager, who will collect your voucher.

Self-Catering Rentals
Self-catering accommodation is the most economic option. In Mauritius most self-catering places are managed by agencies. In Seychelles, they are individually managed. Most require a minimum stay of three nights.

STAYING LOCAL

The tradition of the chambres d'hôtes (B&B) and maison d'hôtes (guesthouse) in Mauritius and Réunion is one of the best ways to experience a slice of local life.

These places are run by locals, usually Creoles or Franco-Mauritians, and offer immersive experiences to local markets and home-cooked meals at their tables d'hôtes. They often showcase some of the island's best cooking. Chambres d'hotes vary from simple, rustic places to more luxurious Creole residences such as Les Grands Monts and La Maison d'Edith on Réunion.

LEFT, FROM TOP: ANTON_IVANOV/SHUTTERSTOCK ©, SASHKIN/SHUTTERSTOCK ©
RIGHT, FROM TOP: INARA PRUSAKOVA/SHUTTERSTOCK ©, VM2002/SHUTTERSTOCK ©

Family Travel

With endless beaches, a temperate climate and safe seas bounded by reefs, these islands are a paradise for children, and their parents. Family is also central to island culture, and kids will be received with a smile everywhere, while resorts cater to every imaginable desire in storybook surroundings with world-class facilities.

Sights & Activities

Swimming, snorkelling, boat excursions, beachside cycling, forest and volcano hikes, and communing with giant tortoises and turtles – these islands are an activity wonderland for kids. Some activities and hikes, particularly on Réunion, aren't suitable for younger children, so check in advance. Kids need to be over 8 or 10 years old for diving. Resorts usually have brilliant clubs and conservation-focused activities tailored to children.

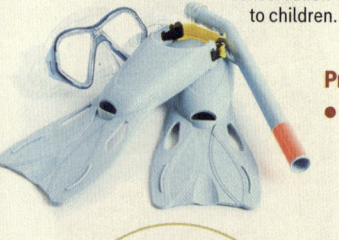

Child Safety

Sunburn and heat exhaustion are the most common risk. Ensure you have high-UV-factor sun cream, hats and UV-protection swim tops. Also, take heed of local advice on safe swimming beaches. On Réunion, check the difficulty of hikes before setting off.

Practicalities

- Most hotels and guesthouses have family rooms; hotels also offer kids menus and babysitting services; and high-end resorts have amazing kids' clubs.
- Cots and extra beds are usually provided free, or at a small extra charge, and most car-hire companies have child seats.
- Nappies are readily available; but specialist baby products are hard to find outside main cities.
- Baby-changing facilities aren't common.
- Breastfeeding in public isn't an issue.

Getting Around

Babies under 2 years old (or 3 in Réunion) usually travel for free on buses, ferries and inter-island flights. Otherwise, children under 12 years old get a 50% discount on public transport and ferry tickets.

KID-FRIENDLY PICKS

Île aux Aigrettes, Mauritius (p115)

A lovely nature reserve and a haven for giant tortoises.

Beau Vallon Beach, Seychelles (p213)

Mahe's best beach has safe swimming and great local restaurants.

Tamarin, Mauritius (p83)

A palm-fringed bay popular with dolphins and local surfers.

La Digue, Seychelles (p242)

Every family's favourite (largely car-free) island, La Digue is an idyllic outdoor playground.

Cité du Volcán, Réunion (p200)

A fabulous interactive museum exploring the dynamics of Réunion's volcano.

KIDS & CONSERVATION

For kids keen on conservation, wildlife, the marine world and sustainability, these islands are a great place to explore unique ecosystems in fascinating, immersive ways. Many high-end hotels provide a base for conservation NGOs, such as WiseOcean and Save Our Seas; alongside these, local conservation organisations are staffed by young scientists, biologists and conservation specialists. They lead excellent tours, guided snorkels and dives, reef and island walks, tree-planting activities, and monitoring programmes for turtles, birds and even manta rays. There are also a number of volunteering opportunities for young adults, such as with the Mauritian Wildlife Foundation and Seychelles Island Foundation.

Health & Safe Travel

INSURANCE

Make sure your travel insurance covers outdoor activities, particularly diving, climbing and canyoning, as well as the emergency transport required to get you to hospital or repatriated. If diving, take out cover to evacuate you to a recompression facility and ensure it includes the cost of hyperbaric treatment. Divers Alert Network, a nonprofit diving-safety organisation, provides a good policy.

MOSQUITO-BORNE DISEASES

There have been outbreaks of chikungunya and dengue fever in Mauritius and Réunion, so check the latest advice.

Beach Hazards

- Swimmers should always be aware of currents and riptides around reefs, particularly on southeastern beaches in Seychelles during the southeast trade winds.
- Many beaches aren't supervised, so heed local advice.
- Sunburn is an issue, particularly when spending hours snorkelling, fishing or kayaking, so bring appropriate sunscreen.
- Finally, be aware of falling coconuts – they can cause severe head injuries.

Marine Dangers

- Above all, watch out for sea urchins.
- Lionfish have poisonous spined fins and stonefish are exceptionally poisonous.
- Fire coral also packs a powerful sting if touched, and stinging blue bottles (jellyfish) appear in Mauritius after cyclones.
- More serious are shark attacks on Réunion. Always heed warnings and stick to lifeguard-patrolled beaches.
- Swim only inside lagoons and protected areas.

HEALTH CARE

Health care is generally good. However, in Seychelles, hospitals are only found on the three main islands. The Outer Islands only have basic first-aid posts. Private clinics have better equipment and more advanced drugs. It is always safest to bring your own medication. If travelling to remote areas and engaging in adventure activities, carry a first-aid kit.

BEACH WARNING FLAGS

Green flag — Low Hazard

Yellow flag — You may remain at the water's edge, but no swimming

Red flag — High Hazard
Two red flags — Water closed to public

Red & yellow flag — Beach is temporarily unmanned

Purple flags — Marine pests present

DECOMPRESSION SICKNESS

A serious condition caused by diving too deep, staying at depth for too long or ascending too quickly. Common symptoms include unusual fatigue or weakness, skin itch, pain in the arms, legs or torso, dizziness and vertigo, local numbness, tingling or paralysis, and shortness of breath. Your last dive should be completed 24 hours before flying.

Food, Drink & Nightlife

EATING CUSTOMS

Eating habits vary across ethnic groups. Some eat with their fingers, others don't eat meat on Fridays, and some abstain from pork.

Breakfast is quick and informal. Lunch, too, is a casual affair, though at weekends a family get-together is typical.

In Mauritius and Réunion, aperitif is a tradition, while eating out is a treat that people dress up for.

HOW TO... ENJOY RÉUNIONNAIS APÉRO

The French tradition of apéritif (or apéro) goes back centuries. French philosopher Diderot first classified it as a medicinal 'drug which opens the way to elimination' of toxins in 1751. But with the proliferation of alcoholic beverages in the 19th century this stimulating pre-dinner drink became a social event.

In Réunion, the tradition is deeply entrenched. More than just a 'happy hour', it is a cultural ritual where friendships and community are reaffirmed. Thus, every meal starts with an aperitif, traditionally a glass of *rhum arrangé* (rum flavoured with fruits and spices), or a Creole *ti'punch* (punch made with tropical fruit, rum, lime and cane syrup).

To avoid inebriation, savoury nibbles are served. These are shareable and dippable and include specialities such as *samoussa cari poulet* (curried chicken pastries), *bouchons* (pork dumplings), stuffed peppers, shrimp fritters, Creole pâté and *bonbons piments* (chilli candies).

MENU DECODER

Carte (en Anglais) The menu (in English)
Carte des vins Wine list
Menu pour enfants Children's menu
Chaise haute Highchair
Petit déjeuner, dejeuner, dîner Breakfast, lunch, dinner
Entrée, plat, salade First course, main course, salad
Apéritif or apéro Pre-dinner drink or cocktail
Fruits de mer Seafood (sometimes a separate menu category to 'poisson', fish)
Végétarien Vegetarian, not usually a category on the menu
Pommes frites French fries
Spécialité locale Local speciality
Saignant, a point, bien cuit Rare, medium or well done (referring to how you want your meat cooked)
Assiette A plate of something, (for example cheese)
Grillé Grilled
Cru Raw
Rôti Roasted
Poêlée Pan-fried
Vin rouge/blanc Red/white wine
Bière Beer
Eau minérale Mineral water
L'addition The bill
Je ne mange pas... I don't eat...

Where to Eat

Restaurants The mainstay of the dining scene; restaurants range from open-air beachside shacks to smart local restaurants and sophisticated international dining in five-star hotels.

Tables d'hôte (host's table) In Mauritius and Réunion these set-menu, home-cooked feasts are served at B&Bs and guesthouses. Book in advance.

Cafes & patisseries A French hangover and feature of Mauritian and Réunionnais towns.

Food stalls & takeaway outlets Extremely popular across the islands, these simple venues serve tasty, affordable Creole food.

HOW MUCH FOR...

a fruit smoothie
€5–10

a takeout curry
€6–10

grilled fish with rice
€20–25

a salad
€8–15

mid-range meal for two
€20–60

a local beer
€2–4

HOW TO... COOK WITH SPICES

Spices are aromatic flavourings from seeds, fruits, bark, buds, rhizomes, stems and other plant parts that are used to season and preserve food. They've been highly valued for thousands of years – the word *spice* comes from the Latin *species*, which literally means 'goods' or 'wares'.

Spices are fundamental to Creole food so this is a great place to learn how to use them and stock up. A key point to note is that spices serve different purposes. Some, like cinnamon leaves, add aroma to food; others, such as garlic, cumin and ginger, enhance taste; and others still, create colour, particularly turmeric and paprika.

Use whole spices for subtle flavour and aroma in stews, braises and infusions, and ground spices where you want to disperse a lot of flavour, such as in baked goods or spice rubs. You can mellow their taste by toasting them, or blend flavours by frying them in oil.

You can buy top-quality spices on all the islands. Ground spices oxidise more quickly and will lose flavour in a few months. Whole spices will last up to a year if stored in an opaque jar or an airtight container in the fridge. The signature spices of these islands are cinnamon, nutmeg, turmeric, star anise, ginger, garlic, curry leaves, chillies and thyme, which lend Creole food an earthy, sweet, warm flavour.

The Power of Ginger

Ginger genuinely deserves its superfood designation. The root's active ingredient, gingerol, fights infections, lowers LDL cholesterol, treats chronic indigestion, lowers blood sugars, reduces joint and muscle pain, and delivers strong anti-cancer benefits.

WHERE TO PARTY

Of all the islands, Mauritius has the most dynamic nightlife scene, focused on the west coast. The options include huge nightclubs (open Friday and Saturday nights, and sometimes Wednesday), beach bars, pubs and casinos. A number of hotel resorts also host beach parties with international DJs and local live music.

The northern beach resort of Grand Baie is the main hub. One of the biggest venues is Banana Beach Club; OMG is another large club with guest DJs. For retro vibes and ocean views, head to the end of the beach in Pereybere to the RedCat Beach Lounge, a 1950s bar with regular live séga sessions.

Further south, in Flic en Flac, popular venues are Kenzi Bar, Shotz and Buddha Bar. Of these, Shotz features international DJs, skilled bartenders and live music performances. The hotels at Wolmar also put on live music gigs and evening events. Further south, Tamarin has a more laidback scene with the popular sports bar Big Willy's featuring live music and big-screen sports coverage; and, Awanam, the beach club at the Veranda Hotel, putting on a great programme from Thursday to Sunday.

In contrast, the nightlife scene on Réunion is fairly small and in Seychelles it's virtually non-existent. On Réunion, the west coast between St-Paul and St-Pierre is where most of the bars and nightclubs congregate, in particular at L'Hermitage-des-Bains. Here, clubs kick off at midnight and roll on until 5am. The top spots are La Villa Club and Beach Club.

Responsible Travel

TOOLKIT

Climate Change & Travel

It's impossible to ignore the impact we have when travelling, and the importance of making changes where we can. Lonely Planet urges all travellers to engage with their travel carbon footprint. There are many carbon calculators online that allow travellers to estimate the carbon emissions generated by their journey; try resurgence.org/resources/carbon-calculator.html. Many airlines and booking sites offer travellers the option of offsetting the impact of greenhouse gas emissions by contributing to climate-friendly initiatives around the world. We continue to offset the carbon footprint of all Lonely Planet staff travel, while recognising this is a mitigation more than a solution.

Restoration vs Conservation

Restoration ecology seeks to repair ecosystems through human intervention. Seychelles Islands Foundation is a pioneer in this field. Mauritius Wildlife Foundation also aims to restore the ecology of Île aux Aigrettes and Ferney Valley.

Tread Carefully

The 115,000 sq km underwater Mascarene Plateau is a top global diversity hot spot. Coral-bleaching events in 1998 and 2016 severely damaged the coral, so take care of fins and feet when diving or snorkelling.

Go Local

Spending your money locally is one of the most responsible things you can do. In Mauritius, hook up with My Moris and Taste Buddies; in Seychelles, check out Domaine de Val des Pres.

WHALE WATCH

From June to October, humpback whales migrate to the Indian Ocean from Antartica for a formidable oceanic show best seen on Réunion's west coast (p153). Help conservationists at Globice by downloading their app and recording your sightings.

10

In 2018 to 2020, US$21.6 million of Seychelles debt was forgiven in exchange for the protection of 30% of its 1.35 million sq km ocean territory, thus helping Seychelles meet the UN's 2030 sustainability goals 10 years ahead of schedule.

There are four Unesco Heritage Sites: Le Morne Brabant mountain and Aapravasi Ghat immigration depot in Mauritius; the Vallée de Mai palm forest in Seychelles; and Réunion National Park.

Wise Oceans provide marine education and conservation services through programmes at partner resorts in Seychelles and Mauritius. They run an online academy and public sessions for young marine enthusiasts.

The Island Conservation Society and Nature Seychelles protect seabird nesting colonies in Seychelles.

Seychelles Outer Islands are home to the last southern fin whale and the Indian Ocean's only dugongs.

BOTANICAL LESSONS

The islands are full of plants with medicinal properties. Find out more at Seychelles' Biodiversity Centre and the Jardin le Roi spice garden; the Mascarin Jardin Botanique on Réunion; and Pamplemousses Botanical Garden in Mauritius.

Routes of Enslaved Peoples

The Intercontinental Slavery Museum in Port Louis, Mauritius, is part of Unesco's Slave Route project. Learn more about the legacy of slavery there, at Réunion's Liberté Métisse festival and the Creole festival in Seychelles.

Responsible Adventures

Yanature and Lokal Adventure (Mauritius) are adventure specialists; Duocean (Réunion) lets you swim with cetaceans responsibly; Nature Seychelles offers tours to see nesting seabirds; Les Ecuries du Maïdo and Turquoise Trails (Réunion, Seychelles) host horse treks.

Reptiles Rule

The giant tortoise is the emblematic species and thrives in Seychelles. It is protected by the Island Conservation Society (ics.sc). Some have also been reintroduced to Mauritius at Île aux Aigrette, La Vanille Nature Park and Chamarel.

PROTECTING ENDEMICS

Seychelles' Vallée de Mai, Forêt de Bébour on Réunion and the Ebony Forest in Mauritius are full of endemic species. To protect them, the islands have strict import laws concerning plants, flowers, nuts and seeds.

RESOURCES

Mauritian Wildlife Foundation
The island's largest conservation-focused NGO.

Marine Conservation Society Seychelles
Provides marine education and research.

Blue Safari Seychelles
Runs research projects in Seychelles' Outer Islands.

Globice Réunion
Protects Réunion's cetaceans.

LGBTIQ+ Travellers

LGBTIQ+ travellers are unlikely to encounter any problems travelling in Mauritius, Réunion and Seychelles. Réunion and Seychelles are among the most progressive African countries with regard to LGBTIQ+ rights, and while Mauritius has a law that bans some forms of gay sex, it is rarely enforced. That said, the islands are still socially conservative, so some discretion is advised.

RESOURCES

Gay Sejour and Mister B&B are useful resources for finding queer-friendly guesthouses and holiday rentals on Mauritius and Réunion.

THE LAW

On all the islands, LGBTIQ+ people are legally protected from discrimination. French laws prevail in Réunion, which means there is no legal discrimination against homosexuals. In 2016, Seychelles also decriminalised sex between men (lesbianism was never a crime), same-sex marriage was legalised, and LGBTIQ+ couples are permitted to adopt. However, community attitudes are more conservative than these laws suggest. **Mauritius is the only island where sodomy (opposite-sex and same-sex) is still criminalised. However, it is unlikely that any issues would arise from same-sex couples sharing rooms at international hotels.**

GAY-FRIENDLY PLACES

In Mauritius, La Mariposa near Tamarin is the only place that advertises itself as gay-friendly. On Mahé, head to Mango House in Baie Lazare. On Réunion, in St Denis, Le Prince and Zanzibar are gay-friendly clubs. Bubbles Sauna Club is a gay-friendly bathhouse and the main beach is Plage de la Souris Chaude, which also has a naturist section.

The Mauritian Scene

Mauritius has a paradoxical relationship to homosexuality. On the one hand, much of the population is young and progressive; on the other, there remains a rigidly conservative streak to Mauritian public debate. Gay life on the island remains fairly secretive, existing on the internet, in private and at the occasional party. Incidences of LGBTIQ+ travellers experiencing any discrimination or harassment are uncommon.

The Réunionnais Scene

French laws apply in Réunion and homophobia is rare, although attitudes are not as liberal as in mainland France and displays of affection may be regarded with disdain. However, attitudes are slowly changing. The focus of the community is St-Denis, St-Pierre and La Saline-les-Bains.

The Seychellois Scene

Although Seychelles has relatively liberal laws, local attitudes are governed largely by conservative Catholic views. There are no issues with regard to same-sex couples booking rooms, but open displays of affection may raise eyebrows. There is no openly gay or lesbian scene in Seychelles.

Accessible Travel

Although infrastructure across these islands is of a high standard, there are few specific facilities for travellers with disabilities, and other than a single beach in Réunion, no beach is equipped for wheelchair access. That said, a range of international hotels can accommodate and support most travellers' needs.

Getting Around

Coastal resorts often lack any pavements, and sometimes pavements in larger towns aren't well-maintained and curb heights may present a problem. Public transport does not offer wheelchair access, so it's best to book a car with a driver through your hotel or travel agent.

Airport
Wheelchair assistance is available at the main airports, which are also well-designed with ramps. You must request assistance at least 72 hours in advance and arrive at the airport at least two hours before departure.

Accommodation
Although most modern buildings conform to international standards regarding disability access, some accommodation has stepped rather than ramped access. International chains like the Hilton are the best bet for accessible rooms.

SEYCHELLES INTER-ISLAND TRAVEL
Cat Cocos and Inter-Island Ferries are both wheelchair accessible and will provide assistance if notified in advance. Most of the Air Seychelles planes flying between Mahé and Praslin are too small for wheelchair users and none can accommodate wheelchairs on board.

ACCESSIBLE SIGHTS

In Seychelles, the ground floor of the National Museum, Mission Lodge and the Vallée de Mai are accessible. Likewise, the Cité du Volcán, Kelonia marine observatory and Stella Matutina museum on Réunion are accessible.

RÉUNION FOR YOU
Lareunionpourtous.re is a useful website with an interactive guide listing accessible hotels, restaurants, museums and activities on Réunion.

Scan this QR code for the interactive guide.

BEACHES

Réunion's St-Pierre beach is fully accessible with two tiralots and a Hippocampe (all-terrain beach wheelchair) available; Plage de L'Hermitage is another good option. Mauritius and Seychelles have no special beach facilities but higher-end hotels can provide you with assistance on the beach. In Seychelles you may want to base yourself on sheltered Beau Vallon beach, which has the highest concentration of restaurants.

ALEXANDER SPATARI/GETTY IMAGES ©

Pilgrims on their way to Grand Bassin (p95), Mauritius

Nuts & Bolts

PUBLIC HOLIDAYS

New Year's Day
1 January

Thaipoosam Cavadee, Mauritius
January/February

Chinese Spring Festival, Mauritius
January/February

Abolition of Slavery, Mauritius
1 February

Maha Shivaratri, Mauritius
February/March

National Day, Mauritius
12 March

Ougadi (Hindu New Year), Mauritius
March/April

Good Friday/ Easter Monday
March/April

Labour Day
1 May

National Day
12 March

Liberation Day, Seychelles
5 June

National Day, Seychelles
18 June

Independence Day, Seychelles
29 June

National Day, Réunion 14 July

Assumption
15 August

Ganesh Chaturthi, Mauritius
August/September

Creole Festival, Seychelles
October

Divali (Dipavali), Mauritius
October/November

Indian Arrival Day, Mauritius
2 November

Abolition of Slavery Day, Réunion
20 December

Christmas Day
25 December

Illegal Drugs

These islands are part of the Indian Ocean drug-smuggling network and drug use is a significant problem.

Travellers are unlikely to experience issues. The only side-effect is petty theft. So, don't leave valuables in cars or on the beach.

Although islanders smoke cannabis recreationally, be aware possession and drug use are strictly illegal.

Toilets

There are free public toilets near many Mauritian beaches; not in Réunion or Seychelles.

Smoking

Smoking is prohibited in indoor public places, at workplaces and on public transport.

GOOD TO KNOW

Time zone
GMT/UTC plus four hours (Mauritius, Réunion and Seychelles)

Country code
Mauritius: 230
Réunion: 262
Seychelles: 248

Emergency number
Mauritius: 114
Réunion: 15
Seychelles: 151

Population
Mauritius: 1.27 million
Réunion: 873,102
Seychelles: 98,462

Electricity 220V/50Hz

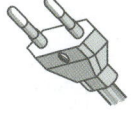

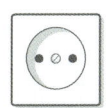

Type C 220V/50Hz

Type G 230V/50Hz

ETIQUETTE

Greetings Shaking hands is the typical greeting.

Clothing Beachwear is only worn on beaches. Nude bathing is prohibited.

Temples and mosques Dress modestly and remove shoes. Women should cover their hair in mosques.

Language

Along with the local Creoles, French is spoken (and official) in all three destinations included in this book. You'll find that menus on the islands are mostly in French, with English variations in some cases.

MAURITIUS
Most people will first speak to you in French and only switch to English once they realise you're an English speaker.

Basics

Hello. Bonjour. *bon·zhoor*
Goodbye. Au revoir. *o·rer·vwa*
Yes. Oui. *wee*
No. Non. *non*
Please. S'il vous plaît. *seel voo play*
Thank you. Merci. *mair·see*
Excuse me. Excusez-moi. *ek·skew·zay·mwa*
Sorry. Pardon. *par·don*
What's your name? Comment vous appelez-vous? *ko·mon voo za·play voo*
My name is … Je m'appelle. *zher ma·pel*
Do you speak English? Parlez-vous anglais? *par·lay·voo ong·glay*
I don't understand. Je ne comprends pas. *zher ner kom·pron pa*

Directions

Where's (the station)? Où est (la gare)? *oo ay (la gar)?*
What's the address? Quelle est l'adresse? *kel ay la·dres*
Could you please write it down? Est-ce que vous pourriez s'il vous plaît? *es·ker voo poo·ryay seel voo play*
Can you show me (on the map)? Pouvez-vous m'indiquer (sur la carte)? *poo·vay·voo mun·dee·kay (sewr la kart)*

Time

What time is it? Quelle heure est-il? *kel er ay til*
It's (8) o'clock. Il est (huit) heures. *il ay (weet) er*
Half past (10). (dix) heures et demie. *(deez) er ay day·mee*
morning matin. *ma·tun*
afternoon après-midi. *a·pray·mee·dee*
evening soir. *swar*
yesterday hier. *yair*
today aujourd'hui. *o·zhoor·dwee*
tomorrow demain. *der·mun*

Emergencies

Help! Au secours! *o skoor*
Leave me alone! Fichez-moi la paix! *fee·shay·mwa la pay*
I'm ill. Je suis malade. *zher swee ma·lad*
Call …! Appelez … *a·play…*
  a doctor un médecin. *un mayd·sun*
  the police la police. *la po·lees*

Eating & drinking

What would you recommend? Qu'est-ce que vous conseillez? *kes·ker voo kon·say·yay*
Cheers! Santé! *son·tay*
That was delicious. C'était délicieux! *say·tay day·lee·syer*

NUMBERS

1 **un** *un*
2 **deux** *der*
3 **trois** *trwa*
4 **quatre** *ka·trer*
5 **cinq** *sungk*
6 **six** *sees*
7 **sept** *set*
8 **huit** *weet*
9 **neuf** *nerf*
10 **dix** *dees*

RÉUNION
French is the official language of Réunion, but Creole is the most widely spoken language. Few people speak English.

SEYCHELLES
Most Seychellois will use English when speaking to tourists, French when conducting business, and Creole in the home.

TOOLKIT

CREOLES

The Creoles spoken in Mauritius, Réunion and Seychelles are a blend of French and an assortment of African languages, with some regional variations. Seychelles Creole is similar to that of Mauritius, but differs significantly from the Creole spoken in Réunion. Note also that the Creole spoken in Mauritius and Seychelles is more comprehensible to French people than that of Réunion, even though Réunion itself is thoroughly French.

Mauritius Creole
How are you? Ki manière?
Fine, thanks. Mon byen, mersi.
I don't understand. Mo pas comprend.
OK. Correc.
Not OK. Pas correc.
he/she/it. li
Do you have ...? Ou éna ...?
I'd like ... Mo oulé ...
I'm thirsty. Mo soif.
Cheers! Tapeta!
Great! Formidabe!

Seychelles Creole
Good morning./Good afternoon. Bonzour.
How are you? Comman sava?
Fine, thanks. Mon byen, mersi.
What's your name? Ki mannyer ou appel?
My name is ... Mon appel ...
Where do you live? Koté ou resté?
I don't understand. Mon pas konpran.
I like it. Mon kontan.
Where is ...? Ol i ...?
How much is that? Kombyen sa?
I'm thirsty. Mon soif.
Can I have a beer, please? Mon kapa ganny en labyer silvouplé?

WHO SPEAKS FRENCH?

97.6 million people speak French as their mother tongue

300 million people speak French worldwide

- Canada
- France
- Switzerland
- Monaco
- Haiti
- Guinea
- Mali
- Niger
- Ivory Coast
- Benin
- Congo
- Democratic Republic of Congo
- Seychelles
- Réunion
- Mauritius
- Vanuatu

STORYBOOK

THE MAURITIUS, RÉUNION & SEYCHELLES
STORYBOOK

Our writers delve deep into different aspects of Mauritian, Réunionnais & Seychellois life

A History of Mauritius, Réunion & Seychelles in 15 Places

Three distinct sovereign nations - yet with shared geological origins and a complex history..

Paula Hardy, Fabienne Fong Yan and Rooksana Hossenally

p272

Meet the Mauritians

Do expect a warm welcome. But don't be put off if people overshare, pry and throw in the odd home truth.

Rooksana Hossenally

p276

Meet the Réunionnais

Close to nature and bearers of traditions, the Réunionnais trace their heritage to all corners of the world. And they love to share it with visitors.

Fabienne Fong Yan

p278

Meet the Seychellois

Sitting just below the equator in the Indian Ocean, the island nation of Seychelles is barely visible on the map, but its Creole culture is one of the richest in the region.

Christophe Zialor

p280

Séga: Mauritian Soul Music

The music that ties together the island's past, present and future.

Rooksana Hossenally

p282

Réunion's Spiritual Heritage

Meet the gods, deities and forgotten spirits who have shaped the island's blend of rituals and beliefs.

Fabienne Fong Yan

p285

Seychelles: Green Pioneer

Seychelles proves that even small countries can take action to create a sustainable future.

Paula Hardy

p288

Kalikambal Temple (p139), St-Denis, Réunion

A HISTORY OF MAURITIUS, RÉUNION & SEYCHELLES IN
15 PLACES

Mauritius, Réunion and Seychelles may be three distinct sovereign nations – Mauritius and Seychelles are independent, while Réunion is a French overseas department – yet they share the same geological origins, a complex history entwined with the colonial plantation system and the Mascarene slave trade, as well as rich Creole cultures with interesting island-specific variations. By Paula Hardy, Fabienne Fong Yan and Rooksana Hossenally

THE VAST, SUBMARINE Mascarene Plateau extends from Réunion in the south nearly 2000km to Seychelles in the north. Seychelles' granite islands are remnants of ancient Gondwanaland, which fragmented 66 million years ago, while epic eruptions in the Réunion volcanic hot spot gave birth to Mauritius eight million to 10 million years ago, and Rodrigues and Réunion two million years ago.

The islands' botanical and marine bounty and temperate climates made them pit stops on trade routes from Arabia and India to East Africa as early as the 7th century. But their remoteness left them largely unknown, and uninhabited, until Portuguese explorers mapped them in the 16th century. The arrival of the Dutch and French East India Companies in the 18th century, and the establishment of a plantation economy in Mauritius and Réunion, transformed the existing trade in enslaved peoples into a business stretching from South Africa to the Far East.

After slavery was abolished, the British drew indentured labourers here from India and China, along with merchants from Southeast Asia. This mix of people, ideas and influences gave rise to the islands' three Creole cultures. Today Mauritius, Réunion and Seychelles are some of the most progressive and economically stable countries in Africa.

1. Vieux Grand Port, Mauritius
DUTCH, THEN FRENCH

It was at Vieux Grand Port that the island's first inhabitants landed. On 9 September 1598, under Dutch admiral Wybrand van Warwyck, the first people formed a colony on the shores of Mauritius. The landing spot is marked by a signposted brick tower, but the fort (the Dutch East India Company headquarters) was built 3km north. In 1710, after the Dutch abandoned the island, the French set up their colony here before moving to Mahébourg and then Port Louis. Today, the Frederick Hendrick Museum, close to the remaining fort ruins, contains artefacts and descriptions of the history of Mauritius.

For more on Vieux Grand Port, see page 117

2. Mahébourg, Mauritius
SANDBARS, DEFEAT AND SHIPWRECK

The sleepy fishing town of Mahébourg, in the south-eastern corner of the island, was Mauritius' first port before French colonial governor Mahé de Labourdonnais moved it to Port Louis in 1736. In these bright blue waters, the 1810 Battle of Grand

Port took place, in which the French defeated the British thanks to their intricate knowledge of nearby sandbars: the British became stuck in the sands of the shallow waters. On the seafloor you can still glimpse the *Sirius*, one of the ships that went down in the battle. The area is now a popular diving spot.

For more on Mahébourg, see page 119.

3. Port Louis, Mauritius
A PLANNED, HARMONIOUS CAPITAL

In 1736 Bertrand-François Mahé de La Bourdonnais (Labourdonnais), an administrator of the French East India Company, moved Mauritius' port from the windy east to the more sheltered site now known as Port Louis. The city is still organised according to Labourdonnais' design, with commerce on one side of the main avenue, Place d'Armes, and the business district on the other. As everywhere in Mauritius, the city is a harmonious mix of cultures and beliefs, with temples, churches and the country's biggest mosque all within a short walk of each other. The cultural blend also comes through in the delicious street food and vibrant murals.

For more on Port Louis, see page 60

4. Aapravasi Ghat, Mauritius
THE INDENTURE SYSTEM BEGINS

About 70% of Mauritians can trace their ancestry to someone who arrived at the Aapravasi Ghat immigration depot from the 1830s. After slavery was abolished in 1835, around 500,000 indentured labourers were drawn mainly from India in the ensuing decades to work on the island's sugarcane plantations. Mauritius went on to become one of the world's leading sugar exporters, and the indenture system was eventually responsible for one of the largest migrations ever seen. Now a Unesco World Heritage Site, the ghat has a visitor centre detailing the squalid conditions the workers endured and their unjust treatment, akin to slavery.

For more on Aapravasi Ghat, see page 64.

5. Cap Malheureux, Mauritius
SCENE OF A SURPRISE ATTACK

Leaving the tourist resort of Grand Baie and following the curve of the north coast, you'll reach Cap Malheureux and its tiny, red-gabled church. The pace of life suddenly slows almost to a halt. It's hard to imagine that this peaceful spot was where the British invaded the island in 1810, triumphing over the French. (The British had failed earlier that year at Grand Port, but this time they attacked from the north, taking the French by surprise, and marched across the island to assume command.) The French later named the tip of the island Unhappy Cape for this turn of events.

For more on Cap Malheureux, see page 105

6. Cave of the Settlement, Réunion
ARRIVING IN BOURBON ISLAND

Until 1663, Réunion was temporarily inhabited only by a few convicts, but then Louis Payen and another Frenchman, accompanied by 10 Malagasians brought with them to become servants, arrived with the intent of 'populating' the island. Among them were the first three women to live there. In the municipality of St-Paul, a grotto known as the Cave of the Settlement is said to have sheltered this first group of voluntary immigrants to Bourbon island after they disembarked. Unsurprisingly, the difference in the number of men and women in the group became a source of discord and the Malagasians soon ran away.

For more on the Cave of the Settlement, see page 273

Auxiliatrice de Cap Malheureux (p105), Mauritius

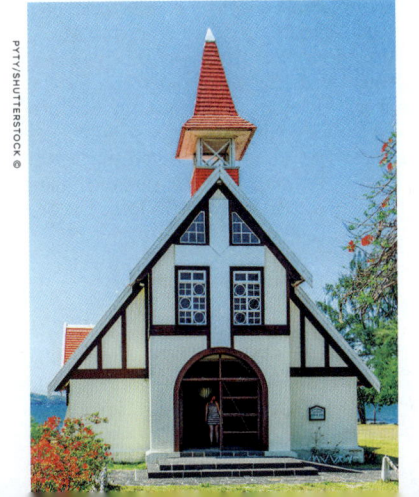

7. Camp Dimitile, Réunion
OF COURAGE AND REFUGE
The names of the cirques are an eloquent homage to the history of marronage (escaping slavery): Cilaos, Mafate and Dimitile commemorate the chiefs who established mountain camps to evade slave hunters such as François Mussard. Relentlessly pursued, these men and women built concealed refuges for their families on high summits and beyond deep crevasses and were ready to flee at all times. Accessible by a hike, the Camp Dimitile site was entirely recreated by a local association as a tribute to those who sought refuge in the area. The summit is named after Captain Dimitile, one of the most renowned runaway leaders from the 1730s.

For more on Camp Dimitile, see page 170

8. Musée de Villèle, Réunion
WHERE HISTORY MEETS LEGEND
At the start of the 19th century, coffee cultivation declined as it gradually came to be replaced by sugarcane plantations. But the system was the same: hundreds of enslaved people working on vast properties at the service of rich landowners such as Mme Desbassayns. Sometimes seen as a providential woman (she established the first hospitals for enslaved people) and sometimes as a bloodthirsty slave owner, she may be the most controversial historical figure in Réunion. One of her former properties, the Villèle estate in St-Gilles-les-Hauts, now hosts a museum dedicated to the history of slavery on the island.

For more on Musée de Villèle, see page 156

9. Stella Matutina, Réunion
A GLIMPSE OF PLANTATION LIFE
From the 1860s to the first half of the 20th century, sugar growing was the main industry in Réunion. Traces of it are still visible everywhere, with sugarcane fields covering the island's slopes, but only two sugar factories are still active today. Although they're open to the public during the harvest, there's no better way to understand how the sugarcane economy has shaped Réunion than by visiting Stella Matutina. Located in a former factory where many old machines remain, it gives a unique insight into what life used to be like and how it has rapidly evolved in the past century.

For more on Stella Matutina, see page 158

10. St-Denis, Réunion
CAPITAL OF GARDENS AND VILLAS
Although the earliest arrivals chose St-Paul as their main settlement in the first few years, French governor Etienne Regnault rapidly moved the capital to St-Denis around 1665, as he deemed the northern coast more suitable to 'gardening' and human activities. It has remained the capital until the present day. With its grid street plan and typically colonial architecture, from preserved administrative buildings (the prefectoral house, the town hall and the former governor's house, now the Natural History Museum) to Creole villas surrounded by luxuriant tropical gardens, the city remains a historical stronghold as well as the beating heart of the island's economy.

For more on St-Denis, see page 136

11. Granite Islands, Seychelles
A LOST MICRO-CONTINENT
The 42 granite islands of Seychelles are the peaks of a submerged microcontinent, a fragment of Gondwana that cracked up 120 million years ago, splitting Antarctica-Australia from Madagascar-Seychelles-India. The latter formed the 300,000-sq-km Mascarene Plateau. Charles Darwin first wrote about Seychelles' unusual geology, and the grey and pink porphyry granite rocks, best seen on La Digue, were central to Alfred Wegener's pioneering 1912 theory of continental drift, which led to the model of plate tectonics. This granite bedrock means there are no springs, so Seychelles sources its water from rainfall and desalination. Rainfall variation due to climate change is therefore a critical issue.

For more on La Digue, see page 229

12. Outer Islands, Seychelles
DISCOVERY-LAND
The eight islands and three atolls of the Amirantes Group were sighted in 1503 by Vasco da Gama. But it wasn't until the 1740s that they were systematically explored by Frenchman Lazare Picault, who had been

Anse Source d'Argent beach (p246), La Digue, Seychelles

sent to find an alternative route to India from Mauritius. He named the main island Mahé, after Mahé de Labourdonnais, the governor of Mauritius, and the French claimed Seychelles 12 years later. The outer islands were subsequently used by pirates and slave smugglers, and when the spice economy collapsed, some became farms for copra and guano. They remain some of the remotest islands on the planet.

For more on the Outer Islands, see page 247

13. Vallée de Mai, Seychelles
BOTANICAL PIRACY AND PRESERVATION

The coco de mer (sea coconut) is the only case of gigantism in Seychelles and has been shrouded in folklore for centuries. In 1769, Frenchman Jean Duchemin discovered the nuts on Praslin and looted so many he nearly destroyed the forest. Poaching has been banned since 1979, but the tree is also threatened by the encroachment of invasive species – such as cinnamon, smuggled in from the Far East by Pierre Poivre in 1772 – and fire, which virtually wiped out the forest on Curieuse. Today the coco de mer is protected in the Vallée de Mai National Park on Praslin.

For more on the Vallée de Mai, see p235

14. Le Jardin du Roi, Seychelles
SPICES, SLAVERY AND CREOLISATION

Although the French laid their Stone of Possession on Mahé in 1756, Seychelles wasn't settled until 1770, when 28 people arrived to start a spice farm. The Jardin du Roi and Domaine de Val de Prés were established on Mahé's protected west coast. But Seychelles mainly made a living provisioning and repairing slave ships en route to Mauritius and Réunion. It also acted as a midway 'sanatorium' for enslaved people who were quarantined on satellite islands. By 1810, when the first official record of a Creole child was filed, the population of Seychelles was 3467, of whom 3015 were enslaved.

For more on the Jardin du Roi, see page 221

15. Victoria, Seychelles
BIRTH OF A NATION

Bearing the name of an English queen from its days under British colonial rule (1814–1976), the Seychelles' capital, Victoria, bears witness to the span of Seychellois history. The National History Museum documents Seychelles' story, the country's flora is showcased in the botanical garden and some of the best Creole food can be sampled at Marie Antoinette. Since 2019 the city's Palais de Justice has also been where the Truth and Reconciliation Committee has been conducting its vital public investigation to heal the wounds of the post-independence dictatorship (1977–93) and find a way to a better future.

For more on Victoria, see page 213

MEET THE MAURITIANS

Do expect a warm welcome. But don't be put off if people overshare, pry and throw in the odd home truth. ROOKSANA HOSSENALLY introduces her people.

WHAT IS IT to be Mauritian? You can be white or Black, Hindu, Buddhist or Catholic, and be Mauritian all the same. Mauritian identity weaves in different strands of the island's rich history as it went from Dutch to French to British rule, along the way receiving an influx of enslaved people from Africa, indentured labourers from India and merchants from China before being granted independence in 1968. Mauritius was uninhabited when the first people settled here, and that might be why all ethnicities feel at home on this island.

Mauritians are affable people who know how to put visitors at ease right away. Island stereotypes don't really apply here, though: the locals are punctual and dependable. The young generation is connected and speaks fluent English (the language of administration), French (the lingua franca) and the local Creole dialect. As well as a shared notion of home, Mauritians' national identity lies in a newfound respect for Creole. The language developed from the speech of enslaved Africans, and today it's spoken and understood by most Mauritians. Despite this, the move by artists and singers of all genres to celebrate Creole culture as a key aspect of national pride is relatively recent.

So what else brings together the country's communities? There's a shared satisfaction that diverse ethnicities live together peacefully in this small place. But more than anything else, Mauritian identity lies in the country's food. Whether it's a tangy *rougail poisson salé* (salt fish in tomato sauce), a delicate pair of *dhal puri* (lentil pancakes filled with curry) or a flavoursome briani (spiced saffron rice cooked in a huge pot), locals' eyes light up at the very mention of Mauritian dishes. They're common ground for everyone, regardless of ethnicity.

Other similarities tie all the communities together. Mauritians in general love nothing more than good gossip, and any piece of news rips through the island like wildfire. This has inspired the popular saying 'To live well is to live hidden'. Mauritians are trusting, which serves to build intimacy almost instantly, but it can also seem to newcomers like prying and oversharing. Locals are cheeky, fun-loving and witty, which finds full expression in Creole turns of phrase. The famous 'ayo!' – which you'll hear frequently – can mean a range of things from wonder to disbelief to anger.

Above all, though, Mauritians switch continually between languages, speaking an insider code understood only by those who have mastered the island's three main languages. In this way locals harness the best of all the island's cultures and hone their adaptability, as they have done since human occupation here began.

> **Mauritian Roots**
>
> Mauritius has a population of just over 1.3 million. The majority (about 70%) are of Indian descent. The remaining 30% are composed of Creoles, Muslims, Sino-Mauritians, Franco-Mauritians and more recently Bangladeshis and South Africans.

Clockwise from top left: Mauritian woman; Local shopkeeper, Port Louis (p60); Mauritian couple in traditional wedding clothes; Model ship builder, Mahébourg (p117)

I'M MAURITIAN...SORT OF

I was born in London, where my French mother and Mauritian father met. My father, the only son in a line of sisters, was expected to follow in the footsteps of my grandfather, a quiet politician with a nose for business who received an OBE from Queen Elizabeth. In the early '90s, we made the move to Mauritius. Even though it's a country of diverse ethnicities, there were so few mixed couples there at the time that my parents (a white woman and a dark man) made the front page of the main newspaper when we arrived. The turn of the millennium marked a new chapter in Mauritius' story, though – one where mindsets loosened. For me Mauritius is still the one place where no one puzzles over the spelling of my name or asks me where I'm from. No matter how long it's been, returning to this little Indian Ocean paradise always feels like coming home.

MEET THE RÉUNIONNAIS

Close to nature and bearers of traditions, the Réunionnais trace their heritage to all corners of the world. And they love to share it with visitors. FABIENNE FONG YAN introduces her people.

FLOREBO QUOCUMQUE FERAR (I will flourish wherever I am carried) is Réunion's motto. Some see in this an acknowledgement of the Réunionnais who left their homeland to succeed across the oceans. Others see a reflection of their ability to settle anywhere, like fugitive enslaved people once did in the cirques. Sometimes, the motto is taken to refer to the island's agricultural fertility. Few know that it was first used by the Compagnie des Indes Orientales, which aimed to make the colony's land productive using the labour of the people it brought in from the 18th century onwards. Like the Réunionnais themselves, the saying is multifaceted.

There might not be a single interpretation of it, but the motto's image remains accurate for an island that's one of the world's richest natural sites. A glance at any market stall tells you how diverse Réunion's vegetation can be, even though only 15% of the land is used for agriculture. But the Réunionnais have their secrets: the typical Creole garden doesn't just hold flowers and plants imported from all continents; it also has an orchard in which fruit trees are grown with pride. It's important to make the neighbours envious of one's vegetal riches, even if the fruit is generously shared when the trees bring forth their bounty.

In a typical meal you can see how the Réunionnais can use absolutely anything to feed themselves, from their gardens and beyond. Take *brèdes* (edible leaves such as spinach, taro or sweet-potato leaves), for instance: they're thrown away in Europe, but in Réunion they're cooked in fricassées or soups. Each part of the island has its emblematic produce: people from the south revel in their vacoa fruit, while in the east it's the edible palm tree and in Salazie it's the chouchou (a kind of gourd). The Victoria pineapple from Réunion has been judged to be the best pineapple in the world! When December comes, the Réunionnais passionately go in search of the best lychees – it's believed a pointy lychee hides a small seed and therefore lots of flesh. (And the big seeds make great old-fashioned spinning toys!)

Réunionnais Creole

Réunion's Creole is a mix of contemporary French, words inherited from languages such as Portuguese, Hindi and Malagasian, and 18th- and 19th-century French terms used by sailors. Spoken by 81% of Réunionnais, it's a living testament to the island's diversity.

If you're lucky, you might meet the most ancient bearer of natural knowledge, the tisaneur. Now a highly regulated profession, the tisaneur is the Malagasian ancestor of the pharmacist. This central figure in former Creole communities knows all local plants by name, their medicinal properties and where to find them. Many still trust the tisaneurs' science and rely on local pharmacopoeia to cure or ease their pain. Between tradition and modernity, proud of their island and creative in the way they use its heritage, is where you'll meet the Réunionnais.

Clockwise from top left: Performer at the Guan Di festival, St-Denis (p136); Réunionnais woman; Muslim man, St-Paul (p147); Tamil women in St-André (p176)

STORYBOOK

RÉUNIONNAIS BY NAME...

Whenever I'm asked where I come from, I explain a little about Réunion, but people remain confused by how I look, the languages I speak, and why my first name sounds French and my last name Chinese. My ancestors were from Guangdong in southern China and came to Réunion in the 1930s. Like my parents, I was born and raised on the island, which makes us Creole-Chinese ('Sinois' to locals). I went to the French Republican school and grew up in an environment infused with Catholicism while also learning my family's traditional rituals, as is common among Réunionnais of Asian descent. My parents spoke mainly French to me (and I don't really speak Mandarin), but I learnt the Creole language in the community. I left my island home at 17 because we believed a mainland university would offer a better education. But after so many years (18!) away from the island, I'm now considering going home.

MEET THE SEYCHELLOIS

Sitting just below the equator in the Indian Ocean, the island nation of Seychelles is barely visible on the map, but its Creole culture is one of the richest in the region. CHRISTOPHE ZIALOR introduces his people.

IN ITS 250-YEAR history, Seychelles has expanded from a small settlement of 28 people to a population of 107,400. Each of us is the product of many different ethnic backgrounds, but we're bound by one nationality: Seychellois.

If you visit the islands, you'll notice that no two Seychellois look alike. Because of this, locals are frequently asked what their family background is.

The truth is that we're a bit of everything. In the late 18th and 19th centuries, the arrival of French, African, English, Indian and Chinese migrants created a mixed-race society as people intermarried and cultures intertwined. These days, if you go to a local Chinese restaurant you'll notice Creole flavours in the dishes – they've been adapted to suit the Seychellois palate. The same is true of other cuisines, such as French or Indian.

To see how the cultures of different ethnic groups have merged here, don't miss the Creole Festival in October. Here you can immerse yourself in the islands' variety of traditions and discover an array of food, drinks, music and dance, all of which have a multiracial influence. The week-long festival pays symbolic homage to the archipelago's vibrant Creole customs and practices.

That's the beautiful thing about a country where diverse cultural traditions have been blended over the centuries to form a harmonious whole. You'll enjoy an interesting fusion cuisine and be exposed to a broad selection of art and music. While you're here, you'll hear Roman Catholic church bells and the Islamic call to prayer. And all Seychellois celebrate Chinese New Year.

The nation's official languages are Creole, English and French. Since the islands became independent from the UK in 1976, the government has actively sought to develop and protect Creole. The Lenstiti Kreol (Creole Institute) was founded in 1981. Lessons at primary school are taught in Creole; after this, English is adopted and French is taught as a foreign language.

Whereas previously most people spoke Creole and a hybrid of French and English, English has recently overtaken Creole among the younger generation. That's because those who grew up watching *Friends* and the Disney Channel are gradually replacing traditional Creole with a Creole-English hybrid. Meanwhile, French has almost entirely vanished from the regional dialect. So, like the Seychellois cuisine, the Creole language is mirroring the islands' contemporary culture: it's becoming a mixture.

Regardless of individual ancestry – whether it includes enslaved people, explorers, exiles or pirates – today all Seychellois enjoy equal rights and a variety of blended cultures that form the rich, evolving identity in the islands.

> **Seychellois Then & Now**
> Most Seychellois are descendants of early French settlers and East Africans who arrived in the islands in the 19th century. In 2023 the Seychellois population surpassed 100,000 for the first time in the archipelago's history.

Clockwise from top left: Hindu temple, Victoria (p213); woman at Carnival, Victoria; Seychellois grilled fish (p46); Fisherman, La Digue (p242)

APPRECIATING SEYCHELLOIS UNIQUENESS

I'm a 24-year-old former journalist and editor who was born in Seychelles. I've recently moved into a new role at a resort called laïla where we promote Seychellois culture by offering immersive experiences with local writers, musicians and artists.

Before I came to write this chapter, no one had ever asked me to describe the Seychellois. It's made me think about our island history. Although I have French, African and Indian ancestry, at my core I'm Seychellois. I'd say the same is true for most of the population: we simply don't have the racial barriers and issues that are so pervasive elsewhere in the world.

This reflection has made me appreciate my country's unique culture. So far I've visited five of the archipelago's 115 islands – you would need a lifetime to fully appreciate the uniqueness of them all. At the very least, in order to really understand Seychelles, you must experience it firsthand.

SÉGA: MAURITIAN SOUL MUSIC

The music that ties together the island's past, present and future. By Rooksana Hossenally

LIVELY SÉGA UNDERPINS a big part of Mauritian history, namely that of the Creole population, mostly descendants of enslaved African people with varying amounts of European ancestry. The word séga originated in the 1820s, when enslaved people spoke of chéga or tchéga, an East African dance. Even though all forms of discrimination are illegal under the Mauritian constitution, it's widely recognised that the Creole minority has been socially, economically and politically marginalised, and séga music was and still is a real outlet for many to bring that state of affairs to light.

Ti Frère & Authentic Séga

One of the oldest and most prominent musical genres on the island, séga is heard everywhere nowadays, but in the early 20th century it fell out of fashion. It was singer Ti Frère, with his gravelly voice, who brought it back. His song 'Anita' remains a classic. Later a hip-swaying séga dance appeared, performed as hotel entertainment by locals wearing long, colourful,

Séga dancing, Port Louis (p60)

flower-print clothing. It's a fun first approach to the music, but the more authentic concerts happen in local bars and at concerts around the island and tend to be charged with political meaning. Popular séga songs include Carino's 'Alimé di fé' (Light the Fire) and 'Mo la po cabri' (My Goat's Skin), Claudio Veeraragoo's 'Amba la ba' (Under, Over There) and summer hit 'Ala li la' by Denis Azor.

Kaya & Political Activism

The majority of séga artists tend to be Creole and sing about their lack of representation. Singer Kaya is credited with creating seggae, a mix of séga and reggae. Like those of international reggae star Bob Marley, Kaya's songs were infused with a revolutionary spirit that brought Creoles together to fight for their rights. Tragically, Kaya died in police custody in February 1999 after protesting for the legalisation of cannabis.

Désiré François, Voice of the Creole People

A huge fan of Kaya and one of the most prominent and respected séga figures of the last three decades, Désiré François is a founding member of legendary band Cassiya.

Like many Creoles, François grew up with limited literacy, yet he's made albums for three decades. 'It's all in my head', he tells me, tapping his black curls. We're sitting in front yard in a small town close to Port Louis, having juice and biscuits at a table covered with a bright cloth. His wife, Evelyn, flits between the table and their grandchildren, who can be heard playing with instruments inside the house. 'I've never forced them to play, but I'm so happy to see that they love music', he tells me, with a broad smile. 'My music questions a lot of things, especially the exploitation of Mauritians, and why those who are out in the fields feeding the country are those who earn the least. Some of my songs are banned here in Mauritius, even though I'm a peaceful activist. I'm not trying to antagonise anyone, just ask questions.'

François was born in Cassis, a district of Port Louis, and grew up taking care of himself. 'It's how it was back then. We had nothing and wanted for nothing. If we wanted to eat, we'd fish or pluck fruit off the trees on the side of the road.'

The First Song: 'Séparation'

During the '60s and '70s, Mauritius was becoming independent from Britain, and there wasn't a great deal of infrastructure or opportunities for much of the population, especially Creoles. There was no compulsory schooling back then, either. Most parents were out working, during which time their kids would take care of themselves. For François, whose parents were both alcoholics, it was tough. 'They had nothing to give us, even if they did love us tremendously', he says. He talks about when his parents gave him to another family in their village to be looked after.

This event was the inspiration for 'Séparation', his first song, released in the '90s with Cassiya. It was followed by hits 'Marlène' and 'Rêve nou ancètre' (Think Back to Our Ancestors).

'I'd been singing and playing guitar and *ravanne* (a local drum) for as long as I could remember. My first band was called Zanfan Cassi (Children of Cassis), but I started to really create songs in the '80s.' Before that, he lived at the pace of the tides, fishing with his older cousins, playing guitar on a roundabout in his village with older kids who reluctantly let him play. 'My dad was a great singer and guitar player. One day he brought home a borrowed guitar that had just a few strings on it. I wasn't allowed to touch it, but I would play it when he was out. When I was older, I played music on the village roundabout with friends, and we later formed Cassiya with Gérard Louis, Alain Ramanisum (now a successful solo séga artist), Alain La Fleur, Bruno François, Damien Elisa and Silvia Ravina. We went on to produce 10 albums together.'

> 'WHAT'S KEPT ME GOING ALL THESE YEARS? THE FEELING OF HOPE PEOPLE COME UP TO ME IN THE STREET TO THANK ME FOR. MAKING PEOPLE FEEL HOPE IS MY SOLE PURPOSE IN LIFE, I KNOW THIS NOW. THAT'S THE POWER OF SÉGA – IT'S THE MUSIC'S HEART AND SOUL.'

Musicians, Port Louis (p68)

'I couldn't understand why, but more and more people would come up to me and ask me to play and sing. Sometimes I'd do events and people would dance, crying. I was the first to be surprised at their reaction', he tells me. 'I never imagined I could have a chance of being a professional singer – it was a dream I hardly dared to dream.' The turning point came when he entered his first singing contest, Starshow, in 1992. 'I didn't win first off, but when I left, the judges deliberated, and I was called back. The audience loved my performance, and that was how it all started.'

This year, François is celebrating his 60th birthday and a three-decades-long career. 'What's kept me going all these years? The feeling of hope people come up to me in the street to thank me for. Making people feel hope is my sole purpose in life, I know this now. That's the power of séga – it's the music's heart and soul.'

RÉUNION'S SPIRITUAL HERITAGE

Meet the gods, deities and forgotten spirits who have shaped the island's blend of rituals and beliefs. By Fabienne Fong Yan

ALL SORTS OF gods, saints and spirits dwell in Réunion as a result of two centuries and a half of immigration – forced or voluntary – from Africa, Madagascar, India, China and Europe. Just like the people, their beliefs met, merged and evolved. Some rituals took the official path, sheltered in churches and temples, while others became discreetly embedded in local ways until their origins were forgotten. Leave the dogmas behind: you're in Réunion, where faiths have merged and coalesced in entirely unique ways.

Authorised Ambivalence

Historically, the coexistence of religions in Réunion was allowed out of sheer economical interest: indentured workers coming from India or China allowed themselves to be christened Catholics in the hope it would ease their integration into early-19th-century Réunionnais society. On the other hand, sugar-estate owners would allow their Tamil workers to frequent their own family temples, which is why you'll often find Hindu temples close to former sugar estates and factories.

This relative freedom of observance slowly paved the way to the establishment of various religions on the island. After the indenture system ended in the 1880s, this gathered pace as more people started to bring in their own beliefs. At the start of the 20th century, the first mosque to be built on the territory was inaugurated in St-Denis. The building was solely funded by Muslim Indian shop owners – and how could the French prefect refuse when they represented such a large commercial group? Pragmatism trumped any kind of dogmatic mindset.

Today, each community generally follows their ancestors' religion (though younger generations tend not to follow any religion). But if most Réunionnais of Tamil descent go exclusively to Hindu temples and celebrate festivals and 'services' (sometimes with goat sacrifices, now highly regulated), you can still see families with Chinese heritage who go to both church and the Guandi temple during major celebrations to pay their respects to their ancestors. Some Chinese graves also bear the mark of these mixed practices, with Catholic crosses next to incense burners beside the headstones.

Popular Beliefs & Animism

I remember once coming across a sea cave in the Wild South that had been transformed into a natural chapel. From the freshly extinguished candles, you could tell

STORYBOOK

it was often visited. Figures of the Virgin Mary and St-Expedit had been arranged on the bare volcanic rock, with various offerings, flowers, coins and ex-votos disposed among them. There were also some Hindu deities, and even the portrait of a pharaoh! It was a strange pantheon that looked just like the Réunionnais: diverse and multicultural.

It's not rare to see such altars in natural alcoves – they're reminiscent of certain animistic practices that strongly tie religion to nature. Especially driving inland, you'll drive past numerous blood-red oratories in mountain holes that host a red-caped Roman soldier. Although the colour red directly comes from the Tamil tradition, where it is the colour of blood, life and death, these sites are actually dedicated to St-Expedit. Originally a Catholic saint whose existence is subject to controversy, he is particularly venerated in Réunion, often in secret. You could say his cult is close to that of a pagan deity now, halfway between Catholicism and popular tradition. Either way, he supposedly grants your wishes quickly. The frontier between religion and superstition sometimes blurs easily.

Local Folklore

Religious rituals form the most visible part of popular beliefs, and they play a major role in the building of identity for various Réunionnais communities. But beyond them is an entire folklore specific to the island, marked with local superstitions. It has been passed down through oral tradition, from one generation of enslaved people to another, ever since the first settlers' arrival. While it's difficult to pinpoint its origins, it's probably safe to assume it was born from the transformation of ancestral knowledge from Africa and Madagascar, mixed with an array of other beliefs over the centuries.

The most popular Creole superstitions have to do with protecting oneself against the Devil or 'evil spirits'. Crossroads have a very bad reputation – not terribly surprising given the density of traffic in Réunion! – as evil spirits are believed to dwell there. Practitioners of black magic say rituals performed where two roads meet will have their impact amplified. But don't worry: if you do happen to meet an evil spirit, all you need to do is cross yourself and say a prayer. If the spirit hangs around, say a bunch of profanities to it, very loudly, and it should disappear for good.

Myths are attached to places and daily life objects. For example, brooms are said to bring bad luck because they're always in contact with the ground, where the dead rest. This belief supposedly has Malagasian origins. (Perhaps it's no coincidence that European superstition says brooms are a witch's favourite mode of transport.) Either way, don't ever sweep a young person's feet with a broom – they might never get married. Don't sweep indoors with the broom dedicated to the yard, because you might bring in evil spirits. Alternatively, if you want to protect your house from evil souls living outside, bar your door with a broom.

Creole poet and writer Daniel Honoré is a typical example of Réunion's blend of cultures: his father is a Chinese shopkeeper and his mother is a descendant of enslaved African and Malagasian people. He has collected local tales, *kroyans* (Creole for 'beliefs'), myths and superstitions into a book in an effort to preserve the Réunionnais Creole language and culture. His book's preface notes that, even though the reasons for this have been forgotten, Creoles still spill a drink on the ground in honour of the *zam non ramassé* (souls not taken care of). Honoré says that all these very specific beliefs are precisely what makes up the Réunionnais Creole soul. You could say our lives are infused with magic.

Oratory dedicated to St-Expedit, Petite-Île

SEYCHELLES: GREEN PIONEER

Seychelles proves that even small countries can take action to create a sustainable future. By Paula Hardy

LIFE ON THESE islands has always been deeply integrated with the natural world. The first European settlers arrived with the aim of exploiting the environmental resources. Empires and the industrial revolution were built on the trade in spices and the labour of enslaved peoples, who were fed on tortoises and turtles.

The spice trees, coconut palms, goats and rats that those settlers brought were invasive species that damaged the endemic ecosystem, and Seychelles is still dealing with their effects today. Tortoises hunted almost to extinction have had to be rehabilitated and turtles protected by law. The industrial revolution that launched our carbon-hungry world has led to the heavy rains, freak tides, coastal erosion and rising ocean temperatures that now buffet the archipelago.

Despite these challenges, Seychelles is leading the way with inspiring, sustainable solutions.

The Blue Economy

On 26 March 2020, Seychelles announced a ground-breaking debt-conversion deal that secured the protection of 30% of the country's 1.35-sq-km marine territory and met the UN's 2030 sustainability goals a decade early. Now 410,000 sq km of ocean – an area larger than Germany – is fully or significantly safeguarded.

Co-designed by global environmental non-profit the Nature Conservancy

Clockwise from top left: Seychelles blue pigeon; Coco de Mer nut; marine biologist at bleached coral reef; Aldabra tortoise (p244)

(nature.org), the deal helped Seychelles buy back US$21.6 million in national debt. The money will be held in trust and repaid at lower interest rates, with part of those repayments funding conservation projects. The trust is expected to generate US$400,000 annually.

Birds Back from the Brink

Nirmal Shah, CEO of Nature Seychelles (natureseychelles.org) and one of Seychelles' most highly regarded conservationists, believes everyone can make a difference. In 1998, when Shah set up the organisation that would become Nature Seychelles, the archipelago had the most threatened birds in Africa. There were just 19 magpie robins left.

Since then, Nature Seychelles has restored entire islands to receive endangered endemic birds. As birds return to islands, rewilding starts to occur, and invertebrate, reptile and other seabird numbers increase. The organisation's work has been an astounding success and the extinction risk to the Seychelles warbler, fody and magpie robin has significantly reduced. Now Cousin Island, where Nature Seychelles is headquartered, is a model of conservation and ecotourism.

Reef Rescuers

Coral reefs are vital areas of marine biodiversity and act as a first line of defence from rising oceans. They're also breeding grounds for the sea life upon which Seychelles relies for food. But in 1998, and again in 2016, Seychelles experienced a massive coral bleaching event as a result of sea temperature rises caused by El Niño.

Beginning in 2010, Reef Rescuer became the world's first large-scale coral-restoration project. So far, the project has cultivated 50,000 coral fragments in nurseries around Cousin and Praslin Islands that are later transplanted onto degraded reefs. This coral gardening requires countless hours of diving to collect and transplant corals and painstaking work to keep them clean of algae and parasites as they grow.

The nurseries now provide a dynamic laboratory where research questions on coral reproduction, growth and resilience can be answered.

Community Gardening

It is accepted in international conservation circles that people power is essential to combating climate change. Many Seychellois already maintain productive gardens, growing fruit trees and vegetables, but the Seychelles Biodiversity Centre has bigger ambitions. Through educational and public tours, as well as an on-site café, it hopes to increase local knowledge about the nation's unique biome and the everyday uses of unusual endemic plants and fruit.

It also has a nursery stocked with endemic saplings for sale. Manager Natasha Einfeldt hopes this will lead to a national movement to improve propagation of rare plants, some of which are endangered. 'We don't want to be in charge of nature', she says. 'We want everyone to care about and enjoy these plants.'

The centre's hopes seem well founded. National botanical icon, the coco de mer, grows only on Praslin and Curieuse, and there are just 8000 mature trees in existence. In 2020 the Seychelles Island Foundation (SIF; sif.sc) launched a scheme offering Seychellois the chance to apply for coco de mer seeds gathered from fallen nuts. They expected limited interest in about 30 nuts, but instead received applications for 422.

Restoration, Not Just Conservation

SIF was established in 1979, three years after independence, to manage Seychelles' two World Heritage Sites: primordial palm forest Vallée de Mai and the world's largest coral atoll, Aldabra. Aldabra's ecosystem is so pristine the island is only accessible to scientists and a handful of visitors.

Conservation biologist and SIF CEO Dr Frauke Fleischer-Dogley describes her first visit to the island as 'like travelling back in time'. She says 'the marine biome there is six times that of the inner islands and you see huge numbers of turtles, sharks and fish, which are not afraid of people'.

Aldabra has a population of more than 150,000 giant tortoises, huge numbers of coconut crabs, the last dugongs in the Indian Ocean and the world's only population of the flightless bird, Aldabra rail.

'All these things have been made possible because there has been commitment in this small country,' says Fleisher-Dogley.

INDEX

ABBREVIATIONS
M   Mauritius
R   Réunion
S   Seychelles

A

accessible travel 265
accommodation 257, *see also individual locations*
activities 15, 48-51, **50-1**, *see also individual activities*
Albius, Edmond 180
Aldabra (S) 250
Alphonse Island (S) 251
Amber Island (M) 107
Amirantes Group (S) 274-5
amusement parks 81
AnneGa 103
Anse des Cascades (R) 184
Anse Mondon Valley (S) 231-2
Anse Royale (S) 33, 228
Anse Volbert (S) 235
Appanah, Nathacha 69
archaeological sites & ruins
    Hell-bourg thermal baths (R) 188
    Mission Lodge (S) 225
architecture 14
Aride Island (S) 240
art galleries, *see museums & galleries*
arts 22
    Seychelles 226-7
arts & cultural centres
    Bactory (M) 71, 74
    Caudan Arts Centre (M) 64, 75
    Cité des Arts (R) 142

Map Pages **000**

EDITH (M) 65, 75
Green Village (M) 86
Institute of Contemporary Art Indian Ocean (ICAIO) (M) 65, 74
La Fabrik (R) 142
Lakaz d'Art (M) 74, 78
Moka Smart City (M) 71
Astove Island (S) 251
ATMs 256
Aurère (R) 195

B

Babani Sound System 102
Bacbotte, Linzy 102
Baie Lazare (S) 226, 228
Bain Boeuf (M) 100
Baissac, Vaco 74, 101
Bassin Blanc (M) 95
bathrooms 267
beaches 12-13, 259
    Anse à la Mouche (S) 32, 222
    Anse Baleine (S) 228
    Anse Bateau (S) 238
    Anse Boudin (S) 235
    Anse Bougainville (S) 228
    Anse Citron (S) 238
    Anse Coco (S) 247
    Anse Consolation (S) 238
    Anse du Riz (S) 218
    Anse Forbans (S) 228
    Anse Fourmis (S) 247
    Anse Georgette (S) 238
    Anse Gouvernement (S) 235
    Anse Intendense (S) 228
    Anse Lazio (S) 235
    Anse Marie-Louise (S) 228, 238
    Anse Marron (S) 246-7
    Anse Parnel (S) 228
    Anse Sévère (S) 247
    Anse Source d'Argent (S) 246
    Anse St Saveur (S) 238
    Anse Takamaka (S) 228, 238
    Anse Volbert (S) 235
    Beau Vallon (S) 213
    Bénares Beach (M) 121
    Flic en Flac (M) 80-1

Fond l'Anse (S) 238
Grand Anse (S) 247
Grand Baie (M) 98-100
Gris Gris Beach (M) 95
La Cambuse (M) 120
La Cuvette (M) 100
La Digue (S) 246-7
La Morne (M) 86
La Preneuse (M) 84
Pereybere (M) 100
Petite Anse (S) 247
Plage de Grand Anse (R) 174
Plage de L'Hermitage (R) 153
Port Launay Beach (S) 218
Trou d'Argent (M) 126
Trou-aux-Biches (M) 100
Beau Bassin-Rose Hill (M) 71
Beau Vallon (S) 32, 218
beer 71, 72, 153
Bel Ombre (M) 93, 95
Bel Ombre (S) 219
Belle Mare (M) 112
Belvédère du Maïdo (R) 151-2
Billy 'King' 226
Black River Gorges National Park (M) 76, 90-1
Blakkayo 102
blowholes 166
Blue Bay (M) 29, 114-16, **115**
    beyond Blue Bay 117-23
boat tours 49, 50-1, **50-1**
    Cap Ternay (S) 218
    Curieuse Island (S) 240-1
    La Digue (S) 248
    Réunion 154
    Seychelles 230
    Tamarin Bay (M) 83-4
boat travel 253
Bois Chéri (M) 95
books 37
    Mauritius 69, 105
Boucan Canot (R) 30, 153
Bourbon Pointu coffee beans 170
Bras-Panon (R) 180
budgeting 256
bus travel
    Mauritius 129
    Réunion 205
    Seychelles 253

C

Calebasses (M) 111
camping 41, 257
canoeing, *see kayaking & canoeing*
canyoning 48, 188, 192
Cap Homard (R) 153
Cap Jaune (R) 175
Cap La Houssaye (R) 153, 154
Cap Lazare (S) 228
Cap Malheureux (M) 29, 105, 273
Cap Méchant (R) 175
car travel, *see also road trips*
    Mauritius 128, 129
    Réunion 205
    Seychelles 253
cathedrals, *see churches & cathedrals*
caves & lava tubes
    Caverne Patate (M) 126
    Grotte des Premiers Français (R) 148
    La Cave Madame (M) 113
    Roche Noire Lava Tubes (M) 113
    Ste-Rose (R) 185
    Tunnel du Bassin Bleu (R) 155
Cayenne (R) 195
cemeteries
    Cimetière Marin (R) 148
    L'Union Estate Cemetery (S) 243
    St-Pierre Cemetery (R) 161
Central Flacq (M) 112-13
Cerf Island (S) 231
Chamarel (M) 87-9, **88**
    beyond Chamarel 92-6
Chauve Souris (S) 235
children, travel with 49, 258
    Mauritius 72-3
    Réunion 40-1
Christophe 103
churches & cathedrals
    Auxiliatrice de Cap Malheureux (M) 105
    Cathédrale de St-Denis (R) 139

290

Cathedral of the
  Immaculate
  Conception (S) 216
Croix des Pêcheurs
  (R) 164
Église du Bon Pasteur
  (R) 161
Immaculate Church (M) 67
Notre-Dame de la
  Délivrance (R) 139
Notre Dame des Îles
  Chapel (S) 238
Notre-Dame-de-Lourdes
  (R) 161
Notre-Dame-des-Laves
  (R) 184-5
Notre-Dame-des-Neiges
  (R) 192
St James Cathedral (M) 67
St Joseph's Church
  (S) 228
St Paul's Anglican
  Cathedral (S) 216
Cilaos (R) 190-3, **191**
Cilaosa Parc Aventure
  (R) 192
climate 15
climate change 262
clothes 8, 11, 13, 36, 267
coco de mer 235-7, 275
coffee 170
Coin de Mire (M) 100, 107
Col des Boeufs (R) 196
Collen, Lindsey 69
conservation 39, 262, 288-9
cooking classes 181
coral bleaching 39
Corps de Garde (M) 77
Cosmoledo Atoll (S) 251
Cousin Island (S) 241
crafts, see handicrafts
credit cards 256
Creole culture 20-1, 35, 276, 278, 280
Creole languages 37, 268-9, 276, 278, 280
cultural centres, see arts & cultural centres
culture 20-1
  Mauritius 276-7
  Réunion 278-9
  Seychelles 280-1
Curepipe (M) 72, 75
Curieuse Island (S) 240-1
currencies 256
Currimjee, Salim 74
cycling
  Cilaos (R) 192
  La Digue (S) 245
  Réunion 166
  Sentier Littoral Nord (R) 145
  Seychelles 253
cyclones 34

D

dams, see reservoirs & dams
de Chazal, Malcolm 74
Denis Island (S) 232
Desbassayns, Madame 155-6
Desroches Island (S) 250
Deux Mamelles (M) 77, 111
Devi, Ananda 69
disabilities, travellers with 265
distilleries
  Domaine de St-Aubin (M) 73, 74
  Lolita Marie (M) 109
  Rhumerie de Chamarel (M) 89
  Savanna (R) 178
  Takamaka Rum Distillery (S) 220
diving & snorkelling 16-17, 38-9, 50-1, **50-1**
  Anse Union (S) 245
  Beau Vallon (S) 213
  Blue Bay Marine Park (M) 115-16
  Cap Ternay (S) 217-18
  Cerf Island (S) 231
  Cousin Island (S) 241
  Flic en Flac (M) 81
  Îles St Pierre (S) 241
  La Digue (S) 245, 248
  La Passe St François (M) 126
  Matoopa Point (S) 218
  Mauritius 38-9
  Praslin (S) 235, 238, 241
  Réunion 39, 154-5
  Round Island (S) 231
  Seychelles 39
  Silhouette Island (S) 232
  Ste Anne Marine National Park (S) 230-1
  Trou-aux-Biches (M) 101
dodos 93
drinks 11, 260-1, see also beer, rum, tea
drugs 267
Dyalah, Amrita 101

E

electricity 267
emergencies 267
Emlyn 102
endangered species 288-9
enslaved peoples 24-5, 263, 272, 274, 275
  Mauritius 64, 77, 86
  Réunion 139-40, 155-6, 170, 188
  Seychelles 218-19, 225, 226

Entre-Deux (R) 169
environmental issues 39, 122, 288-9
etiquette 11, 13, 36, 267
events, see festivals & events

F

family travel, see children, travel with
farms 172
Ferney Valley (M) 122-3
festivals & events
  All Waves (M) 35, 59
  Anba Pie (M) 59
  Cavadee (M) 58, 106
  Cavadee (R) 168
  Chinese New Year (M) 35, 58
  Chinese New Year (R) 35
  Diwali (M) 59, 106
  Diwali (R) 135, 177
  Donn Sa (M) 102
  Feast of the Assumption (S) 35, 211
  Festival Kiltir (M) 59
  Festival Kreol (S) 35, 211
  Fet Arik (S) 210
  Fête de Pandialé (R) 134, 178
  Fête du Choca (R) 169
  Fish Festival (M) 126
  Ganesh Chaturthi (M) 59, 106
  Grand Raid (R) 35
  Guandi Festival (R) 139
  Holi (M) 35, 58, 106
  Kafe Kiltir (M) 102
  Kréol Festival (M) 126
  La Isla 2068 (M) 35, 59, 102
  Laguna Art Prize (M) 78
  Madmen's Diagonal (R) 162
  Maha Shivaratri (M) 35, 58, 106
  Mama Jaz (M) 59, 102
  Mauritius 58-9
  Meme Pas Peur (R) 173
  Momix (M) 59
  Nou Le Morne (M) 86
  Ocean Festival (S) 211
  Père Laval (M) 35, 59
  Réunion 134-5
  Sakifo (R) 35, 163
  Salon de Mai (M) 59, 78
  Seychelles 210-11
  Spring Festival (R) 134
  Teemeedee (M) 59
  Trou d'Eau Douce (M) 35, 59
  Underground Rock (M) 59
  Vinayagar Chathurthi Festival (S) 211

films 173
fishing 34, 49
Flat Island (M) 107
Flic en Flac (M) 79-81, **79**
  beyond Flic en Flac 82-6
Floréal (M) 72
food 11, 21, 42-7, 260-1, see also individual locations
François, Désiré 102
French language 37, 268-9
Froget, Gaël 75

G

Gabriel Islet (M) 107
galleries, see museums & galleries
gardens, see parks & gardens
gay travellers 264
giant tortoises 167, 241
Glacis (S) 218
golf 48, 93, 96
Goodlands (M) 73, 105-6
gouzous 162
Grand Anse (S) 238
Grand Baie (M) 97-103, **98**
  beyond Grand Baie 104-7
Grand Bassin (M) 95
Grand Coude (R) 171
Grand Étang (R) 183
Grand Gaube (M) 106
Grand Peak (M) 111
Grand Place (R) 195
Grande Barbe plateau (S) 232
granite islands (S) 274
GREG 103

H

handicrafts
  Mauritius 67, 72, 123
  Réunion 155, 201
  Seychelles 227
health 259
Heerah, Jason 103
Hein, Priya 69
helicopter tours 49, 156
Hell-Bourg (R) 187
highlights 8-25
hiking 8-9, 48-9, 50-1, **50-1**
  Anse Major (S) 218
  Belvédère du Maïdo (R) 152-3
  Black River Gorges National Park (M) 76, 90-1
  Cap Noir (R) 151
  Chemin des Anglais (R) 145-6
  Cilaos (R) 193
  Corps de Garde (M) 77

INDEX

H-M

hiking *continued*
Curieuse Island (S) 241
Deux Mamelles (M) 77
Ferney Valley (M) 122-3
Forêt de Bélouve (R) 189
Haut Mafate (R) 196-7, **197**
Îlet-à-Vidot (R) 188
La Digue (S) 244-5
La Roche Écrite (R) 146
Le Maïdo (R) 152
Le Morne (M) 77
Le Pouce (M) 76
Lion Mountain (M) 77
Mafate (R) 195
Mauritius 76-7, 120-1
Morne Seychellois National Park (S) 224-5
Nid d'Aigle (S) 244
Piton d'Anchaing (R) 188
Piton de la Petits Rivière Noire (M) 76
Piton des Neiges (R) 192-3
Pont Naturel (M) 120-1
Réunion 40-1, 168
Rivière des Marsouins (R) 182
Roche Verre Bouteille (R) 151
safety 41
Sentier Littoral Nord (R) 145
Silhouette Island (S) 232
Ste-Suzanne (R) 144
Tamarind Falls (M) 85
historic buildings & sites
Aapravasi Ghat (M) 62, 64, 273
Ancien Hôtel de Ville (R) 138
Bois Chéri (M) 74
Camp Dimitile (R) 170, 274
Cave of the Settlement (R) 273
Château de Bel Ombre (M) 73, 96
Château de Labourdonnais (M) 73
Château de Ville Bague (M) 111
Chateau Réduit (M) 73
Chemin des Anglais (R) 145
Demeure St-Antoine (M) 73

Domaine de St-Aubin (M) 73, 74
Domaine de Val des Près (S) 218-21
Domaine des Tourelles (R) 201
Domaine du Grand Hazier (R) 144-5
Domus (S) 217
Dutch Landing (M) 118
Eureka (M) 71, 111
Governor's House (M) 107
Grann Kaz (S) 231-2
Grotte des Premiers Français (R) 148
House of India (R) 168
Lakaz Rosa (S) 219
Les Aubineaux (M) 72, 74
L'Union Estate (S) 243-4
Maison Carrère (R) 138
Maison Folio (R) 187
Maison Morange (R) 187
Marie Antoinette restaurant (S) 217
Martello Tower (M) 84-5
Mon Désir (M) 73
Mon Plaisir (M) 73
Préfecture (R) 138
Rault Biscuit Factory (M) 119
regional office (R) 138
SSR Memorial Centre (M) 65
Stella Matutina (R) 274
Victoria clock tower (S) 216
Vieux Domaine (R) 169
Vieux Grand Port (M) 272
Villa Angélique (R) 138
Villa du Département (R) 138
history 24-5, 272-5, *see also* enslaved peoples
Mauritius 64, 116, 272-3
Réunion 139-40, 155-6, 170, 273, 274
Seychelles 218-19, 274-5
holidays 267
horseriding 48
Réunion 152, 201
Seychelles 228
hot springs 191
hydroelectricity 182

I

Île aux Cerfs (M) 107, 109
Île aux Chats (M) 126
Île aux Cocos (M) 126
Île de la Passe (M) 107
Île des Deux Cocos (M) 116
Île Hermitage (M) 126
Îlet à Bourse (R) 195

Îlet à Malheur (R) 195
Îlet Bethléem (R) 182
Îlet-à-Cordes (R) 192
illegal drugs 267
Îlot Bernache (M) 107
Îlot Mangénie (M) 107
insurance 259
internet resources 263, 265
islands 18
itineraries 28-33, *see also individual locations*
Mauritius 58-9
Réunion 134-5
Seychelles 210-11

J

Jacotet Bay (M) 93
Jacotet River (M) 96

K

Kaya 102
kayaking & canoeing
Mauritius 83
Réunion 154
Seychelles 247
kitesurfing 49, 106

L

La Digue (S) 33, 242-8, 274, **243**
La Gaulette (M) 86
La Grande Chaloupe (R) 145-6
La Nouvelle (R) 196
La Plaine des Tamarins (R) 197
La Roche Écrite (R) 146
L'Abattis des Cipayes (M) 93
languages 21, 37, 268-9
lava tubes, *see* caves & lava tubes
Le Grand Brûlé (R) 184
Le Morne (M) 77, 85, 86
Le Pouce (M) 76, 111
Le Tampon (R) 171
L'Éperon (R) 155
Les Avirons (R) 167
Les Makes (R) 167-8
Les Trois Roches (R) 197
lesbian travellers 264
Levantard, Raymond 74
LGBTIQ+ travellers 264
lighthouses 145
Lion Mountain (M) 77
literature, *see* books
Long Mountain (M) 111
lookouts, *see* viewpoints

M

Mafate (R) 194-7, **194**
Mahé (S) 212-28, **214-15**
accommodation 218, 219, 220, 221, 226
activities 213, 217-18, 224-5, 228
beyond Mahé 229-32
drinking & nightlife 220, 227
food 216, 217, 219, 221
shopping 217, 227
tours 222, **222**
travel within Mahé 228
Mahébourg (M) 28, 119, 272-3, **119**
maloya 163
Mapou (M) 73
marine reserves
Baie Ternay (S) 217-18
Blue Bay Marine Park (M) 115-16
Port Launay (S) 217-18
Ste Anne Marine National Park (R) 230-1
markets
Bras-Panon (R) 181
Central Flacq (M) 112
L'Éperon (R) 155
Mahébourg (M) 119
Port Mathurin (M) 126
Quatre Bornes (M) 71
St-André (R) 181
St-Benoît (R) 181
St-Paul (R) 148
St-Pierre (R) 162
Victoria (S) 216
Marla (R) 197
Masson, Henri 74
Mauritius 55-129, **56-7**
climate 34-5, 58-9
culture 276-7
festivals & events 35, 58-9
food 42-4, 46
history 272-3
itineraries 28-9, 58-9, **29**
music 102-3, 282-4
navigation 56-7
people 276-7
population 276
travel seasons 34-5, 58-9
travel to/from Mauritius 56-7, 128
travel within Mauritius 56-7, 128-9
visas 128
weather 34-5, 58-9
microlight tours 167
Moka (M) 71
money 256
Mont Choisy (M) 100

Map Pages **000**

292

Mont Dauban (S) 231
monuments & statues
  Père Laval's shrine (M) 67
  Yvrin Pausé statue (R) 195
Morne Blanc (S) 225
Morne Seychellois National Park (S) 224-5
mosques
  Mauritius 67
  Réunion 139, 161
Moyenne Island (S) 230-1
museums & galleries
  Bank of Mauritius (M) 65
  Blue Anytime (M) 101
  Blue Penny Museum (M) 64
  Café des Arts (S) 235
  Château de Labourdonnais (M) 73
  Cité du Volcán (R) 200
  Curious Corner (M) 89
  Eden Art Gallery (S) 226
  EDITH (M) 65, 75
  Frederik Hendrik Museum (M) 118, 122
  Galerie Passerose (S) 235
  Galerie Raphael (M) 101
  House of Turmeric (R) 172
  Ilha do Cirne (M) 101
  Imaaya Gallery (M) 75
  Institute of Contemporary Art Indian Ocean (ICAIO) (M) 65, 74
  Kaz Zanana (S) 216, 226
  Kenwyn House (S) 216, 226
  L'Artothèque (R) 138, 142
  L'Aventure du Sucre (M) 73
  Lieu d'Art Contemporain (R) 171
  L'Usine à Gouzous (R) 162
  Mahébourg Museum (M) 119
  Maison Carrère (R) 142
  Michael Adams Gallery (S) 226
  Musée de Villèle (R) 274
  Musée de Villèle in St-Gilles-les-Hauts (R) 156
  Musée des Arts Décoratifs de l'Océan Indien (R) 168
  Musée d'Histoire Naturelle (R) 142
  Musée Léon Dierx (R) 138, 142
  Museum of Slavery (M) 64
  National Museum of History (S) 216
  Natural History Museum (M) 64
  Photographic Museum of Mauritius (M) 64-5
  Pop Gallery (M) 101
  Postal Museum (M) 65
  Shay Hewett's Fine Arts (M) 101
  SSR Memorial Centre (M) 65
  Stella Matutina (R) 158
  Toile d'Art (M) 101
  Very Yes Art Gallery (R) 162
  World of Seashells (M) 96
music 24, 37, 282-4
  Mauritius 102-3
  Réunion 163

N

national parks & nature reserves 50-1, **50-1**, see also wildlife reserves & sanctuaries
  Black River Gorges National Park (M) 76, 90-1
  Bras d'Eau National Park (M) 113
  Daruty Forest (M) 105
  Forêt de Bébour (R) 200
  Forêt de Bélouve (R) 188-9
  Forêt de Mare Longue (R) 173
  Kestrel Valley (M) 123
  L'Étang St-Paul (R) 149
  Morne Seychellois National Park (S) 224-5
  Ravin de Fond Ferdinand Nature Reserve (S) 238
  Réunion 204
  Silhouette Island (S) 231-2
  Unesco Biosphere Reserve - Bel Ombre 93, 96
  Vallée de Mai National Park (S) 275
nature reserves, see national parks & nature reserves, wildlife reserves & sanctuaries
nightlife 260-1, see also individual locations
North Island (S) 232
North, Marianne 226
notable buildings, see historic buildings & sites
Nouvelle Route du Littoral (R) 146

O

Outer Islands (S) 249-51, 274-5, **249**

P

pagodas 67
Palmar (M) 112
papangue 183
paragliding 15, 49, 156
parks & gardens 23
  Botanical Garden (S) 217
  Domaine du Café Grillé (R) 171
  Jardin de l'Etat (R) 140-1
  Jardin du Roi (S) 221, 275
  La Vallée Heureuse (R) 145
  Le Jardin des Parfums et des Épices (R) 172-3
  Mascarin Jardin Botanique de La Réunion (R) 157
  Sir Seewoosagur Ramgoolam Botanical Garden (M) 68, 69
  Vanilla & Spice Gardens (M) 113
Pas de Bellecombe (R) 199
Patel, Shenaz 69
Patyattan 102
pearls 238
people
  Mauritius 276-7
  Réunion 278-9
  Seychelles 280-1
Pereybere (M) 100
Petit Raffray (M) 105
Pierrefonds (R) 171
Pieter Both (M) 111
Piton d'Anchaing (R) 188
Piton de la Fournaise (R) 198-201, 202-3, **199**
Piton de la Petits Rivière Noire (M) 76
Piton des Neiges (R) 192-3
Plaine des Cafres (R) 198-201, **199**
Plaine des Palmistes (R) 198-201, **199**
Plaine des Sables (R) 199
planning
  clothing 8, 11, 13, 36, 267
  etiquette 11, 13, 36, 267
  Mauritius, Réunion & Seychelles basics 36-7
plantations 24-5, 272
  Mauritius 73-4, 95, 96, 273
  Réunion 171, 180. 274
  Seychelles 218-21, 231-2, 243-4
Platte Island (S) 251
Point d'Azur (M) 100
Pointe au Sel (R) 158
Pointe aux Canonniers (M) 100
Pointe du Bourbier (R) 181
Poivre, Pierre 68, 69
Pont Naturel (M) 120-1
population 267
  Mauritius 276
  Seychelles 280
Port Louis (M) 28, 60-9, 273, **61**
  accommodation 62, 64-5, 67, 68
  beyond Port Louis 70-8
  food 68-9
  tours 62, 63, 66, **63, 66**
  travel within Port Louis 69
Poudre d'Or (M) 106
Praslin (S) 33, 233-8, **234**
  beyond Praslin 239-41
Prophecy, The 102
public art
  Port Louis (M) 66
  St-Denis (R) 142
public holidays 267

Q

Quatre Bornes (M) 71
Quatres Bornes (S) 228

R

rafting 49, 182
religion 21, 106, 285-7
reservoirs & dams
  La Nicolière Reservoir (M) 111
  Mare Longue Reservoir (M) 91
  Takamaka I and II (R) 182
responsible travel 39, 262-3
Réunion 131-205, **132-3**
  activities 35
  climate 34-5, 134-5
  culture 278-9
  festivals & events 35, 134-5
  food 44-5, 46
  history 272, 273, 274
  itineraries 30-1, 134-5, **31**
  money 204
  navigation 132-3
  people 278-9
  travel seasons 34-5, 134-5
  travel to/from Réunion 204
  travel within Réunion 132-3, 204-5
  visas 204
  weather 34-5, 134-5
  wi-fi 204
Rivière Noire (M) 84-5

293

road trips
- Mahé (S) 222, **222**
- Mauritius interior 111, **111**
- Mauritius south coast 94-5, **94**
- Mauritius southeast coast 120-1, **121**
- south coast Réunion 174-5, **175**
Rodrigues (M) 124-7, **125**
Rose Belle (M) 71
Round Island (S) 231
Route du Thé (M) 74
rum
- Mauritius 73, 74, 89, 109
- Réunion 178
- Seychelles 220

S

safety 13, 258, 259
Salazie (R) 181, 186-9, **187**
séga 163, 282-4
Seychelles 207-53, **208-9**
- climate 34-5, 210-11, 252
- culture 280-1
- festivals & events 35, 210-11
- food 45, 46
- history 218-19, 272, 274-5
- itineraries 32-3, 210-11, **33**
- navigation 208-9
- people 280-1
- population 280
- travel seasons 34-5, 210-11, 252
- travel to/from Seychelles 252
- travel within Seychelles 208-9, 252-3
- visas 252
- weather 34-5, 210-11, 252
- wi-fi 252
SeyTé Factory (S) 225
sharks 13
shopping 22, 24, 67, 85, 99, *see also* handicrafts, markets
Silhouette Island (S) 231-2
Skizofan 75
slavery, *see* enslaved peoples
smoking 267

snorkelling, *see* diving & snorkelling
Sohun, Evan 74
souvenirs 22, 24
spices 23, 46, 261
- Mauritius 68
- Réunion 172
- Seychelles 221
St Joseph's Atoll (S) 251
St-André (R) 31, 176-8, **177**
- beyond St-André 179-85
stargazing 167-8
statues, *see* monuments & statues
St-Aubin (M) 95
St-Benoît (R) 180, 181
St-Bernard (R) 145-6
St-Denis (R) 31, 136-42, 274, **137**
- beyond St-Denis 143-6
- festivals & events 139-40
- food 139, 140
- tours 138, **138**
- travel within St-Denis 142
Ste Anne (S) 230
Ste-Rose (R) 185
Ste-Suzanne (R) 144
St-Gilles-les-Hauts (R) 155
St-Joseph (R) 172, 174
St-Leu (R) 156, 157
St-Louis (R) 168
St-Paul (R) 147-9, **147**
- beyond St-Paul 150-8
St-Philippe (R) 172, 173
St-Pierre (R) 30, 159-64, **160**
- beyond St-Pierre 165-73
street art, *see* public art
sugar
- Mauritius 62, 64, 73-4, 93, 96, 111, 123, 273
- Réunion 158, 168, 170, 178, 274
surfing 49
- Mauritius 83
- Réunion 154
- Seychelles 228, 248
swimming 171-2, 175, 259, *see also* beaches

T

Tamarin (M) 28, 83-4
tax refunds 256
tea 24
- Mauritius 74
- Réunion 171
- Seychelles 225
temples
- Arul Mihu Navasakthi Vinayagar Hindu Temple (S) 216
- Kalikambal Temple (R) 139

Shiv Mandir (M) 112
Shri Maha Badra Karli (R) 161
Sockalingum Meenatchee Ammen Kovil (M) 68
Temple Chane (R) 139
Temple du Front de Mer (R) 145
Temple du Petit Bazar (R) 177
Temple Guan Di de Terre-Sainte (R) 161
Temple Lisi Tong (R) 139
Temple Maryen Péroumal (R) 177, 181
Temple Pandialé du Colosse (R) 178
Temple Tamoul de Bois Rouge (R) 177
Temple Tamoul Narassingua Péroumal (R) 161
Terre des 7 Couleurs (M) 88
Terre-Sainte (R) 164
textiles 22, 192, 227
thermal pools 191
Ticot, Jace 162
time 267
tipping 256
toilets 267
tours, *see* boat tours, helicopter tours, microlight tours, road trips, walking tours, *individual locations*
trade winds 35
travel insurance 259
travel seasons 34-5, *see also individual locations*
trekking, *see* hiking
Trou-aux-Biches (M) 99-100
Trou d'Eau Douce (M) 29, 108-9, **109**
- beyond Trou d'Eau Douce 110-13
turtles 157

U

Unesco World Heritage Sites
- Aapravasi Ghat (M) 62, 64, 273
- Le Morne (M) 77
- Vallée de Mai (S) 235-7

V

Vacoas-Phoenix (M) 72
Vallée de Mai National Park (S) 275

vanilla
- Réunion 144-5, 180
- Seychelles 244
VAT refunds 256
vegetarian & vegan travellers 43
Victoria (S) 32, 213, 216-17, 275
Vieux Grand Port (M) 116, 118, 122
viewpoints
- Avenir Viewpoint (M) 111
- Belvédère de l'Eden (R) 182
- Belvédère du Maïdo (R) 151-2
- Dioré Forest (R) 182
- Gorges Viewpoint (M) 94
- Le Gouffre de l'Étang-Salé (R) 166
- Petite-Île (R) 174
- Point d'Azur (M) 100
- Pointe Cabris (S) 237
volcanoes 19
- Mauritius 77
- Piton de la Fournaise (R) 30, 173, 198-203, **199**
- Réunion 184-5
Vrot, Françoise 101

W

Wakashio oil spill (M) 122
walking, *see* hiking
walking tours
- Mahébourg (M) 119, **119**
- Port Louis (M) 63, 66, **63, 66**
- St-Denis (R) 138, **138**
waterfalls
- Alexandra Falls (M) 85, 94-5
- Anse des Cascades (R) 184
- Bassin Boeuf (R) 144
- Bassin Grondin (R) 144
- Bassin La Mer (R) 181-2
- Bassin La Paix (R) 181-2
- Bassin Nicole (R) 144
- Bassin Vital (R) 148
- Cap Noir Waterfall (R) 193
- Cascade Biberon (R) 201
- Cascade de 500 Pieds (M) 85
- Cascade de Grand Galet (R) 172
- Cascade des Délices (R) 144
- Cascade Mamzelle (M) 121
- Cascade V (M) 121
- Chamarel Waterfall (M) 85, 88

Niagara Fall (R) 144
Rochester Falls (M) 85, 121
Tamarind Falls (M) 85
Trou de Fer (R) 189
Waterfall of the Dog (R) 182
water sports 49
weather 15, 34-5
websites 263, 265
whale-watching 49, 153-4, 262
white-water rafting 49, 182
wildlife reserves & sanctuaries, *see also* national parks & nature reserves
  Ebony Forest (M) 88
  François Leguat Reserve (M) 126
  Le Jardin des Tortues (R) 167
  Tortoise Breeding Centre (S) 241
windsurfing 49
wineries 96, 192
Wolmar (M) 81
World Heritage Sites, *see* Unesco World Heritage Sites

Y

Yip Tong, Kim 75

Z

ziplining 88
Zulu 102

"Visit Port Louis' handful of small museums and centuries-old architectural gems to dip into the fascinating past of this bustling port city and capital (pictured; p60) at the heart of multiculturalism in Mauritius."

"Discover the clear turquoise water, diverse coral reefs (pictured) and plentiful aquatic life of Baie Ternay and Port Launay (p217), adjacent marine parks on either side of Cap Ternay at the western tip of Mahé in the Seychelles."

All rights reserved. No part of this publication may be copied, stored in a retrieval system, or transmitted in any form by any means, electronic, mechanical, recording or otherwise, except brief extracts for the purpose of review, and no part of this publication may be sold or hired, without the written permission of the publisher. Lonely Planet and the Lonely Planet logo are trademarks of Lonely Planet and are registered in the US Patent and Trademark Office and in other countries. Lonely Planet does not allow its name or logo to be appropriated by commercial establishments, such as retailers, restaurants or hotels. Please let us know of any misuses: lonelyplanet.com/legal/intellectual-property.

Mapping data sources:
© Lonely Planet
© OpenStreetMap http://openstreetmap.org/copyright

THIS BOOK

Destination Editor
Annemarie McCarthy

Production Editor
Esther Luettgen

Book Designer
Virginia Moreno

Cartographer
Corey Hutchison

Assisting Editors
Sarah Bailey, Peter Cruttenden, Jennifer McCann, Mani Ramaswamy,

Maja Vatrić

Cover Researcher
Hannah Blackie

Thanks Ronan Abayawickrema, Sofie Andersen,

Daniel Bolger, Melanie Dankel, Karen Henderson, Alison Killilea, Amy Lynch, Sandie Kestell, Saralinda Turner, Christophe Zialor

Paper in this book is certified against the Forest Stewardship Council™ standards. FSC™ promotes environmentally responsible, socially beneficial and economically viable management of the world's forests.

Published by Lonely Planet Global Limited
CRN 554153
11th edition – Nov 2023
ISBN 978 1 78868 447 7
© Lonely Planet 2023 Photographs © as indicated 2023
10 9 8 7 6 5 4 3 2 1
Printed in China